APOCALYPTIC GOOD NEWS

Apocalyptic Good News

Christ in the Cosmos

R. DEAN DRAYTON

RESOURCE *Publications* · Eugene, Oregon

Resource Publications
An Imprint of Wipf and Stock Publishers
199 W. 8th Ave., Suite 3
Eugene, OR 97401

www.wipfandstock.com

PAPERBACK ISBN: 978-1-5326-9026-6
HARDCOVER ISBN: 978-1-5326-9027-3
EBOOK ISBN: 978-1-5326-9028-0

Manufactured in the U.S.A.   JUNE 13, 2019

DEDICATED TO SANDRA DRAYTON

Contents

Preface / ix

Introduction / xi

1   The Pale Blue Dot / 1

2   Rediscovery of the Apocalyptic / 19

3   A Denominational God / 39

4   Uncovering the Denomination / 54

5   The Self Within / 79

6   Toward an Apocalyptic Self / 106

7   Finding the Apocalypse / 132

8   The Apocalyptic World / 151

9   The Apocalyptic I / 166

10   The Apocalyptic Message / 186

11   InChrist / 209

12   The Apocalyptic Image of God / 229

13   The Apocalyptic Church / 255

14   Epilogue / 281

Bibliography / 287

Preface

THIS BOOK IS ABOUT the discovery of a different sort of apocalypse in an age which knows only one form of apocalypse, the cataclysmic ending to civilisation as we know it. This apocalypse was unexpected. It has led to radical changes in the foundations of the familiar faith of our era. It took time to happen, however, for what is considered ordinary and known, mask the extraordinary and the unknown in our midst. Five of the most common words in the Christian faith actually screen access to vital elements of the New Testament gospel and the Christian life. Over the last forty years these screens were slowly dismantled. As that happened the power of previous cultures and our contemporary culture to hide key aspects of the gospel was laid bare.

First was "kingdom" in the kingdom of God. Then came "heaven" as in the heavens were opened. This was followed by the centrality of individual "decision" for the mode of Christian life. After this, was the "apocalypse" that defied the accepted understanding of apocalypse. Finally the way "revelation" was used to hide this form of apocalypse from view.

Each opened up new issues for the Christian faith. It was like walking in a fog that was slowly dissipating, with a sense of expectation that there was a new landscape somewhere up ahead. Or like a detective novel, the finding of each clue pointing toward a possible resolution of a puzzling case. Or, working past a screen, that blocked the way to a doorway, that led into a further room with another screen, and on and on. It is the journey itself that is so vital, for then the final view is clearer as a result of the critical un-coverings along the way. Each of the steps then high-light the final disclosure of grace.

Despite the back page of this book, do not expect the quick one page summary. There is much to come to terms with slowly, until the masks can be seen for what they are.

I invite you to drill down with these key words, and be as surprised as I was by "who" is released into our presence. I use this image of drilling down advisedly for it is informed by a powerful memory from my past. In the summer of 1966, I was one of two geologists "sitting on" a drill site in Sturt's Stony Desert, toward the center of Australia. The rig was about half way between two red sand dunes south of the newly discovered Moomba gas field.

It takes a few days to drill through the layers to a target horizon over a kilometer deep. The diamond bit slowly cuts through the layers of rock, lubricated by mud pumped down through the inside of the drill pipe, through the bit, and then up to the surface on the outside the drill pipe, carrying the crushed rock particles up to the surface. There the mud flows through a sieve that separates out the small pieces of rock. With a microscope the geologist describes the rock and determines the layer and its depth. When the bit reached the target horizon we were all disappointed. It was a most unpromising dirty non-porous mixture of shale and sandstone, not the clean porous sandstone horizon hoped for as a reservoir for gas or oil. We gave the go-ahead for the required Drill Stem Test for this exploratory well. The drill pipe was withdrawn and stacked in the rig, section by section. A side valve replaced the bit, and over the next few hours, section by section, the pipe was lowered to the horizon to be tested. The valve was opened. At the surface the drill pipe was connected to a flow line that discharged into a long pit about a hundred metres from the rig. It was twilight.

In less than a minute there was a rumbling that grew louder and louder, until the whole rig was shaking beneath us. We stared at each other, incredulous, amazed, then alarmed. With a deafening, thunderous roar, a horizontal column of white vapor screamed from the end of the flow line over the pit, under immense pressure. But, the burning rag, supposed to be at the end of the flow line, was not there. The gas, pouring out in huge volumes, was already pooling between the two sand-dunes. Next it would slowly roll back on the rig. With numerous motors running, a massive fireball threatened.

The drill foreman shouted at a hapless rig hand, "Light a rag. Throw it into the pit." He ran and threw, but the force of the gas blew it out. "Do it again"—the same result. Then the even more desperate shout, "Do it again." The flaming rag, a pinpoint of light, arced into the gas, and VROOM, there was a fifteen meter blow torch lighting up the desert scene. We all started to breathe again. Soon, orders were given to slowly close the test valve. The blowtorch gradually lessened, until it was only a meter long, then finally snuffed out.

Soon after we all stood around the pit, still glowing red from the tremendous heat, the red sand of the desert fired to terracotta. What a demonstration of awe-inspiring power from an unprepossessing source. Those minutes have never left me. It was worth drilling! That uninspiring reservoir rock eventually supplied gas to major cities of Australia as part of the Moomba gas field.

Unexpectedly for me, the thundering of cross and grace has exploded into view, in this decade after retirement, after years of direct involvement in evangelism and the mission of the church. The basic categories of faith and experience have been recast, heralding a new apocalyptic paradigm for the church, not just on Earth, but in the cosmos. Too big—yes, but what an astounding story of grace.

R. DEAN DRAYTON
June 2019

Introduction

The book has been a long time in the writing, heading down promising trails that petered out, only to realise it was necessary to start again and again until the underlying issues became clearer.

Though the author should not be center stage, the reader nevertheless should know something of the context out of which this work has emerged. I am Caucasian, the eldest son of a builder and his wife who moved from a rural town in Australia to a regional steel town Whyalla during World War 2, where I was born in 1941. The family then moved to a major city, Adelaide, in South Australia. After school in the forties and fifties, it was on to university to study geophysics and geology. I worked with a French oil exploration in a desert in central Australia. I married Sandra and responded to a call to the Methodist ministry and was ordained in 1969. With our two children we moved to the United States for post-graduate work in philosophical theology before returning to minister in Australia. In 1977, while I was working in a congregation, the Methodist Church became part of the Uniting Church. After positions in evangelism in the state church, I was called to a leadership position in the field of mission in Sydney. I retired in 2009 after state and national leadership positions and a decade teaching missiology and theology. It was clear to me that I was retiring during the death throes of the western denominational church, having begun my ministry in the death of God era. In spite of this I had had a profound sense of the way in which God in Christ, in the power of the Holy Spirit, brings new life to those who respond to the Good News of Jesus Christ. And yet, being a geologist, the awareness of deep time and deep space, as these realities are now called, never left me.

It is that realization that gave birth to this book. What was happening? I wandered in the metaphorical 'desert' for a long time until I realized I was asking the wrong questions. I had focused on how the church needed to change. I finally realized there were bigger matters here that had constrained the way the church had responded to the Good News of Jesus Christ. But it was a surprise, quite late in the process, when the role of the 'apocalyptic' in the message of Jesus grew to be so significant.

As an older child I had been sent to Sunday School. I was given a Bible by the Black Forest Methodist Sunday School when I was thirteen and encouraged to spend some time reading the Bible everyday. I have been reading the Bible daily ever since. It was not long before I discovered that even then, few in the churches, let alone those in the wider society, ever read significant parts of this book. It was a book often cited but rarely read. As the church was being progressively more sidelined from the rest of society, the Bible was collecting dust on bookshelves.

But I kept reading. If one accepts there is a God, then it is really a no brainer that it is worth spending time each day with one of the primary source books. The rumbling took a few years to start, but it is now obvious to me that this book is about God's apocalyptic eruption in the midst of history. The Scriptures bear witness to how this shaking has occurred before, and indeed will occur again, shaking the very foundations of everyday life. In an attempt to share key times of that shaking with the reader, each chapter of the book begins with a particular event that was significant to the author as well as illuminating the subject of the chapter itself.

It is not surprising that the church is facing tough times. At the end of the twentieth century, many agree that "what can be said with certainty about the Christian faith is very little."[1] The choices Sallie McFague pointed out for the church and the believer are either to make a hasty conservative retreat into a ghettoized church, or head towards more abstract language that renders faith sterile. She sought to construct a metaphorical theology that "is a post-modern, highly sceptical, heuristic enterprise, which claims that in order to be faithful to the God of its tradition—the God on the side of life and fulfillment—we must try out new pictures that will bring the reality of God's love into the imaginations of the women and men of today."[2]

This book starts from a very different premise. It is not that what can be known about the Christian faith is very little, but that our Enlightenment worldview drastically limits what it is possible for us to know. The restriction of knowledge to what we can know about the self and the world has led to the apocalyptic, the dynamic element of the message of the gospel, being effectively excised from the biblical message. It is time for this exclusion to be redressed. It is time to rediscover the very power and presence of "the word made flesh" that pulsates in and through history, vital for our own future, the future of the church, and the future of more than the planet itself.

In this writing I have mostly been supported by Sandra who has paid the price for a husband alongside her who is often elsewhere in his thoughts and often intensely preoccupied. One day fuller retirement will come. John Oldmeadow may well have forgotten his generosity in loaning me one of the Great Lecture series on Louis J Martynn's commentary on Galatians. It started a long process of uncovering the vital importance of the apocalyptic that is hidden from view. And I was also greatly helped by a study scholarship to Bridwell Library at the Perkins School of Theology at Southern Methodist University in Dallas, and the many friends on the faculty there. My colleagues at the United Theological College, the seminary for the Synod of New South

1. McFague, *Models*, xi.
2. McFague, *Models*, xii.

Wales and the Capital Territories of the Uniting Church in Australia, and part of the School of Theology in Charles Sturt University, were always willing to stop and answer queries and provide new leads and suggestions to consider, especially Jeffrey Aernie who read a draft of some chapters.

Thanks to the Camden Library for their unfailing support, always willing to do more to find a particular text I was searching for, especially Moira Bryant, the Chief Librarian. I have appreciated the ongoing relationships with members of the Public and Contextual Theology Research group of Charles Sturt University to which I belong. Thanks to Bruce Lobb who opened the door to the Order of Jacob's Well and subsequent conversations with Mike Endicott. For friends who went the extra mile in busy lives and read and gave helpful insights in the process of publication, namely Rev Dr Rodger Bassham, Dr Jeffrey Aernie, Dr Ben Myers and Dr Damian Palmer, and especially Rev Ian Price from Mediacom. I am greatly indebted to Professor Clive Pearson, who as a theological editor read and re-read these chapters and over many cups of coffee made creative suggestions re titles, the structure and content that led to vital discussions and significant changes. It is a remarkable process to publish with WIPF and Stock. Thankyou to those who have guided me and shepherded this project, especially, Matthew Wimer, Daniel Lanning, George Callihan, and the marketing team.

This book covers extensive fields of learning and expertise and must, in the attempt it makes to highlight the importance of the apocalyptic gospel, choose between many options and highlight particular points of view with which many will not concur. I bear the consequences of the choices made, and hope the quotes are in context and the errors few. I pray that the apocalyptic good news has surprises for us all who seek to be faithful to Jesus Christ.

R. Dean Drayton
June 2019

1

———

The Pale Blue Dot

THE EXPERIENCE OF NON-BEING

IN 1995 I WROTE,

"The sense of human insignificance had continued to grab hold of me in the profoundest of ways. Yet rarely have I heard of others who talk about this sense of nothingness. For most of my life this was a threat, a shadow to be kept at bay, as this background of immensity seeped into my life. It is only in the last five years that I have realized just how central it really is for me, and the planet. I have begun to think that the growing realization of the fragility of spaceship earth, the way a younger generation take for granted the need for conservation, weapons control, and justice for all human beings, are signs of the way this background is slowly but relentlessly exploding inwards upon the human situation.

But how to bring home the almost soul-destroying intensity of the experience of nothingness that was my travelling companion in life—sometimes more so, other times less so? I knew that I had to start with this core issue of non-being, the critical issue that has to be faced if we are to live in the universe rather than hide our head under one grain of sand (astronomically speaking). But a vital part of my story, too, has been a series of profound God-moments that have had the effect of intensifying the issue of non-being and have pushed me towards finding some resolution.

What do I mean by non-being? Over the last four decades this experience has kept edging its way into the foreground of my life, as I have worked first as a geophysicist and then as an ordained minister studying philosophy and theology and later serving the church. It intrudes mostly as I lie on the pillow waiting for sleep to come. I start to think about the future, first near, then further and further.

An ineluctable pull sucks me into thinking about time, the vast geologic and astronomic aeons that have given birth to the elements in great suns and the almost endless pinwheels of billions of galaxies. It is the experience of this that slowly leaches out the significance of my few pulse beats in the cosmos. Not only is death but a day away in thought, but the mind quickly races on to the extinction of the planet, and the utter meaninglessness of all life when there will be nothing to remember, for there will be nothing. It is the annihilation of everything.

As I think about this infinite non-reversible nothingness, my mind recoils in the anguish of the loss of self and history. Involuntarily my hands reach out and touch the bed, anything, in a longing for the reality of the present. It is as if my mind and self recoil from nothingness to want to hang on to the present with ever greater intensity. If this is all I have, then I will cling to it and live with what I have got. Yet still the idea of nothingness lurks, overshadowing everything, like the rolling black clouds of a thunderstorm blanking out the horizon. How is it possible to escape the ultimate denial of significance? The only way I know is to stay touching the now, and live with what I have at the moment, and console myself with the fact that we all share in this world that will cease to be. And gingerly keep my mind from thinking about time again for a little while, sometimes months, and sometimes only days or even minutes.

This sense of horror grew slowly with each passing year. It wasn't always like this. It is possible to see its beginnings earlier. At the same time, it was the next frontier that always scared me, but it could not be avoided."[1]

THE PALE BLUE DOT

It was Carl Sagan who made the implications clear for a global audience. On 14 February 1990, at his suggestion, NASA had instructed the tiny Voyager 1 space craft to turn its cameras around and take a photo of Earth as it left the solar system. It was 6 billion kilometres from 'home'. In the photo, the Earth is a Pale Blue Dot, an insignificant pixel in one of the scattered light rays barely seen against the black background of space. Sagan would later write:

> [f]rom this distant vantage point, the Earth might not seem of any particular interest. But for us, it's different. Consider again that dot. That's home. That's us. On it, every one you love. Everyone you know. Every one you ever heard of. Every human being who ever was lived out their lives. The aggregate of our joy and suffering. Thousands of confident religions, ideologies, and economic doctrines. Every saint and sinner in the history of our species lived there, on the mote of dust, suspended in a sunbeam.[2]

From somewhere else looking this way it is a nothing, but from here it is almost everything of value.

---

1. Drayton, *Pilgrim*, 9.
2. Sagan, *Pale Blue Dot*, 15–16.

A quarter of a century later the fundamental awareness of the human place within the enormity of the cosmos and its timeline has become more deeply embedded in human awareness. Yet it is still part of the background. It is not yet at the foreground of human thought, even though the reports of other Earth-like planets keep appearing in news headlines, while the realization grows that the human impact on the Earth threatens the planet itself.

I believe this awareness will soon bring about another of those transition points in human history when the perspective that we bring to our personal, social and community life changes in unforeseen ways. In the last five centuries there have been two such points—the first the Reformation which divided a unified Europe into a patchwork of different nations, and the second, the impact of the Enlightenment which gave rise to the democratic revolution. I predict this new transition will lead to a form of global self-consciousness that is already underway. It will give rise to fundamental changes in social and individual life, national and global life as our location in the universe comes home to the human race in a new way.[3] We are in the midst of a step-change in the human perspective.

How will the human race respond to this cosmic view of its home as an infinitesimal grain of dust? The sheer scope of it all can shock us into speechlessness—it is so alien to our daily life. It can bring an experience of dread as the insignificance of our planet and 'my' life hits home. It can imply the meaninglessness of all human life.

The Voyager camera helps us see all human history in a new way, condensed into a pixel on a photo, overwhelmed by the solar system, let alone the Milky Way galaxy and the billions of galaxies beyond. Whether we like it or not, this is the universe in which we are embedded. What will be the response of the human race to these vast perspectives of the universe, and perhaps multiple universes? This perspective has only been taught in western secular schools for the last two generations of students, and popularised by films such as Stanley Kubrick's 2001, the Star Wars series, Star Trek and others. Yet most of this way of seeing things has been absorbed into our traditional worldview without dramatically affecting the perspective of persons. Even the search for extra-terrestrial intelligence (SETI) and the findings of the first spacecraft designed to find planets around other suns (Kepler Space Telescope[4]) have not impacted greatly apart from a few headlines and articles that are part of the media background. As yet the vastness of the universe has not really hit home to the citizens of the west or the east. The ongoing disclosure of planets around other suns, and plans for new telescopes with greater capabilities in the search for intimations of life, the implications do not seem to sink in. Are they trivialized by the noise of more immediate

3. Such predictions are not new, with various claims that a new social order is imminent such as, the discovery of the interdependence of biological and human life, the perspective of post modern philosophy, the use of the internet, or, as posited in 1922 by Teilhard de Chardin, the eventual emergence of a 'noosphere' enveloping the Earth. Chardin, *The Phenomenon of Man*, 181.

4. The search area for Kepler was limited to a small envelope of 6,000 light years around our solar system compared with the radius of our galaxy of the order of 50,000 light years.

and pressing matters such as wars, elections, sport and advertisements? And particularly what will be the response of the major world religions in which the scope of the universe is limited in their own primal accounts to that of the Earth.

Sagan went to the heart of the matter. Death is the ultimate horizon for everything. For him the individual is born and dies just as the universe was born and will die. There is no meaning in life. The search for meaning on a pale blue dot in the cosmos is a meaningless exercise. All human attempts to find an ultimate meaning for the universe, are themselves meaningless.

When Sagan looked at this universe he was both overwhelmed with wonder, and disappointed that the search for meaning goes on. "Life is but a momentary glimpse of the wonder of this astonishing universe, and it is sad to see so many dreaming it away on spiritual fantasy."[5] In keeping with many who take seriously this cosmic perspective, Sagan saw religion as wishful thinking:

> I would love to believe that when I die I will live again, that some thinking, feeling, remembering part of me will continue. But much as I want to believe that, and despite the ancient and worldwide cultural traditions that assert an afterlife, I know of nothing to suggest that it is more than wishful thinking. The world is so exquisite with so much love and moral depth, that there is no reason to deceive ourselves with pretty stories for which there's little good evidence. Far better it seems to me, in our vulnerability, is to look death in the eye and to be grateful every day for the brief but magnificent opportunity that life provides.[6]

Sagan speaks for many in a world in which love and moral depth are but features of consciousness, with attitudes and values produced from the particular evolutionary history of life on this planet. All that can be known is the unfolding story of life in the cosmos.

How will the world religions respond to the perspective of the pale blue dot? It is a crucial question. The matter will not go away; it will continue to haunt those who believe that meaning can be found.

In the past, religious thinking has had to adapt to major new discoveries, even if that adaptation took decades or centuries. Now we are faced with a dilemma: will the sheer scope of this cosmic perspective herald the end of religion as we know it? Will the religious mind find ways of insulating the self from the shock of an infinite universe, or is there a way that meaning can be found on the pale blue dot?

The question of the meaning of life is a quest that has its own history. A thousand years ago in the west the world was described quite differently. The world was created by God and structured by God. The Earth was at the centre, (or, after Copernicus, close to the sun as the centre) of the planets and stars that circled around it. Humanity

---

5. Sagan, in McAfee, *No Sacred Cows*, fn 11.

6. Sagan, *Billions and Billions*, 258.

was created and placed by God in this world, with a divinely appointed beginning and end. The rulers were the agents of God.

Then, in the eighteenth century Enlightenment, the human perspective became pre-eminent. The rights and achievements of the individual were emphasised, leading to the emergence of written encyclopedias, and summaries of human knowledge, in order to describe the world and the story of human history. In the nineteenth century Lyell provided geological evidence that the Earth was very old, and Darwin extended the story of life's beginnings back into this newly found geological past of the planet. In the twentieth century, the discovery that stars created the elements, pushed the story further back to the beginnings of the universe. This historical perspective tells the story of how through deep space and deep time[7] the pale blue dot came into being, an evolved world on which all that is now known, all knowledge, culture and civilization, is a human creation, the product of human conscious thinking brains. And if that happened on the Earth, there exists the possibility that perhaps there are other brains or forms of consciousness elsewhere in the cosmos. The search widens so that space telescopes have, as of 2016, discovered well over 3,000 planets circling suns within a few light years of the Earth in the local arm of our own galaxy.

Sagan located the basis for the source of religion in the desire to live beyond death. It is possible that there are also other aspects of human life that have led to a search for meaning that transcends life and death. Sagan himself touched upon some of them—morality, the awareness of goodness, and the experience of love. He affirms that such experiences can be explained within an evolutionary universe as creations of the human brain.

The primary philosophical framework that gave rise to the Enlightenment was the radical discovery of René Descartes (1596–1650). He posited the key insight, "I think, therefore I am." In doing so he divided experience into the subjective self, the 'I' and the observed objective 'world'. Prior to this split the world was divided into a divine transcendent heavenly realm and a human immanent earthly world. Within a century of Descartes the philosophers had shown that it is not possible for us to reason to a transcendent realm beyond the processes of cause and effect. The God of heaven and earth gradually began to disappear as human knowledge and understanding of the world replaced theological assertions about God. Now each individual 'I' experiences their own subjective feelings within, privately, and can only use words and reason to describe the objective world in terms of cause and effect. These categories are taken as given by most of us. Sagan, for example, sees the "I" as part of the cosmic story of the astronomical world. For him there is no transcendent realm at all.

In describing life on this planet it is possible to emphasize either the objective world or the subjective 'I'. In the twentieth century other approaches emerged such as phenomenology and existentialism which instead draw the cosmic story into the

---

7. In the last decade the term deep time has been assigned by some to the geological spans of time on the face of the planet, and deep space, to the astronomical dimensions of the universe.

subjective 'I'. The claim is made that the experience of the subjective self is all that we can really know, thereby absorbing the world into the subjective experience of the self. Sagan dismisses these and other approaches out of hand. For him and most in the science and technologically driven world, the subjective self, and a cause and effect objective world, is the default position that is the operating world-view that each person inherits. Individually I am aware of myself here in the present moment while I am awake, and I can reason, read, learn about the processes that brought the world into being. We find ourselves as a human race so far limited to one planet, in a remarkable universe. Yet we are unable to reason why we are here, or what the future is beyond the eventual destruction of the universe.

In the past it was accepted that God was the creator of both the transcendent and the immanent worlds, heaven and earth. God resided in the heavens and the human race lived on the Earth. It was God who held both the transcendent dimension and the earthly dimension together in God's being. It was accepted that we live out our lives on the Earth, and depend upon God to bring us to heaven after we die, depending upon the sort of life lived here. Each of the three Abrahamic faiths presume this structure; they differ with regard to what is required to find approval with God. With the Enlightenment, however, God became an unnecessary hypothesis, and heaven, or a transcendent dimension, wishful thinking. For those who describe the history of the universe there is no place for these previous categories of a God-given creation.

This Enlightenment way of knowing and believing leaves the human race without answers to the fundamental questions about the meaning of life: where do we come from, what is the purpose of life, and what is our destiny, have no answers. The death of self-conscious life and the oblivion of the universe are the only certainties. Is it not an extraordinary fact that a self-conscious human race, a product of the evolution of this universe, seeks to describe the universe in which it finds itself and ask questions that cannot be answered? This observation means that the universe is conscious of itself through at least the human brain! Not only is the earth reduced to a pale blue dot in an almost infinite universe, all knowledge and consciousness within the universe as we know it is reduced to the operation of the brain, a blob of pale grey jelly. How is it possible that creatures on a planet can determine the origins of the universe itself?

It is presently accepted that the creation of the universe happened through a 13.8 billion year process of atoms, galaxies, stars, planets and the emergence of self-conscious life. There are questions about the initial conditions, but they are considered as part of the process. For example, if there are an infinite number of universes, then this universe we are in is one generated from one of an infinite possible set of initial conditions. The rational rigor of describing all processes in terms of cause and effect rules out any reference to a divine realm.

But does such rational rigor rule out the possibility of the divine? What if events that emerged within the process uncover hidden factors in this evolutionary story—events that happen within the evolutionary process that point beyond the process and help the process to be seen in a different light. Rather than seeing such events having their origin in a transcendent realm, this alternative posits that experiences that happen in the midst of emerging self-conscious life bring into being new categories that call in question the Enlightenment acceptance of the categories of self and world. Events may happen which gives rise to the development of beliefs in some other reality that exists with, beyond or behind the historical process. The major world religions, and most other religions, point to such primal events that have happened to people or groups of people that have given rise to particular beliefs, practices and traditions. Various meta-narratives have arisen which involve creator beings, gods, or an overarching understanding of life and human awareness. While thought and rationality are valued, it is experience and reflection upon these particular experiences that is considered vital. What has been deduced comes from experience within the evolutionary process and not only from the rationality or logic of cause and effect.

One of these primal forms of events is that of the apocalypse. The English word "apocalypse" is made up of two Greek words, which together mean 'to take off a cover'; it is a noun meaning to 'uncover' or 'disclose'. An apocalypse breaks in upon a person(s) in a particular situation uncovering or disclosing a radically different perspective to those person(s) for living in the world. An apocalyptic event is not as such a philosophical or intellectual framework; it is an event that 'happens' to persons and groups that gives rise to experience, words, thoughts, traditions and frameworks within history.

The word apocalypse has a long history that has directly affected the present meaning of the word. It is not a common word in most peoples' vocabulary and, when it is used, has a particular meaning that has been modified and massaged by other subsequent dominant world-views or meta-narratives over millennia. The end result is that the word apocalypse has come to be understood in terms of future cataclysmic events that threaten the life of the world. In the Christian tradition the word apocalypse came to be translated by the term revelation, further masking the meaning, as subsequent chapters will show. This substitution effectively changed event language into events in the mind or the world, derived as such from the transcendent perspective that informed previous dominant world-views. This translation has effectively put a cover on the meaning of apocalypse and precluded it from being part of the discussion about meaning. It will be affirmed that a renewed discovery of apocalypse provides a promising approach for wrestling with this question as to how it is that the universe is now conscious of itself in and through human awareness. Such apocalyptic events will become the basis for the affirmation that God can speak to people on a pale blue dot within the cause and effect of an immanent objective world, and the subjective field of the self.[8]

8. Since the Enlightenment the possibility of God addressing the human race has had to be posited as a rational possibility. This has traditionally been discussed theologically in terms of Pascal's wager. For Pascal (1623-1662) a person cannot rationally know if God exists. It is a rational wager to believe

Yet before that can be done the discoveries of the last three centuries have to be faced head on so that today's context can be addressed directly. There can be no going back behind the discoveries of the Enlightenment. It is only when this cosmic setting is taken seriously that it is possible to explore whether there can be a renewed approach to the deepest of questions concerning the human race living out its history on a cosmic mote of dust on a sunbeam.

The rational search for knowledge to which the Enlightenment gave impetus, has placed the human story within an evolutionary history of the universe and the planet. The Earth as the pale blue dot encapsulates this story. in 2016 a planet pin-pointed around the star closest to the Earth was named the pale red dot, heralding a colourful series of names if and when other motes of dust are found in this astronomical region.

It is less than a century since this dramatically different context for the Earth has been known. In 1929, Hubble discovered the red shift in the spectra of stars, the Doppler effect of their movement, that led to his realization that the Milky Way galaxy in which the solar system is found, is but one of billions of galaxies moving at incredible speeds in an expanding universe of almost unimaginable dimensions. That enabled Hubble and others by carefully measuring the rate of expansion of the universe, to determine that at one time the source of all the galaxies was one point at a time that could be calculated. It was thus possible to calculate when the universe began. This moment has since been called the Big Bang.

One year earlier Paul Dirac, a mathematical physicist, was seeking to work out how to describe an electron in terms of what had, till then, been irreconcilable views of reality, namely relativity and quantum physics. Dirac used quantum physics on the sub-atomic scale, and Einstein's theory of special relativity for space and time on the atomic scale. He developed a complex relativistic formulation in quantum mechanics that for the electron had an unexpected outcome. It took him a while to see that his equation predicted the existence of a positive electron in addition to the usual negative electron. Dirac had discovered the possible existence of a universe of anti-matter.

This discovery led to the realization that there was no such thing as the 'nothingness' of a vacuum. Experiments showed that a vacuum in space is a frothing creation of particles of matter and anti-matter popping into existence and cancelling each other out. With one of those giant leaps of imagination and logic, Dirac realized that this discovery provided a mechanism for the creation of what came to be called the Big Bang. The universe started at a singular point at which matter and anti-matter did not immediately cancel each other out, but instead rapidly expanded. The first second of this creation, calculated to be 13.8 billion years ago, is described in great detail by astrophysicists. Matter and anti-matter annihilate each other with perhaps one in a

---

in God with one's life, for if one is right, all is gained, and if wrong, nothing is lost. This argument has been found in various religious traditions. Nietzsche's (1844-1900) claim that God is dead, destroys the point of the wager. These points of view are expressed in a transcendent immanent view of heaven and Earth rather than an evolutionary perspective. Sagan sees such thinking as spiritual fantasy.

billion particles surviving to give the mass of the present universe. This extraordinary primeval explosion then moves through three particular phases as the immense energy involved cools to produce the universe as we know it.

In the first phase (0—500 million years) the expanding universe was in darkness. During this phase photons were actively involved in creating complex fields of energy that gave rise to the formation of neutral hydrogen, the simplest of all atoms which vibrates at a frequency of 21 cms. The emergence of hydrogen atoms led to further interactions that released photons thereby ending the darkness and making the universe transparent. The background radiation from this time has been mapped as the Cosmic Microwave Background (CMB) that shows how early perturbations in the expanding universe gave rise to the structure of the galaxies.

In the second phase (500 million—7 billion years) vast clouds of hydrogen collapsed to form first quasars, then galaxies. The stars turned the hydrogen first into helium and lithium and then further into heavier elements before exploding in supernova. In this way the early stars seeded the cosmos with heavier elements. New stars formed from these dispersed elements that created still heavier elements within them, that again, through supernova, were spread through the universe. Galaxies on the move also merged and cannibalized each other. The Milky Way galaxy is estimated to have formed 9 billion years after the Big Bang.

It was during the third phase (7 billion—present) that the solar system came into existence 9.2 billion years after the Big Bang, or 4.6 billion years ago, rich with heavy elements and a range of planets. Early signs of life appear on Earth at least 4 billion years ago. An oxygen rich atmosphere developed as a result of biological life 2 billion years ago. Then 600 million years ago there was the sudden appearance of vertebrates in the seas between the continents that had formed on the face of the planet. From then on life appears on land as well as in the sea. Bacteria, animals, birds, and insects appear. In the last 5 million years a series of forms of self-conscious life culminated in the emergence of *homo sapiens* as a species 100,000 years ago. The last 60,000 years brought the emergence of a human culture that led to the origins of farming life 10,000 years ago as the last ice age receded. In various river deltas the first cities were built. The rest is the history of various peoples and places culminating in the first ordered cities of the Roman Empire. In 100 BC Rome reached 1 million people, but it was not until 1900AD that London was the first city to reach a population of five million people. In 2000 there were 18 cities greater than 10 million people.

Looking to the future it is estimated that by 2050 more than 70% of the population of the planet will live in cosmopolitan cities, interconnected with one another digitally and physically. In the long term, calculations show the biosphere of the earth has an estimated life of a billion years, and the earth itself 5 billion years, in a universe that continues to gradually cool toward oblivion. Michio Kaku[9] sets out to show that it is necessary for humanity to spread beyond the pale blue dot if human life is to be

9. Kaku, *The Future of Humanity*, 2018.

sustained. Energy sources will need to be harnessed on an ever increasing scale so that human civilizations can expand to fill, first the solar system, then the galaxy, and beyond. This, he posits, is the only way self-conscious life on this planet can outrun the death of our species in a dying universe and hope to find another universe!

More immediately Jacob Berkowitz[10] claims that at present we are in the throes of the third great scientific revolution. The first was the Copernican Revolution at the time of the Reformation that removed the Earth from the centre of creation; the second was the Darwinian Revolution showing the emergence of the human species as part of an evolutionary world. The third revolution is the Stardust Revolution that brings together the results of the two previous revolutions and further discoveries in astronomy and evolutionary biology to place life within an evolving cosmic context. Slowly the realization is spreading that our bodies are made up of elements that were created in the midst of stars billions of years ago in the second phase of the Big Bang. We are "children of the stars,"[11] made of stardust.

Remarkably Berkowitz focuses on scientific revolutions without mentioning the Enlightenment which provided the basis for much of the ongoing scientific discoveries. The Enlightenment was a consequence of Descarte's philosophical revolution in making the individual the fundamental reference point for rationality and experience. This revolutionary turning point helped create an historical perspective that released a scientific and technological revolution, as well as provided the basis for a new political perspective that destroyed the *ancien regime* of kings and church and gave rise to a worldwide democratic revolution. This scientific and technological revolution has led to the globalization of human society and the realization that the impact of the human race on the planet may well have created a new geological epoch, the Anthropocene.

THE SELF-CONSCIOUS UNIVERSE

There is a profound mystery inherent in this human consciousness of history. From an historical perspective the universe has become conscious of itself on this planet through the brain of an evolved creature. How is it that a creature of the universe can describe the universe in which the creature finds itself?

What constitutes this self-consciousness awareness, and from where is it derived? This raises all sorts of questions for this Enlightenment duality of self and world, matter and consciousness, body and mind. The separation of the subjective self from the objective world is the subject of discussion for both philosophers and religious thinkers. How remarkable it is that a product of evolution can question the very purpose of the evolutionary process. What does that mean for the distinction between self and world?

10. Berkowitz, *Stardust*, 2012.
11. Berkowitz, *Stardust*, 307.

It is also a fundamental issue from a scientific point of view that pushes beyond the bounds of the scientific world. In the quantum world the presence of a self-conscious observer affects any measurement attempted. The early cosmos was in a quantum state of probability. What then was the act of measurement that caused the quantum world to shift into the classical gravitational world of stars, galaxies and planets? Who or what is causing this to happen? In a recent article David Sudarsky is cited as asking, "What's playing this role in cosmology? If I don't want to invoke God, or something external to the universe, which I don't, I have no place to locate this measuring device." [12] A self-conscious observer within the cosmos, raises huge issues for cosmology. Is self-conscious awareness in some way a potential property of the matter of the universe?

The discussion about the brain, consciousness, thought and reason, has a long history prior to the Enlightenment. In traditional Christian tradition, thought and reason are signs that we are made in the 'image of God', the God in heaven who brought creation into being. Humans are able to be open to this God because they are created in God's image and are thus able to have a relationship with God. Usually this has been posited in terms of knowledge of a transcendent heavenly realm from an immanent earthly realm.

In the Greek search for wisdom there were two dominant positions which had similarities with Hebrew thought. The first was that of Plato (428-348 BC) who emphasized the reality of the divine oneness of being with pure forms, a transcendent realm parallel to heaven in Hebrew thought. The second was Aristotle (384-322 BC), who emphasized the importance of deductive logic with regard to the forms of order in the world, parallel to the immanent this-worldly world of the Hebrews.

At the time of the Enlightenment Plato and Aristotle provided the two major perspectives for theologians and church leaders with regard to the role of rationality and thought. Plato was understood to claim that our thinking is but a shadowy copy of the really real of a divine reality that the brain dimly perceives. The transcendent eternal realm of the unchanging divine is only tenuously linked to the changing temporal realm of the passing age. Augustine (354-430 AD) was the great fifth century thinker influenced by Plato who affirmed the importance of the person made in the image of God being able to discover the beatific vision of salvation that the transcendent God could give.

Aristotle placed the forms of order, or universals, within the matter of everyday stuff and developed deductive logic to describe the beginning, ends and ethics of events in the world. It became the way of determining the good for the political realm. Aquinas (1225-1274AD) was the medieval theologian who in Aristotelian terms saw the world in terms of the eternal law of God. The natural law was derived from the potential of the rational being to act in accordance with both eternal law and human

12. Ananthaswamy , "Perfect Disharmony," 35. Ananthaswamy explores the so far unsuccessful attempts to unify nature's forces.

law through the four cardinal virtues of prudence, temperance, justice, and fortitude; the divine law was given by God through the scriptures, the church and its tradition.

What is clear from these descriptions is that the Platonic—Augustinian and Aristotelian—Aquinas perspectives were describing the nature of the world and thought in terms of transcendence and immanence, rather than in terms of the brain of the individual. Enlightenment attention turned toward the role of human perception, with the brain seen as the source of that perceiving and assessing.

The Mind/Body Issue

Descartes stated that mind and body were both substances[13], two distinct forms of reality. Philosophers have since taken each possible option when relating the mind to the body. Idealists give priority to the mind and claim that all is seen through mental constructs; realists give priority to the body, asserting that mind is derived from a particular way matter is organized. Bertrand Russell claimed that mind and body are the same.

At present most neuroscientists are realists who claim that it is the organization of the cells of the brain that gives rise to the mind, consciousness, and the experience of the self. It is difficult, still, to describe an identifiable physical meeting point between the cells of the brain, and the experience of consciousness and thought. As regularly noted in the literature, the pulsing of extra blood through the capillaries of a certain section of the brain is a different reality to that of the subjective experience of consciousness and or thought.

As the twenty-first century unfolds the conviction grows in the fields of neuroscience, socio-biology, and computer science, that all the characteristics of the brain, and self-consciousness, will be described in terms of biology, chemistry and physics. The result will be that religious and philosophical claims declaring that there are other realities and other dimensions will be explained as creations of the human mind within the evolutionary story. Though many scientific accounts now take this for granted, there has been no breakthrough to show that this is the case. "Nowhere in science have so many devoted so much to create so little consensus," writes physicist, author and presenter Michio Kaku.[14]

This fascination with producing consciousness keeps researchers beavering away. Stanislau Dehaune gives an illustration of recent work where an observer focuses on

---

13. Brown and Strawn, *Physical Nature*, 47. In fact Descartes distinguished the soul from the body. "Given the current state of knowledge in neurology and neuro-science, it is no longer necessary to attribute rationality, relationality, morality, or even religious life to the presence of a non-material soul, simply because we can't imagine how a physical system would do this." I have used the term mind rather than soul for that is the way the discussion ensured after Descartes. That the mind is embodied is now accepted. What is still contested is the relation of subjective experience to the observation of a physical element of the brain.

14. Anderson, "Corridors of the mind," 46.

a quickly flashing visual stimulus, such as a word, between masking images. At first the word is perceived as a flickering pattern, but as the duration of the flash is increased, there comes the moment when the word is first consciously seen and the person shouts out that it is seen. Scanners inside the brain, and EEG machines on the surface, show an 'avalanche in the brain' when this threshold for consciousness is crossed, sending messages back and forth between high level areas of the brain with a characteristic 'P3' wave. The interpretation is that in the moment of consciousness this word becomes available to high-level decision-making areas through a brain wide broadcast that results in brain wide intercommunication. The time it takes for this avalanche to occurs may explain why consciousness seems to run about a third of a second behind reality.

Anderson comments:

> Could the rich experience of consciousness, which feels as though it brings together sensation, interpretation, memories and language, really be no more than this 'global sharing of information'? The metaphor is certainly attractive but some will disagree. For these critics, the mental 'feel' of the colour red, say, will not be found by adding up the firing of brain cells which detect red, the association of red in your memory, and the labeling of a colour with a word. How the firing of cells can 'feel' like something is the philosophical 'hard problem' of consciousness. And it is a problem researchers think needs wholly new kinds of answers."[15]

As yet there is still a great mystery at the heart of individual and social human experience.

We have discovered that this universe happened from a single point that gave rise to billion year processes that eventually evolved into brains made of stardust. From the human perspective this single point in our history eventually gives rise to a self-conscious thinking person. The brain, an organ in the human body, is where the mind emerges with awareness, thought and reason, to create self and belief and community and culture—and eventually to the unraveling of the nature of the world that enfolds it including the discovery that our brains made of stardust create religion, beauty, truth and love.

There is no evidence, yet, to simply collapse the perspectives of the mind into the body. So far no one has been able to show that the category of the mind is the same as the category of the body—or putting it another way, that the subjective can be collapsed into the objective world, as the historical perspective of an evolving universe presumes has happened.

The history of the mind/body problem indicates that this issue cannot be so simply dismissed. In this approach the evolving world and the appearance of the mind are

15. Anderson,"Corridors of the Mind," 47.

understood to be two separate categories that cannot be collapsed into each other, but are integrally related and depend upon each other in the experience of consciousness.

So, despite two hundred years of philosophical reflection and later research the relationship between mind and body is still a mystery. That there is a relationship is evident, but as yet it does not seem that the category of mind involved in consciousness, can be collapsed into the category of the body as matter. Prior to the Enlightenment it was God as the creator who integrated both mind and body through the creation of creatures in the image of God. Without God in the picture this integration of both mind and body in self-conscious awareness has become and remains a mysterious duality.

The Religious Realm

If the mind itself cannot be explained in terms of the universe, what then is the role of the mind in the source and role of religion? Since the Enlightenment the two basic Christian responses in the religious realm have been, either to affirm the earlier Thomist affirmation of the world as the place of natural and revealed law, or to locate with Augustine religious experience in the mind or the feeling of individuals. The first response by Protestant theologians was to focus on the self and the mind as the place where God is experienced. The focus on individual experience came to the fore for most worshippers. The democratic revolution changed the nature of the church from an integral part of the former religious state, to a voluntary society. Now a person had to choose to belong to and support this group of people. Thus the Enlightenment created a new form of church, the denominational church, in which either convictions about God, or the experience of conversion, provided the basis for attendance and membership.

What is also clear is that the world in which Christian believers lived still included a transcendent heaven and an immanent earth, with the continuing belief that at death the faithful believer went to heaven. At the same time the unfolding discovery of the evolutionary history of the Earth raised serious issues for the understanding of the scriptures. The Protestant Church was divided in the last half of the nineteenth century with most members still believing the biblical account was true and rejecting the scientific account as a dangerous worldly delusion. Mainline churches were more likely to accept the scientific account and focus more on Jesus' teaching in terms of Christian values and a more rational account of the call of God for social justice in the world. Conservative churches tended to hold to a more literal view of the Bible affirming some form of a seven day creation account. In the nineteenth and twentieth century the spread of the church world-wide, led to the growth of denominations in many different cultures with a range of social, spiritual and cultural insights. This basic split about how to interpret scripture has been exported world-wide without most church members realizing that a stardust revolution has already happened. As the Protestant churches lose members in the west, their ability to share gospel with a post-modern world is progressively constrained by a reluctance of those in the pews to come to terms with the findings of astronomy, geology and biology.

If the churches now are still in denial about a cosmic perspective, perhaps we should look to the past to see what can be learnt from previous changes to human society in the history of religion. Over the last millennia religious awareness and experience has given rise to many ancient and worldwide cultural traditions as well as major world religions. What can we learn from this evidence?

One approach would be to proceed with a thorough going history of the forms of religion, starting with the description of the role of religion in hunter gathering societies, then farming societies through the Neolithic Age, and moving to the origin of the world religions in the Iron Age and the Bronze Age. Such an enquiry could then be augmented by a study of the role of religion in various societies as Weber, Durkheim and Diamond—and, more recently, Robert Bellah, have done. To do this would be helpful but it does not address the primary issue of the nature of religious belief itself. Those who conduct this sort of enquiry usually presume that religious belief is a function of the mind, with the result that the descriptions are seen as wishful thinking, or psychological projection, or a necessary creation of society to legitimate morality, or some other function of the mind. The religious dimension is explained as some function of the mind or society, for the God dimension does not fit into the historical perspective.

The Pale Blue Dot forces upon us the need to ground the origin of religious experience in another way. Are in fact, the seemingly fundamental categories of mind and body, self and world, in and of themselves the issue? They lead to a focus either on cosmology or on the mind. What if the categories of self and world are not adequate to explain the sources of religion. What if the mind itself is as problematic as the world for the reality of religion? As documented, the empirical cause and effect scientific understanding of the world excludes the possibility of God acting in any way. With regard to the self, it was not long into the Enlightenment before the soul/body discussion became the mind/ body discussion.

Over the last 200 years the mind has become a contested space in which talk about God is more and more often explained away, or internalised within the self. Firstly Schleiermacher rewrote theology in terms of the internal feelings of absolute dependence. Secondly Immanuel Kant showed that any thoughts of God can only be concepts. Thirdly, psychology explained away the divine in terms of the super-ego. Fourthly neuroscience described religious experiences in terms of blood flow in certain parts of the brain.

It is the argument of this book that it is the re- discovery of the category of the apocalypse that opens a way look beyond the mind and the body and give credence to the experience of billions in the religions and religious cultures of the pale blue dot.

APOCALYPSE

As outlined, the word apocalypse refers to an uncovering or disclosing of that which is either covered or not yet known. That disclosure happens in the midst of a particular context and a particular person or group of persons. For our purposes what is vital is that such a happening is not just about the mind, or a description of the world; it is an event that impacts on both, often in unexpected ways.

There is, however, a major issue with suggesting that the word apocalypse may open a way of discovering meaning. There is good reason why over the last two thousand years the word itself has come to be associated with catastrophic events in the future. The book of Revelation (Greek:Apocalypse) is the last book in the Bible and describes an apocalypse of God's final purpose for the whole creation. It has had a profound and pervasive influence in the understanding of apocalypse over the last two millennia. Then, in the last century the word apocalypse was secularized to mean events that threaten the future of the planet. It is not surprising that the usual understanding of the word now is that threats to the life of the planet are called apocalyptic events. Such events confront the normal human experience of people in space and time with an ultimate threat that is not about disclosing God but portend the extinction of the human race. The result is that the word apocalypse in the public mind is now almost exclusively associated with catastrophes, events that overwhelm the individual, and the existence of human life on this planet.

This common description of apocalypses as end time events masks the fact that an apocalypse can also happen in history. The key fact of an apocalypse is that it is an event that uncovers or discloses new realities rather than only being associated with end time events. From the perspective of those involved in an apocalyptic event, it would be a life-changing event in which purpose and meaning are found, uncovered, and disclosed. This book affirms that apocalyptic events in the past, in the early history of the human race, have disclosed the presence of the reality of God in the midst of history. Rather than positing the need of a prior transcendent realm, an apocalyptic event has the character of an historical event. Such an event could set in train possibilities that reinforce and legitimate what has been uncovered or disclosed. It would provide a way to find meaning on the pale blue dot.

It is not surprising that apocalyptic events are embedded in human history in the rise and fall of civilisations, and key events in the history of major world religions, raising the fundamental questions about God, meaning and the purpose of human life.

What is remarkable is that it was not until the beginning of the twentieth century that scholars began to unpack the significance of the category of the apocalypse in the events of the New Testament, and the significance of the apocalyptic for the religious history of the Middle East. In particular it is extraordinary that the apocalyptic dimension of the kingdom of God in Jesus proclamation of the gospel has mostly lain dormant for nearly 2,000 years. Over that time there have been episodic end time apocalyptic outbursts, derived principally from the imagery of the book of Revelation. These events only reinforced the way apocalyptic imagery was recast in terms of cataclysmic endings. That the gospel of Jesus Christ is an apocalyptic announcement that is not focussed on such 'end times' but is about the disclosing of the kingdom of God clearly requires a dramatic re-appraisal of the category of the apocalypse. It is tragic that the primary reality of an apocalyptic event that is meant to uncover, has itself been covered over for so long and in the process masked the core message of the gospel, which is the kingdom of God. Only in the last 100 years has this become apparent.

As will become evident the eclipsing of the apocalyptic kingdom of God has had a major impact on the way the church understands the message of Christ—and, indeed, on its life and organization.

A SOURCE FOR MEANING

I remember walking with a charismatic friend beside the largest mud pool at Rotorua in New Zealand. The plop of the bubbles in the mud breaking to the surface with their sulphur rich gas was a primeval setting for our conversation. The Rev Jim Wallace, a New Zealand Presbyterian minister was sharing the wonder of how it is that some people have found themselves addressed by God. It was the wry comment that followed that was so important. He said something like, "How strange it is that when they share what happened, they include in God's word so much about themselves and their setting as part of the divine declaration."[16] He did not doubt the core of an experience of God, but saw that it was enshrouded with the personality of the hearer and the nature of the world and culture in which they lived. That should not be surprising if we are addressed from within the world by an apocalyptic event.

The possibility that God addresses us in the midst of history focuses attention on the way an event happens, or a word is heard, as a word, but also includes a commentary on those involved in the event and the perspective of their time. While this book is focused on God as the one who is disclosed, it is clear that in terms of the early religious experience of the human race there are at least three ways that the word has been heard in particular contexts that open new perspectives and provide new frameworks and new syntheses for exploring the religious dimension.

First, the oldest continuous human culture in the world is that of the Australian Aboriginal people having arrived in Australia from Asia at least 70,000 years ago. The word heard in their culture was of the spirit at work in the dreamtime, creating

16. The conversation with the Rev Jim Wallace was on the 11th September 1990. Checking with him in 2017 he remembered the place and comments. "I am happy with the way you worded it as I think I was probably a bit more cynical about the overlay of human perceptions that can sometimes cloud the call and words of God."

country, and giving the Aboriginal people the task of maintaining and nurturing the dreamtime stories in which they live. Second, in Asia, and later in the Americas, the word that was heard was from the shaman, sharing the awareness of the light and dark, the blessing and curse of the Spirit world. And then third, in Europe came a focus on the word itself making clear the divine tragedy of human life in the grand epics remembered by the Greeks, alongside the call and promise inherent in the word of the Hebrews.

In these various ways humans were addressed in events that shaped them and held them as *a priori*, archetypal experiences. It is possible to dismiss these as projections of particular minds in particular cultures. Yet that is not the way these experiences impacted on various peoples. These events gave rise to the sustaining reality of these happenings that welded mind and world together in new ways.

In each of these regions of the globe specific ways of understanding the word of God and the meaning of life unfolded. The focus of attention in this book is quite particular. It is to recover the importance of the category of apocalypse involved in the message and person of Jesus and explore why it is that the church at the beginning of the twenty-first century cannot yet hear the amazing good news of the apocalyptic Kingdom of God in a cosmic setting.

For, as Sagan makes plain, if we are left with the categories of self and world, mind and body, then the pale blue dot floating like a mote of dust on a sunbeam is the sum total of all that can be known. It is destined for oblivion with the universe itself. The category of the apocalypse posits a way that God can be involved in an evolutionary universe so that discussions about the meaning and purpose of life cannot be dismissed as just religious superstition and spiritual fantasy. Further, the exploration of the role of the apocalypse in human history opens up the way for further discussion between world religions, beyond the realm of both thought and, or cosmology, involving the assessment of the importance of historical events in the development of world religious history. Indeed, what if God is the key event in our history, through irruptive events, not able to be explained in terms of the two other irruptive events—the Big Bang and consciousness, neither of which as yet can be explained in terms of the other?

2

Rediscovery of the Apocalyptic

I AM SPEAKING TO YOU

As a minister of *the Uniting Church in Australia, serving in the state of South Australia, we were nearing the end of a time set apart to write resources. Sandra and I were clear that our next appointment should be in an inner city area of the capital Adelaide. I had been into the church offices in the city for the afternoon. On the way home I stopped in at the Epworth Book Depot and, after browsing, bought a book on prayer by Oswald Sanders titled 'Intimacy with God'. Being a little early for the bus, I decided to walk along the route, reading as I went. There was a very slight drizzle of rain. After five minutes I reached the bus stop in front of the Royal Adelaide Hospital on North Terrace, and stood there reading in the shelter. Buses were coming and going, with people briefly queueing for their particular bus. I remember reading of God's love for me, and, as I did so, telling the Lord that I loved him. I was aware that at that moment I was alone on the hospital side of the divided bus shelter, standing looking west, when I heard a deep authoritative word, 'I am speaking to you', from my right and slightly behind. I can remember turning to look towards the hospital rose garden at the spot from which the voice had come and being surprised at finding that there was no-one there. I knew clearly that I had been spoken to. Some months earlier I had read one of 'The Chronicles of Thomas Covenant, the Unbeliever', about a leper transported into a subconscious world, who, when anything happened, would mentally check himself all over to see if he was alright. At that moment I remember quite self-consciously systematically checking out where I was and what had happened and thinking, 'I am not feeling strange or anything'. I had a sense of surprise, wonder, and questioning all at the same time. Then there came a distinct impression in my mind, a thought: 'The bus you are waiting for will not stop'. I suddenly felt relieved, thinking: 'That at least can be tested'.*

A minute or so later my bus, the 551, came into view and three or four people in a short queue on the other side of the bus shelter looked up and stepped forward ready for it to stop. It nosed in towards the bus stop, and then, as it slowed down, shut the doors that had just opened, turned back into the main stream of traffic, and headed on without stopping. 'Lord you have my attention!' was all I could think to say. Certainly it had been an audible word that had come from outside me, and it was also certain the comment about the bus had been an inaudible word. I was left in a quandary. I kept on reading, wondering if it was the book that was important. I waited half an hour until the next 551 arrived, feeling somewhat elated and let down. Why, Lord?

I walked home from the bus half an hour late for the family evening meal. Unlocking the front door, I could see through into the kitchen that Sandra, Jane and Jeremy were already well into the main course. As I put down what I was carrying, Sandra said there were some letters for me on the kitchen bar, so I walked across and reached for the one on top and opened it. It was a letter from the Riverina Presbytery Mission Committee chairperson, stating that they had nominated me for the position of general secretary of the Board of Mission in the New South Wales Synod located some 1400 kms to the North East. As I read the letter it hit me: 'So this is what it is all about'. Apparently my face must have fallen, for either Jane or Jeremy said, 'What's wrong, Dad?' I looked up and said, 'This is an invitation to go and live in Sydney'. They said something like that would be great, or wow, as Sandra said, 'What's in the letter?'

After I had read out the details Sandra said, 'Do you remember saying that would be the only synod (state) position you would ever be interested in doing?' Four months previously I had been invited to give a teaching weekend at the Board of Mission. It had been a throwaway line. I had said it because of the resources of the Board of Mission had, but I had not known that the position was becoming available. Sandra went on to say, 'I believe that is God speaking to you'.[1]

A REDISCOVERY

The telling of personal stories in the doing of practice of theology used to be frowned upon. It was reckoned that this way of doing theology could direct attention away from the proper subject—that is God. The turn to the autobiographical would instead put Karl Barth's "puny little man" at the centre of the discipline's enquiry. There is merit in this claim. The telling of personal stories needs careful discernment and should not seek to render captive the otherness of God.

There is a wrestling with this tension in this particular event. It is included, nevertheless, for a reason. It seemingly bears witness to the irruptive presence of God in the midst of everyday life. This occasion has been a continuing source of reflection. From a much later perspective it is clear that my first response was as an Enlightenment person, questioning what was happening, checking the context and what was happening within myself, for there is no place for such moments in an Enlightenment

1. Drayton, *Pilgrim*, 91.

framework. And, then, secondly there was the presupposition that this moment was a spot in time with God speaking from some divine dimension. It was not until much later, with the discovery of the category of the apocalypse, that I realized this event might be called an 'apocalyptic moment'. It was not in the sense of it heralding the ending and winding up of history in some sort of cataclysm, but the uncovering or disclosure of that which would otherwise be hidden—the 'otherness' of a God personally apprehended, in an unexpected event. It was a good example of Jim Wallace's statement that it is possible to hear the word of God, but that it is received within the cultural and personal filters we each have.

In terms of my own journey this experience has been a decisive moment that has had disturbing ramifications for living the gospel in subsequent years. It has been the equivalent of one of Jurgen Moltmann's 'companion experiences'. This particular incident I have previously written about in an earlier book published under the title of *Pilgrim in the Cosmos*. There the questions were framed in terms of the role of faith in searching for the meaning of life and the purpose of life before a cosmic God. Since then this search has continued to reverberate in the present setting of deep space, deep time and the meaning of life on a pale blue dot.

The discovery of the apocalyptic as disclosure rather than an end time catastrophe came much later. It led to the realization of the restrictive power of the en-globing frameworks provided by the world-views of the past, involved in Christendom and the present day Enlightenment. They are the world-views given expression in what can be defined as the National Church Paradigm and the Denominational Paradigm. This book is the attempt to name and unpack the way these world-views are now limiting, and restricting the discovery of the good news of the apocalypse known in Jesus Christ.

There is a double irony here. I had worked as a geologist and geophysicist, a scientist trained in empirical methods of deduction, at home with the Enlightenment paradigm, before ordination and then after had become a process theologian. This background experience made the sheer anomaly of this apocalyptic event so obvious. And, as well, it was this irruptive happening that led to me exchanging a position in one state, for another in another state of the same denomination. The work there was to raise vital questions about the nature of the denominational church and the denominational paradigm. Some three decades later it was this apocalyptic event that led eventually to the realization of the inadequacy of the missionary structures of the denominational church. The events of that day set the direction for a future working in the mission of the Church that was to disclose the implications of the apocalyptic for the mission of God.

When an apocalyptic event happens to one it is not forgotten. There is no option but to work through what the event means for we are meaning-seeking creatures. The experience of such an apocalyptic God not only shocks the human psyche into new pathways and possibilities, but raises questions about so much that is posited and believed in the name of God.

From a human perspective the word God has come to be the repository of so much history that includes belief, conviction, and social wisdom. It can also function as a shadow side of protection, projection and bigotry. For Martin Buber, God

> [i]s the most heavy-laden of all human words. None has become so soiled, so mutilated. Just for this reason I may not abandon it. The generations have laid the burden of their anxious lives upon this word and weighed it to the ground; it lies in the dust and bears their whole burden . . . We cannot cleanse the word 'God' and we cannot make it whole; but, defiled and mutilated as it is, we can raise it from the ground and set it over an hour of great care.[2]

For Buber this word, this name, this appeal to a God who hears is too important to lose, but it requires a profound sensitivity to hear the pain and hope borne as part of the human condition. What an immense mysterious word this word 'God' is. It binds us to the experience of space and time and holds us before the source of all space and time.

For here too are stories of how the creation came into being, accounts of those who dared and those who were faithful against all odds. "For the language about God has a history. . . . words about God are cultural creatures, entwined with the mores and adventures of the faith community that uses them. As cultures shift, so too does the specificity of God-talk."[3] New issues emerge, and society faces new threats, that lead to further wrestling with the historical open-endedness of God's mysterious being. Even now, as global warming threatens the planet, there are voices calling for resources from our religious heritage to provide a new ethic for society.

And yet the very importance and scope of the word God leads many to a deep resistance to any changes in our thinking or experience of God. So easily God becomes identified with, and even legitimates, a particular world, that inculcates particular values, beliefs, organizations and attitudes. In time God enshrines a steady-state description of reality that becomes the basis of people's life. For such societies the experience of the apocalyptic is that of a God who both affirms but also betrays the world-view that God had formerly inhabited.

Not surprisingly the understanding or even the experience of God is of inestimable importance for the church. Even here there is a wide range of understanding and expression. As it happens, the mission of the church has also dramatically affected the understanding of God. The church's proclamation of the message of the gospel in the language and the world-view of the Greco-Roman world has had unintended consequences for a later Enlightenment time. God was framed as a transcendental God in the terms of the Greek understanding of being. The mission to the Roman world

2. Buber, *Meetings*, 60.
3. Johnson, *She*, 6.

resulted in the fifth century translation of the Greek New Testament into the Latin Vulgate. An important consequence was that, the appropriate word to translate the word "apocalypse", was the word "revelation", reflecting this particular understanding of God. Such a view of God had the effect of masking, or hiding the reality of any apocalyptic happening within history. In Greek, the Book of Revelation is the 'Apocalypse' of John, but when translated into Latin becomes the 'Revelation' of St John. The word apocalypse was removed from the biblical record and replaced with the word revelation. Now that the church finds itself in a radically different world, even universe, in which the transcendent is dismissed, the possibility of revelation as usually understood is called in question. The nature of revelation is a major issue for the twentieth and twenty-first centuries.

It is fascinating to see the way in which the authoritative Kittel's Theological Dictionary of the New Testament makes a clear distinction between an apocalypse and a revelation. The author of the section on Revelation (Albrecht Oepke) is very much aware of the 'unusual difficulties of method' involved and lists 'ecclesiastical dogmatics', 'some philosophy of the period', and 'unclarified pre-understanding of the subject' as matters that are 'often imported into the normal translations 'to reveal' and 'revelation.'[4] The core definition given is "revelation is a manifestation of deity", which requires further 'precision' in the light of studies of Greek Roman culture, the Old Testament and the New Testament uses of the word.[5] Oepke states directly that apocalypse "corresponds better to the strict biblical concept of revelation", but the definition of revelation as an act of God, or manifestation of deity, allows revelation to be the dominant word that incorporates the concept of apocalypse within it.

On theological grounds too, the decision is made on the basis that revelation best describes what is happening as the 'manifestation of transcendence within immanence.' Here, the Platonic categories that dominated the interpretation of the

4. Oepke, "Revelation," 3: 563–592.

5. A concise summary of the article follows. In the Old Testament, Revelation is not to be identified with supernatural knowledge or numinous feelings, it is the action of Yahweh, though knowledge and feelings may be involved. For the Hebrew Bible "in the strict sense revelation is always and everywhere the act of God." 574.

In the New Testament the apocalyptic "to a very large extent furnished it (Christianity) with its basic concepts."580. Revelation is the act of God. Jesus "does not merely proclaim the coming kingdom of God. He himself is this kingdom in person." 580. For Paul, "God used revelation to convince him of the resurrection of the Crucified." 584. For Paul and the early Christian community, "the whole earthly life of Jesus bears the character of eschatological revelation." 584. Reflecting on the word 'apocalypse' Oepke states that apocalypse "corresponds better to the strict biblical concept of revelation." 591.

The theological summary is quite direct. "In the New Testament, too, revelation denotes, not the impartation of knowledge, but the actual unveiling of intrinsically hidden facts, or, theologically, the manifestation of transcendence within immanence. . . . By derivation, however revelation is also the message, which transmits the comment. . . . It thereby becomes revelation for individuals, but from the very first it comes with the claim to be heard in the name of God." 591.

In this summary the end result is that an apocalyptic event in the midst of history, the manifestation of deity, is re-described as a revelation of a transcendent message heard by an individual in an immanent world.

scriptures from the third century on are being projected back on to the understanding of apocalypse. The result is the future directed eschatological message of the New Testament as the unveiling of the hidden is presented in terms of transcendence and immanence. In addition the description of the action of God in revelation as a message received or heard by the individual, reflects the Enlightenment restriction of religious experience to the individual.

A number of questions follow. Does this matter? Is not an apocalypse a revelation? In most cases yes, but it cannot be said that a revelation is an apocalypse. In the scriptures an apocalypse is an event, a happening in which an individual or a group are confronted with the action of God with which they have to grapple, and not only a message received or heard by an individual. Has this eclipsing of the word apocalypse by revelation happened for any other words in the scriptures? Yes, in the Johannine writings the Greek word for manifest is also translated as revelation. "What we have seen with our eyes, what we have looked at and touched with our hands, concerning the word of life. This life was revealed (Greek: *manifest*)."(1 John 1:1-2a) Is a manifestation a revelation? Yes, but again a revelation is not necessary a manifestation.

How did this happen? It is a result of the way world-views impact upon the meaning of words—the meaning of a word in a new language does not necessarily have the range of meanings that it has in its original language. In the case of apocalypse there are three distinctive times in history that have affected its translation; the first century in the life of the Church; the third and fourth century when the scriptures were translated into the Roman language, culminating in the Latin Vulgate; and finally the impact of the Enlightenment. The consequence of these three phases resulted in the translation of the word apocalypse as revelation. This change has had enormous ramifications for the understanding of religious experience. And with this history the meaning of the word apocalypse has been obscured.

REVELATION

The word apocalypse did not disappear over the last two millennia; instead as previously stated a very particular view of an apocalypse triumphed—cataclysmic events that herald the end of the world. It is important to reflect on this use of the word, especially if it overwhelms in public understanding any other way of understanding the dominant New Testament view of apocalypse.

The New Testament book of Revelation has had an extraordinarily powerful role in defining the word in the public imagination over many centuries. This, the final book of the Bible unveils a cataclysmic future, describing the calamity and destruction which is a sign of the coming end of the world. With extraordinary imagery the book lays out the seemingly imminent end of the world. It heralds the judgement of the human race and the creation of a new heaven and new earth. After describing signs and tribulations including the four horsemen of the Apocalypse, Revelations 20:3 states that the serpent, the Devil after being defeated is to be bound for a thousand years, and then 'let out for a little while'! Such biblical statements have provided a ready source of end time imagery for literature, religion and the public mind ever since.

The power of this imagery was especially evident in the anxiety that preceded the decades in European society before 1000AD, when it was feared the Devil would be let loose in the world once more. The structure of the medieval church that followed reflected a divinely structured world in which all power was given to God, who could end the world when God chose. Apocalyptic imagery was used especially when times of chaos threatened the known world.

The sixteenth century Protestant protest during the Reformation was replete with apocalyptic language and imagery. As the threat of the Ottoman Empire loomed large, Luther used the book of Revelation to make one of his central points, that the papacy was the Antichrist, and the end of the world was coming. A series of woodcuts as illustrations show the whore of Babylon wearing a papal crown, the seven-headed beast wearing a papal crown. The people got the message. And again, during the seventeenth century Civil War in England, Protestant preachers declared the King to be the anti-Christ and believed they were in the last days. The Enlightenment in the late seventeenth century, led to a turn from God to the individual, with the emphasis on the individual and society, and a focus on technological progress. It was a time that was not comfortable with this sort of apocalyptic language. This kind of discourse was disowned in the public sphere and left to the vocabulary of religious sects. The more general religious focus was on personal conversion and morality in this life as the prelude to death and judgement at the end of life rather than the threatening imagery of the apocalyptic in the present, as in the book of Revelation.

It was the twentieth century nuclear arms race after World War 2 that brought the fear of an apocalypse back into the realm of public consciousness. Up until then only God could bring an apocalyptic end. When Russia and America realized that the only way to work through the threat posed by nuclear weapons was to negotiate in the face of MAD, that is Mutually Assured Destruction, a whole generation grew up aware that it was possible for the human race to destroy or irreparably spoil the planet. Novels and films graphically portrayed the apocalyptic nuclear consequences. In the last third of the twentieth century other apocalyptic scenarios have emerged and gripped the public imagination: The possibility of a pandemic sweeping the globe, a large meteorite smashing into the Earth, the effects of global warming, the discovery of alien life, the destruction of the ozone layer, overfishing the seas and other crises in a hierarchy of calamitous possibilities. Fortunes have been made writing novels with the hero or heroine battling against tremendous forces that threaten to destroy them and the world as we know it. There is always the race against time to find the key, or unlock the secret that will save the planet or the nation and themselves and us all. It is action packed, tension filled and makes for thrilling film or television scenarios.

The Biblical use of the word apocalypse, however, is not restricted as is generally thought to the book of Revelation. In the Hebrew Bible the word apocalypse is used for Daniel's visions in which the Archangel Michael discloses the fate of empires and kingdoms to come. Even more significantly in the New Testament Jesus good news is about the apocalyptic kingdom of God, and for the apostle Paul the word apocalypse is central to his message. This apocalyptic perspective is also there in the Johannine writings where the word 'manifest' is used instead of apocalypse to describe how the apostles saw, touched and knew the Lord.

What are the significant differences that are lost when these two words for 'uncover' and 'disclose' in the Greek, are translated by the word revelation in the English?

A closer look at the understanding and meaning of the word revelation helps.

Revelation is now understood to be the supernatural communication of knowledge by God. The *Oxford Dictionary* states that a revelation is,

> The disclosure or communication of knowledge to man by a divine or supernatural agency: Enlightenment. A striking disclosure of something not known or not realized.[6]

A revelation then is the disclosure or communication of 'knowledge' to 'man' by 'God'. A revelation is about the knowledge God gives to a person. In the New Testament when the word revelation is used it is read as disclosure or communication of knowledge from the divine. It concerns God and the mind. Two illustrations are given of revelation in the dictionary that do not involve God but arise from a striking disclosure of something not known or realized in everyday life. It can be used to cite a 'revelation in science', or 'the daily life of everyone of us is a perpetual revelation of his inner self,' citing first an instance from the world, and second from the self. What is important to notice is that these references assume the Enlightenment divorce between self and world.

This dictionary definition is a problem for the understanding of apocalypse, or manifest, as presented in the Biblical record. An apocalypse or manifesting of God is an event that breaks in upon a person, persons or a society. It is an act of God in the midst of history. It is far more than the communication of knowledge to an individual. In the Biblical world not only is the word apocalypse about the threat of an event that will happen, such as the destruction of the temple or the end of the world, it is also about the coming of the kingdom of God announced by Jesus, and a miracle or a sign from God. Of course such an event gives rise to revelation, but is more than a revelation, more than the communication of divine knowledge, and it involves an act of God.

It is not surprising that these two words, apocalypse and manifest, do not fit well into an Enlightenment world-view in which the scientific understanding of the world of cause and effect makes any notion of divine intervention in happenings and events,

6. "Revelation", Oxford Dictionary, 594

suspect. Revelations in the mind are not so difficult to accept in a scientific age, for they can be claimed to be true by the person concerned but at the same time dismissed as projections of the mind itself by the scientific observer

APOCALYPSE AND THE KINGDOM OF GOD

A positive effect of the Enlightenment was the renewed focus on determining the history of the New Testament books, authorship, and context as well as the history of the interpretation of the content of the books. It was a shock when, at the beginning of the twentieth century, two New Testament scholars, Johannes Weiss and Albert Schweitzer, affirmed that the heart of Jesus core message about the Kingdom of God was an apocalyptic announcement and demonstration of the coming kingdom already happening in their midst. They repudiated the interpretation that scholars of the previous one hundred years had given, that Jesus message about the kingdom of God was to be understood in ethical terms.

It also brought to light a strange feature of the way the early Church had taken attention from the message of the kingdom and focused on other aspects of the good news. Wolfhart Pannenberg's overview of the use of the word 'kingdom' in church history is telling. Within a hundred and fifty years in the life of the early church the theme of the kingdom was rarely used. For most disciples the Christian hope for the future was "the resurrection and the conforming of believers to the likeness of Christ"[7]. God was Lord of the present rather than a coming Kingdom. The basic world-view became a Platonic one, emphasizing the transcendent world of the eternal God over the immanent world of passing temporal life.

As highlighted earlier, in the Greco-Roman world of the empire, the Platonic world-view led to the understanding of revelation as the communication of knowledge about who God is and what God has done in Christ. The message was essentially an a-temporal message focused on the individual trajectory from earth to heaven. Death was the escape from life to the afterlife of heaven.

This message was still in place at the coming of the Enlightenment. The Enlightenment further reinforced this individual perspective from an historical perspective with the consequence that "hope of individual fulfilment in the hereafter went hand in hand with the doctrine of the immortality of the soul."[8] This view is still widely held in popular spirituality. In the nineteenth century era of reason and science the enlightened individual was the reference point, and the focus was on how religious truth was individually received and morally lived out.

The experience of God was either that of God as the transcendent one and the source of revelation of divine rational truth, or in the words of Friedrich Schleiermacher, the individual's experience of the 'feeling of absolute dependence' on the

7. Pannenberg, *Systematic*, 528.

8. Pannenberg, *Systematic*, 533.

transcendence of God. For John Wesley the message was of the way his 'heart was strangely warmed', sung by the converted in the moving hymns of his brother Charles Wesley. The Enlightenment splitting of truth into the objective and the subjective is operative here with the individual either experiencing rational transcendental truth or the subjective feeling of the transcendent. The result was that in the second half of the nineteenth century the gospel was presented in terms of the pietistic experience of conversion or the revelation of truth and morality[9].

It is an amazing fact that the apocalyptic dimension of the Kingdom of God in the Gospels lay dormant for nearly two thousand years leaving the book of Revelation as the primary source for end time apocalyptic language and imagery[10]. Even now writers and tele-evangelists continue to develop this scenario.[11]

Johannes Weiss' *Jesus' Proclamation of the Kingdom of God* (1892) and later Albert Schweitzer's *The Mystery of the Kingdom of God* (1901) showed how important apocalyptic expectation was to the message of Jesus and the early church. This came just before two World Wars that heightened the apocalyptic dimension of wars fought on a world-wide scale never seen before. The apocalyptic dimension was brought into the theological discussion first by Barth with the revelation of God as the 'Wholly Other' calling in question the self as the reference point of the previous century. And then later the eschatological theologies of Moltmann and Pannenberg start from the apocalyptic nature of Jesus message as a proleptic forerunner of what was to come in the eschaton, at the end of the Age. Yet the result was that the apocalyptic was still seen as a revelation of what was to happen in the future.

In New Testament scholarship there was a rediscovery of the importance of Jesus announcement of the Kingdom of God. Now the church and individuals are to be caught up in what God did in Christ, towards God's final bringing into being a new heaven and earth in the future. Suddenly, Jesus message had consequences for the future in time and space. No longer was the individual released by death from time into the eternity of a transcendent heaven. Instead the message of the Bible and orthodox Christian doctrine were released from these dualistic assumptions to show holistically, "God's rescue of the created order itself, rather than the rescue of saved

---

9. In 1917 Rudolf Otto inverted this focus on creaturely feeling to claim that an experience of the numinous precedes the claim to the experience of absolute dependence. He described this as individuals experiencing the overpowering presence of God in a way that is more than rationality, but not irrational, within the same a-temporal framework. It is the subjective response to the transcendent God that encompasses the individual. It is described as a form of mysticism that is not concerned with time and space, but the experience of God.

10. The book of Daniel also echoed a similar understanding of the apocalyptic as the unfolding of world history in the kinds of empires to come.

11. Writers such as Hal Lindsey, *The Late Great, Planet Earth,* forecasting the rapture of faithful souls, and Tim LeHaye, the "*Left Behind*" series of apocalyptic novels. An internet search with the word rapture brings up a plethora of United States TV shows and evangelists. There is such a thing as a Rapture Index, at an all time high in 2016.

souls *from* the created order."[12] The common understanding of most Christians is still, however, caught in this past *cul-de-sac* of being rescued from the created order, rather than rescued for the created order.

What a difference it makes when the future is "grounded firmly in the entire biblical story, beginning with God's original intent for earthly flourishing and culminating in God's redemptive purpose of restoring earthly life to what it was meant to be—a purpose accomplished through Christ."[13] But even this earthly focus is still too limited. In the twenty-first century the reality of the pale blue dot requires the consideration of God's purposes within the creation, not only for the Earth, but for the universe itself. We need further reflection and action in coming to terms with the apocalyptic nature of the Kingdom of God that is unfolding in the present time. After all, this was Jesus prayer, "Your kingdom come!" Yet this language is a shock to most in the life of the Church and unknown in the wider society.

In the 1960s Ernst Käsemman, further modified the apocalyptic emphasis, showing the apocalyptic in Jesus ministry was not only about the future, but the bringing of God's reign into the present. His thesis modified Weiss's end of time view of the apocalyptic, highlighting the possibility of God being known apocalyptically by the self in the present. Yet by 1998 Stephen Patterson in *'The End of Apocalypse: Rethinking the Eschatological Jesus,'* was willing to dismiss the importance of the apocalyptic as of primary importance for the interpretation of Jesus message in the gospels, on the basis of John Dominic Crossan's study of Jesus. "Far from Weiss's apocalyptic prophet of the end times, Crossan's Jesus is a radically countercultural social critic who proclaimed immediate access to an unbrokered reign of God for persons marginalised from the conventional means to humane living."[14]

He was denying the role of the apocalyptic in Jesus message and seeing instead that the focus was on the kingdom of God providing a radically new ethic for the individual over and against the Roman Empire. It is ironic that the apocalyptic was split once more into Jesus opposition to the Empire (world) and offering a particular experience or ethic (the self's access to the reign of God). Here is the apocalyptic continuing to be explained away in terms of Enlightenment categories.

AN APOCALYPSE OF JESUS CHRIST

In 1999 a friend loaned me a copy of lectures by Louis Martyn which led to his important 1997 commentary on Galatians. The word apocalypse is used here in a present and different way as a happening, an event experienced by Paul. The apocalyptic is not about the content of Jesus message or Jesus expectation concerning the future; it is the way the risen Jesus appears to Saul of Tarsus. It is an event in the present for Paul.

12. Wright, *God became King,* 17.

13. Middleton, *A New Heaven,* 312.

14. Patterson, *God of Jesus,* 170.

Paul wrote the letter Galatians to the congregation(s) in Galatia he helped establish. They were being torn apart by new leaders who replaced his gospel with another message about the Law. Galatians is one of the oldest documents included in the New Testament. In this epistle Paul defends his calling and states that the good news which he received did not come from any human authority; it was an 'apocalypse' of Jesus Christ (Galatians 1:12). All present translations of this passage translate this word as a 'revelation' of Jesus Christ to Paul. Martyn shows how all subsequent translations have followed the fourth century Latin Vulgate in which the Latin *revelo* is used to translate the Greek apocalypse. He not only points out that apocalypse is the appropriate translation here, but emphasizes that Paul's use of the apocalyptic is not about waiting for God to act in the future as the apocalyptic had come to be understood, but it is about God acting apocalyptically in the present to Paul.

For Paul this is not the transcendent communication of knowledge to him, the unveiling of something hidden, it is not even a waiting for God's future to unfold, it is a confronting event that happened to him while he was with others. The key difference between revelation and an apocalypse is clear. Revelation as the communication of divine knowledge is quite different to the irruption of an apocalypse to Paul. Revelation assumes the self as the receiver of the transcendent message,[15] whereas the apocalyptic is a present event in which God appears within space and time.

The same word apocalypse is also used in Gal 1:16. In Martyn's words, "So when it pleased him (God) apocalyptically to reveal his Son to me, in order that I might preach him among the Gentiles, I immediately kept to myself, not asking advice from anyone."[16] (Gal 1:16)

Note how the word reveal creeps in to Martin's explanation as he makes it plain that it is not a mind event but an apocalyptic disclosing of Jesus Christ.

> In this sentence there is no syntactical ambiguity. God is the subject of the verb *apokalypto*, being the actor who carried out the invasive revealing. Christ is the object of God's revelatory act. And Paul's receipt of the gospel is the result. . . . In a word, the gospel *happened* to Paul, when God stepped on the scene, invading his life in Christ.[17]

> Paul's glad tiding happens because in it God himself steps on the scene, addressing the hearers directly. This glad tidings does become a message, but at no time and under no circumstances can that message be separated either

15. Heath, *God Unbound,* 36. In a popular book written by a theologian and scholar to encourage Christians it is taken for granted that the only category available to describe the apocalyptic in Galatians (and other experiences of the revelation of Jesus Christ in the New Testament) is that these were revelations to those who were mystics, having revelatory transcendental experiences in themselves. "Paul, Mary the mother of Jesus, Joseph the husband of Mary, and all the other apostles were mystics. They were mystics because they experienced revelations of Jesus Christ that absolutely changed their lives and the world." p. 36.

16. Martyn, *Galatians,* 152.

17. Martyn, *Galatians,* 144.

from its real author (God) or from the person about whom it speaks (Christ, the Son of God). On the contrary, this glad tidings is the active power of God, because in it God himself comes on the scene, speaking his own word-event. For this reason Paul draws a contrast between a gospel that would come via a line of tradition and the gospel that came to him by God's own apocalyptic revelation. Strictly speaking, God's gospel is not an it; the gospel is the good event that God is causing to happen now.[18]

For Paul the cross of Christ is an apocalypse, "as the divine, that changes not only the cosmos but also one's way of perceiving it."[19] For the rest of his life every event and every day was seen in the light of what God had done in Christ. This invasive act of God had turned his life upside down. How was he to share this?

The experience of the apocalyptic is much more than the unveiling of truth, a belief, a mystical experience or a rational appropriation of the message. It is the uncovering or disclosing of a divine cosmic happening. This is so different to the understanding of revelation that emerged in modernity, where revelation is subjectively seeing into a transcendental divine realm dominated by reason, values feeling and belief, and has no categories for this sort of breaking into the midst of life, in the midst of history. The apocalyptic is an archetypal event that happened to Paul. It was an uncovering or disclosing of the voice of God heard and known by an event on the Damascus Road in which the Risen crucified Christ disclosed himself to him. "Last of all, as to one untimely born, he appeared also to me." (1 Cor 15:8)

There has been a great deal of research and scholarship with regard to this category of the apocalyptic and its effect upon the understanding of faith and conversion in the Church. Schweitzer's ground-breaking discovery led to Bultmann and then Käsemann. More recently there has been the rise of the so called New Perspective movement that includes Martyn, Dunn, Wright, Barclay and others.[20] The power of the Enlightenment paradigm is evident in as much as the apocalyptic is considered either from a world perspective or a subjective perspective. Originally Schweitzer described the apocalyptic in terms of Jesus expectation for the coming world, but then Bultmann described the apocalyptic in terms of subjective existentialism. It was not until Käsemann focused on the apocalyptic as an event in the present that affects the future, that the Enlightenment categories were challenged. Since then Martyn, Dunn, Wright and others have emphasized God's act as an event that irrupts upon Paul dramatically affecting all that followed in his life.

Paul's experience was radically different to that of the disciples. The life, death and resurrection of Jesus was for them God's event that happened after three or so

18. Martyn, *Galatians*, 131.

19. Martyn, *Galatians*, 32

20. The New Perspective movement is now attacked by those defending what they claim is the Old Perspective enshrined in the Enlightenment pre-apocalyptic era holding on to the category of revelation as given in the form of written scripture.

years of walking with him. They found themselves within the grand narrative of God's covenant with Israel, dramatically changing the expectations of the people of God and involving not just Israel, but all peoples.[21] For Paul this was condensed into one extraordinary confrontation. The apostles, including Paul were living in the apocalyptic announcement.

The scholars themselves involved in this re-assessment have to be careful not to let their discussions be a form of knowledge about the nature of an apocalypse without actually realizing that articles about the apocalypse are no substitute for apocalyptic moments in the life of discipleship and the experience of the Church. One can write a history and exegete the passages but still be trapped in the mind. The subject matter can however open a person to the possibility that that which is uncovered or disclosed can enable the world and our own lives to be experienced in a new way. For then the apocalypse is not an event waiting to happen, but has already happened.

APOCALYPSE—BEYOND SELF / WORLD

So what then is an apocalypse? It is a divine event that unexpectedly beyond expectation and knowledge happens to a person or a group of people that helps them confront a new framework, a different or developing world-view. It is such a divine event that involves them integrally as part of what is happening. From a first century perspective this cannot be divided into a self-world dichotomy, but involves, instead, a seeing of the self in a new world made possible through the apocalyptic event. In the life, death, resurrection, and ascension of Jesus, the apocalypse has already happened. It is an irruption into space and time that lets space and time be seen in new ways. An apocalypse gets religion out of the head into events that happen.

What the debate about the apocalypse has made plain is that for most of the last two thousand years the preaching of the church has been for the individual essentially a-temporal. There was no expectation of an apocalyptic kingdom, only the possibility of an-end time scenario of the second coming of Jesus Christ. The mission of the church was locked into a vertical movement of saving the individual for heaven with the creation only a backdrop, the stage on which this drama occurred. During the Middle Ages and in the two centuries after the Reformation the church was the gateway to heaven for both the Medieval Church and the Protestant Church. The believer escaped from creation to the paradise of heaven. The creation did not really matter.

We nearly all live with what is accepted as the traditional up and down view of reality, with God in heaven up there above humans on earth, the transcendence of

---

21. Wright, *Paul and Interpreters*. In terms of scholarship the apocalyptic is a contested space with as yet no final agreement with regard to details. This book provides a valuable overview of the voluminous state of discussion and research about the apocalyptic. The central issue here for the purposes of this work is to show the uniqueness of the category of apocalypse over against knowledge derived from the apocalypse for which the term revelation is more appropriate.

eternity beyond the temporal nature of our existence. It is a denial of the situation we find ourselves on the pale blue dot. Paul Wallace tells of a lecture he was giving in which he said that the unaided eye can see 3,000 stars above us, and if we could move the earth there would be 3,000 stars beneath us. He noticed a student with a look of horror on his face. When he inquired the student said, "It's just that you said there are stars under my feet, and I had never really thought of it like that before. Wow! . . . The words *up* and *down* momentarily lost all content. Perhaps he felt a faint flutter of vertigo."[22] The reality of our spinning earth in its orbit had never hit home before. The apocalyptic needs no up or down, only God to appear in the midst of an evolutionary universe.

When the apocalyptic is not collapsed into revelation, but seen as the Biblical witness clearly states in passage after passage, to be events, happenings which break in upon people unexpectedly in the midst of life, resulting in lives turned upside down, inside out, and world-views shattered. Once the apocalyptic is recognized it is quite strange to read the key biblical events and find that they are not the result of personal revelations, ideas or new thoughts or convictions that generate action, but events that irrupt upon a person or groups of people or even societies. It is a shock to read again so much of the Biblical record and see how much western Christianity has been reduced to ideas, thoughts in the head, attitudes and values (though these are important as well). What then is at work in these apocalyptic events within history? As Paul discovered the apocalyptic is first a confrontation with the living God and not about life after death, or subjective wishes. The category of the apocalyptic opens the pale blue dot, to the importance of creation, history, and the way God is at work in the midst of the creation and history.

It is either a disturbing thought, or an encouraging possibility, that beyond our naming of God, beyond the metaphors for power, for care, for love, God is actually the ultimate disturber at work in the midst of human history. The apocalyptic puts God as the ultimate reference point, and brings self and world into one reality in relationship to God. This God then is at work in history and in the great religions, the source of events that bring self and world into new possibilities for the future. The God who created us to respond to new visions and dreams, is continually stirring up our sense of beauty and truth in the world and stimulating self-consciousness and thought. God at work in history, draws humanity on beyond static views of the past and the legitimation of existing structures.

Once, however, that we admit the 'otherness' of apocalyptic events occurring in history, the very creativity of the human mind can find in such events undreamed of possibilities and potentials that can be worked through to radically new ways of doing things. Maybe in the mists of time and pre-history the emergence of spoken language might be more than the evolution of grunts and musical awareness and also involve the otherness of the apocalyptic. Or, as recently suggested, the great revolution that

22. Wallace, *Stars*, V11.

brought hunter gatherers to become farmer settlers in the Middle East was a result of religion, rather than being a case of farmer settlers inventing religion as a means of maintaining order and morality.[23]

Once the possibility of a God or gods is admitted, new perspectives are possible. If God is beyond the structures of perception of what we can experience and know, then to confront or be confronted by God must come with sensory overload, (experiences of awe, and dizzying awareness) that cannot easily be shared or fitted into human experience. It is likely these events will be massaged and shaped in ways that make them possible to be shared in a particular place at a particular time. It would indeed not be surprising if various elements of such impossible happenings are picked up in different ways by various cultures, various religions.

The discovery of this sort of anomalous apocalyptic God explains why, when the reports of these events are written up, they become texts and values that are held to be so precious by the culture, that they are seen to be at the heart of their understanding of reality itself. Such happenings give rise to reflection, philosophizing, meditation. With the Greeks there was the logical working through of what such events mean in terms of gods and being. In other cultures, such as the Hebrew and the Arabic, the Bible and the Qur'an document religious traditions that lie at the heart of the experience of God and the life of the individual believer and the community or nation. In the East likewise the sacred books bear testimony to the power of archetypal events and persons and their experience that have influenced and shaped the following millennia. These apocalyptic events can bring new possibilities, but too, over time there is also the possibility that the event and the penumbra of interpretation and experience associated with it can become ossified, a straitjacket locking individuals and groups into the past and finding it difficult to be the source of these new possibilities in new situations.

APOCALYPSE

How important it is to realize what the implications are of the apocalyptic event of Christ for our reading of scripture. What difference does it really make? First it leads to a re evaluation of the foundational texts in the biblical story. It is a re-evaluation that places them within the possibility of a cosmic perspective and not just an earthly or a personal perspective. Paul's apocalypse of Jesus Christ leads him to a visionary apocalypse that Abram (Abraham) had as the founding father of the Jewish and Arabic

---

23. At Göbekli Tepe a series of sanctuaries built by hunter-gatherers 9,500 years BC provided a place of pilgrimage and meetings for rituals and feasting in large numbers. It is believed that it was the building of amphitheatres and a temple with huge faceless T figures at the centre in elaborate structures that required hunter-gatherers to live together for extended periods. It is claimed it was these settlements that led to the domestication of grains and animals, and the Neolithic farming revolution that followed. Rather than farming giving rise to religion, it has led to claims that it was religion that gave rise to farming.

people, revered in three major world religions, Judaism, Christianity and Islam. Paul finds in the account of Abram the archetype for the way God is experienced. This same God at work in Abram, Paul sees is the same God at work in the apocalyptic event of the cross of Christ.

In both the early letter to the Galatians and the later letter to the church in Rome a particular passage in the experience of Abram—Genesis 15: 6 in the first book of the Torah—provides the key to his own experience of what happened to him. He presents faith in terms of this former event in Galatians, and develops this experience of faith further in Romans. In Romans 3 he introduces the need for faith. In Romans 4 the account of Abram in Genesis 15:6, becomes the key passage for understanding faith. We do well to give our attention to this passage about Abram, a passage that in a way brings us back to a perspective not so different to that of the Pale Blue Dot, the cosmos and God.

Abram was a pilgrim, leaving his homeland with his family heading into the unknown for a land God would give. In Palestine Abram rescues his nephew Lot and his property in a fight between kings, and receives a further word. "After these things the word of the Lord came to Abram in a vision, 'Do not be afraid, Abram, I am your shield; your reward shall be very great.'" (Gen 15: 1)

Abram confronts God. The promised reward that his offspring will be like the dust of the earth[24] is denied him and his barren wife Sarai. There is a vital missing link to the possible fulfillment of this promise of God—he has no offspring. Then the word of the Lord comes to him again and in the vision he is taken outside,

> "Look toward heaven and count the stars, if you are able to count them." Then
> he said to him, "So shall your descendants be." And he believed the Lord; and
> the Lord reckoned it to him as righteousness. (Gen 15:5,6)

These are momentous words for they provide the basis for the definition of faith by the apostle Paul—it is a definition of faith in a cosmic setting. Your children will be as many as the grains of dust on the Earth, and as many as the stars in the night sky—beyond counting in fact.

Considering this passage twenty years ago, I wrote: "These are foundational promises that envisage such huge numbers. This God delights in an incredible harvest of conscious awareness in the universe. Four hundred billion sand grains, equivalent to the number of stars in our Milky Way Galaxy, each one a cubic millimeter in size, would make a slab a kilometer square and forty centimetres thick!"[25]

God loves big numbers. As Abram looked at the stars in the night sky and considers his promised progeny, so now the human race finds itself on a pale blue dot circling one star amongst billions of stars. In a similar way to Abram the stars provide

---

24. Genesis 13:16. "I will make your offspring like the dust of the earth; so that if one can count the dust of the earth, your offspring also can be counted."

25. Drayton, *Pilgrim,* 166.

us with the clue to the majesty of God and the cosmic scope of God's purposes. As the numbers were breathtaking for him, so they are even more so for us.

The numbers provide the setting, but there is something here that is even more important for Paul. It is what happens to Abram in this vision encounter with God. When the vision began, Abram was a pilgrim with a promise for the future unfulfilled. When the vision ended Abram was in a new and different relationship with God, a promised future already fulfilled in faith. "And he believed the Lord: and the Lord reckoned it to him as righteousness." For Abram what a surprising unexpected apocalyptic act of God, for he now is reckoned as righteous by God—by God's act able to be in relationship with a righteous God. Abram's initial protest led to an event that happened unexpectedly and changed his future forever.

From Abram's perspective, having no offspring and then faced with the vast numbers of stars as a sign of how many his descendants would be, he is presented with an option either to dismiss this vision as a fantasy, a projection of hopes, or believe the cosmic one who has made the promise. Abram believes the author of the promise. That is obvious. What happens then is what makes this verse so important for Paul and the New Testament. It is God who acts in the situation and reckons Abram's response to him as righteousness—that is, God declares Abram as righteous. This is an extraordinary moment. The righteous God creates a new possibility. In making Abram righteous, Abram is then able to be in relationship with God. This is God's act, not Abram's doing. There are two actions here. First, Abram's belief in God opens the way for the second, God's act in reckoning Abram righteous. It is the second act of God that bursts beyond the bounds of individual belief to open the possibility of God acting upon the believer. God and Abram continue on from this vision in a new way together.

Walter Brueggemann's commentary on this passage underlines two vital issues. The first is the issue of reward. "Clearly, trusting is not the cause of fulfillment, for that would reduce things to *quid pro quo*. On the other hand, it is clear that only those who hope will be given the gift. This does not make a very logical argument. But it is a key insight of biblical faith. It has been learned not as a theoretical matter but as an experience of God's grace. The gift of God is given especially to those who trust and who will risk according to what is promised."[26]

The second concerns the nature of God's gift.

> But the sign proves nothing. How could it be that the multitude of stars is a promise of a son? We must not misunderstand the universe of discourse here. It is not an argument, but a revelation. This is a vision, a disclosure that surprises old reality. We are struggling, as was Abraham, with the emergence of a certitude that is based not on human reasons but on a primal awareness that God is God. And that certitude is given in this dark moment to Abraham.

---

26. Brueggemann, *Genesis*, 141.

He knows, and the knowing can only be credited to the work of God's brooding care.[27]

It is not an argument, but a disclosure that surprises old reality, a certitude given from a primal awareness of God as God, a result of God's brooding care, what Brueggemann calls a revelation. But it is better named as an apocalypse, 'a disclosure that surprises old reality'.

In Romans chapter 4 Abraham becomes the prototype for faith for Paul, and thereby the father of many nations. The defining characteristic is not a particular background or culture, circumcision or lack of circumcision, but the discovery of what God has brought into being.

Paul makes this connection for the church in Rome, a connection we will explore in greater detail later, for it constitutes the core of the gospel of God.

> Therefore his faith 'was reckoned to him as righteousness' Now the words, 'it was reckoned to him' were written not for his sake alone, but for ours also. It will be reckoned to us who believe in him who raised Jesus our Lord from the dead, who was handed over to death for our trespasses and was raised for our justification. Therefore, since we are justified by faith, we have peace with God through our Lord Jesus Christ, through whom we have obtained access to this grace in which we stand. (Rom 4:22-5:2)

Paul declares the parallel. Abraham's conviction that God will give a multitude of children results in Abraham's greater discovery that God brings him into relationship with God's righteous self. The believer who sees that God brought the resurrection of the crucified Jesus from the dead finds the greater discovery that it is God who establishes this new relationship of righteousness with the believer. It is the amazing act of God bringing peace with God through Christ in the grace of this new relationship.

The apocalypse that happened to Paul, seeing the light and hearing the Risen Lord on the road to Damascus, was much more than hearing a voice. "In a word, the gospel *happened* to Paul, when God stepped on the scene, invading his life in Christ."[28] He was in the presence of the Risen Lord through whom God had destroyed death in the cross and resurrection and brought a new reality into being. The very nature of reality, as he knew it, was ripped apart because God was at work in the midst of history.

What broke in upon him then led him to see, know, experience and discover that these were elements already there in the Torah. He could say to others, and I paraphrase, 'Put yourselves in Abraham's shoes, but don't look at the night sky, look at the cross of Christ. As he saw the stars and believed God, God brought Abraham into relationship with him, so brothers and sisters, the place for us to look is the cross of Jesus Christ and believe this is God's act and we will find that God will bring us into this relationship God makes possible.' This is God's act of grace.' This is what faith

27. Breuggemann, Ibid., p. 143.
28. Martyn, Galatians, 144.

is—believing that the cross of Christ is God's act for all humankind, discovering the reality of being the recipients of God's peace and grace as a gift given us in Jesus Christ.

This redemption in Christ Jesus is available for all. It is the apocalyptic reality. As a result Paul had to deal with all history, because the apocalyptic act of God in the cross of Jesus Christ causes a re-evaluation of all previous ages. This is so clearly evident in the letter to the Romans. Most attention in our churches is given to Romans chapters 7 and 8 in order to describe how the individual experiences living out the gospel. But in Romans 9 and 11 Paul re-evaluates the history of Israel in relation to God's acts, alerting the newly emerging church to the fact that it is grafted into this history, and does not supplant it. Romans chapter 11 puzzles most readers because they have not understood Romans chapter 4 and the importance of Abraham. It is all there, implicit in Genesis 15:6. Abraham believed God's promise for the future, and God reckoned it to him as righteousness and fulfilled the promise, that "In you all the families of the earth will be blessed." (Gen 12: 3b). For "Abraham's faith was faith in the God who had promised, not merely in what had been promised."[29]

Here is a global perspective that places the individual before a God who addresses all life on this planet. Over two thousand years a number of other world-views have shaped, massaged and modified the experience and understanding of faith, however. Most believers presently experience their faith through the church produced by the Enlightenment, in which faith is primarily limited to private personal subjective matters. It is more often than not experienced with a church that is organized on a denominational basis. If we are to rediscover a global perspective of faith we need to explore how these changes came about, and the effect of these changes on the church and the gospel.

---

29. Cranfield and Emerton, *Romans*, 249.

3

A Denominational God

THE LIFE/DEATH CYCLE

IN A STUDY BOOK *"The Workbook in Mission" written in 1983, I described the "death cycle" of a congregation in the urban setting and pointed out what the "life cycle" would look like. In the newly developing suburbs on the edge of the city, the new congregations in the young family areas grow their congregations by starting and sustaining a Sunday School, enlisting teachers from among the young parents who want a Sunday School for their own children. It is tough work, and becoming tougher as the competition for parent's time increase with the added demands for a couple to work to pay for their new home. Then, after a decade or fifteen years, the youth groups are formed and are bright centres of life for all, with camps and special events. Then, at 25 years, the weddings start and slowly the burgeoning youth groups decline, as the newly married couples move to the newer outer suburbs to buy a new home.*

The congregation plateaus, and for the next 20 to 25 years remains about the same size, with people moving in and others moving away. There is no way though to engage with the people who live down each street when there is no Sunday School. Women's and men's fellowships wax and wane, but do not seem able to do more than cater for the needs of the members of the congregation. Occasionally a brilliant preacher, or a community figure emerges who can spark up the life of the congregation, but after a while that person moves on. So often I hear from members of such congregations. "If only we could get the Sunday School working again people would come." Or, "The Rev John was such a great organizer or preacher. If only we could find someone like that again."

And then members of the congregation begin to retire and move away to retirement homes, or downsize, or move closer to the grandchildren. Over the next 20 years the congregation slowly declines in numbers of members. Ironically, with universities closer to the older core of cities, and the singles who have moved out of home and taken an apartment close to the city and their workplace, these congregations are actually surrounded by a younger generation who walk past, but do not enter the building. The dominant memory for most older members was the days when the annual Sunday School service had platforms reaching to the top of the back of the sanctuary. If only that could happen again. The church building is more and more associated with a traditional world that is gone, surrounded by modern apartment blocks. Old people attend as the younger generation walks by.

In the mid- 80's a conference used the book for study purposes and arranged a series of train trips from the centre of Melbourne through the established suburbs to the new homes skirting the city. Those not used to thinking in such terms came back somewhat traumatised having seen this pattern so clearly demonstrated as they travelled from sector to sector, starting with the dead centre through to the young congregations in the outer suburbs.

This pattern holds true for all the major cities in Australia. And yes as suburbs are rejuvenated, the pattern becomes less recognizable and the growth and decline of congregations in various suburbs is not as clear. Rural congregations are even more subject to a death cycle in terms of the periodic generational changes in farm ownership with the succeeding younger generation far less involved in participating in the church. But the death cycle of congregations is a given if the primary way the congregation interacts with the wider society is through the Sunday School. Since the Sunday School has declined massively in the last quarter of the twentieth century, the issue for ministry is to find how it is possible for the church to begin to grow again, rather than just ministering to the existing members as they continue to age.

Church members hated the term 'the death cycle of congregations'. I kept pointing out that the "death cycle" is the other side of the "life cycle" of congregations. When the church discovers how to relate the good news of God to the whole community, then the congregation is not defined by the age of those who live in the surrounding suburb, and the congregation will be able to share actively and dialogue with local community and those beyond. For the denominational church the almost complete dependence upon ministry with children has left the church voiceless in a society in which at least the 30% of the population who put 'no religion' in the national census are dominantly the younger parents of the children in their community. These are the parents who no longer send their children to Sunday School, since they no longer give the church the authority to teach their children.

But even when I spoke of the "life cycle" of the congregation what people heard was the "death cycle". In a state wide meeting talking about mission I said publicly, from a microphone on the stage, that I had decided not to use the term "death cycle" anymore. To my amazement there was a sudden surge of sustained clapping. In hindsight it was a mistake. I should have kept on. After all it made me complicit in the denial of what was underway.

THE DENOMINATIONAL PARADIGM

We are now at a cross roads for the church. At the beginning of the twenty-first century the churches in the west are locked into an individual—and church—centered view of faith. There has been a minimal response from the wider community to the gospel itself. It is now time to examine critically the implications of the denominational paradigm for the Western church and its influence on nearly all churches. It is time to ask why the church has not been able to respond to the insights derived from the rediscovery of the apocalyptic kingdom of God in the late twentieth and twenty-first century.

Life cycles and death cycles are part of what it means to live in a changing world and society. We now know that stars and planets possess their own life and death cycles. Life forms and civilisations rise and fall. From the perspective of the pale blue dot, it is not the death of a particular form of life or civilisation that is as important as asking what form of life or society is emerging. The apocalyptic has been introduced as a vital if not essential category for religion, and particularly the church, to rediscover hope for the future at a critical time in a global and cosmic setting when the possibility of meaning itself has been called in question. The emergence of the apocalyptic frames the mission of the church in a fundamental new way that has not impacted, however, the life of worshipping congregations. The denominational church seems locked into long term patterns that resist change, leaving the church caught in its own death cycle.

The Enlightenment gave rise to churches which function as come-structures rather than go-structures. The very language used week by week is that we go to church and go out into the world. Our task is to get others to come to church as we do. Most of the sermons, the hymns, and the organization, continually reinforce the maintenance and protection of a centered come structure.

The western culture into which we are born, and live, privileges the role of the individual, and the role of institutions. Both individuals and institutions are seen as centers from which all else flows. It is a consequence of the dualism inherent in the divorce between self and world, mind and body. It is not surprising then that faith is my subjective commitment to Jesus Christ as Lord as the center of my life, and the church becomes the center of life, as God's house in our midst. The result is a denominational God concerned with individual conversion, personal morality, and the growth and preservation of the church, either through the role of missionaries in other cultures, by evangelism of the individual, or upholding Christian values in the wider society.

The language of mission has been taken over by our society and made to be a servant of the center, used not only for personal aims and objectives, but also for the aims and objectives of institutions, in business, health, education, and voluntary groups. Whatever walk of life we are in we are caught up in a series of mission statement and missions. What if the fundamental matter of mission is not derived from either the self or institutions as the center? What if the plurality of so many missions

sent out from these many centers is a result of the de-centering of society. It is a consequence of democratic individualism, that first separates individuals from each other,
and then requires a coalescing of individuals and plans about vital centers in society.
The only way any overall plan can emerge is derived from the consideration of the
population in elections, and the assessment of needs and trends in society. In fact this
multiplication of centers is both a consequence of the loss of meaning, and a substitute
for any overarching meaning. William Neill was seeking to to reframe this accepted
understanding of mission with his prophetic comment that "the age of missions is
over and the age of mission has begun."[1] He is pointing to God as the source of mission and meaning.

The apocalypse of Jesus Christ refocuses attention on the action of God in our
midst. God's action provides a radical new framework for the understanding of mission, and especially the mission of the Church?

This came home powerfully when I was asked to present the Tuesday bible study
for the students at the seminary where I lectured. After a little thought I was quite
clear what I wanted to focus on. A student, months before, had said he was not going
to take a course on mission for the word mission was not in the Bible. And of course
the student was right, from a technical point of view, but wrong in fact, for the word
"*mission*" is the Latin equivalent to the Greek "send", and the scriptures from Genesis
to Revelation are about the sending God. I decided to do a word study on Jesus' use
of the word send in the New Revised Standard Version of the scriptures (NRSV). I
turned to one of the first passages in which Jesus sends the disciples on the road before
him, namely Matthew 9: 35—10:16.

The word send occurs three times in the passage. The first is in Jesus' words in
Matthew 9:38. "The harvest is plentiful, but the laborers are few, therefore ask the Lord
of the harvest to send out (Greek: *ekbale*—literally throw out or forth) laborers into
his harvest."

The second and third times are in Matthew 10:5 in which the disciples are "sent
out (Greek: *apestellein*) with instructions", and then again in v16 when Jesus says he is
"sending you out (Greek: *apostello*) like sheep among wolves." It was clear from these
readings that the contemporary understanding of mission was 'to send out disciples'.

When comparing versions I discovered there was a different translation in the
King James Version. There both Greek words are translated in the three verses with
the same phrase, 'send forth disciples', instead of 'send out disciples'.

It took a while to realize why these same words were translated differently. Send
out and send forth are not the same, for there is a different spatial orientation involved. Send forth is to go from one place to another in the same realm without crossing any boundaries, whereas send out is to go from one place to another crossing the
boundary between in and out. 'Send forth' made sense of the fact that when the King
James Version was published in 1611 the Church of England was the national church

---

1. Bosch, *Transforming Mission*, 39, quoting Stephen Neill.

in a time of Christendom. A person or group could be *sent forth* from a cathedral in London to York or Southampton or whatever. Wherever they were was in Church of England England!

The NRSV was published in 1989 in the time of the denominational era. No longer was the dominant form of the church the cathedral. When the church was separated from the state, each denomination built its own chapels, now, in most places, called churches. No longer was the defining mark of religious affiliation the nation in which a person was born; now the defining mark of the denominational era is the chapel of a particular denomination to which a person has chosen to belong. It is the individual's decision which is the critical dividing line between those who belong to a particular chapel (church) and those who do not belong to that chapel (church). A person is either inside or outside the chapel. The result is that evangelism and mission become part of the way the chapel 'sends out' its members and message to 'reach out' to the society to gain new members.

The translators have translated the two Greek words as '*sending out*', reinforcing the denominational paradigm itself. How remarkable to discover that the translation of the Greek words actually reflects the chapel structure of the denominational paradigm. There is a better translation than 'sending forth' or 'sending out', simply, 'send'! The key to this passage is what Jesus sends the disciples to do. "As you go, proclaim the good news, 'The Kingdom of Heaven has come near.'"(Matthew 10:7) They are given authority to demonstrate the signs of the kingdom, namely healing, exorcism and raising people from the dead. Neither the so called 'Christian space of Christendom' or the church itself is the reference point, but the in-breaking apocalyptic kingdom.

It is remarkable that the translators use these words 'send out' instead of the word 'send', thereby reinforcing the denominational paradigm. They are as such translating a Greek word into the church culture of which they are part. How extraordinary it is that the church has seen itself as the reference point for many centuries, rather than the kingdom of Heaven or kingdom of God. That tendency is reflected in the practice of the church's mission to the so-called 'un-churched'! Those not in the center are defined negatively in terms of the center!

The mission passages studied make it abundantly clear. There is no "in" or "out" boundary around the local chapel, church or congregation. We are not sent to those out there, or even to others who share a Christian framework; we are sent as followers of Christ to bear witness to the Kingdom of God wherever we go. "And you will be my witnesses in Jerusalem, in all Judea and Samaria, and to the ends of the earth."(Acts 1:8b) Now, however, the ends of the earth extend beyond the pale blue dot to a vast universe.

NEARING THE END OF THE DENOMINATIONAL PARADIGM

I have been greatly helped by David Bosch and his description of two millennia of church history, or rather mission history, in terms of six paradigms. This set the language of death cycles and life cycles into a wider and more comprehensive mission framework. The word paradigm is used here in the sense pioneered by Thomas Kuhn as the framework presumed in all perception and experience.[2] It was Hans Kung who applied the language of paradigms to church history, subdividing all of Christian history into six major paradigms.[3] Bosch has further developed the descriptions of those paradigms.[4] At the end of each paradigm there have been fundamental tipping points in society which bring not only change, but change that leads to a new way of society organizing itself, and consequently results in the church operating in a different way.

This happened with the Emperor Constantine who established Byzantium as an eastern capital of the Empire, and instituted succession through his sons. Before he came to power the church was more of an underground movement that was persecuted at times, and tolerated at other times, because it was seen as a threat to the gods of the empire. He legitimized the church in the Edict of Milan in 313AD while allowing other pagan religions to continue in the public space. Then, in 380AD, Emperor Theodosius I invoked imperial law to require all citizens to be Christian—as the Empire was splitting into the east and the west and was threatened by the Barbarians from the north. This century was a key tipping point between two drastically different contexts for the life of the church. The church changed from a subversive movement with a hidden organization, to a Christendom in which the church legitimated the structures of the empire with a church in every community.

---

2. Kuhn, *Scientific Revolutions*. This revolutionary book described the change between the Newtonian physics of the nineteenth century and the quantum relativistic world post Einstein as a change in a scientific paradigm, that required a new framework. A paradigm in this sense is a framework which is adequate to explain any experimental result. As experimental difficulties emerged with the Newtonian perspective they were initially rejected as problems of the experimental approach rather than calling in question the Newtonian framework. The guardians of the Newtonian perspective resisted the new evidence until overwhelmed by it. Others have applied this understanding to the past, seeing history as a series of paradigm shifts rather than a linear history of incremental changes. Bosch's description of the mission of the church as a series of paradigms in which major changes in society led to changes in the message has been widely influential and is used in this approach.

3. Bosch, *Transforming Mission*, 181. Kung's 6 Paradigms are as follows. 1. The Apocalyptic Paradigm of primitive Christianity; 2. The Hellenistic Paradigm of the patristic period; 3. The medieval Roman Catholic paradigm; 4. The Protestant (Reformation) paradigm; 5. The modern Enlightenment paradigm; 6. The Emerging Ecumenical Paradigm.

4. Bosch's six paradigms: 1. New Testament models of mission; 2.The Missionary Paradigm of the Eastern Church; 3. The Medieval Roman Catholic Missionary Paradigm; 4. The Missionary Paradigm of the Protestant Reformation; 5. Mission in the Wake of the Enlightenment; 6, The Emergence of a Postmodern Paradigm. It is important to realize that the form of the church in the Protestant Reformation was that of the National Church, and the form of the church in the modern Enlightenment paradigm is that of the denominational church.

The emergence of paradigms is associated with times of dramatic change when society itself is changed in the way it is organized. So much of the present discussion about the need for the church to change assumes a form of continual change in society and attitudes that has left the church in a previous era, and the task of the leader is to help the church 'catch up' with the present, or critique the present state of society. But the discussion of paradigms raises the possibility that beyond incremental change there are times of massive change in society that leads to radical new questions for the society and for the church as well. The sort of change which brings in a new paradigm is change into an unknown future, bringing new ways of seeing the world, society and the role of the individual within it.

Writing in 1991 Bosch described the emergence of a postmodern paradigm. The word emerge is critical. No one knows what the new paradigm will be until it becomes obvious, but the elements emerge well before it is obvious. Bosch documented a series of elements that he saw as bringing an end to this modern era, the Enlightenment era, in which the rights of the individual are foundational for societal organization. For the church it will be an end to what is described here as the denominational paradigm. The good news of an apocalyptic gospel for the cosmos is a key to the emergence of a different in-breaking paradigm that focuses on the mission of God rather than the mission of the church.

The word paradigm is now used in a variety of ways, many superficial, but in terms of mission history as understood here, paradigms are extraordinarily powerful world-views providing the individual and the society with frameworks that are like the air which we breathe, or the sea in which we swim. When a new paradigm emerges it puts everything into a different context. As a paradigm is breaking down, there is no welcome sign for the new to emerge—quite the contrary there is a powerful resistance to the signs of a new era. That should not be surprising. There are some echoes of this resistance in the psychological issues involved for individuals in extreme religious or political worlds who go through a process of being de-programmed. Such members do not give up easily their chosen world-views. For someone who has grown up in a political or religious sect it is a very delicate and sensitive operation to introduce that person to the 'normal' world. There are parallels, but differences when it is society itself, or the church, which hold to particular views that no longer do justice to the scriptures, the experience of faith, and the changing world in which people live. The threat of a new paradigm is far less intense but in a way more difficult to deal with because the issues are far more diffuse. A paradigm change is like helping people face the issue of climate change. The scientific evidence may itself be obvious that it is vital to lessen the human contribution to the rate of increase of carbon dioxide in the atmosphere. Karie Norgaard[5] shows how quite dramatic changes in the climate attributed to climate change do not necessarily lead to acceptance or action. The scale and reality of climate science is known in the abstract but is disconnected from political, social,

5. Norgaard, *Denial.*

and private life. The outcome is that there is little individual or social response to the threat. This goes hand in hand with powerful social forces that are heavily invested in maintaining the status quo which call in question the evidence through the use of the public media that they own.

Yet, while there is a continual hemorrhaging of members of the western church over the last three or four decades—and an inability of congregations to share faith with younger generations—the service of worship and the hymns and message still focus on the 'house of God' as the center of the 'come' message. It is familiar and comfortable, and to those who attend all that they have ever known. It is not easy to convince the leaders in the congregations, the gatekeepers responsible for the life of the congregation, that the world is changing and the issues for younger generations are different. The very understanding and experience of living in a rapidly changing society, faces the congregation with new and different roles as they respond to the mission of the living God.

It has not been for the want of trying. Theologians, missiologists, mission consultants, church planners and developmental mission agencies have been sounding the alarm, offering programs and working with congregations. The difficulty of reorienting congregations and ministry, however, is sabotaged by the denominational paradigm that subtly but directly reinforces the paradigm through the accepted structures of the congregation.

FUNDAMENTAL ISSUES FOR THE DENOMINATIONAL PARADIGM

A remarkable example of this difficulty in re-orientation, is the detailed work done in the 1960s and 1970s by the World Council of Churches. Task groups in Europe and the United States set to work studying and evaluating what they called "The Missionary Structures of the Church." Colin Williams summarized the results of this thinking in his book *Where in the World*.

> Most Christians today seem to hold an unexamined assumption—that the local congregation, centering around the homes of the members, with an ordained minister (or ordained ministers) and a church building, is and has been and will be the normal and basic form of church life. Is it? Turn to the New Testament and you will not find it. There is no word for the "congregation." The "saints" gathered regularly; but there seems to have been a remarkable flexibility in the forms of gathering. They saw themselves as one body; one household; one temple; one building; but they gathered apparently, wherever their secular life brought them together: in communities of occupation ("in Caesar's household"), in communities of residence ("the Church of God in Corinth," but meeting in houses), in communities of alienation (in the catacombs). For the first three centuries or more, they had no buildings, and in the early years there is remarkable flexibility about ministries and orders. They as

Christians were on the move, taking the gospel to the ends of time and space, and declaring everywhere—in all the highways and byways—the purpose of God, already revealed and now being made manifest, to gather all things in heaven and earth alike in Christ.[6]

Williams saw that the missionary form of the church needs to be 'on the move'. By the middle of the twentieth century the male breadwinner in the rapidly growing cities of the world spent more waking hours away from the home, travelling and at work. And, as Williams was writing, another revolution was under way. The invention of the contraceptive pill freed women from the traditional role of women as carers of children and the custodians of the home. In the post world war 2 generation the participation of males in the church dropped dramatically, and what was even more revealing was that women who had a job beyond the home, or followed a profession, had church participation rates the same as males. The car, the development of dormitory suburbs and work in jobs in a moneyed economy dramatically affected the life of the 'local congregation', the operating unit of the denominational paradigm. The local congregation was left focused on the family and the essential 'private' areas of life, while there was little way of relating to the work place which had become the 'public' domain in the secular world. The local congregation became the center for Christian worship occupied with the matters of private and personal morality, while there was little involvement with the issues of the world and the role of work in society.

In *Planning for Mission*[7], the compilation of working papers prepared in this new quest for missionary communities, Johannes Christiaan Hoekendijk stated that even in missionary thinking and planning the church puts itself in the center. He believed it necessary to,

> [s]top thinking from the inside towards the outside.... Moreover this movement from the inside to the outside, from the alleged center to the periphery (and the real center) will more often than not distort and pervert the Mission into PROPAGANDA: the attempt to make man in *our* Christian image and after our ecclesiastical likeness.[8]

We also 'must refuse to take for granted the Church and its institutions', and 'that we refrain from the customary mental movement from the ministry to the laity.'

The denominational paradigm uses this center to the periphery language, and turns it into a divorce between private and public in an inner/outer dynamic. The fact that over half a century later this inner/outer language is still as strong as ever, implicit in the translation of scripture as we have seen, shows the power of the denominational paradigm. Add to this language the common expectation, that if there is to be change,

---

6. Williams, *Where*, 4.

7. Wieser, *Planning*. The book comprises the working papers on the New Quest for Missionary Communities covering a period from 1963–1965.

8. Hoekendijk, , "Meaning of Mission(ary)," 45.

it will be in changes to the organizational structure of the church. It is still assumed in most councils of the church that the message of the gospel remains the same as it has always been. There is virtually no awareness of the way the gospel has been subjectivised in the denominational paradigm. When crises come, in the form of not enough money available to continue doing what was done before, the usual response is to restructure the institutional councils of the church, placing a bigger load on fewer people as budgets are cut, while in the local congregation, ministry is still placed at the center of the local life, with the hope that somehow the laity will be grasped by the message which they are convinced that they already know.

Hans Schmidt, another of the contributors to *Planning for Mission* puts the matter in a more technical way. He noted that there is a particular attitude to time and space implicit in these points of view, an attitude founded in Plato and Parmenides of a closed universe and a static view of truth and time and space. It is a view that triumphed until the Enlightenment and is still present in the structures of the church. The faith and the institutional forms of the church were, "acquired at the time and in the context of the structures of ancient society; they have been developed under the Platonic axiom of the unchange-ability of the truth, and have claimed a timeless validity. But truth is always happening. Therefore nobody can make an image either of God, or of man, or the world."[9] "It is the same contrast between the Greek concept of the world as a measured cosmos enclosed in itself and an Israelite-Christian understanding of the world as a mandate in history. The God of Abraham, Isaac and Jacob is not a God of the fathers, but a God of the grandfather, the father and the son—a God of the generations, who calls his people in order to work with them."[10]

This God is a God with a history who calls in space and time, and calls each generation in their particular situation. Schmidt asked basic questions for the church. "How did Jesus as the Christ claim and proclaim the universal Lordship of God? How does Christ reign in the world?"[11] Once the religiously legitimated divine hierarchies prior to the Enlightenment were dismissed by the new historical perspective he saw that people would,

> [f]all into a self-made prison in a world of their own knowledge and desires (even religious desires), and they will fall prey to the orphic (mystic) temptation to be only organ and function of the then-existing conditions. . . . society needs a church which is free for its world mission in order to assume its responsibility for the continuing world events; and every individual needs the liberating word which places him in the service of righteousness away from hopeless concern for himself. [12]

9. Schmidt, *Planning,* 112.

10. Schmidt, *Planning,* 116.

11. Schmidt, *Planning,* 112.

12. Schmidt, *Planning,* 112. Note that the word 'orphic' can also be translated as 'mystic'.

Or, put another way, for the Hebrews the temple was the place where the tabernacle came to rest. In Exodus it was the way God journeyed with the people. It was the way God was in the world. The Platonic world-view developed a series of hierarchies with God as the transcendent really real, and the earth as the place of temporality and change. This changes the role of the temple. In this perspective the temple becomes the portal in the midst of life to worship the transcendent God above. God is not journeying in the world but resides in heaven. In a similar way in the middle ages the church became the gateway to this eternal heaven above. The Enlightenment dismissed these hierarchies. The church, however continued to maintain this vertical relationship between the individual in an immanent world and God in heaven above. The result is that the believer finds themselves in a self made prison of their own knowledge and desires about God with the added temptation to accept the existing conditions of life as the background of life and not the concern of God

What happened to this search for missionary structures? It has gone on in some way, but not directly in terms of this formulation of them. In the international councils of the church it would seem that the discovery of the mission of God has not led to further reflection on the missionary structures of the church, but more in the direction of the need for further ecumenical initiatives, the need for peak bodies to speak into the world situation, and the on-going issue of the continuing viability of such organizations in a time when their support base continues to erode. The focus of attention has moved back to liturgy and ministry in the world.

For whatever reason I was astonished to read this penetrating analysis half a century after it was published, and realized this search for the missionary structures of the church in the world has not continued. The church is still locked in a time warp in its understanding and experience of God. Many search for fresh expressions of church, but by placing the church in the center they are still captive to the God of the Enlightenment church, expressed in the form of the denominational paradigm. Is not this resistance to the call of an anomalous apocalyptic God? It is apocalyptic, because God speaks in the midst of history to give a purpose and a future for the pale blue dot and not only for the church, and anomalous because it is God who in Christ who calls our present structures into question. The resistance shows so clearly how the Enlightenment has actually cut down God to an individual church perspective. Schmidt argues that "society needs a church which is free for its world mission in order to assume its responsibility for the continuing world events; and every individual needs the liberating word which places him in the service of righteousness away from hopeless concern for himself."[13]

These questions do not go away but renew in intensity and variety. As the perspective on the world continues to change, and as the perspective from space becomes more well known, the missionary structures adequate for the mission to the pale blue dot become more urgent.

13. Schmidt, *Planning*, 112.

Why is it that discoveries about the sheer size of the universe, the evolutionary view of the universe, and the Earth as a planet, have not made any impact on the views of most worshippers in the pews on a Sunday morning? Few are aware of the way these radical new views of the world impact on religious thinking. We have seen that the denominational structure of the church is taken for granted by the Protestant church. It is presumed by nearly all, that the mission of the church is to reach out to the community, that members are called to be committed to the Lord and the church, to invite others to come to church and to witness to them. Even the older pre-Enlightenment churches, such as the Roman Catholic Church and the national churches have slowly had to come to terms with this denominational view of the church.

We have, however, reached the stage where it is evident that worrisome deep and pervasive trends are happening to all denominations in the west. The response to religious question(s) in national censuses of the population showed that until the 1970s, all answered the question positively apart from a small minority. Since then those marking none, or not answering the question at all, has increased dramatically. Even in the United States where church attendance is highest in the west, the 'Nones' increased from 8.2% to 14.3% in the decade 1992–2002. In Australia the rise has been far more dramatic, increasing from 5% to 30% in the period 1971–2016. Analysis shows an increasing number of the younger generation disown denominational identity with the result the church is predominantly made up of older generations. The use of such sociological research has helped gain a sense of what is happening in the Church. The results of the National Church Life Survey in Australia (1991–2016) provide a careful twenty-five year longitudinal study of the life of all churches in the nation, which shows that the churches of all denominations are declining and getting older. A few Pentecostal churches bucked the trend for a while in the last decade of the twentieth century, but they too are now losing members. This is not only true of Australia—it is true for Europe and North America as well. A vital and growing Protestant church in the middle of the twentieth century has lost touch with most in the society 50 years later as the twentieth century ended.

It is no wonder that there is a helpful consultant industry available to help congregations find new ways to connect with their message and their immediate community. For the last thirty years I have either been involved in new experiments or researching attempts to do church in new ways. There is now a growing literature on 'the emerging church' that is important if not compulsory reading for church leaders and ministers. A decade ago I resolved to read as widely as I could about these new attempts at ministry in the contemporary world. At first it made exciting reading. Throughout the world there are many groups attempting to find new forms of worship and service that see the importance of the church ministering to the world as it becomes ever more global, interconnected, facing planetary issues. Many of these practitioners and writers call the existing structure of the church into question on the basis of its identification with western culture.

After a while I became strangely dissatisfied. It became apparent that much of what was being done was a reaction to the church as it now is. There was much type-casting of the church as an institution, a monument or a system, or some combination of all of these. Repeatedly the conclusion was that the church needed to become a movement, a dynamic community, an organic body able to be in mission to the world.

What became obvious was that there were a limited number of views of what constituted the heart of the movement, and a limited number of views of what the real issue was that had to be addressed. I began to think that most were still trapped within the predominant denominational paradigm that has created the present context for ministry. Leaders were searching for other ways to do ministry, without realizing that the categories they were using, and the way they were seeing the issues, were predominantly a creation of the Enlightenment.

The consultants, speakers and writers in this field had one of three primary ways of calling the church back to its task. The first approach was to learn from the nature of society as it now is, and attempt to find new ways for those searching for a more authentic experience of church in terms of new forms of inter-relationship, community, or life style derived from the gospel. The English group Ikon are very much aware that they are pilgrims and sojourners on a journey 'building relevant contemporary churches'. Brian McLaren also has written much about the way the form of the church has been shaped by many historical contexts, and the need for the church to ask again what was Jesus' message and mission and its implications for today.[14] The second approach was to look back to the Reformation and seek to base the life of the church on the local congregation. It was a call to explore different forms of church through a more dynamically appropriate stress on justification by faith and the need for a substitutionary understanding of the atonement. The third way was to claim that the church has to return to the New Testament message in order to rediscover the message for the present day as Michael Frost and many others have persuasively argued. The church must get back before Christendom. "We must begin with the example of Jesus himself. Before we begin strategizing or scheming, we twenty-first-century Christians must reposition ourselves chiefly, first and foremost, as people of the way of Christ." [15] Other writers speak of this emerging church as the development of a post-denominational church, a post-evangelical church or a missional church, taking seriously the worldwide issues of society and the importance and willingness to forge new structures.

In a way all are right, yet each in their own way are not taking seriously the way the most recent history of the church has affected our context. The lack of awareness of the impact of both Christendom and the Enlightenment on the present situation was a great surprise.

---

14. Brian McLaren has written, *A Generous Orthodoxy*, *The Secret Message of Jesus*, *A New Kind of Christian*, *Everything Must Change*, and other books outlining this approach.

15. Frost, *Exiles*, 27.

Those who are reacting to the church as it now is, fail to see how the shape of the present church takes for granted fundamental values that have shaped the present era. Those who want to return to the Reformation not only have to ignore the historical context that the Enlightenment brought into being; they also are presuming the discredited God ordained 'chain of being' assumed by the *ancien regime* endorsing the divine right of kings to rule, that was swept away by constitutional democracies. As *Planning for Mission* makes clear the church has not faced the way science, technology and a radically different cosmology have impacted on the belief and the shape of the church. For those who want to return to the New Testament, there is an enormous leap into a different world across a 'hermeneutical ditch' of two thousand years, from one worldview to a radically different worldview involved in translating the message. Each of these approaches takes for granted the importance of the individual and faith as the key elements to be unpacked, without stressing sufficiently the importance of the changing all embracing worldviews in which the individual is found. The rediscovery of the importance of the kingdom of God and the apocalyptic reality have shown how these later world-views mask and hide vital elements of the original message.

I remember the moment of realization that came from a comment of the Rev Donald Elliot of the Council of Churches for Britain and Ireland during a visit to London in 1994. "In our time you cannot go around the Enlightenment; you have to go through it."[16] It is not a matter of repudiating human experience and discovery, but a need to take seriously the consequences of those discoveries and the way they now have impinged upon the life of the church.

What stood out in the writing about the 'emerging church' was the lack of awareness of the role of Enlightenment on the perception of the self and world and the role of religion. It was not seen to be significant for these writers. As noted earlier David Bosch has detailed six paradigms in the life of the church. Each comes and irrevocably brings changes to the message and the form of the church as it seeks to come to terms with radically new societal contexts. Each of these paradigms has impinged upon the message of the gospel, the church, and society as we know experience it. The attempt to short-circuit these effects and return to the New Testament is admirable in wanting to go to the heart of the apostolic message. It is, however, difficult to dis-entangle the results and effects these subsequent paradigms have had. The desire to find the core of the gospel in the Reformation is attractive. That too is caught up with the breakdown of the medieval Roman Catholic missional paradigm and the creation of the missionary paradigm of the Protestant Reformation at a time in which there was a radically different understanding of the world, God, and society. Bosch's desire to look to the future and explore the elements of an emerging ecumenical missionary paradigm seems to offer promise. This attempt to discern a new structure has to become aware of the Enlightenment foundations the church has incorporated into its own life and that are now taken for granted.

16. Drayton, *Pilgrim*, 161.

The first task is to take seriously the present day context, and begin the process of discovering how the Enlightenment denominational church came into being. How does the form of the church in society both affirm and reinforce key aspects of the church, society and the message, and at the same time, mask and hide key aspects of the church, society and the message? It is vitally important to come to terms with the denominational paradigm that is the en-globing reality that provides a view of the world and informs the experience of the individual and the church of the present. There is the present 'death cycle' in the life of congregations that place themselves in the center not able to hear that they are 'sent' rather than the sending agents. There is the subjectivisation and privatization of faith that locks believers and the congregations into private morality and local neighborhoods. And, then, there are the troubling questions concerning the missionary structure of the church that have been left unanswered. It is absolutely necessary to come to terms with the nature of the denominational church. The next chapters dig deeper into the historical context, and the nature of the self that came into being. This exploration will show how the gospel and the church was shaped by this new revolutionary view of society.

Only then will it be possible to understand why the denominational churches have in the main, not been able to come to terms with the twentieth century rediscovery of Jesus apocalyptic message of the kingdom of God. At the same time the denominational church now finds itself in a radically different twenty-first century world from the world and world-view in which the denominations were first formed. The Earth, once at the center of the world, is now a pale blue dot in a universe of galaxies.

4

Uncovering the Denomination

TWO FLAGS

AS AN AUSTRALIAN MINISTER *arriving to serve in a Mid-West congregation in the United States, I found two flags present at the front of the church—and all other churches where I worshiped. There alongside the pulpit was the American flag, and on the other side, in the matching position, the Christian Flag. I had never heard of the Christian flag! One day in the seminary library I randomly stumbled upon an account of how the flag was created. Elaborate preparations had been made for a special Methodist Sunday School rally in New York in 1904[1]. With only minutes to go the superintendent was shocked to be handed a late last minute telegraph message. The distinguished speaker would not be arriving on the train as expected. What was the superintendent to do? Rather than cancel the special event he decided to go ahead and deliver the key address himself. He spoke about the need for a Christian flag to fly alongside "Old Glory".*

> *The ground is white, representing peace, purity and innocence. In the upper corner is a blue square, the colour of the unclouded sky, emblematic of heaven, the home of the Christian; also a symbol of faith and trust; in the center of the blue is the cross, the ensign and chosen symbol of Christianity: the cross is red, typical of Christ's blood.*

He did not forget this improvised speech. Eventually in 1907, he and a Methodist youth leader had the flag made, and promoted its use in churches throughout America. It spread rapidly across many Protestant churches and was eventually endorsed nationally and ecumenically by the Federal Council of Churches in 1942. Subsequently a hymn, and a pledge of allegiance, were created by others.

---

1. I rued the day I replaced the book without taking down the details. More recently a Wikipedia article and other pages on the Christian flag give a different date, that of September 26 1897, but in all other respects confirms this account.

I did not believe it was appropriate to preach under the American flag. Each week I would push it back a little, but at the end of the month the cleaner always put it back into its "right position" without ever realizing what I had done. It was a cultural given. And in the basement Sunday School I later found that our two pre-school children were expected, with all other children, to pledge their allegiance to the American flag and the Christian flag.

When I discussed this practice with our church members they found it difficult to accept my unease. It seemed to me the importance of the American flag in this culture had created a need for a parallel Christian symbol that involved the individual making public declarations of faith, in a similar way to the citizen's declaration of allegiance to the national Flag. It all seemed to be earthed in a form of civil religion. The colours in both flags are the same. White is for purity in both, red is for the blood of Jesus in the Christian flag and hardiness and valor in 'Old Glory'. Blue in the Christian flag focuses on the sky, heaven, baptism and faith and in the American flag vigilance perseverance and justice. Faith and nationality seem to be operating in a similar way in these acts of individual and corporate allegiance.

A NEW WORLD

A flag is a powerful way to provide a rallying point, and a symbol to give identity to a place, people or religion. The Christian flag is a practical symbol of the Enlightenment denominational paradigm.[2] The origin of the denominational form of the church had its roots in the new world continents of the Americas. It took a long time for this different form of church to come into being and later give expression to this unique new Christian flag.

Soon after the discovery of North America by Christopher Columbus, Amerigo Vespucci discovered South America and published his report in letters entitled 'The New World.' These adventurous explorers went to the ends of the Earth and found a world that was not supposed to be there—and it is not surprising that Vespucci called it a 'New World' over and against the 'Old World' of Europe. Soon after these lands were called the Americas after his first name. This new world raised new issues. Were its inhabitants human or sub-human? Could they be civilized? What did the church have to say to these people? It took a Bartolomè de Las Casas, in the name of their God given humanity, to protest the conquistadores massacre of millions of those they dismissed as "sub human" Indians.

It is never easy to address the new. One thousand years prior to this discovery the assertion that people could live south of the equator was dismissed on the authority of scripture in the 'doctrine of the antipodes'. In the 5th century Augustine responded to suggestions that the world was spherical by declaring, that if it was, there could

2. The fifth paradigm Bosch describes is the modern Enlightenment paradigm that followed on from the Protestant (Reformation) paradigm.

be no life in the antipodes—such peoples could not exist! "Augustine had learnt that the words of God had been proclaimed to the 'ends of the earth'; but here there was a problem. There was no record of these preachers having been to the antipodes. The authority of scripture was thus such that, in effect, Augustine concluded that since 'we find it constantly declared that, as those preachers did not go to the antipodes, no antipodes can exist.'"[3] In the twenty-first century the ends of the earth is the universe itself that contains a seemingly insignificant pale blue dot. In the near future these past events may well be analogies to remember when there are results from the findings of probes to other planets in space beyond the Earth.

Over the next 200 years, as settlements multiplied along the east coast of America, the religious issues of the old world were imported into this new setting. Would this new mission field open new ways of discovering other aspects of the gospel, previously hidden, perhaps recover past perspectives, or lead to a continuation of the practices of the old world? Few, however, envisaged the radical change that would eventuate as a result of the American Revolution in the new world that would then dramatically impact upon the old world of Europe.

On this edge of the known world there was a patchwork of colonies from various nations, but no one nation. There was a plurality of religious groups inter-relating with one another. In the old world various religious groups had split or been suppressed by the dominant National Church structure in the various nations of Europe. It was the Peace of Augsburg in 1555, following the collapse of the Medieval Roman Catholic Empire, that led to the agreement that 'each region has to follow the religion of its ruler'. In England, a civil war protesting this agreement led to a reinstating of this doctrine in 1660. After this, gradually a policy of tolerating non-conformist groups developed in England and some European nations, but in others these groups were still being persecuted by national churches. The result was, that in the eighteenth century, along the east coast of the Americas there were numerous national settlements, each with their particular national church, as well as settlements of other religious groups fleeing persecution. When this polyglot region became a nation these numerous and diverse religious groups would have to find a way to live together. The Enlightenment view in this new world setting led to a major revolution in society and with it a new form of church. No longer was the religion of the ruler the religion of the subjects. Now the ruler or leader was a result of the free choice of citizens in the two new realms that emerged—in politics and also the church. In terms of the church it was up to the member to choose the particular church to which they would belong. Each time a new paradigm has come into being it has done so as a result of great societal change and religious questioning. What is surprising is that the radical emergence of denominational churches at this time is a history that is not widely known. Here was a revolution in the structure and the form of the church unlike any other in the history

3. Pearson, "Christ's Sake," 208

of the church. Today, most in the church take it for granted that the denominational form of the church is the way the church has always operated.

It was to take 50 years to rip apart, irrevocably, the accepted order and fabric of church and society that had been in place for the three hundred years in Europe prior to the American Revolution. It would see the emergence of a new religious view of the world in which the church was separated from the state. The critical date for this separation is 1786 and the decisive place was the new state of Virginia. It took a decade of tough politics between determined opponents in the Virginian Legislature, before legislation first proposed by Thomas Jefferson in 1776 was finally passed a decade later.

It is not surprising that after the American Revolution the fledgling United States had reasons for seeing itself as the New World over and against the Old Order of Europe. A democratic government, and a voluntary church brought a fundamental change in the way people saw themselves. They were no longer subjects of monarchs but free citizens responsible to choose what the nation should do, and responsible to choose and support voluntarily their churches. No longer was there an "established" church that could use the laws of the land to outlaw as "nonconformists" anyone who disagreed with an established church policy or doctrine. Now people were free to meet in whatever church they chose and decide what they would believe.

The background to this decisive legislation in Virginia was a result of the particular way that the religious settlements responded to a call for religious conversion, a new approach to the declaration of the gospel. It began with what came to be called the 'Great Awakening' that broke out during the ministry of Jonathan Edwards (1733–1735) in his congregation in Northhampton, Massachusetts. His powerful defence of the events is in his widely read *A Faithful Narrative of the Surprizing Works of God in the Conversion of Many Hundreds of Souls in Northhampton and the Neighboring Towns and Villages.*

In 1739, Edwards sponsored the visit of the English evangelist George Whitefield to New England, enabling him to enter this Puritan stronghold, which prior to this time had barred travelling preachers. Wherever Whitefield preached thousands came to hear him speak about the need to be "born again." During the following decade other evangelists followed and many people were converted, bringing tensions to local congregations which were part of the local Puritan town-church covenant. Splits began to occur between the conserving "Old Lights" and the enthusiastic "New Lights". It was not long before these new groups joined with the so-called General Baptists. There were now at least two different churches in many communities, radically dividing and fracturing the Puritan Commonwealth, an indication of what was to come.

Over the next three decades tensions with England increased over what the northern colonists believed were unfair taxes, imposed without representation, by the English Parliament. Whitefield continued to visit, travel, and preach through the colonies in a total of eleven visits, and finally died and was buried in Newburyport, Massachusetts in 1770. Some historians "have suggested that the Great Awakening provided a cluster of ideas which informed revolutionary discourse. Indeed they argue that most men and women explained revolutionary issues to themselves and others more through evangelical than Enlightenment language."[4]

Whitefield's declaration of the new birth was reported widely by the newspapers, recently freed from censorship. His language provided an evangelical, revolutionary, religious, and social vocabulary for people. He helped develop a new public awareness in communities that spread beyond individual colonies. Lambert cites the pilgrimage of some soldiers to Whitefield's tomb during the Revolutionary War; "The soldiers desired to see the tomb of George Whitefield, which they knew lay in the crypt beneath the altar. After the sexton opened the coffin, the officers began to cut off small pieces of Whitefield's collar and wristbands. As they marched off on a dangerous mission, they carried with them amulets taken from the body of one whose life and ministry had become a symbol of hope and salvation."[5]

Whitefield spent little of his time in the southern colonies in the 1740s even though the primary purpose of his travels was to raise money for an orphanage and a theological college in Georgia. The colonists had gone to Georgia to grow tobacco and cotton, provide a place to send convicts, and also keep the French and Spanish at bay, with the blessing of the English Parliament. The Church of England provided there, as it did in England, the religious framework for a deferential society. Isaac Rhys[6] outlines this different world in terms of the gentry in their large homes, the planters in smaller homes, and the huts where Afro-American slave workers formed their own communities. He carefully and deliberately shows how religion and law mutually joined and reinforced each other in such a society.

In the southern colonies it was the law that provided the vital basis for a deferential society that at first able was able to keep the consequences of the Awakening at bay.

> All the different forms of gentry domination were subtly concentrated and institutionalized in the system of local government. The seats of the country courts and parish vestries were held by members of the ruling elite, who served without salary and filled up their own vacancies by co-optation. They thus simultaneously embodied "liberality" and the rightful rule of those whom distinguished property, family, and learning set above the common folk. Command of the law sustained this social supremacy of the gentry.[7]

The same persons were both lawgivers and law enforcers.[8] Such control of the law maintained the order of society but as a God-given order. "Association with institutionalized divinity helped to give law a sacrosanct character. The raised benches in

---

4. Lambert, *Pedlar,* 215.

5. Lambert, *Pedlar,* 215.

6. Rhys, *Virginia.*

7. Rhys, *Virginia,* 133.

8. Rhys, *Virginia,* 135.

the court-houses and the magistrates' pews at the front of the churches gave formal precedence and authority to the leading gentlemen who headed great households, commanded large credits, and had an assumed familiarity with the books in which the essentials of law and divinity were stored."[9]

From 1745 on two fundamental matters emerged in Virginia that the gentry were not able to easily solve. The first was the desire of the ordained Church of England ministers to have guaranteed stipends, settlements and an appropriate status in society independent of the 'liberality of the gentry'.

The second was the appearance of Presbyterian 'awakened' itinerant preachers, and later 'Separated Baptists', who had migrated south, gathering groups together, including slaves, the ignorant and the poor, and in the process vilifying 'established religion'. The gentry used the courts and other violent measures to stop this revolutionary activity—their preachers were hounded and groups suffered persecution. Then, in the mid 1770s, the Methodists appeared, complicating matters further, raising up new groups of people with their call for vital religion within the Church of England.

Voices started to be heard in public calling for the freedom to gather for religious purposes. In a speech given in 1772 student James Madison, the cousin of the later President, voiced the thoughts of the rational clergy and professors of his College. "I am well aware" he declared, "that even the Idea of a free Toleration in Matters of Religion, has been a Source of endless Apprehensions," and that "to some, this Freedom of Mind . . . may seem the ready Avenues to Corruption and Depravity. Human life, thus unhinged, the universal Fabric appears already dismembering."[10]

With the onset of the Revolution imminent and the Legislature disbanded by Britain, the gentry called for large gatherings at the courthouses similar to that of the Baptist association meetings. Virginians came to sign the 'provincial association', elected by acclamation their representatives, and raise money for the Bostonians. When victory was won, Virginia still had not decided what it would do about the dissenting religious groups that had grown stronger during the Revolution. The Baptists grew rapidly in numbers and strength with many former members of the Church of England joining their congregations.[11] The reforming Methodist Church also grew quickly as the Church of England ministers left their congregations for Canada or

---

9. Rhys, *Virginia*, 136.

10. Rhys, *Virginia*, 203.

11. In 1771 the Baptists formed a "General Association" bringing together many Baptist groups. They saw the opportunity to challenge the religious establishment in Virginia and perhaps believed that they could bring about change if they remained united. They were strongly in favor of independence, hoping that the Declaration of Independence would see a victory for the United States, and not a return to even more intensive religious persecution under the Church of England, if England should win. They rightly sensed that the return to England of many Church of England ministers, and the feeling against Britain and its national church was an historic opportunity to free the Baptist Church from the persecution it had experienced for centuries, and free the Church from interference by the State. The Baptists saw their own principles embedded in the Constitution, prepared by men who had other reasons for espousing their cause, such as Jefferson, Franklin, Madison.

England. Virginia was still caught up in a social conflict that "was not over the distribution of political power or of economic wealth, but over the ways of men and the ways of God."[12]

SEPARATION OF STATE AND CHURCH

In 1786 the Baptists joined with the Deists to support a section of the Thomas Jefferson Bills that had languished for nearly a decade after the Revolutionary War. The result was overwhelming support for the radical separation of church and state. It was a relatively simple step. The state ceased to fund churches. Free and equal citizens were able to choose the church they wanted to belong to, but they would have to pay for its operation.

Jefferson did not completely carry the day. The Baptists refused to support his three Bills that preceded the Bill for Establishing Religious Freedom. These Bills sought to replace the "parish" by the "hundred" and replace pulpits with publicly supported teacher's positions. Instruction was no longer to take place from the Bible as a primer, but from republican texts. "A new Virginia republican "establishment" would replace the old Anglican Christian one."[13]—It would mean replacing an ecclesiastical hierarchy with an educational hierarchy, leaving the educated and cultured still at the pinnacle of society. The Baptists would have none of this, having suffered from ruling elites for centuries.

In 1791, four years after the United States Constitution was ratified, it was the Baptist Church which petitioned Washington for the religious amendment included in the first amendment of what came to be called the Bill of Rights. It was finally passed in the following form. "Congress shall make no law respecting an Establishment of Religion, or prohibiting the free exercise thereof." The Baptists had helped bring an end to the legislative persecution of religious minorities by established churches that they had suffered since the Reformation, and in doing so ushered in a new form of church.

The American Revolutionary War led to the separation of the church from the state in the English speaking world. Or more correctly it was the state that removed religious bodies from being part of government, as they were previously in the time of the national church paradigm. It saved a lot of money for government now that they did not have to build churches, support clergy, and decide where they should minister. The law of the land defined by the Constitution then stood in its own right as the responsibility of the legislature of this new nation (under God) without the need for legitimation by church or religion. The law was emancipated from religion.

The churches, were no longer bound by the decisions of the state with regard to belief—religion was defined in terms of the free exercise of what individuals did with

12. Rhys, *Virginia*, 162.

13. Rhys, *Virginia*, 294.

their belief. Socially it was to become a matter of self-funding voluntary participation in religious bodies. These fundamental changes are now taken for granted, and not fully appreciated for the consequences, both intentional and unintentional, that flow from them.

The religious energy from the Great Awakening and the independence that flowed from the American Revolution were the critical factors in ripping the old fabric of society apart, resulting in the separation of the church from the newly formed state. The events in Virginia gave emerging groups such as the Baptists and Methodists the opportunity and the framework to take advantage of a new mindset, a new way of being church in a new society.

Thomas Jefferson requested that his memorial cite this legislation as one of his three most important achievements. 'Author of the Declaration of Independence; of the statute of Virginia for religious freedom; and Father of the University of Virginia.' The fact that he had been foreign ambassador to France, then President for two terms, and had added the extra territory of Louisiana to the United States did not rate a mention! But he was right. Two of these were statutes that changed the world.

What would this freedom mean for the individual citizen and believer? The implications are summed up so well in a letter Jefferson wrote on the occasion of the opening of a synagogue. "Jefferson observed that while tyranny reveled in religious unity, freedom flourished in multiplicity. In civil government, one repeated the words 'United we stand, divided we fall.' In religion, said Jefferson, the opposite was true: 'Divided we stand, united we fall.'"[14]

When religion was a matter between a person and their God, Jefferson had no problems. For him it was organized religion that threatened the freedom of the citizens of the state. As he put it when acknowledging the religious persecutions of Jews in the West in 1818: "your sect by its sufferings has furnished a remarkable proof of the universal spirit of religious intolerance inherent in every sect, disclaimed by all when feeble, and practiced by all when in power."[15]

He had bought a Qur'an in 1765 and read widely with regard to Muslims (20 percent of Afro-American slaves were Muslim) as a way of working through how the freedom of citizens could be protected from organized religion in the Constitution.[16]

Jefferson presumed that the wider society was Judeo-Christian in values and that citizens were free moral agents. As trade, travel and immigration opened each nation to the world, his form of religion left open the possibility for other religions to find a place within the state. In later life Jefferson created his own New Testament, cut and pasted from the four gospels, to form his own ethical picture of Jesus shorn of miracles and divinity. Because of his Enlightenment focus on the state as the governing body

14. Gaustard, *Altar of God*, 205.

15. Jayne, *Jefferson's Declaration*, 157.

16. Spellberg, *Jefferson's Qur'n*,

and his emphasis on ethics it is likely, given the right circumstances, he may have also created a Jefferson Torah, or a Jefferson Qur'an.

THE NEW DENOMINATIONAL PARADIGM

In one sense the denominational structure had been a long time coming, but it came as a massive shock to the religious institutions of the day. The Pietists and the Baptists had long been used to meeting in homes and out of the way places, far from the cathedrals and churches that dominated the cities and villages of their day. What a difference for them to wake up and find that no longer did they have to seek permission to meet, or were penalized socially for belonging to a suspicious group. They were free to meet as citizens, not penalized subjects.

Within fifty years, in nearly every democratic country, the state had refused to fund churches. Each country dealt with the churches in different ways to bring about this freedom of citizens to worship as they chose. In Europe, England and Germany the former established national churches continued to be privileged in some way, such as the church having a say in parliament in the House of Lords in England, or finances for the church collected by a general religious tax by the state, as in Germany.

For national churches the established practices of centuries were changed overnight. They were now only one church among many in their nation. No longer supported by the nation, they were faced with the need to finance ordained ministers and maintain their church buildings, let alone build new ones. Access to power through parliament and privilege was removed in most countries.

The Methodists and the Baptists were the churches that first worked best in this new American setting. The Methodists pioneered the use of camp meetings and class meetings on the frontier, being there alongside the pioneers with circuit riders supporting and fostering leadership. The Baptists were no longer a clandestine organization so they could now openly invite people to be part of their associations and congregations and did so with gusto. After the initial shock of this new way of operating other churches began to adapt to this new religious, political and social environment.

In the United States the Constitution creates what Jefferson later called a wall of separation between state and church. Jefferson was convinced that institutional religions should not be involved in the political realm, for the sake of the political realm. He was seeing the matter from the political side of the wall of separation. Most discussion about political theory and constitutions is from this perspective. There is not a lot written about the profound impact of the wall of separation on the life of the church. There is a widespread awareness that citizens have the freedom to worship in the way they choose. Often in worship someone prays, 'We give thanks that we are free to meet and worship.' There is little reflection about the effects of the state separating the sphere of the church from the state. In fact, the denominational church, is a creation of the state by the decision of the state. Most constitutions of democratic nations now affirm the right of the individual to worship in whatever way they choose, and limit the role of the state to legislate in the religious sphere. The result is there are a number of important factors that need to be taken into account when describing the nature of the denominational church.

There is now a variety of churches from which a citizen can choose.[17] The separation of the church from the state by the state effectively destroyed the authority of any church's claim to primacy. Religion was relativized. It is up to any specific church or denomination to convince the individual citizen to join and participate. Some denominations seek to affirm their credibility on the basis of their ordained leadership being part of the apostolic succession reaching back to the New Testament. Other denominations claim their form of organization is the true church in terms of their understanding of the early church and the Bible. Some emphasize the truth of the doctrine they profess, while others the commitment of members and their particular experience of Jesus Christ.

The decision of the state results in a particular denomination having little direct say in terms of the political process. Further, denominations must define themselves over and against the political world, and over and against other churches. In a democratic society the individual is both a free citizen and equal with all others before the law. The wall of separation protects the individual from the state legislating about religious matters, and decrees that citizens are free to choose whether to meet together in churches. It is up to the individual to choose whether they will belong to a particular church or no church at all. That seems such a simple thing to say, but it has extensive consequences. It introduces a spatial element into the life of the church. In a technical sense the national church of the of the previous era has become a local chapel of the denomination. The result is that in any area there are many chapels or congregations, each with their own distinctive emphasis, that gives rise to a 'competitive piety' between congregations. There are then a series of boundaries between each of the chapels, and each chapel and the society of which it is part. This denominational reality has enormous ramifications for each congregation.

It is important to explore the features of this setting in some detail. What are the consequences of having say ten denominations each claiming to be the true church within the one state? The nineteenth and twentieth century effectively provided a social laboratory that describes the various ways that religions, or more precisely denominations, have impacted on each other and carved out a role for religion in the wider democratic society

Firstly, the wall of separation does not entirely separate state and religion. When most denominations agree together, the state has to listen, not because of their

---

17. It is difficult to decide how many separate denominational organizations there are. A common figure states 40,000, but generally in the West there are of the order of say 10,000 with six major groupings, namely Roman Catholic, Anglicans, Protestant, Orthodox, Charismatics and Independents.

combined statements so much as the power of their members to influence the majority of the opinion of voting citizens in the state.

Secondly, in Jefferson's time, there was still widespread acceptance of the authority of the Bible, even if interpretations varied significantly. It was not yet a time of literary and historical criticism of the text. That meant citizens in the state at least shared a common source for religious belief. With the Enlightenment came the rise of an historical critical consciousness of the biblical text. Research into the text, the viewpoint of various scholars, a greater emphasis on the context, and a growing awareness of history, evolution and psychology, called the authority of the Scriptures into question and divided the way that the Scriptures were interpreted in the church and in the wider society. There were a proliferation of bible translations, further emergence of new denominations, and a wider range of beliefs. As the nineteenth century gave way to the twentieth, there was less of a common religious language, less of a basis for denominations to share together, and less of an opportunity for denominations to make an impact on the state. Add to this the effects of migration and the development of multi-religious states, with more than one holy book, each with its followers meeting in groups, and clearly there are new issues involved in the organizational separation of church and state. It is not surprising that as this growth in diversity of groups happened, there was a realization in some churches that this lessened the influence of the gospel in the wider society. The importance of churches working together ecumenically began to grow.

Thirdly, while the law of the state was emancipated from religion in this democratic order, the law of the nation became a vital issue for the denominational church. For those on the church side of the wall, God was still the lawgiver, but with a difference. Rather than as in the previous paradigm, in which one church divinely legitimated the law of the land, now each denomination has its own particular view of the divine law and the way that law should be upheld not only within the denomination but also within the wider community. There will always be a tension between the laws of the land as prescribed by a denomination and those prescribed and created by the state. The result is a continuum, from denominations that accommodate with the state, to those who are in tension with the state, and in the case of some sects, in opposition to the state. For many churches and religious groups there is the expectation that since the ten commandments and the principles of the New Testament are from God, then the rest of society also should acknowledge these laws. Vital divisive issues for future horizons flow from this expectation—racism, sexuality, abortion, euthenasia, genetic engineering, conservation, global warming, ecology and the response to other forms of life.

Fourthly, in the denominational paradigm, each denomination is a divine commonwealth unto itself, determining the God-given laws for its life and its members; since they are God-given laws they are seen to apply to all, even if the denomination is the only group that actually is faithful. From the perspective of the state and the wider society the denominational churches are just another group of public voices, often in competition with each other, or arguing against each other, or even sometimes agreeing together. The danger of this confessional approach to the world is that such churches presume, in the name of God, the right to be heard. In a democracy all voices are deemed equal. As Martin Marty saw, there is a need for the churches to work together and discover a public theology that enables churches to speak with a distinctive voice amongst the many voices involved in public debate about the common good. While this would be helpful, the actual outcome has been to intensify the differences between conservative and liberal voices in the public arena.

In practice, then, each denomination presumes it is the state church even if the state does not recognize this and constitutionally is opposed to the claim. The result is that there is a need for the denomination to create structures parallel to the state in its own life, such as governing groups, parliamentary bodies, and a judiciary in some form or another. There is a gradation from denominations that develop such a divine commonwealth, right the way through to a local group that has no organizational structure at all beyond its local meetings.

Fifthly, it did not take long for observers to realize that the competitive spirit between denominations and within denominations has a long-term detrimental impact on the message of the churches. In Australia three different sorts of Presbyterian Church had been imported into the growing colonies in the second half of the nineteenth century. Leaders realized that the message would be enhanced if the three groups sought to unite, which they did. They became convinced that reconciliation lay at the heart of the gospel, not division, and became initiators of further union with other denominations. Over the last 1,000 years the splits between East and West, the subsequent schism between Roman Catholic and Protestant in the Reformation, and the competition between denominations opened by the separation of the church from the state, continued to multiply the number of denominations. By the middle of the twentieth century there were voices throughout the world calling for greater ecumenism for the sake of the churches integrity and for greater clarity in addressing and listening to the issues of the world. As church growth declined in the last half of the twentieth century the importance of the ecumenical movement grew, alongside the life of the denominations. The ecumenical movement's call for reconciliation between people who have different points of view and the call for the churches to be one, runs headlong into the free choice of individuals that is at the heart of the denominational paradigm. At the beginning of the twenty-first century the ecumenical movement faces uncertain times, looking for a way to deepen a faltering movement, or as Michael Kinnamon puts it, *Can A Renewal Movement be Renewed?*[18] Writing as a former staff member of the World Council of Churches Faith and Order Commission and a General Secretary of the National Council of Churches in the United States, he gives "a qualified yes (with the help of God)."

18. Kinnamon, *Renewal Movement*, 3.

Belonging to a denomination does not just happen; it involves quite specific decisions. In the former national church era everyone was a member unless they ruled themselves out of membership and suffered the social consequences of being a nonconformist. Now the denomination could not presume any one was a member unless they actively and voluntarily ruled themselves in as a member. The transition from passively belonging by birth to a national church, to actively being involved in a local congregation or denomination involves extraordinary social change. Membership became and still is a form of voluntary participation that is dependent on the on-going decision to belong.

For the family who regularly attended their church and kept on attending in this new era it was not such a radical difference. Within a generation or two it soon became apparent that the family would not necessarily continue to support such voluntary participation. But what about those in the wider society who did not regularly attend apart from special events, perhaps occasionally, or who never darkened the door of a church? There was now less cultural and social pressure to be involved. The family and the new culture of the state no longer fostered attendance. This new religious setting required active decision, and the willingness to join a group and participate in worship and giving. Each of these steps involves a change in the beliefs, the practices, and the habits of a person. It is a series of quantum steps forward for any member of the community to move from no involvement to become involved actively in a congregation.

The most direct challenge the denominational paradigm created was the requirement for each denomination to finance its own life. Each local congregation had to provide what the state used to provide, namely payment for leadership, housing, travelling and church buildings, and do it by seeking voluntary participation and voluntary contributions. Congregations had to find ways of paying the bills. Most congregations require an ongoing program of raising money from offerings at services, through special events, running various sorts of markets, seeking pledges, selling donated goods, finding sponsors, seeking bequests, and other imaginative ways. To become a member is to become part of the fund raising task, giving one's time, talents and money to support the ongoing infrastructure for a group of people to meet regularly in their own building. Of course if a person actively fund raises for their local congregation, they may consider that they are active members without ever being involved in the worshipping congregation! From an organizational point of view the emphasis on membership can take the place of discipleship.

And a stark new possibility emerged. If it is up to the individual to choose to belong to the local congregation then it is not possible to presume the individuals of the next generation will make the same choice. In this setting no denomination could assume the next generation would attend and continue to believe in the particular identity of their denomination. It did not take long for leaders to realize that unless a congregation or denomination has a stream of new members it will fail to maintain its own life and the level of funding required for its life. In any congregation people are being born, moving in or away, or dying. Numbers are never going to be static for very long. This did not matter previously when the national church congregations were financed by the state. When there are many congregations or churches in the one region, it is obvious that they each need a stream of new members over time and that they are each competing in the same market to convince people to opt in to their group.

Recruitment of new members is vital. How could this happen in this era of individual choice? The two of immense significance for the denominational church were the emergence of evangelism and the creation of the Sunday School.

1. Evangelism.

Within 50 years a new way of sharing the gospel emerged. It was a result of changes in the message that emerged in the Second Religious Awakening in the United States, a result of the impact of democracy on the population. Evangelism, a word that first appears in its modern sense in a quotation from the time of the English Civil War, became by the 1830s a common and popular way of describing how the message is to be made known as a means of recruiting new members. Evangelism is the method, or 'ism', by which the evangel—that is the gospel—is made known. First an important distinction needs to be made to highlight how an earlier way of preaching was modified.

It will surprise many to find that John Wesley, the founder of Methodism in England in the mid–1700s, was not involved in evangelism. He was a minister of the national Church of England in the previous paradigm. His was a national perspective, not a denominational one. If people responded to the message, he gathered them into a society, or later a class meeting that was part of a reform movement in the Church of England. Along with George Whitefield, Wesley called individuals to salvation by faith, and the nation to scriptural holiness, through God's converting power. For him the time when a person was regenerated, that is 'saved' in modern parlance, was the great mystery of God's grace. It happened in God's time. Recent research shows that many did not experience the converting power of the gospel until they had been in a class meeting for two years or more. For Wesley the focus was on the individual's response, in line with his own experience. "I felt my heart strangely warmed. I felt I did trust in Christ, Christ alone for my salvation, and an assurance was given me that he had taken away *my* sins, even *mine*, and saved *me* from the law of sin and death." [19] This deepening focus on the personal was given expression in Charles Wesley's hymns.

A further intensification of individual experience came with the development of evangelism as a specific method early in the 19th century. A way was needed to recruit

19. Ward et al, *Works of John Wesley*, 249.

individuals as new disciples of Jesus Christ and new members for the denomination. The result was that the declaration of the gospel to the individual came as part of a total package. It is necessary to believe in Jesus in the way in which the denomination presents him, with its history, structure, saints, and its specific literature as well. It goes without saying that a growing denomination will need to have control of its own publishing and distribution as it identifies itself as distinctively different from other denominations.

One person more than any other is responsible for the method of evangelism as it is now practiced. In 1820 a young lawyer, Charles Grandison Finney aged 29, was profoundly converted from shame in his own pride, in a wood outside a village called Adams (he subsequently became a Presbyterian Church minister).

> The sin appeared awful, infinite. It broke me down before the Lord. Just at this point this passage of scripture seemed to drop into my mind with a flood of light. 'Then shall you go and pray unto me, and I will hearken to you. Then shall you seek me and find me, when you shall search for me with all your heart.' I instantly seized hold of this with my heart. I had intellectually believed the Bible before, but never had the truth been in my mind that faith was a voluntary trust instead of an intellectual state.[20]

The passage was Jeremiah 29:12,13. Finney was to lay extraordinary stress on this aspect of searching with all your heart to find God. That verse is caught up in his belief that there is nothing mysterious about a revival. "A revival is as naturally a result of the use of the appropriate means as a crop is of the use of its appropriate means."[21] At the heart of the preparation for revival was prayer, praying and searching with all the heart to find God. Finney in his democratic setting was advancing the basic tenet of republican political ideology into the realm of theology, namely, that just rule must be with the 'the consent of the governed'. God whose rule is perfectly just, will govern only with the full participation of his people. Salvation, said Finney, involves a 'change in the choice of a *Supreme Ruler*.[22] Finney brings a republican revolution to the process of salvation. As a leader of the 'second awakening' in the United States he is considered a father of modern evangelism and revivalism. "The evangelism of Charles G. Finney was based on his conviction that every person 'has the power and liberty of choice' in the matter of who they will serve and how they will live."[23]

The answer to the problem of sin is not 'a constitutional alteration, and the implantation of a new principle, in the substance of [our] soul': it is, rather, 'a change of heart' that 'consists in changing the controlling preference of the mind in regard to the *end* of pursuit.' Finney preached, "You have all the powers of moral agency; and

---

20. Wessel, ed, *Autobiography Finney,* 17.
21. Finney, *Revivals of Religion,* 5.
22. Hambrick-Stowe, *Finney and Evangelicalism,* 80.
23. Hambrick-Stowe, *Finney and Evangelicalism,* 80.

the thing required is, not to alter these powers, but to employ them in the service of your maker."[24]

It all rests upon our decision, to voluntarily choose in our heart the kingdom of Christ instead of the kingdom of self. The power of the political culture has thus drastically affected the form of the message and the shaping of the message. Previously the fallen person was not free to choose, but depended upon God to rescue them. Now the person is able to respond and take the vital step to change their life as a result of this appeal to the affective subjectivity. Thus,

> 'the actual turning, or change, is the sinner's own act,' but 'the agent who induces him, is the Spirit of God' and 'a secondary agent, is the preacher,' while 'the truth is an instrument, or motive, which the Spirit uses to induce the sinner to turn. . . . the masses easily grasped—and were gripped by—Finney's explanation. Tears came to their eyes, and they fell to their knees in anguished repentance, when he looked them in the eye and said, 'The fact is, sinners, that God requires you to turn, and what he requires of you, he cannot do for you. It must be your own voluntary act. . . . Another moment's delay, and it may be too late for ever.'[25]

Many deep streams of the nation's life come together here. The free acts of commitment, choice and decision that the political realm requires of the citizen, were now also operating in the realm of the religious citizen. Jefferson's conviction that morality provided the common bond between church and state was reinforced by Finney's similar emphasis. Finney's support of women in leadership, and abolition of slavery show the political morality that flowed from his religious morality. Conversion becomes a rational and emotional act of the individual to decide now, to say no to the past and yes to a new view of God. Religion takes a giant leap into the realm of the rational, and the personal, and the democratic.

This theology of decision had consequences. It led to Finney's use of the penitent's bench in the service, and the invitation to those who wanted to, or were in the process of making a decision, either to come forward, and/or attend the "after meeting". Now that conversion involved a human decision rather than a divine experience of regeneration, it was possible to expect human decisions, and evaluate whether a person was effective as an evangelist. It was the beginning of the revival movement, now known worldwide as the principle form of evangelism. Once it is possible to measure whether people had responded or not, it is possible to evaluate various methods—and many have been developed. The democratic era and the denominational church gave rise to evangelism, a very particular, time-specific, context dependent way of making the gospel known. Since the time of the Second Awakening, there have been many famous practitioners, none more famous than Billy Graham. He used city-wide crusades that

---

24. Hambrick-Stowe, *Finney and Evangelicalism*, 81.

25. Hambrick-Stowe, *Finney and Evangelicalism*, 81.

enlisted the churches in a process which culminated in the call for commitment in huge stadiums. The call was given, counsellors walking forward, and the music from massed choirs singing songs like "Just as I am," helped the person take the decisive step forward and walk to the front.

Later day evangelists have evolved creative ways for listeners and viewers to respond to their evangelical messages over radio, film and television. Now the immediacy of the internet provides new opportunities to help the audience participate in the cause of 'spreading the gospel'. Evangelism has been the primary way that the denominations have sought to bring adults to commitment and church membership from the wider democratic community.

2. The Sunday School.

It had soon been realized that it was important to prepare the next generation for membership while they were young. The vehicle for this was the adaptation of the earlier Sabbath Schools of Robert Raikes. In 1780 Raikes started a school to teach boys in the slums how to read and write using the Bible as a text book. Since most worked in the factories six days a week, Sunday was the only day available. Despite concerns that boys were being taught on the Sabbath, the movement grew. Later girls were also included. The schools were a creative attempt to help children be given the basics—such as clean clothes, with lay teaching of reading, writing and hygiene—so that they could be good subjects of the crown instead of delinquents on the streets. As part of their instruction they went to church and learnt the catechism.

As Jefferson had foreseen, those who control education control the formation of the citizen. While depending upon evangelism in the form of revival meetings and camp meetings on the frontiers, the denominational church was aware that it had to be involved in the task of educating the young about the gospel, even as the state was taking a greater and greater role in educating the citizens of the state with public schooling.

The Sabbath School was adapted to become the Sunday School. By the mid-1820s, instead of teaching the poor, churches taught the children of the community about faith. The day of the Sunday School was just beginning. "A large supply of church workers existed to serve as agents for joining the child and the message to effect salvation. Conversion soon became the great refrain of Sunday school workers. The Decision Day was instituted by the Sunday schools as the annual event for encouraging the spiritual redemption of young scholars."[26]

It was Finney's language that led to the emphasis on the need for a Decision Day for the students. The Sunday School however changed the dynamics of the churches interaction with society. Where the camp meeting was on neutral or non church

26. Hambrick-Stowe, *Finney and Evangelicalism,* 202.

territory, the Sunday school retreated into the religious compound of the denominational church.

In the United States and elsewhere many denominations came to rely on the Sunday School as the new dynamo for recruitment. "By 1890 the Methodist Episcopal Church alone had more Sunday schools than churches (27,000 Sunday schools to 23,000 churches), with 300,000 teachers instructing 2.5 million students; since 1866 the number of Sunday schools had doubled. As Sunday school scholars swelled the ranks of church members, clergy and laity alike agreed that the Sunday school had become the nursery of the church."[27]

The Sunday School became the principle training ground for discipleship for the teachers as well as the pupils. It became a lay led, lay involved movement that required the adult resources of the congregation to run it week by week. The minister was responsible for church worship, the lay leader for the Sunday School. It was the way so many believers expressed their faith, sharing with those of the next generation. Not only was the Sunday School the nursery for the church, it was another important reason to focus the church's mission on the church property. The need to get children to come to Sunday School, paralleled the adult need to get adults to come to Church. It reinforced the come structure of the denominational paradigm.

The Protestant Church created these two effective ways for the congregation to "reach out" into the community, and invite individuals to cross the boundary between chapel and society, and become a member. In so doing they shaped in a very particular subjective and individual way the understanding and experience of God's dealing with humankind. Over the last 200 years, however, the differences between the church and society have deepened with advances in knowledge. In the latter part of the nineteenth century and the beginning of the twentieth century, evolutionary, psychological and sociological discoveries raised serious, important, and for many, threatening questions about the Bible, the church and Sunday School textbook, and fundamental matters of faith. The divide between the church and the world has intensified. More and more the church is tempted to be a safe refuge in a dangerous world, the house of God providing an alternative to the ways of the world. Yet for the sake of the gospel it becomes even more important for the church and believers to face these issues. A cartoon showed a moat around a church building crossed by a narrow bridge, the only way out to the en-circling world. The image highlights two crucial issues. It is difficult for those who outreach in the name of the gospel to make this crossing, and it deepens the mystery in the wider community as to what happens inside the church.

What happens when the two principle means of people crossing that ever narrowing bridge into the church falter? The Sunday School is still offered but taken up less and less by succeeding generations, and the evangelistic or revival meetings in the community are not well attended and fall back to being run in the church for the faithful. It leaves the local congregation finding it ever more difficult to engage with

27. Hambrick-Stowe, *Finney and Evangelicalism*, 201.

the society in these denominational ways of the past. While more people still attend church on a Sunday than go to any other public function, the church is increasingly marginalized in the media and the public domain as an ageing institution that is rarely reported apart from a conservative response to issues of sexuality, drugs, drinking, abuse and misconduct.

What does the church do now that these methods are no longer effective? It is a disturbing indication that the days of the denominational paradigm are nearing an end.

LEADERSHIP

One of the wider less obvious consequences of the denominational paradigm is that it creates a form of ecclesiastical competition in which citizens within the state can be considered as consumers in a religious market, as well as buyers in the wider market place. It would seem inevitable particular denominations relate to particular market groups within the society, and as a result are more tuned in to the particular values of those groups. From a sociological perspective, the members of denominations and the denominations themselves reflect the socio-economic structure of the society.

In fact the focus on the need to choose to belong affects the way the message is shared in both direct and subtle ways. It is not possible to become a Christian, one has to become a Roman Catholic or a Church of Christ, or a Baptist or as in the United States, one of thousands of particular denominations. Each reflect to a degree particular social niches in the wider society reflecting age, education, work, ethnicity and other characteristics.

As in the wider market place, not only do businesses rise and fall on the power of their brand name, so also do churches. In a time of growing diversity the religious consumer will choose what makes sense to them or what feels right. The post World War 2 generation, educated further in the school system, have shown an increasing interest in spirituality rather than organized religion.[28] In the face of so many options the introversion of religious choice can easily give rise to a private do-it-your-self religion, focused on feelings. In this setting effective denominations need their own publishing companies, newspapers, schools, hospitals, counselling services and finance organizations if they are to appeal to those who are not in their congregations. The church needs to be, in the jargon of the market, vertically integrated in providing a complete service that emphasizes the uniqueness of their product, and the vitality of their message. The indications worldwide are that this organizational superstructure is in serious decline. What is crucial is the service provided by the local agency, the congregation. Whatever the wider organizational network, it is vital that the place where people meet the organization is customer oriented. So much depends upon

---

28. Bouma, *Australian Soul.*

the life of the local congregation, the shop front as it were for the denomination and inevitably the leadership of the local congregation. The falling membership of most Protestant churches indicates the churches lack of effective communication of the gospel in a competitive consumer-oriented world of organizational success and failure.

Leadership in the church, however, needs to be placed in a wider setting than an organizational view of the church. After all leadership is about God's call to a very specific role in the life of a congregation. As Dietrich Bonhoeffer states,

> The calling is the call of Jesus Christ to belong wholly to him; it is the laying claim to me by Jesus Christ at the place where this call has found me; it embraces work with things and relations with persons; it demands a 'limited field of accomplishments' yet never as a value in itself, but in responsibility towards Jesus Christ.[29]

Thus the calling of the minister is inextricably linked with the life of the congregation. Together they have the responsibility to fulfill the proclamation of the message in two ways. "First by the adaptation of the whole organization of this community for the effective proclamation of Christ to the whole world, which means the congregation is merely an instrument, merely a means to an end; secondly by virtue of the fact, that precisely through the congregation's acting on behalf of the world in this way, the purpose is achieved and the divine mandate of proclamation has begun to be fulfilled."[30]

The leader of a congregation has the task to work with the congregation so that its life is consistent with its discipleship, thereby being a means toward the effective proclamation of Christ for the world. Ministers are called to be leadership followers of their Lord. The temptation is to make the congregation a value in itself, concerned with its own growth or survival. In this competitive consumer world there are profound pressures to adapt the gospel proclamation to the wider world. The risk then is that the congregation becomes the end in itself rather than an instrument in the effective proclamation of Jesus Christ in the world.

The role of leadership is pushed to the fore in the denominational church for so much depends upon the minister, given that membership is a voluntary individual decision. The finances raised from the members pay the stipend or salary of the leader. The minister is seen to be responsible for the quality of the life of the congregation, the maintaining of financial support and the long-term recruitment of new members. Spiritual vitality and financial vitality are seen to go hand in hand with growth in membership, or at least maintaining membership. Leaders need to have gifts that tend in the direction of engaging attractive entrepreneurs who encourage people to join, give and support the denomination. Conversely, if those who give leadership are

29. Bonhoeffer, *Ethics*, 257.
30. Bonhoeffer, *Ethics*, 300.

uninspiring, uninteresting, and relate poorly interpersonally, there will be difficulties for congregations both spiritually and financially.

Leaders in the churches are ordained as ministers or selected for the role in which they are responsible for preaching, sacraments and pastoral care. Yet the denominational dynamic and organizational reality is that the paid ministers with other leaders within the congregation have to take responsibility for raising the finances of the congregation and making sure new members are recruited. From the perspective of the members or attenders, however, they are choosing to participate in a voluntary organization. The attender makes their own contribution but expect and are dependent upon the leadership to grow a group ethos that enables a person to feel at home, and as well, encourages group leadership and the ability to develop a group mission, that makes a person want to belong. These expectations are part of the leadership role. For most Protestant churches the key expectations of those in the pews turns out to be good preaching, and effective recruitment of new people.

Such expectations result in a serious tension in the preparation of leaders for congregations. Will they have the gifts and be given insight into how to declare the gospel and support the congregation in its own perception of its present needs? Will they also have the gifts and the insight into what the congregation needs to hear about the gospel and the future of the congregation in the next generation? Even when leadership roles are clearly understood there is always a tension between congregational needs and goals and the expectations of the members. The ongoing danger is that key elements of a gospel of grace and truth are eclipsed by the needs, goals and expectations of the congregation. That tension and danger is massively increased in a time of rapid change and falling membership.

In this setting the two poles for ministry are that of chaplain to the faithful, or the promoter of a vision for the future. When membership is decreasing it is almost impossible not to be the chaplain to the faithful. The attempt to promote a vision of growth, let alone one that is missional and theological, is far more difficult because it involves new approaches or attitudes that risks alienating existing members and thereby further limiting the future of the congregation. The leader as chaplain is pushed toward a co-dependent situation knowing that more needs to be done, but also knowing that the expectations of the membership that their own Christian lives be nourished is foremost in most minds. The introverted dynamics of the denominational paradigm push any congregation towards a focus on its own congregational life and the life of its members. Even the plans for mission events and evangelism become a means to get new people to come, who will help pay the bills to continue worship and keep the church doors open.

The leader who attempts to promote a vision for the future has to convey a view of what constitutes church that is different from the view the overall majority of members initially own. It is the beginning of a pilgrimage into the unknown. The implementation of such a vision is a minefield, negotiating who will help create the vision, who will own the vision and who will implement it. If the vision is the creation of the leader or a small group within the congregation enormous issues of power arise. What if the vision involves a different theology, a different view of the Scriptures and different roles for attenders? What happens to those in the congregation who are not interested in these new ways forward? There are many consultants[31] who work with congregations searching for new ways forward. Much has been written to provide resources for the continuing education of leaders grappling with these issues.[32]

Whether a chaplain or a vision caster, still the overall expectation is that the leaders will be the ones who bring in new members. Members know that if new members come then the congregation will survive and grow. It is not surprising that the functional issues of leadership easily usurp the responsibilities stated in the ordination vows.

It is far easier to minister in a time when there is a ready response from the wider community to the gospel and congregations are growing. The issues become far starker when congregations are declining and the wider community is less inclined to make the decision to opt into faith communities.

It is salutary to read the written history of any particular denomination or the history of a particular congregation. Other religious groups and denominations are only mentioned incidentally as background to their denominational story. This need for a denomination to affirm its own life and recruit people in the face of ecclesiastical competition with other denominations affirms the view that the church is the religious center of life for its members and fosters the view that civil society is an alien parallel universe. When the church is strong and growing it is seen to influence the rest of society, but when it is weak and declining it becomes more like a religious ghetto.

THE HOUSE OF GOD

The evangelical emphasis on conversion, and the Sunday School decision day depend upon a God—Me introverted relationship. The relationship with others is of less significance, than my internal subjective commitment, an internal experience of the saving God. There is then a tension, if not a divorce, in the believer's world between self and world, a tension between the individual conversion or subjective religious experience, and the communal nature of church life. Yet it is the church where the Christian faith is lived for most members. There the sacraments of the church, namely baptism and eucharist, are the ways the individual is received into community and lives in a community of thanksgiving.

---

31. The author spent more than 30 years as a consultant for congregations, and while recognizing the important work of consultants is also aware how difficult it is for most congregations to respond to new directions.

32. The Alban Institute was one of the first of many ventures started in the 70s to provide such resources, but closed in 2014. The book lists are still available from Rowman and Littlefield.

Avery Dulles[33] describes the life of the church in six possible communal models: the institutional church of clerics and laity, five forms of community, as the body of Christ, as sacramental witness to Christ, as a herald of the gospel, a servant people, and finally as a community of discipleship. The divorce between self and world can render these descriptions of little relevance from the perspective of the individual believer. When belief is a individual choice the emphasis is placed on individual expectations rather than the ways individuals gather with other believers.

In the denominational church it is in fact the act of worship in the church building that provides the 'container' that brings individuals together. There are very few congregations who do not have a fixed location. The overwhelming majority of congregations focus their life on the building in which they worship. It is worship in the church building that is the constituting element of congregational community life. Worship creates a world of sacred space within the building over and against the secular world of non-faith or other faiths beyond its walls. It is not surprising that without fail the church building becomes in the Christian life the "house of God."

What is truly remarkable is that this flies in the face of the New Testament witness to the nature of the church. There is a dividing line between the Hebrew Bible and New Testament over what constitutes the holy and the location of the holy. In the Hebrew Bible the holy is associated with God, and the times, places and objects particularly associated with the Temple. In the New Testament the holy is associated with the Holy Spirit and the character and values of the gifts and fruit of the Holy Spirit. Those who are beloved of God are called to be 'saints'. Apart from the temple in Jerusalem there are no particular sacred spaces in the New Testament.

In normal Christian life, it is the language of the temple that is used for the church building. It is the place where God dwells. We come to church to meet with God, talk with God, hear from God. As the temple was the centre for the life of Israel, so the church building becomes the centre for the life of denominational congregations. The importance of the church as the 'house of God' for most in the pews overwhelms the theological categories that Dulles provides.

It is the faithful who come to church to worship. The language of gather and scatter permeates Christian language and theological language. It is revealing language. We come together as God's people, and then we go out to witness in the world. The missionary task is to reach out into the world. The missionary task is described in terms of a series of concentric circles with regular worshipers in the central circle with those less regular further out, and the Christmas, baptism, wedding and funeral attenders further out again bridging into the 'non-churched' who do not come. It is assumed the task is to reach-out with the gospel to get people to move from the outer circles through to the inner circle. Of course the negative of that image shows the individual denominational congregation to be a religious ghetto which requires people to choose to become more and more involved as they move toward the centre.

33. Dulles, *Models.*

The language of the house of God has continuity with the preceding national church paradigm, though the cathedral was also meeting place for the whole community. In the denominational paradigm each denomination calls people out from the community to enter into the inner space of their own particular temple.

When worship is made the constitutive act of the church, and is seen to take place in a temple, the leader is placed at the top of a hierarchy of power and responsibility. Such a hierarchy is a given and rarely questioned—but it has consequences. In any church a great deal of authority, and with it power, is given to the ordained, to be used in the service of the gospel.

This hierarchy of power also attracts those who desire and seek to exercise power for their own ends or needs, and who interpret the gospel in terms of authoritarian truth. The more the church focuses on worship in God's house, the more the ordained are placed at the center and vulnerable to the attraction of power rather than the serving authority in witnessing to Christ

If the other facets of being the church are placed second to a focus on worship in the building, then the worship of God forms the community in particular ways. It locates God in the church building. In conversation and experience, the sign of ongoing faith is 'going to church'. So much is reinforced in this simple summary. "God, whom I know in the inner self, I choose to worship with others in the sacred space of my local church building, as a voluntary participant in a particular denomination that is dependent upon my attendance and my giving."

A proviso is required at this point. The reader may have concluded that this is a bleak and negative picture that does not acknowledge that the ministry of the church has been effective and that many individuals have had a profound experience of Jesus Christ that has fundamentally changed the way they have lived out their lives. Thank God that has happened, and continues to happen.

The denominational paradigm ushered in an amazing era with an explosion of religious freedom for individuals and families free to worship as they believed. For millions this opened for them the personal discovery of the grace of God in our Lord Jesus Christ in a way that revolutionized their life and faith and enabled them with decision and commitment to make a great contribution within the church and the wider society.

Secondly, many discovered in and through this framework a Risen Lord who was Lord of the World as well as their personal Saviour. So many set out in response to their Lord into new worlds, new ministries, new discoveries of justice and healing. They became disciples of a Lord who led them on in bold ministries of worship, witness and service that brought the gospel to nearly every place on the planet.

Nevertheless there is now a profound malaise in the denominational churches in the west that has to be addressed. As time has passed it has become plain that most who confess the name of Jesus Christ in the denominational churches are constrained by the individualism of belief, dependent upon leaders to lead and bring church growth, and caught up in the church as a 'come structure' centered on the church building as God's house. The very structure of a church made up of democratic Christian individuals has become a religious straitjacket.

As the twenty-first century unfolds the church now finds itself on the sidelines in a society having to address a plethora of issues affecting the world such as global warming, international conflict and local wars, multi religious and racial tension, increasing disparity in wealth and new means of communication. As well there has been a major change in the attitude to the church with a greater religious diversity in society, a greater critical awareness of the life of institutions, a deep caution about the interpretation of scripture, and a greater suspicion of the church by younger more educated generations. Add too, the way the wider media and common public comment have accepted that the message of the Gospel can be explained away in psychological terms and dismissed as a superstitious means of finding certainty in an unsure world.

It was the denominational paradigm that focused attention on the life of the congregation. As such the life of each congregation is different as it holds together the gospel within the practicality and the ordinariness of each unfolding week. Yet it has become clear that the Enlightenment world and the denominational paradigm itself has dramatically affected the gospel that is celebrated within the warp and woof of congregational life. What would it mean to hear about the kingdom of God in the midst of history, instead of being limited to the kingdom of God within? Uncovering the denominational paradigm is a necessary step in the ongoing task of proclaiming the gospel on this planet, supposedly a speck of dust in a meaningless universe.

5

The Self Within

STATUS ANXIETY

THE EXPRESSION WAS UNWIELDY, *but it made sense of so much that I had found was at the heart of church and social life. We were all to some degree democratic religious individuals, atomic religious units, with our own beliefs and convictions. It was summed up while visiting a friend in Pennsylvania. We were enjoying a time relaxing around a swimming pool. I found myself talking to someone I did not know who asked what I did for an occupation. When told I was a minister, he said, "I do not attend any church. I guess you could call me a 'one person church'". He was definitely a religious democratic individual! For some time I wondered how to further describe this issue in relation to social atomic units and not just religious atomic citizens.*

When I read Alain de Botton's 'Status Anxiety' it slowly became evident that here was a description of a view of self that is taken for granted, presumed in the atomic life of citizens and the 'new world' of denominational life. The great democratic vision is that we are all free and equal, and that we have the power to choose who we will be. In a mass society of individuals we are each constantly bombarded with images and examples of what constitutes a desirable house, car, television set, style of clothing and holiday destination to name some of key components. Technology continues to offer new options in travel, communication, personal comfort and the latest must-have gadget. The rate of change keeps opening up new enchanting markets to visit and buy.

The quintessential American psychologist William James described this quality so well. "The more people we take to be our equals and compare ourselves to, the more people there will be to envy."[1] James explains that for our self-esteem we do not have to succeed in all that we do, only that which we set out to do. "Our goals determine what we

---

1. de Botton, *Status Anxiety*, 47.

will interpret as a triumph and what we must count as a failure."[2] *"Our self-esteem in this world depends entirely on what we back ourselves to be and do."*[3]

So Self-esteem = Success/Expectations

"James equation illustrates how every rise in our levels of expectation entails a rise in the dangers of humiliation. What we understand to be normal is critical in determining our chances of happiness. Few things rival the torment of the once famous actor, the fallen politician or, as Tocqueville might have remarked, the unsuccessful American."[4]

There are then ways to raise our self-esteem. Either we try to achieve more, or we reduce our expectations. There are some who swim against the tide of 'normal expectations' and opt out of the 'rat race'. Overwhelmingly though, the opportunities before most of us beckon alluringly for us to be a some-body, and to be able to show others that we have succeeded. "The price we have paid for expecting to be so much more than our ancestors is a perpetual anxiety that we are far from being all we might be."[5] *Instead of God-created hierarchies in the outer world, now human hierarchies are projected within the inner world.*

THE SELF

There has been a dramatic change in the understanding of what it means to be a self in the last three centuries. The so-called plausibility structures that underlie the everyday life and world of society changed when an hierarchical society became a democratic society. The previous chapter showed how the coming of the Enlightenment radically changed church structures, the religious role of the individual and the view of the self as described by de Botton.

But what if fundamental changes are now underway in the experience of the self far beyond what de Botton presents, as we move into the new era of the pale blue dot? What happens to the experience of the self when Voyager 1 carried the human artifacts of Da Vinci's drawing of an individual and a recording of the Earth's music beyond the solar system, into the winds of interstellar space. The only horizon humanity has ever known shrinks inexorably to a dot in an infinite universe. The scale of human awareness is assailed by such vistas. At the same time the exploration of the sub-atomic scale of matter and life expose the quantum structure as another unimaginable realm. In terms of the self, scientific and technological breakthroughs have led to instruments that probe the brain in new ways that are unravelling its neural wiring. What happens to the view of providence, that God provides fore-sight-ful care of the Earth for the sake of his creatures? If a person has grown up singing, "God's hand is my perpetual guide", and "all creatures are subject to your care," they may not be aware of the doubt

2. de Botton, *Status Anxiety*, 55.

3. de Botton, *Status Anxiety*, 55.

4. de Botton, *Status Anxiety*, 55.

5. de Botton, *Status Anxiety*, 63.

that those of a younger generation may experience in hearing these words, if civilization on Earth is thought to be but another 'pop up' of self-conscious life in a universe of many pop-ups—some no longer existing, and others to come.

The plausibility structures supporting the Enlightenment view of the self as the unalterable center of human awareness, however, have proved remarkably resilient. It is important to explore why this is so. How and when did the move to the inner self begin? Much earlier than most expect.

THE INVENTION OF THE INNER SELF

Phillip Cary's claim that Augustine invented the 'inner self' in the fifth century AD is a dramatic and important claim[6]. It raises the possibility that the roots of the later Enlightenment self/world bifurcation are found here.

Augustine was the first to document his own conversion. There is a sense in which he anticipated Luther's view of faith that gave rise to the Reformation, Wesley's view of conversion in the eighteenth century, and Finney's fashioning of the commitment view of conversion that triumphed in a democratic age. Some fifteen hundred years after Augustine, conversion language is now expressed as a personal experience in the inner self. In the last two hundred years of the denominational paradigm, conversion has become as important, if not more important than baptism, in the understanding and experience of the overwhelming majority of Protestants in the West.

Cary claims that Augustine was the first to describe human experience in terms of an inner self and an outer world. Previously the heart was seen as the total human response to what was happening in a person's life and world. The Psalms speak of the hidden thoughts in the heart that can be expressed in speech. The Apostle Paul speaks three times in his writings of the 'inner man', but there is no hint "of an inward turn, no suggestion that we should try to find Christ inside ourselves by looking within our hearts."[7] Rather Christ is in our hearts by faith through the good news of preaching that comes from beyond ourselves, in hearing the word of Christ.

I had always thought that the *Confessions of Augustine* was one of his early writings. It is in fact one of his most mature works. It was only when Augustine was clear about the essential core of the Christian experience of God, that he could write the account of his conversion. It is vital to see that his conversion was about his turn to the Church rather than a turn to Christ.

What is extraordinary about Cary's claim is that it illuminates an issue that I had previously seen in terms of the democratic revolution flowing from the Enlightenment. What Cary says about Augustine provides a deeper underlying feasibility structure for the intellectual pinnings that are presumed by both the Reformation and the Enlightenment.

6. Cary, *Augustine's Invention of the Inner Self*.
7. Cary, *Augustine's Inner Self*, 50.

The Inner Self

The missiological issue for these first centuries of the church was different from that of the twenty-first century. Then the fundamental issue was, how could the unchanging oneness of the light of the eternal divine being, be present in the darkness of a changing imperfect world? Hence the critical issue facing the early Church Councils was how Jesus Christ could be both divine and human at the same time.

Augustine lived within this world informed by an earlier Platonic framework that had been further developed by Plotinus. A series of quotations from Cary provide four snapshots that signpost the way this move to the self happened prior to Augustine and then developed after his time in western history. The first two signposts are important, but strange to modern readers and show a very different world to the historical perspective that is now presumed.

> The oldest snapshot is Plato's picture in the Allegory of the cave: an eye that has escaped from bondage in the lower darkness is now gazing upward, away from itself, at the sun. There is no inwardness here, but there is a key concept, intelligibility or intellectual vision, which will be at the heart of later Platonist inwardness.[8]

Plotinus's (210-270 AD) worldview is a modified view of Plato. From a transcendent place of pure being, there are a series of emanations which provided a descending series of intermediate worlds ending in the last most imperfect, time constrained, and distorted world in which we find ourselves. The first emanation is the Divine Mind (*nous*) that wills the good; the second emanation, the World Soul, is subdivided into an upper Soul turned toward the Divine Mind and a lower aspect of Soul involved with nature including individual human souls; the third and final emanation is matter. "Plotinus asserted the ultimately divine nature of material creation since it ultimately derives from the One, through the mediums of *nous* and the world soul. It is by the Good or through beauty that we recognize the One, in material things and then in the Forms."[9] Plotinus sees humans as faces on the Divine Soul looking outward to the external world of temporal things, able to see through the changing world to the beauty and the good that found its source in divine being. How then is it that beauty is recognized by particular souls?

> The next snapshot gives us the much less familiar picture of Plotinus: the soul is a like a sphere revolving about the source of all light at the center of the universe and turning inward to see it. Our particular souls are each points of light on the revolving sphere, capable of looking out on the darkness or turning into the inside to behold the realm of light. This inner world is the Platonist's

---

8. Cary, *Augustine's Inner Self,* 5.

9. Porphyry, " Life of Plotinus", I.6.6–1.6.9.

"intelligible world," which has now become an inner world—although unlike Augustine's inner space it is common to all, not private. [10]

For Cary the key to understanding Augustine is his understanding of how a human person could discover the beauty and goodness of the divine. The big difference between Plotinus and Augustine was that, for Plotinus the soul was divine and could see the beauty and goodness of the divine, for Augustine the soul was a part of a fallen creation and was not divine. How then is it possible for a person to "see" the beauty and goodness of the divine if it is fallen? Since it did not seem possible for the eternal beauty and goodness of the being of God to be experienced through the senses Augustine turned to another feature of human existence. He saw that the experience of God was like the inner seeing of a theorem, the 'aha' moment in which the mind perceives the truth of a mathematical statement—in that moment the description of a triangle is suddenly seen as a triangle.

> Augustine's picture comes third, and it is of an inner palace, with great courtyards opening to the sun. To see the light means both entering within and looking upward—combining Plotinus's inward turn with Plato's ascent to vision. The result is that what you find when you turn inward but not upward, is your own private inner space. [11]

Inner Space

There has been a long history of writing about the hiddenness of the heart. Homer and the Hebrew scriptures speak of the way we can choose to hide our thoughts and desires in our heart or speak them out. Cary states,

> Augustine gives new rigor to this talk by identifying the hidden heart with private inner space and conceiving speech as an expression of what lies in that space. It was an epochal innovation when Augustine classified words as a species of signs, and treated signs as external indications of the inner will of the soul—thus laying the groundwork for medieval understandings of word and sacrament as well as much of modern semiotics and theory of language. [12]

What Augustine was doing was making the private inner space the reference point for all else. Here it was possible to see the beatific vision of God. The experience of the outer world was always to be interpreted from the perspective of the inner world. Cary argues this inner space was the fundamental revolution Augustine introduced into Western thought.

---

10. Cary, *Augustine's Inner Self,* 5.

11. Cary, *Augustine's Inner Self,* 5.

12. Cary, *Augustine's Inner Self,* 4.

For each person there was an inner space, a private, individual world for which memory was like a vast inner palace, with courtyards open to the sun of the divine above and a divine light shining down into it. So the self "turns inward, then upwards", first entering into the private inner space of the self, and then looking up at God shining above the soul. Augustine then added the effects of sin. He was the first to describe that inner world as a private world because of the consequences of sin, that not only separates us from God but separates us from others, leaving us alone within.

Since this inner world is not a spatial world, but an inner world within us, the result of our darkened will is that this subjective world or soul is a realm separated from the light of God above, and separated from others, because of the conflict between our will and the will of others. In terms of God, while the soul is a separate entity, it is not dark, but bathed with light from above. In terms of others, because of the fall, the body is opaque, resulting in souls being hidden from each other. It is because of this opacity that words and outward signs are necessary to communicate with one another. The very privacy of this inner world is a result of sin. In heaven there will be no separation between souls because the separation will be overcome and we shall see into each other's minds and enjoy God together.[13] The true reality for Augustine is not the external world but the world of God within. No wonder Christians say, after Augustine, 'the Kingdom of God is within you'. One and a half millennia of the use of this framework, has woven it into the warp and woof of the way we use the words we have to describe our experience of God.

There is now a fundamental division between this inner space and the outer world for each person. In the inner world there is a non-divine soul that is the center of the human being. As Augustine grew older in his position as a Christian bishop he had to wrestle with the Scriptures and the inherited faith that underlined belief in the incarnate Christ and then the resurrected Christ. In baptism and the eucharist he realized that it is not possible to turn away from all outward things.

In one sense it is not surprising that Augustine becomes a forerunner of a systematic theologian. He works with the mind and the faith. He has to reflect and consider what the biblical story and the church's reality mean for the time in which he lives. He makes teaching the core of his contribution, providing Christian doctrine with the intellectual firepower to take on the best minds of his time. And, in doing so, he provides a definition of the self that is peculiarly Platonic and Christian.

But then, late in life, Augustine reflects on his own calling, his own what he calls 'conversion', in his *Confessions*. And, in doing so, he creates a new language for the Church to use about the way God acts in our lives that is to have enormous implications for subsequent generations. Firstly, Cary shows that the Protestant church has read into Augustine's account the conversion accounts of a later time. The conversion narrated in *Confessions 8* is thus not a decision to believe in Christ but a decision to join the church, acquiring newness of life by becoming a baptized member of Christ's

---

13. Cary, *Augustine: Philosopher and Saint*, 46.

Body. This is conversion in the ancient ecclesial sense of turning away from all other religious affiliations and being fully incorporated into the Catholic Church. The power of the narrative consists in the coinciding of this ecclesial sense of conversion with the Platonist sense of conversion as turning from love of temporal goods to love of eternal goods. That in turn coincides with the Pauline transition from life under law to life under grace. According to Augustine these are all one conversion: they all consist in the power of charity, turning the heart to love God above all things, as well as one's neighbour in the church, the community of those who love each other in the deepest way possible for human beings—by strengthening in each other the love of God.[14]

So, here it is a fundamental turning, with conversion or *conversio*, the Latin translation of the biblical word for 'turning'. It signifies turning from one belief or attitude to another, rather than the later particular Protestant understanding of conversion as being 'born again', or 'justified', or more lately 'saved'.

Secondly, as Cary makes plain, for Augustine there were three parallel processes that occurred when his heart was turned upwards to love God. The individual turning from a form of Christian belief to membership of the church, the Platonic turning from the love of temporal goods to the love of eternal goods, and the Pauline turn from law to grace. All of these facets of turning are a result of his turning to his inner self and then looking up to the God who is accessible from within, who enables him to know grace, love the eternal church, and live in eternal goodness. It is a very particular process that has implications for the will, human decision-making and the grace of God. For Augustine sin is that act of will that chooses temporal goods other than the goodness of God, resulting in a life separated from and cut off from others, and at variance with God. But when the inner self, through God's prevenient grace, is able to will the will of God, then the inner self is opened to love God above all things and one's neighbour as one's self. It is this creation of the inner self as the field where the self resides that is his revolutionary contribution to the understanding of the person in society.

Augustine was the first to describe his own private conversion. In the New Testament the word conversion only appears once. In Acts 15:3 Paul and Barnabas, while on their way to Jerusalem, report to the church in Phoenicia and Samaria the 'conversion of the Gentiles'. In this context it is the turning of the Gentiles to Christ. Augustine's account is quite different. It is a careful theological description of conversion to the church made possible in the inner self as a gift of the grace of God.

What would happen if the focus on the inner self is cut free from these Platonic roots?

It is not surprising that as the centuries pass, the concentration on the individual response and the nature of the self is highlighted and reinterpreted. One thousand years later the conversion language is given a different emphasis by an Augustinian

14. Cary, *Inner Grace*, 65.

monk, Martin Luther. For him the focus is on the individual and the anxiety of the inner self.

> The beginning of faith means repeatedly beginning again and conversion means turning back to faith in a repentance that should take place daily. So for Luther the Gospel is always prevenient, coming to Christians while they are still unbelieving sinners and turning them around yet again.[15]

In Luther's theology, 'all Christians are both justified and sinners at the same time', 'believers and unbelievers at the same time'. The wills of all are in bondage to sin. It is only in the inner self that the Christian finds the freedom of faith. The individual is pushed back into the inner self, dependent daily in faith upon God for their conversion.

Eberhard Jungel's commentary[16] on Luther's view of freedom is helpful. Usually the inner world of the self mirrors the external world. The gospel however gives rise to the possibility that the inner world could be quite different to the outer world. That is, the inner world of the person could either be a clone of the outer person or radically different from the outer person.

> For Luther, faith gives a new identity to the inner person and the possibility that the outer person is no longer controlled by its experience of the world. The new person is actually generated from within the inner world by the Spirit of God (received from God in the gift of faith enabling that person to believe), and then is able to live freely and creatively as a faithful person with a new identity in both the inner and outer world.[17]

These words were a result of my own search for the roots of Wesley's faith that came firstly from reading Luther and Jungel, as a result of reflection on Wesley's experience of a 'warmed heart'. A decade later, it was such a shock to read Cary's unfolding of the inner self, for it was clear from Jungel's description just how much Luther's description of the inner self had its roots in Augustine.

While there is continuity between Augustine and Luther, there is also a drastic discontinuity. It was Krister Stendahl who pointed out that the law was reinterpreted by Luther in terms of an "introspective conscience" that transposed the experience of the law to an experience within the inner self.

> Paul's argument that the Gentiles must not and should not come to Christ via the Law, i.e., via circumcision, etc. has turned into a statement according to which all men must come to Christ with consciences properly convicted by the Law and its insatiable requirements for righteousness. So drastic is the reinterpretation once the original framework of 'Jews and Gentiles' is lost, and

---

15. Cary, *Inner Grace,* 102.

16. Jungel, *The Freedom of a Christian.*

17. Drayton, *Pilgrim,* 144.

the Western problems of conscience become its unchallenged and self-evident substitute[18]

For Luther the conscience rules in the inner self, the place of introspection and the place of anxiety, guilt, and conversion. This view triumphed through the Pietists and with variations lasted through the Enlightenment. It is still at the heart of much Protestant evangelism.

The Enlightenment Self

Sometimes it helps to put things in stark outline without all the nuances that the philosophers have to make. For Plato, the world was open at the top to the ideal world of unchanging being, that enabled human souls to see the eternal forms and values from below, in a changing, decaying world. Augustine's genius was to present the Christian faith as a turn to the inside and then up toward God. The inner self was now a private space within a soul set with other souls in the wider public world open to the reality of God's truth and order. The result of sin was that each soul was isolated from all others and from God. Over the next thousand it came to be accepted that creation in the outer public world was a hierarchical world ordered by God. It meant that a person by birth was given a particular place within a public hierarchical world, while the private inner self was open to God in their inner space. With the coming of the Enlightenment this outer public hierarchical world was replaced by an external world of history brought into being through a scientific understanding of cause and effect.

This is the background to the presentation of Cary's fourth snapshot derived from John Locke (1632-1704). The Enlightenment perspective has arrived.

> Last there is John Locke's picture of a dark room where there is nothing to see but images projected from within. No sun shines into this room from above, and even the windows afford no direct view of the external world but only serve as a lens to project images of what is outside on a blank inner wall.[19]

From then on the inner self and outer world are different realities, soon historically to morph into the categories of self and world, then mind and body.

> The thread of continuity tying these pictures together (like four beads on a string) is the metaphor of the soul as an eye, based on the Platonist notion of intelligibility as the visibility of something to the eye of the mind. Plato's picture is intellectual vision pure and simple. Plotinus's is intellectual vision construed as inward turn, Augustine's is intellectual vision resulting from a turn first in then up, and Locke's picture is of a self with no direct intellectual

18. Stendahl, "Introspective Conscience", 87.

19. Cary, Phillip, *Augustine's Inner Self*, p. 5.

vision of anything but its own private inner world, seeing only images of things outside.[20]

In the Enlightenment, life in the inner world is about our thoughts and desires in relation to the sensations from the outer world where the focus is on the laws of cause and effect that make perception possible in the world. The inner self at the center need acknowledge no other authority other than their own individual conscience and desires, which is the same situation for all other selves in the world. Kant showed the world was limited in another way. Since thought occurs within space and time it was not possible to think beyond space and time to God, irrespective of whether God be in the inner world or the outer world. God is then shut out of the experience of the inner and outer world.

> Hence Western inwardness can be traced back to the Platonist inward turn, represented by Plotinus, which is adopted and modified by Augustine to produce the concept of private inner space, which later undergoes modifications of its own in Locke and others. As we go from Plotinus to Augustine to Locke, we find the inner world shrinking—from a divine cosmos containing all that is ultimately real and lovely (in Plotinus) to the palace of an individual soul that can gaze upon all that is true and lovely above (in Augustine) to a closed little room where one only gets to watch movies, as it were, about the real world (in Locke). It is a progression in which the inner self contains progressively less of reality and divinity—from Plotinus's divine inner self, to Augustine's inner self in which God can be found, to Locke's inner room where there can be literally no idea of God.[21]

The end result is that the self finds itself alone in inner space, enclosed in a world of cause and effect that can only be deduced by language and reason from other lonely selves. The 'I' is the one point of self-certainty. In this world it is impossible to discover God or really be at one with another. There can be no certain answer to the why of existence and the purpose of life. Instead the desire to create identity leaves the individual with de Botton's status anxiety, living in terms of the internal hierarchy of values and accomplishments that an outer society helps to create.

The Democratic Self

This new way of thinking about the nature of the self in terms of free and equal inner selves, in a non-hierarchical outer world, was incredibly powerful. So powerful in fact, that it led to the overturning of the hierarchies of divine order that had defined the outer and inner worlds for more than a millenia. The *ancient regimes* succumbed to revolutions in the eighteenth century that led to the emergence of democratic nations

20. Cary, Phillip, *Augustine's Inner Self*, p. 5.
21. Cary, *Augustine's Inner Self*, p. 5.

defined by constitutions. In each case the constitution defined an agreed basis for a nation of free equal individuals to live together. This is now the dominant view among nearly all nations. Still vestiges of the other two views remain with some convinced of the created orders of the world, and others maintaining that the self is still open to God. What constitutes reality though, are these two sorts of fundamental perspectives, self and world, specifically the perceptions involved in experience, the categories of 'the inner world' and 'the outer world'.

The development of the cinema is an amazing demonstration of the philosophical underpinnings of the world. The movie is watched in a darkened movie theatre, and the story is projected onto the screen, catching up the moviegoers in the story. It is as though the story derived from outside the individual, is projected onto the inside walls for the individual to experience. All that can be known of the 'outside world' is that which is perceived by the eye of the camera, and recorded for showing in the 'inner world' of Locke's 'inner room'.

This inside/outside view is written in to the way reality is now seen. It gives rise to the self as the center of the individual life with life being ordered in terms of what is best for the individual, and the group or institution as the center of its life, with a series of concentric circles that move further and further out from the center describing the relative participation in the group or institution.

Once the Enlightenment view of the world triumphed, the church, which had previously been at the center of power, was separated off from the affairs of the nation and political life. This parallels the separation between self and world in the individual. In terms of the inner world, the Church defied Hume and maintained that the inner world was still open to God so that the inner self could be open to the action of God. This individual relationship with God was the key to worship. There was still the task of convincing others that God was still important to the life of the wider society, if only they would be willing to be converted and discover God's role in the inner life. In terms of the inner-self, the emphasis was on the revelation of God given through knowing the Scriptures, and in the wider world the need to convince others of the importance of the God of the inner self, being the same as the God of creation.

This revolution had differing consequences for the church in different places. In Europe the church became an active minority that performed a form of "vicarious religion" on behalf of the rest of the society. In the public domain the church was still supported by the state in a limited way.[22] The rituals and expressions of belief were accepted as a framework by society that saw their individual freedom as a "freedom not to believe". Whereas in the United States in the new democratic world this new freedom was celebrated as a "freedom to worship" with the church separated from the state. Much of the Christian world tends toward this view of freedom that gives rise to the privatization of religion. As the democratic era has unfolded the continued stress on choice as a fundamental human right has focused on belief as an individual

22. Davie, "Is Europe an Exceptional Case?" 247–258.

right and led to a lessening of the ownership of responsibility for the wider patterns in society.

Of course there are other philosophical frameworks for the understanding of the self. Phenomenology and later existentialism have affirmed the given-ness of the self in the experience of the being of the world in which the self finds itself. These views deny that the experience of the self can be reduced to the scientific world of cause and effect. Idealism and Realism maintain that the Platonic and Aristotelian thought still provide more comprehensive frameworks than the Enlightenment world that succeeded them. Also evolutionary thought, psychology, and sociology, each provide other accounts of the emergence of thought, the structure of the self and the influence of society.

These other perspectives have had a limited impact on the awareness of most individuals. It is the acceptance of the Enlightenment view of the individual that lies at the heart of the cultural understanding of the self. The individual is the atomic unit of society, experienced from the inner self. In this setting the congregation becomes a gathering of individuals, and the church building the place for the sharing of their experience. It is not all surprising that the building becomes the house of God for the congregation, for a place is required for communal worship to happen.

The denominational paradigm maintains that the inner world of the individual is still open to God. How was that understood? The belief that the human race had been created in the image of God meant that a relationship was possible between humans and God, though marred by the fall. Traditionally that relationship had been understood in terms of a shared rationality. And it was early in the Enlightenment that Schleiermacher provided another basis for this relationship—the particular experience of the feeling of absolute dependence within. Rudolf Otto later affirmed the inner experience of being open to God through the mystic experience of the transcendently numinous. The inner self then was open to rational belief, profound feelings, and the possibility of mystical experiences. These each reinforce that the life of faith and belief is focused on what happens in the inner self.

The focus on the inner self gave rise to quite particular evangelical approaches in the late eighteenth and early nineteenth century. The first was during the first great evangelical awakening when Whitefield and the Wesleys declared that if a person was willing to repent, God would act to justify and redeem them in Christ Jesus, and they could know an inner assurance of this. For Wesley that moment could never be predicted however. The inner self waited, sometimes for years, for the 'warmed heart' moment of God's action, independent of the person's own thinking or desires. Thus conversion was primarily a waiting on the activity of God.

It took a further hundred years before Charles Grandison Finney discovered another option for the inner self. Rather than wait for God to act, the individual human person could act to commit their life to God in Christ. The common way of describing this experience is to place Jesus Christ as Lord on the throne of one's inner life. This emphasis on the subjective commitment of the individual then is the key factor that opens the inner self to God. It is a private subjective act of the individual. The greater the focus on commitment, the greater the presumption that the individual self is at the center of the inner world. It is the end product of seeing the self as a Lockean 'inner room'. The New Testament story has been cut down, modified, and massaged to fit into a Lockean inner room!

The Socially Constructed Self

In the wider society, beyond this inner room of the self, the technological revolution that the Enlightenment brought into being, gave rise to an industrial revolution that remade the face of social life. The cities were the new centers for society, with markets becoming shopping centers, the growth of educational centers, research centers, healing centers, and the development of cultural centers, such as libraries, art galleries, museums in the center of the cities. The cities were ringed by suburbs that first with trains, and then cars, were enabled to grow exponentially. A whole range of new forms of service provided what was needed for the family unit in the home. The home became the family inner room for the overwhelming number of families who now lived in suburban communities.

The self was at the center, of so many different settings as the irreducible atom of democratic society. There is a sense in which each self is a multiple self, depending on which center they are in, or another way of putting it, which role they are fulfilling. For a very few, psychic stress, can give rise to multiple selves. The ultimate private room is the irreducible atom of the inner self. Only the self knows how a person adapts their self to the context in which they find themselves.

In the twentieth century the description of the outer world beyond the self continued to grow, understood in terms of cause and effect. The laws of science, through psychology, medicine, sociology and biology began to rebound on the very notion of this self, as the basic unit of the democratic view of the world.

The logic and inquiry first applied to the outer world, were then applied to the study of the inner self in terms of functions of the brain. Psychology and sociology began to slice and dice the solid self, in terms of the conscious, the preconscious and the unconscious. The roles of the individual, both as a person, and in terms of their roles and positions in society, were carefully described. The study of ethnography showed the parallels in the awareness of those animals close to humans on the family tree with humans themselves. The study of the brain identified similar processes and behaviors that are associated with human consciousness. The study of human and biological systems indicated that the human race was inter-related with the rest of life in an inter-dependent way. The analysis of human DNA and DNA of other mammals showed how each depend upon the same basic building blocks of life. And the realization began to dawn that the earth is not the stage on which the human story is to be told, but the human race is an inter-related and inter-dependent expression of the fabric of life that evolved on this planet.

The generation born since the beginning of the stardust revolution increasingly takes it for granted that the self is socially constructed. In the second half of the twentieth century attention has focused on the self in new and revealing ways. First books, then television, journals and experts spruke the need for self-fulfillment in life and how to find it, stressing self-assessment, self- awareness, self-presentation, and even the spiritual self and the possibility of self-transcendence. With this search for the self goes the shadow side of self-mutilation, self-medication, addictions and anxieties that beset people. In the public domain marketing highlights the I-Phone and the I-Pad, while the ubiquitous 'selfie' then emerges when nearly everyone carries a camera in their phone.

The impact of the wider social world reverberates on the self in many ways not previously realized. Sociology has described the impact of the collective upon the individual as the self. Emile Durkheim points out that when the integration of society is less effective and more tenuous there is a rise in the level of aimlessness in living that is expressed as *anomie*. Max Weber showed how class and role in society affect the perspective of each individual in terms of culture, gender, place, language and history. It is now almost expected that a particular presentation is not really complete without the history and the location of the person involved also being included. The social construction of the author or presenter involved is an integral factor.

As the atomic "I" of the inner self has frayed into a number of social, scientific and psychological threads, a more general way of speaking about the individual as a unit of society has emerged in terms of human rights. Such language is now part of the human condition. Remarkably it was not until 1948 that the United Nations Declaration of Human Rights codified what rights given to the self should be universally protected.

Since then the suggested extension of this rights language to animals and machines raises fundamental questions as to what it is to be human, that is, a 'self-conscious self', with a private subjective inner self. Experiments in ways to augment bodies is proceeding apace, using what Steve Fuller describes as converging technologies for "the purpose of extending the power and control of human beings over their own bodies and their environments."[23] Advanced computers and the technology to manipulate the human genome will continue to push the envelope for what is considered to be human and self conscious awareness.

Many scientists now accept that the self will be explained on the microcosmic scale when computers are developed that will share consciousness with the human self. And macroscopically since self-conscious life has emerged on the Earth, the possibility grows that as thousands of planets have already been discovered around other suns, it will be found that life is not necessarily unique to the earth. Rational processes

23. Fuller, *Humanity 2.0*, 103.

of cause and effect will have explained the increasingly accepted social view of the self in terms of the processes of the world. These are major questions that impact upon this division between the inside world and the outside world. Is the inner self really anything different to that outside it? What is human self-consciousness if it can be made from the materials and processes learnt from studying the 'outer world'?

What is clear is that the denominational church has faced an increasingly sceptical intellectual response from the world of science and learning. It may be that despite the attacks, faith still remains reasonably resilient in the inner world of the self, even if silenced somewhat in the discourse of society. Not only has such questioning pushed the church further to the margins as an institution in western society, the structure of the denominational church has been further eroded by the stress on the autonomy of the individual in democratic society. Stephen Warner points out that there is a convergence across all religious traditions toward a *de facto congregationalism*[24] that does not relate to the regional or national structure of the denominational churches to which they supposedly belong.

As Robert Putnam showed such compartmentalizing in the long run weakens social structures as individuals disconnect with each other.[25] Late in the twenitieth century Martin Marty realized that the Protestant church had so turned inward with its emphasis on the life of the inner self that it had resulted in a retreat of congregations and believers from the wider world. His alarm that private believers were locked into confessional churches, speaking to themselves, led to an epic call to churches to become a 'public church' speaking across mainline, evangelical and catholic boundaries. His assessment of individual belief is telling.

> So each individual who cares for the holy must be a steadfast eccentric who builds a private castle or fortress inside the mind. In the mental stronghold the last and only shrine survives, and from it individuals may draw strength, but they can never share this strength, only live off it.[26]

Marty called for a Public Theology to face the en-globing issues that now threaten the planet, like global warming, nuclear devastation, a sustainable human future, bionic adaption of the body, and other developments that raise ultimate questions about the meaning of life itself. In the twenty-first century theologians are beginning to speak about God again in the public realm. Increasingly the world horizon of human society rebounds upon the individual with these matters that bring to the forefront the survival of the individual and the human race. As a result questions about the meaning of life and the future of the human race come from many directions and cannot so easily be avoided. Discussion in the public square is now more open to talk about the creation and the creator.

24. Wind and Lewis, *American Congregations*, 54.

25. Putnam, *Bowling Alone*.

26. Marty, *Public Church*, 47.

It is time to ponder Fuller's question in this radically changing context. What "would it mean to live "in the image and likeness of God" in the twenty-first century—not the thirteenth or seventeenth century?"[27]

CHOICE AND COMMITMENT

The implications of a democratic view of the 'inner self' as the billiard ball core of who we are as people, however, still lie at the heart of the religious democratic individual who lives within the world-view of the denominational paradigm of the last 250 years. How is it that the denominational church can see itself with a message for society in the public square when its members are caught up in a world lived out in terms of status anxiety derived from commitments made in the inner self?

There is an extensive body of work grappling with the need for the church to escape these structures and attitudes that the denominational church once legitimated and rendered plausible. The primary ways the church used to recruit and influence society are no longer effective.

Evangelism has failed as a means of reaching adults since World War 2. There were (and still are) many evangelistic programs and congregational revival weeks, but the evangelist is principally relating to the existing members of the congregation and not the members of the society "out there" as once happened. These are events that seek a deeper commitment from existing attenders who in 'the castle of their minds' are unsure as to whether they are Christians. They provide an opportunity to make a more overt decision and say yes. Very rarely in the late twentieth century have evangelists in the west made an impression on wider western society. Billy Graham is the exception. Yet even he struggled to get beyond the attenders at the local congregation. His innovation was to carefully organize preparation with church leaders in advance of the rallies. Together they made sure that the logistics of getting people to a large stadium or center were carefully worked out and followed through.[28]

The Sunday School too has failed as a means of recruitment. Throughout the western world the generation born after World War 2 grew up with a different attitude to authority than their parents had. The 1960s were a turbulent time politically with student riots in France and the marches against the Victnam War elsewhere. Contraception, and a more open attitude to drugs, as well as the availability of tertiary education for many more than ever before, has seen the emergence of a more critically aware generation, who have a keen sense of their right to choose. When this group became parents themselves there was a profound change in their willingness to let their children be sent to Sunday School. In Australia[29], Sunday School attendances

---

27. Fuller, *Humanity 2.0*, 4.

28. Johnston, *Graham's Theology of Evangelism.*

29. The results of comparative research show that the attendance of people at church in Australia sits between higher rates in the United States, and much lower rates in Europe. The trends in Australia

in the 1970s dropped to less than a quarter of those in the preceding decade. In the national census, which includes a question about religious identity, the 0–5 year olds overwhelmingly put 'no religion' or did not answer the question! Of course this was their parents answering for them. By the end of the century more than a third of the population had put 'no religion' or did not answer this question about their religious identity, with this parental generation heavily over-represented in this category. This phenomenon did not emerge until the 1970s, paralleled in North America—and to an even greater extent in Europe.

With the two principal means of recruitment or "outreach" of the denominational church having failed, the average age of church attenders gets older. Even among church attenders, a question asked in the National Church Life Survey[30] saw a devastating change in the attitude of members to their particular denomination. When asked, "Do you believe in life-long membership with your denomination", one in two, over fifty, said yes, quite a remarkable figure in itself, with only half seeing loyalty to a denomination as appropriate. For those younger than fifty, every denominational result was the same—only one in seven believed in life long membership with their denomination. And those answering the question were already attending a congregation!

Something deep and profound has happened in society. It has resulted in those sitting in pews younger than 50 not being willing to give allegiance to the denominations to which they presently belong, while the same age group in the wider society provide the overwhelming majority who put 'no religion' or did not answer the question in s national census. These statistics are a disaster for denominational churches. It is not that issues of religion are dead in the 21st century. In the wider society there is a great deal of interest in spirituality, but it exists alongside this aversion to the denominational form of the local congregation. Indeed in Australia, where attendance at church has dropped to 7.5% of the population,[31] Bouma sees a resurgence in forms of spirituality that reflect a more pluralistic society with greater diversity in understanding and experience. "At the core of spirituality is the encounter with the other, some other, be it God, nature, a tree, the sea, some other person or the core of our own being."[32] Individuals are working out for themselves what they believe, picking and mixing from what is available. Bouma further argues that "while in the twentieth

---

cited in research are echoed in all regions.

30. The National Church Life Survey in Australia is a longitudinal study from 1991–2016 of the attitudes of those of nearly all who are in church on a Sunday (>600,00) of all denominations near the National Census, enabling the results to be compared with national perspectives.

31. The best surveys of weekly attendance in the period 2012-2013 have United States 23%, France 15%, United Kingdom 10%, Australia, 7.5%. There are many lists of attendance derived from self reporting surveys such as Gallup in 2013 in the United States which showed 37% attending weekly or near weekly. Clearly many people in the US see themselves as churchgoers but over report their attendance.

32. Bouma, *Australian Soul*, 12.

century religion and spirituality often provided and identity and meaning for people, in the twenty-first century the core is the production and the maintenance of hope."[33]

While the understanding of religion has been caught up into broader definitions of spirituality, it is the personal encounter with the "other" that is most significant. Some sort of God is back, but what sort of God? Once more it is still primarily a 'God and Me' framework. More are interested, but this interest goes along with greater agnosticism and apathy in society as well. It is as though the God question, or the search for the experience of some sort of "other", has been pushed back deeper into the dimension of the self.

The greater the expectation in society that the individual has the right to choose, the harder it is for those in the church and the wider society to escape from the loneliness of the inner self. At the same time as the belief in an interventionist God involved in life has almost evaporated, the hope of finding a 'spiritual other' in the midst of the world has grown. The more the billiard ball of the self is replaced with a socially constructed view of self, the greater the need there is to find some center for the self. Whether this need to find a sure center is a response to uncertainty, or an expression of a profound longing in the human self, it is evident that the power of religion has not waned so much as being expressed in new ways. The widespread influence of New Age spirituality finds meaning in and through forms of the spirit of God immanent in the world rather than from former views of a transcendent God. In a similar way the focus in the church on the divinity of Christ has been replaced with a stress on the humanity of Jesus.

This change raises major questions for the denominational church. In that strange way that major events coalesce about themselves, the events of 9/11 drew a line under the twentieth century. It has become a sign of how we are now living in a different twenty-first century. Once more religion has returned to the front page. Something radically new had happened. No longer could any western nation turn a blind eye to religion when it was seen to be the source of forms of radical terrorism that threaten everyone. This shift meant that churches have a new context in which to work. What had been there in the background came to the foreground. Churches had to come to terms with the fact that a global world was now a multi-faith world. Denominations now have a responsibility to relate to other world faiths, as well as help congregations become more open to the religious diversity that migration has made such a part of the western world.

Hardly anywhere in the west can there be business as normal, yet there is an impatience with established polities. In most denominations as congregations age, the sources of money derived from giving in congregations lessens year by year. The operations of the local congregation and the organizational structure of the wider councils are threatened and seek new ways of meeting the crisis. Many new programs and approaches are tried; there is restructure after restructure of organizations. There

33. Bouma, *Australian Soul*, 30.

is a desperate focus on the training of new leaders, hoping that such leaders can make a difference, without the opportunity for reflection about the deeper issues involved.

For 1800 years baptism was the rite of entrance into the faith. In the denominational paradigm individual decision took the place of baptism as the basis of being a Christian. It is assumed that faith is an individual commitment that leads to the choice to join a particular denomination. It is a gospel of choice. When the individual is at the center the very act of decision makes the relationship of faith an individual—God relationship. Only I can decide to follow Christ. Rather than entering a community of faith by profession in baptism, one opts to join with others who have decided to be Christian in a particular way that I accept. Even in Asian and African 'we' cultures the emphasis of the gospel is still on the individual. We each live our individual Christian lives during the week, then return to the House of God, the building that is the 'container' that holds us together, for worship on a Sunday. The committed core are convinced that what is needed is a deeper more decisive individual commitment to the gospel in the inner self if individuals are to live a life of dedicated discipleship. At the same time in the wider society individuals consider themselves committed to their own view of the spiritual or the 'other', but see no need to attend a church, and stand free of the need of any institutional or communal expression for what they believe. It brings to the fore a critical question. Is an emphasis on commitment the way forward or a dead end from the denominational era?

In the last decades of the twentieth century at least three powerful movements emerged, each of which has many followers and proponents who see their movement as an indicator for the future of the church. What is the role of commitment in these developments?

The Mega-Church

First is the rise of mega-churches, defined as a Protestant church with more than 2,000 members[34]. The largest mega-church is the Yoido Full Gospel Church in South Korea with more than 800,000 members, and in the United States Lakewood in Texas with greater than 40,000 members. There are many mega-churches in Africa and India. While there were large churches prior to the 1950s, it is generally recognized that this movement began with the TV era, and is focused on urban areas with economic resources. To grow a mega-church requires a careful working through of the matters that enhance church growth. The great emphasis is on the sort of leadership required to grow a church through successive stages of mission—growth in buildings, development of ministry teams, with critical issues emerging at particular levels of attendance as the size of the services grow.

---

34. There are many Roman Catholic churches with more than 2,000 members. These large congregations are the result of rationalizing resources to provide regional centers for members to have access to the sacraments.

How significant is this movement? The percentage of members of a denomination involved in a mega-church in the United States gives some idea of the scope of this phenomenon. "While almost 10% of Protestant churchgoers attend a mega-church, these churches represent only about half of one percent of the roughly 320,000 Protestant churches that exist in the United States."[35]

Advocates of the movement see the importance of training a new form of leader for the church, able to grow larger congregations, utilizing the insights of business leadership, market surveys re belief, able to have a voice in the media. Critics of the movement claim that this worship-oriented approach is more entertainment than religion, captive to business leadership models, market aware, and more concerned with personal morality and affirming the faith of those who attend.

In a way the mega-church is the end product of the denominational church paradigm. The key to the life of the church is that of church growth. The mega-church emphasizes the mission, to "reach out" and make new disciples, using all of the available tools for growth in preaching, music, and an integrated small group ministry. The mission is to grow a larger and larger congregation which can then have a greater impact on the society in which it finds itself. The senior minister is the key person. Such a leader has to be an engaging preacher, able to inspire individuals to grow spiritually, and give the money needed for media ministry and the large church buildings required. This gives the leader great power and great responsibility. It is however very difficult both to grow a large mega-church and also raise questions of social justice that have the potential to be contentious amongst those who attend, for such churches have large building programs and large debts and the budget is dependent upon maintaining the allegiance of members. High profile mega-churches are vulnerable to critical media attention when problems emerge. In South Korea and Singapore, high profile mega-church pastors have been convicted of fraud, casting a pall over the movement in those countries. Since most mega-churches are built through the ministry of one leader, the question of succession is not easy. One of the earlier and most well known mega-churches was the Crystal Cathedral in California that had more than 20,000 members at its peak. A split over the question of succession in leadership led to the church filing for bankruptcy in 2010, with debts of more than $50 million.[36] Mega-churches can and do get into serious financial and organizational trouble.

So much depends upon the leader being able to build a supporting team of other leaders, while maintaining the central role of preaching that enables the week by week contact with the membership that is essential if a vision is to be shared. It is vital to build small group networks, and often multiple services of worship, that provide the relational support needed to help members grow in participation. Research by the

35. For more information with regard to size, see the Hartford Institute for Religion Research FAQ's.

36. The Crystal Cathedral has since been bought by the Roman Catholic Church and consecrated as a Cathedral.

Hartford Institute for Religions Research on 406 of the 1650 mega-churches in the United States indicates that,

> [c]ontrary to expectations, these congregations promote intense personal commitment in a majority of their members but also contain a large percentage of anonymous spectators in their ranks.[37]

Note the emphasis on 'intense personal commitment' and 'anonymous spectators' underlines the importance of individual choice. There remains the vital question as to how the message of Jesus has to be massaged to serve the needs of growth, numbers and success. The mega-church is a special case of the denominational paradigm targeting their message to the core attributes of a "God and me" religion. In fact most large mega-churches become 'non-denominational' denominations in their own right. Mega-churches have a wide range of theological backgrounds, including Pentecostal, Evangelical and Liberal theologies though most are in the Pentecostal and Evangelical streams. The leader must be able to draw upon a specific segment of the community and relate the gospel message to that group in a profoundly personal way that encourages members to give to the shared vision

The Charismatic Movement

In 1906 in Azusa St, Los Angeles, William Seymour began a multiracial meeting that gave birth to the Pentecostal Church. Over the next 50 years the Pentecostal flame spread through the rest of the world, as visitors attracted to Azusa Street returned to their homes and new Pentecostal Churches were formed in city after city. The key to the movement is each individual's direct experience of God through the baptism of the Holy Spirit.[38] The initial emphasis on speaking in tongues and the expectation of healing were focused in the revival meeting or Pentecostal meeting. The Pentecostal movement continued to grow world wide significantly decade after decade. In the 1950s David DuPlessis, a South African Pentecostal Pastor, felt called by the Holy Spirit to relate to Roman Catholics, and in 1952 he also spoke to the World Council of Churches International Missionary Council in Willengen. He can rightly be called the one through whom the charismatic movement came into being, a Holy Spirit movement wider than the Pentecostal Churches, a wild fire in many denominations, with the Holy Spirit experienced individually by millions of Catholics and Protestants. In 1960 an Episcopal Priest Dennis Bennett published his autobiography *Nine O'clock in the Morning*[39] that widely publicized his experience of speaking in tongues. In the second half of the century the charismatic movement stressed the experience of the Holy Spirit and the discovery of spiritual gifts, an experiential form of faith, with an

37. Bird et al, Decade of "Megachurches."
38. Poewe, *Charismatic Global Culture.*
39. Bennett, *Nine O'Clock in the Morning.*

experiential way of reading the scriptures that is different to the rationalism of the fundamentalists and the liberal focus on values. Since then Charismatics like Tom Smail, Gordon Fee, and Amos Yong have provided a more reflective insider's assessment of Charismatic theology. By the end of the twentieth century it is estimated that there were more than half a billion charismatics world wide, about a quarter of the world's Christians, with large numbers in Latin America and Africa.

In the west by the beginning of the twenty-first century, the immediate effects of the charismatic movement had passed their peak. Some of the larger denominations in the United States resisted acknowledging the movement though all denominations were considerably affected by it. One of the effects of excited new believers was, once more, division, especially in church youth groups, or among young families, leading to a minority of members separating from the congregation when there was resistance to the experiential nature of the movement or criticism of its practices. In many ways the charismatic experience of the Holy Spirit intensified the individuality of the believer, and led to the formation of many new smaller denominations. But also the charismatic experience led to a new openness to scripture and an openness to other denominational traditions in a way that helped the ecumenical movement. There are a significant number of charismatic mega-churches emphasizing either worship, blessing or healing. The first 'mosh pit' in front of the musicians on stage occurred at Hillsong in Australia, a charismatic mega-church whose songs and CDs circle the globe.

At its heart this was a new form of the "God and Me" theology emphasizing commitment and personal success, that underlies the Protestant movement during the Denominational Paradigm. A sign of a deeper commitment to God was the willingness to seek the spiritual gifts such as speaking in tongues, though as the twenty-first century unfolds there is less of an emphasis on this particular gift and more on others. The Charismatic movement provided a third way beyond that of the fundamentalism—evangelism wing, and the social justice—liberalism wing, that had polarized the Protestant churches up until the last third of the twentieth century. The movement, however, continued to accept the primary aim and requirement of the denominational paradigm to grow the church. It became another form of church growth. One of the hallmarks of the charismatic movement beyond the Pentecostal church was that it was primarily a people movement that occurred with or without the approval of the leadership of the church.

The missio Dei

If leadership is key for the mega-church, and the experience of individuals is vital for the charismatic church, then the *missio Dei* has emerged from those working and reflecting on the various missionary councils of the churches. In the two decades after the 1910 Edinburgh missionary conference, with its stirring theme of the 'Evangelization of the World in this Generation,' the basic differences in the missionary approach between America and England on the one hand, and Europe on the other, became apparent. The Anglo-American approach was seen as imperialist in its emphasis on the need for conversion as its primary message. In the focus on the individual response of persons in another culture the Europeans claimed the Anglo Americans were blind to the way their own culture and history was presumed in the message. The Europeans were convinced that in sharing the message the key was to take seriously the cultural heritage of the listener and find ways that the revelation of Jesus Christ was already implicit in that culture. It was up to the missionary to discern the pattern of Christ in the culture and use that as a bridge for the message. Then, in the 1930s, the German Church's silence in the face of the Nazi attempts to rewrite Christmas (the Christmas tree topped by the Swastika instead of the star, and the creation of German legends to take away the focus on the manger's son of a Jew) made it obvious that this approach also was a way of freighting in the assumptions of the missioner and the culture. In 1934 the German Confessing Church took its stand against this denial of the centrality of Christ in the Barmen Declaration principally authored by Karl Barth.

At the 1952 International Missionary Council meeting in Willengen the missionary community faced the resistance of the new emerging nations on the colonial mission field to the continuing reception of western missionaries. These nations could see the cultural issues the missionary agencies were bringing with their message—the European stress on the medium of culture, and the Anglo-American emphasis on the role of the individual. The term *missio Dei* (mission of God) emerged in the missionary movement as a way of holding both positions together reflecting the prior reality that the source of mission is found in God. That led to a wrestling with the understanding of the Trinity and its implications for the missionary task of the way the church was to relate to the world and announce the possibility of faith to all peoples.

Yet, perhaps not surprisingly, it was still the church at the center determining the task of God's mission. It was Barth who made the decisive critique of the church as the source and center of decision for the mission. "Neither the Christian nor the Church is 'a goal in it itself, and end in itself . . . Where there is Christianity or a church institution, piety, inner life, going to heaven, which is an end in itself, that is no Christianity, even if it appears in a very strong form.'"[40]

The church is not a goal in itself, or the deciding agent of the gospel between the time of the cross and resurrection, and the time when the creation acknowledges the Trinitarian God. Theologians and Christians meeting in international meetings of the church began to see that if it is God's mission, then God is a missionary God. And, if God is a missionary God, then not only is God the sending God but it is the church that is sent. What a revolution for the church. The individual disciple, or the church is not at the center, for it is the individual disciple and the church that are sent by God, the missionary God. The Christian and the church in its apologetic, proleptic, public, pastoral and liturgical ministry are, in fact, caught up in God's missionary purposes.

40. Barth, "Fragebeantwortung, 433–444

A whole host of matters come to the fore. It is perhaps not surprising that attention focused on who it is that the Church is sent, and in what manner does the Church go? Over the twenty years from 1950 to 1970 in the meetings of Vatican 2, the World Council of Churches, Lausanne and Pentecostal events, there was a convergence in understanding that the disciple and the Church are the sign, the witness and the sacrament of God's mission.

THE MISSIO DEI

Of these three movements, the mega-church, the charismatic, and the *missio Dei*, it is the last that is more explicitly grounded in the understanding of the gospel of Jesus Christ rather than the self as the center of the religious self, as in church growth or the individual experience of the Holy Spirit. This movement is a worldwide discovery that builds upon the core doctrines of the church, which occurred ecumenically across Protestant, Pentecostal, Catholic and Orthodox councils of the church in the last third of the twentieth century. The central feature of the denominational paradigm, the importance of commitment and choice in a "God and Me" primary relationship presumes a view of both God and the self that we have found to be inadequate on scriptural, historical and theological grounds. The *missio Dei* is a massive change in perspective that opens up new possibilities for the experience of discipleship and church life, and a way beyond the dominant paradigm most Christians take for granted. Further reflection is required about this key notion that de-centers the church and places God back in the center of the church's life, in a time when a cause and effect view of the world makes it more difficult to speak of God. What does this mean for the church and our understanding and experience of God? What sort of God is implied in the *missio Dei*? And to which world is the church sent?

It was not long before different emphases emerged within the understanding of the *missio Dei*. First, at the Willengen meeting of the International Council for Mission 1952 from those who stressed the Trinitarian source of the mission of God.

> The classical doctrine of the *missio Dei* as God the Father sending the Son, and God the Father and the Son sending the Spirit was expanded to include yet another 'movement': Father, Son, and Holy Spirit sending the church into the world . . . Willengen recognized a close relationship between the *missio Dei* and mission as solidarity with the incarnate and crucified Christ.[41]

But there were those who saw the *missio Dei* as far larger than the mission of the church. The church was not necessary for God to be "working out his purpose in the midst of the world and its historical purposes."[42] Those working for justice, peace and

---

41. Bosch, *Transforming Mission*, 390.
42. Bosch, *Transforming Mission*, 392.

the common good, saw the *missio Dei* in terms of God's preferential option for the poor as the hallmark of the coming Kingdom of God.

It was not surprising this split emerged between this world mission perspective and the religious role of the church. Once again the self-world bifurcation at the heart of the Enlightenment perspective was at work. Whether it is seeking the conversion of individuals, pastorally caring for the community, or creating a community that is a sign of the kingdom, or the need for liberation theology, involvement in social justice, or witnessing to God's vision for the creation, there are different understandings of the *missio Dei,* and the role of the church and other agencies within it

Again it was Karl Barth who saw to the heart of this matter. Rather than the mission of God being mediated through the inner self or the world society, Barth derived the mission from God's mission to the creation in and through Jesus Christ, who is both Son of God and Son of Man. The Church derives its mission directly through the humanity of Jesus Christ, (and indirectly through the union in Christ with the God who sent him).

> The resurrection is the visibility of the new creation, and the Christian community is called to live within this future reality. She exists here and now as human beings determined by the promise of the Spirit, and takes the concrete form of liberation for missionary service.[43]

This brings alive the discussions of the early church Fathers re the two natures of Christ. For Barth the union of the two natures is not meant to be understood statically as a balancing of the transcendent and the immanent, but as a uniting in Jesus Christ, that leads to the mission of the church to the world.

> All this is from God who reconciled us to himself through Christ, and has given us the ministry of reconciliation; that is in Christ God was reconciling the world to himself, not counting their trespasses against them, and entrusting the message of reconciliation to us.(2 Cor 5:18,19)

The Church in Christ is entrusted with the message of reconciliation.

> Any reification of the church and her practices forms Christian witness after the mode of propaganda constitutes a denuding of the 'actual' community. The existence of the community is missionary service to the gospel, not an occasion for propaganda. . . . This task is her holiness in the world, the one task the world cannot do for itself. . . . In serving God, the community serves the world.[44]

This was Hoekendjik's warning in the discussions about the missionary structures of the church, cited earlier. How hard it is for the church to take itself out of the

43. Flett, *Witness of GOD,* 290.
44. Flett, *Witness of GOD,* 275.

center and let its witness to Jesus Christ be its life in Christ, not church growth, or the source of help for spiritual growth, or the celebration of the sacraments, or the agent of social justice in the world—though all of these are important. As Bosch states,

> Mission is, primarily and ultimately, the work of the Triune God, Creator, Redeemer, and Sanctifier, for the sake of the world, a ministry in which the church is privileged to participate. Mission has its origin in the heart of God. God is a fountain of sending love.[45]

The great danger is for the mission to become a new process of making decisions—for the sake of mission—fashioning plans to express the love of God in terms of worship witness and service. In this way the church sneaks back into the center of the decision making! In the *missio Dei* the missio can take pre-eminence at the expense of the experience and knowledge of God. In the denominational paradigm God is known through decisions within the self. The Enlightenment world has no categories to describe God at work in the midst of history. There is no place here for the apocalyptic kingdom of God that is at the center of Jesus message. The apocalyptic had long ago been collapsed into the categories of history. As Moltmann states,

> What we have to learn is not that the church has a mission, but the very reverse: that the mission of Christ creates its own church.[46]

This happens through the apocalypse of Jesus Christ in his life, death upon a cross, resurrection and ascension. It is God with us in his Son Jesus Christ, who is the defining center of the *missio Dei,* bringing into being the redemptive existence of the church as a reconciling witness to God's purposes.

In 'God's being in becoming' the *missio Dei* can provide the healing source that transcends the schizophrenia of self and world inherent in the Enlightenment view and the religious focus on decision. This rediscovery of the *missio Dei* by Barth, came as a result of his calling in question the Enlightenment theology of the nineteenth century on the basis of the revelation of God from a new reading of Paul. Later it was discovered that the revelation of which Barth speaks is for Paul an apocalyptic happening manifested within history. This apocalyptic reading further underlines the critical importance that it is Christ's mission that creates the church. The way is open in Christ for a rediscovery of the apocalyptic kingdom of God in our midst.

The form of the self will be different in an apocalyptic paradigm. The long process of the intensification of the experience of the self will develop further or even change. What will come after Augustine's view of the self as the turn within and up, the Enlightenment atomic center, and the growing awareness of the social sources of self? Any change has enormous implications for the experience of God and the life of society.

45. Bosch, *Transforming Mission*, 392.
46. Moltmann, *The Church in the Spirit*, 10.

What is surprising is how introverted this discussion about church growth and mission has been. And even when it is focused on God's future shalom in a new heaven and a new earth, this transformation is most often presumed to occur on this planet. As the twenty-first century unfolds, God's mission to the world can no longer be restricted to planet Earth. The missionary God who created the universe has a mission to a universe, or maybe even universes. What a different horizon lies before us as we consider that the missionary God relates to the universe on a scale that theology has rarely before envisaged. So while the *missio Dei* is found in the cross as the event that makes plain who God is, the purpose of God's redemption there has implications that go far beyond the pale blue dot where the human race lives—thus far.

6

Toward an Apocalyptic Self

THE HEAVENS TORN OPEN

THE PREPARATION FOR AN *address on the baptism of Jesus in Mark's gospel was not going well. Why was there such attention on the sequence of events that happened as Jesus came up out of the water? First the heavens were torn open, then the Spirit came down and Jesus heard he was the beloved son of the Father. I had heard a lot about being born again and receiving the Holy Spirit in the Christian walk, but nothing about the heavens being torn open.*

In fact the message that brought me to stand at the front of the Adelaide Town Hall to accept Jesus Christ as Lord was that in Jesus Christ I could be born again as a child of God. The Chinese evangelist said, "Come forward and receive what is your divine birthright." The famous texts used were John 3:3b, and John 1:13 from the King James Version. "Except a man be born again, he cannot see the kingdom of God" and to those who received Jesus "which were born, not of blood, nor the will of the flesh nor of the will of man, but of God". It has been a powerful message over the last three hundred years since the time of George Whitefield. God will adopt me as a son or daughter. So many millions have responded to that call like I did.

Then sixteen years later in the charismatic movement the invitation was to be baptized in the Holy Spirit. I had said yes, and ministry in the power of the Holy Spirit had come alive in working with the congregation.

But what was the sense of the first act of God in Jesus baptism. God "opened the heavens". That was the puzzle. I remember, driving past a famous hotel in Adelaide, mulling over these words, when the question came. "If the heavens were opened for Jesus at his baptism, when were they closed?"

Putting the question that way pointed directly to the answer. The heavens once opened, remained open throughout his ministry. Arriving home I checked to see what the Greek said. Yes, the tense of the verb 'to open' indicates that once opened, the heavens stayed open. Like a door opened, and kept open. I always have had the image of a door ripped off its hinges unable to be closed again. And in Matthew and Luke, the parallel passages have the same sense. (In John it is presented differently for the heavens are already opened, since Jesus is the Word of God, the Lamb of God, on whom John "saw the Spirit descending from heaven like a dove, and it remained on him." (John 1:32))

This was a different way to look at Jesus' ministry. I could not wait to re-read the gospels. There was a new significance in many of Jesus words, but especially this comment in the Beatitudes. In a statement about vows Jesus says, "You have heard that it was said, . . . but I say to you,"

> *You shall not swear falsely. But I say to you, Do not swear at all, either by heaven, for it is the throne of God, or by the earth, for it is his footstool, or by Jerusalem, for it is the city of the great King. (Matthew 5:34,35)*

The throne of God here in heaven is connected to God's footstool on earth. Heaven and earth are open to each other.

And even when Jesus cries out from the cross, "My God, my God, Why have you forsaken me"(Mark 15:34), the sense of separation indicates that he has lost the awareness of what he had experienced during his ministry, his openness to God, yet he still says, My God!"

It took a few months to realize that the heavens torn open is another way of speaking of the presence of the kingdom of God, and many years to discover that this was an apocalyptic beginning to Jesus baptism that has great significance for the way we receive the gospel.

THE APOCALYPTIC SELF

No one said anything about an apocalypse when I was at Sunday School. The lessons emphasized a gentle loving Jesus meek and mild who called us to commit our lives to him. An apocalyptic Jesus announcing the Kingdom of God was far from the teacher's mind and the church's understanding. In their own way the Sunday School teachers were the body-guards of the Enlightenment Jesus, keeping our attention on commitment and faith.

When the unveiling or disclosing of the hidden occurs with God, the conscious experience is super-saturated, overwhelmed, like a thimble before a waterfall, by the very reality of a presence that ripples with other possibilities as yet not known. These events are not fantasy—they ring with the intensity of an experience that the person has not known before. People do not forget these moments, they are life-changing events.

And many people have such events implode in upon them. The apocalyptic event shared earlier disclosed a future that was as surprising as it was unexpected. When I left home that morning our future directions were clear—a new place of ministry in inner city Adelaide. When I went to sleep that night it seemed there was a call to minister in a different state in a new role, that within a year had us as a family moving 1400 kms from South Australia to New South Wales. There have been other events in my life that have had 'this otherness yet presence of God' about them, but this particular event is unique in the sequence of events that unfolded.

This occurrence, hearing a voice from God, cannot easily be dismissed as just a creation of the mind in response to reading a book about prayer. It is in a setting in which many elements quite independently of one another happened: hearing a voice, thinking a thought, a bus closing its doors to travellers, arriving home to a letter heralding a new beginning, and without knowing what had happened in the previous hour, Sandra's comment 'This is God speaking to you'. There are five separate and independent events, occurring sequentially and capable of being analyzed separately, and with a sixth further fact, the potential appointment to a position, of which I was unaware at the time, in another state.[1]

There is the juxtaposition of event, mind, context and comment about a possibility I did not know was open. It is always possible to explain away any event as a psychological event, or chance occurrence, or projection of thoughts, or just plain mysterious. For me there was a line in the sand drawn that day at that spot. Yes, I have been back there.

I do not have to crucify the mind to accept that this disclosure was not a creation of the mind. My mind was on the receiving end of what happened: I was more of an observer than a creator of what was happening. It is the discovery with Simone Weil, of the possibility "of a real contact person to person, here below, between a human being and God"[2]. It points clearly to the existence of the other, where the other is not the creation of the mind, or only known by mind. The creation of the relationship is dependent upon the other, upon God, to be a reality. It depends upon the other to make clear in the event that it is more than an idea of the mind, or a projection of the mind. It is an uncovering of the hiddenness of God. The normal response to such an event is that it is seen as extreme, mystical, unreal and not really rational.

This is light years from the autonomous self that is presumed in our denominational culture which is focused on decision and commitment and is puzzled by any suggestion of such events as involving the action of God. The gospel is restricted, cut down, to a gospel of choice—"I am free to choose" my beliefs, and to choose which congregation I will attend with its particular set of beliefs about Bible, conversion, doctrine, gender, welfare etc.. Brueggemann indicates just how difficult it is to move

1. Probability theory states that the number of probable outcomes involved in 6 points or 6 players is 6x5x4x3x2x1=520. That this happened by coincidence will surely be affirmed by some. For me, what more rock solid evidence could one receive of the presence of God within the creation, with six separate events unfolding one after another, but then in retrospect seen to be interdependent and leading to a conclusion that I did not know about? At the same time it is vital to test such events as far as one can with any non-repeatable event.

2. Wijngaards, *Sense of God*, 227.

beyond this cultural view of the self that is inherent in the dominant narrative of the society, presumed in services of worship.

> The dominant narrative—one I have characterized as "therapeutic, techno-logical, consumerist militarism"—is committed to the notion of *self invention* in the pursuit of *self sufficiency* . . . Thus it is an acting out, in quotidian ways, of the modern sense of an autonomous self that eventuates in a rat race that readily culminates in violence if and when that self is impinged upon in in-convenient ways. The dominate narrative is seldom lined out, rarely seen in its coherence, and hardly ever critiqued in its elemental claims.[3]

A telling question makes this plain. I am still surprised by the consistent response to a question I have often asked churchgoers, "What was Jesus' message?" There is the normal range of answers, such as, forgiveness, the new commandments, love, recon-ciliation, etc., nearly all individual matters that the member needs to choose to put into practice. Most are puzzled and surprised by when the summary is read from any of the three Gospels.

> Jesus came to Galilee proclaiming the good news (gospel) of (from) God, and saying, 'The time is fulfilled, and the kingdom of God has come near (is at hand), repent and believe in the good news (gospel).(Mk 1:15)

When asked what they know about the kingdom of God, the answer usually comes, quick as a flash, from deep within somewhere, "The kingdom of God is within you." In one fell swoop the power of the reinforcing effect of the Enlightenment, de-mocracy and religious individualism within the dominant narrative is laid bare. Belief and faith are reduced to internal subjective states of the individual, for God is found within. "Let Jesus be in your heart, or Lord of your heart, or sit on the throne of your life". The Christian is called to put into practice personal kingdom values from within. Religion is centered in the inner self, the 'I.' As the issues that confront the planet are presented in an increasingly apocalyptic way the message of Jesus that most have heard is to commit yourself to change your personal attitudes to others and the world.

What the first three books of the New Testament declare is that the Kingdom of God is at hand and available. Jesus teaches how one enters the kingdom of God: The kingdom of God is not in me, instead he teaches how we may enter into the kingdom.

But then comes the rejoinder from those who know their Bible a little: does not Jesus say somewhere that the kingdom of God is within you? Well yes, there is a passage, only one passage amongst more than fifty about the kingdom of God. "The kingdom of God is not coming with things that can be observed; nor will they say. 'Look, here it is!' or 'There it is.' For, in fact, the kingdom of God is among (within) you. (Luke 17:20a, 21)" The key word can be translated among or within. The one doubtful exception only proves the rule. The overwhelming pressure of the culture

---

3. Breugemann, *Prophetic Preaching*, 4.

of choice is to still locate the kingdom of God within. As a result the discovery made by biblical scholars that Jesus' message is an apocalyptic kingdom message that is "at hand", can hardly be heard.

Once more it is apparent that vital and central words used in describing the gospel have had their meaning and content changed over the course of time under the impact of various world-views. Not only revelation, but gospel, and apocalypse, have been affected. The kingdom of God also has tremendous historical baggage.

The kingdom of God is a term that carries with it at least two sorts of difficulties. The first is the history of past kingdoms in which the power of the king or ruler was upheld by force and repression. From the perspective of a democratic era many of these kings were little more than dictators in which citizens had few or any rights. When Jesus announced the kingdom of God he was well aware of the way most saw kings, since Israel was suffering under this sort of rule at the time. He carefully contrasted the kingdom of God with the kingdoms of this world. We need to do the same.

> So Jesus called them and said to them (the disciples). "You know that among the Gentiles those whom they recognize as their rulers lord it over them, and their great ones are tyrants over them. But it is not so among you; but whoever wishes to become great among you must be your servant, and whoever wishes to be first among you must be the slave of all. For the Son of Man came not to be served but to serve and to give his life as a ransom for many. (Mk 10:42–45)

Secondly the history of Israel and the wider world show kingships are almost always patriarchal structures in which a woman's role is almost always subservient, if recognized at all. A feminist perspective rightly critiques the notion of kingship from this point of view. At his baptism when the Father declares Jesus to be his beloved Son, and subsequently in his ministry, supported and sustained by women, Jesus demonstrates how the kingdom of God is a kingdom of equals and loving family relationships.

The importance of the kingdom of God is absolutely basic to any understanding of his message. After all this kingdom of God is a radical alternative to all kingdoms in the midst of history. It is vital to assess the kingdom of God on its own terms in relation to Jesus ministry rather than give too much weight to the historical experience of other kings and kingdoms. The re-discovery that this kingdom is an apocalyptic kingdom makes it even more urgent if we are to understand the central facts of the gospel.

THE APOCALYPTIC JESUS CHRIST

Albert Schweitzer's announcement of the role of the apocalyptic in Jesus ministry at the beginning of the 20th century was such a shocking claim that, for a while, New Testament scholars denied the possibility in the gospel accounts. He exposed the Kantian Jesus as an historical fantasy,[4] drawing on Weiss's work from a previous decade which argued that "Jesus central message was that the kingdom of God was coming soon, a kingdom brought by God's intervention in history, not one built by human effort."[5]

Käsemann and Martyn showed in the last half of the twentieth century that an apocalypse is not only at the heart of the gospel accounts, but also at the heart of the message of Paul.

> [d]rawing on Käsemann's reading of Paul as an "apocalyptic" theologian, Martyn reacts strongly against readings of Paul focused on the individual, refuses to demythologize Paul's language of "powers," and emphasizes that the Christ-event and its aftermath are the enactment of divine power, not the opening of human "possibility".[6]

As Paul states, he received the gospel directly from the risen crucified Jesus as an apocalypse.

> I want you to know, brothers and sisters that the gospel that was proclaimed by me is not of human origin, for I did not receive it from a human source, nor was I taught it, but I received it through a revelation (Greek: *apocalypse*) of Jesus Christ." (Gal 1:11,12)

The apocalypse of Jesus radically re-orientates his world and his future as he discovers what God has done in and through his Son. Paul discovers there is a new creation, a new world in which God has reconciled all things already in his Son. Martyn points out that this apocalypse is not an end time cataclysmic event heralding disaster and judgement as in the Book of Revelation or a secular disaster threatening the planet and all who live on it. This is an apocalypse in the midst of history, a *kairos* moment within the *chronos* of cosmic time.

The Revelation scenario and the cataclysmic end of world threats are but one way that uncovering or disclosing happens. The gospels declare through prophecy, witness and sign that God is disclosing the fulfillment of God's promises in a person. These are apocalyptic accounts with Jesus having an apocalyptic message, uncovering

---

4. Walls, *Handbook of Eschatology*, 9.

5. Walls, *Handbook of Eschatology*, 9.

6. Barclay, *Paul and the Gift*, 147.

God's purposes for the present and beyond. Martyn[7], Wright[8], and Barclay[9] have shown the importance of this apocalyptic understanding of Jesus ministry, cross, resurrection and ascension. A new perspective emerges of the bearer of the apocalyptic kingdom disclosed in the Jewish world.

It is one thing to read and study such writings; it is another matter to integrate the significance of these discoveries into one's own lived experience of being a Christian in the present era. As I look back, I realize that the 1981 bus stop event was an apocalyptic life-changing event, though I did not use the word apocalyptic at the time. It was not a term that I would use then because of its end-time imagery. In the previous decade the discovery of Jesus message that the Kingdom of God was at hand had been the liberating centre for my ministry, preaching, evangelism and personal life. Instead of basing sermons on the character and the experiences of the disciples and other biblical characters, I described the way that disciples, crowds, leaders, priests and other biblical characters responded to the kingdom of God as they heard it in the ministry of Jesus. It meant starting with the Good News and finding the individual and societal responses to such news. And then came that day. The significance that the heavens were torn open in the Mark reading of Jesus baptism came like an epiphany. Even then the realization came slowly over the following months, that this was a description of the kingdom of God being at hand, with an apocalyptic dimension directly involved in this moment. It led to the working through of what this apocalyptic kingdom was all about. The emphasis though was still on the Kingdom more so than the fact this was an apocalypse. It was not until twenty years later that the importance of Paul's apocalypse of Jesus Christ imploded upon me deepening the dimension of the apocalyptic kingdom. It took a long time to unpack these events before the profound significance of the apocalyptic Jesus and the apocalyptic Kingdom became clear. This time of gradual uncovering was most important, not only for what was to come, but

---

7. Martyn, Galatians, 132. Note 140. "The Galatians are sure to have noted that Paul sees the execution of Christ by crucifixion as apocalypse, as the divine, revealing invasion that changes not only the cosmos but also one's way of perceiving it."

8. Wright, *Jesus*, 322. "The early Christians re-used the language of Jewish apocalyptic eschatology to describe, and hence to interpret, the events of Jesus' death and resurrection and the sending of the divine spirit. In doing so they expressed their belief that the decisive 'end' for which Israel had longed *had already happened*, and that the consummation for which they still waited was simply the final outworking for the now-past event. I now wish to suggest that the early Christians thought like this not least because Jesus himself had done so."

9. Barclay, *Grace*, 443. "Much of what Martyn wishes to emphasize in deploying the category of 'apocalyptic,' and much of what Luther asserted with the slogan sola gratia, I have attempted to explore in different terms through the motif of the incongruity of grace. In each case, what is at stake is the denial that God's action in Christ is the recognition or reinforcement of a human narrative of worth—whether that narrative concerns Israel or anyone else. Whereas Luther explored this dynamic primarily at the level of the individual (who no longer looks to himself or herself to elicit the grace of God) and Martyn at the level of the cosmos (through the invasive 'apocalypse' of Christ), my goal was to draw out the original social ramifications of a gift that disregards and therefore subverts the normative schemas at the core of cultural systems of worth."

over time, the opportunity to discover the strength of the power of a democratic culture that bound and restricted religious experience to the inner self. What huge issues have to be confronted if we are to find the wonder of God's role in the world in gospel, church and society.

THE APOCALYPTIC KINGDOM

What is truly remarkable in the synoptic gospels, Matthew, Mark and Luke, is that Jesus ministry begins at his baptism with the heavens being 'torn open.' The heavenly realm, has the Holy Spirit and Father God as the Trinitarian source of all that is to come! Jesus in his ministry declares this in-breaking apocalyptic Kingdom of God as the basis of his teaching, parables, healing, and life. In a remarkable way he does not draw attention to his own person. From the perspective of the disciples he comes as a mysterious one, incognito.

His apocalyptic message brings into the open the issues in the lives of those around him, the response of those who come to him, and starkly illumines the use of power in Jewish society. He exposes the systemic and societal powers that wreak their violence upon him culminating in the cross.[10] The apocalypse of one life brings down upon him the apocalyptic violence of his enemies. Then comes the unexpected, the unbelievable resurrection by God. He is raised from the dead and ascends to God. God discloses the apocalyptic one who was in their midst, and endorses all that happened in his life and death. The apocalyptic event then is hidden first in a life announcing the kingdom of God, and then disclosed in a resurrection, and fulfilled in an ascension.

There is no powerful otherness let loose at first in his ministry, but a person whose identity is not fully known until the end of his life, when the message of the apocalyptic kingdom he proclaimed is disclosed in his own person as the Son of God. The metanarrative of power that usually introduces the apocalyptic is absent. Instead there is one who, in the absence of power bears witness to the source of all power, namely the king of the kingdom of God.

After his baptism the Spirit drives him into the wilderness where in the temptations, "he is denied the economic, political and religious means for a 'seizure of power.'"[11] In declining this power, mediated by the Spirit, he is given a public power that "remains unrecognizable and incomprehensible to the world all the way to the cross and resurrection."[12]

Jesus lives in the apocalyptic life of the kingdom of God, hidden in his very humanity. It is not disclosed until the resurrection and ascension refocused attention on

---

10. Myers, *Binding the Strongman.*

11. Moltmann, *Way of Jesus,* 93.

12. Welker, *God the Spirit,* 187.

the one who is discovered to be of God. The day of resurrection illumined not only that day, but every day of Jesus's life prior to that day. James Breech writes:[13]

> One of the most striking characteristics of Jesus' core sayings and parables is that he remained basically silent about himself. Only two of the core sayings make any reference to Jesus, the saying that states he came eating and drinking, and the one that indicates he liberated persons from the demonic. Nor did Jesus tell stories about himself. In that respect, he is the opposite of most contemporary storytellers who say, 'An interesting thing *happened to me* on the way to . . .' Jesus does not organize his experience in the re-active mode, in terms of what happens *to* him. Rather, the perspective that comes through in all of his parables is that of someone who is intensely observant of what happens in human life, quite apart from any reference to his own ego. "This combination of characteristics . . . explains why Jesus sayings and parables reflect nothing of what Baudelaire points out as both profoundly human and Satanic in man, that attitude arising from the miserable condition of feeling oneself superior and thinking oneself inferior . . . His behavior was that of a free person grounded in the kingdom of God."[14]

Jesus was truly a free person, grounded in the apocalyptic reality of the Kingdom of God. His identity was given in the kingdom of God. His identity was not founded on any hierarchy, whether external to himself or within himself, to generate a sense of superiority or inferiority, but a relationship given in the context of the Kingdom in which he lived.

We learn about the kingdom of God from him in his ministry, not from the understanding of the word kingdom as it is describe in previous world-views and current practice. It is not a hierarchy of power that is modeled on the kingdoms of history; it is the unique archetype of a kingdom of God in which God is called "Abba."[15]

Various understanding of Jesus as well as the kingdom live on from the world views of the past. Anselm of Canterbury asked in *Cur deus homo?* "Why did God become human?" As Niels Gregersen surprisingly points out,

> [i]t is nowhere said in the New Testament that God became human, though in Paul we hear that Christ was bearing "human likeness" (Phil 2:7). It is rather that 'the Word (logos) became flesh (*sarx*)'. (Jn 1:14) . . . For that God has a

13. Breech, *Silence of Jesus*, 217.

14. Breech, *Silence of Jesus*, 219.

15. It is far richer to stay with Jesus use of the term as the totality of God's living, future reality breaking into the present. The earth is the Lord's not ours. The psalms have the trees and the fields praising God. Terms like 'kindom of God' and 'family of God' actually restrict our understanding of the kingdom of God to 'a human and relational perspective'. And as important as this is, the kingdom of God is far greater than that. The kingdom of God is God's rule over the creation, the domains of heaven and earth, and as well amazingly and devastatingly shown in the life death and resurrection of the Son. The kingdom of God is where we find a healing, redeeming and restoring perspective for God's creation, with God's people and God's purposes as the ultimate framework of life.

human face can only be maintained if God assumes a real human body, situating him in continuity with the rest of the material world.[16]

Anselm asks that question from a different perspective influenced by the early Christological discussions about the two natures of Christ. How is it possible for someone of divine substance to be found in human substance? This question, vital for the missionary setting of Augustine's time fashioned Anselm's view in a later time and still is seen to be relevant in the radically different missionary setting of the present. The Church fathers wrestled with the Platonic intellectual issue of how can the substance of the eternal unchanging divine be mixed in with the substance of a temporal decayed humanity. In 451 AD the Council of Chalcedon eventually said, the two natures cannot be mixed or separated, that Jesus is not a compound of divine and human, half human and half God.

After more than a millennia of focusing on the importance of the divine substance, the Enlightenment inverted the issue and instead focused on the human substance. In the twenty-first century this language of substance has led to a radical separation between divine and human, with the language of the human taking over as the language of life, and talk of divinity a problem within the historical perspective.

The twentieth century search for the historical Jesus attempted to get behind this post-resurrection perspective from which the gospels were written. It illustrates the power of the historical perspective in which Jesus is 'an individual in a bygone past'. This search for an historic individual shows how both the individual and the historical become the dominant reference points. Both are informed by powerful and particular understandings of what it means to be an individual and what the historical perspective can allow to have happened. It should not be a surprise that the Enlightenment perspective now presents Jesus as the wandering "sage", the sharer of the spirit of wisdom, in an individual mode, or as the one who challenges the kingdom of the Emperor with the kingdom of God, in the context of the world mode. These flow from the mind body split presumed in the dominant narrative. The apocalyptic Jesus, however, brings to the fore the presence of God as the prior reality who addresses not only the individual but the world, in a way that takes seriously the concrete view of the self in all its actual and potential relationships.

What is being affirmed here from the post-resurrection perspective is that the very nature of the apocalyptic happens in the midst of life in all its inter-relationship. We see Jesus living in the hidden kingdom of God that is the presupposition of his teaching and declaration. We need a recovery of this apocalyptic reality from which the early Church gradually retreated. We need an apocalyptic reading of the gospels and the letters. There the apocalyptic acts of God are fleshed out in the midst of the witness to this kingdom life of the Son.

---

16. Gregersen, 'Christology,' 44.

The apocalyptic is there in all his ministry, first in his baptism then in teaching about the kingdom, his own self identification, when he is accused of being Beelzebul, the transfiguration, his healing presence, his response to people's needs and questions, his concern for the crowd and those pushed to the edge or rejected by society. It is no wonder that the disciples were not sure what was happening. Peter's confession at Caesarea Philippi that Jesus is the Messiah and the consequences of that disclose the confusion. The closer the disciples came to seeing that he might be the Messiah, the more in Mark's gospel, Jesus declares that they are to keep the messianic secret. There is an event to come, which is beyond the framework the disciples can as yet conceive, that will help them see who it is that is present with them

We have seen how powerful are the paradigms that are brought to the reading of scripture and the reading of the gospels, especially in the denominational era. The apocalyptic kingdom provides us with a way to address a vital change that has occurred in the way the world is seen that is not only different from the substance view, and the historical view of recent times, it opens the way for Jesus to be seen in terms of the inter-related nature of the world. The kingdom perspective helps us enter more fully into the nature of the incarnation which places Jesus into a profound network of inter-relationship. The incarnation makes it necessary to take seriously the relation between history and theology, Palestine and the kingdom. Gregersen makes clear, "The kingdom of God is the extension of the body of Jesus, just as much as his body is a crystallization point of the divine reign.[17]"

> Obviously the biblical writers did not have to hand any ideas of evolutionary biology. . . . After Darwin, we have gradually learned to overcome the distinction between humanity and nature, as well as the wedge between human history and human prehistory. Just as philosophical ecologists, such as Arne Næss, speak of the human embedment in larger ecological systems in terms of *deep ecology*, so recent historians speak of human culture in terms of *deep history* while emphasizing common features such as kinship relations, sharing of food and land and co-evolutionary spirals in the community between humans, animals and plants, thus leading to gradual changes in ecological systems.[18]

As Gregersen remarks, Jesus names himself the Son of Man, that is the Son of the 'Son of the earth' (the meaning of Adam as the one made from the earth—stardust), while at the same time defining 'kinship relations with those who do the will of God (adopted by God) rather than by genetic kin.'[19]

> The evangelists do not regard Jesus from a purely horizontal perspective, of course. Jesus is the crystallization point for the reign of God and for the power

17. Gregersen, 'Christology,' 40.
18. Gregersen, 'Christology,' 39.
19. Gregersen, 'Christology,' 40.

of the Holy Spirit that fills him and radiates from him to alter his surroundings. The ecological space, the social space and the religious space belong together in the gospel narratives. It is in the midst of this world—not as a supplement or a theological superstructure—that Jesus preached the gospel that 'the kingdom of God is among you'.(Luke 17:21) Similarly, the resurrected Christ returns to be among his disciples (Luke 24:36). Christ is the Immanuel (in Hebrew, 'God with us').[20]

Or this may be put more theologically in terms of the Trinitarian missionary God in whom the Son is sent. He called himself the Son of Man with a double allusion to the heavenly One coming on the clouds, the Messiah, and also in his baptism claimed identification with the human race. Given this apocalyptic reality how can we read and respond to the gospel accounts in this new setting.

The Heavens Were Torn Open

What do we learn of Jesus from his first public act, being baptized by John the Baptist? In him we see disclosed an apocalyptic self.

> In those days Jesus came from Nazareth of Galilee and was baptized by John in the Jordan. And just as he was coming up out of the water, he saw the heavens torn apart and the Spirit descending like a dove upon him. And a voice came from heaven. 'You are my Son, the Beloved; with you I am well pleased.'(Mark 1:9-11)

The emphasis is not on the mode of baptism, but what God did in conjunction with the baptism. God acted in three ways. First, God 'opened the heavens', second, the Holy Spirit descended on Jesus and third, God calls Jesus 'his beloved Son' (echoing the words in Psalm 2:7, used in an anointing of King David's successors and Isaiah 42:1 affirming the suffering servant as the one whom God upholds).

The heavens are torn open for him at his baptism. This is a different sort of apocalyptic event. A new dimension of God's presence is present as the hidden nature of this act is disclosed.

> In Mark God directly speaks twice and acts twice. At Jesus' baptism, God tears open the heavens and declares Jesus "my Son, the Beloved." At the transfiguration God again declares, "This is my Son, the Beloved"(9:7), and at the moment of Jesus' death, God tears the veil of the temple in two (15:38). Two proclamations and two tearings: God breaks open barriers and identifies Jesus as God's beloved Son.[21]

20. Gregersen, 'Christology,' 40.
21. Placher, *Mark*, 23.

This rarely commented on phrase, 'the heavens were torn open', is the first event of his public ministry.[22] The order of these three acts of God is important. It became even more important when the realization followed that the 'kingdom of God was at hand', is another way of declaring what happened in his baptism, that the 'heavens were torn open'. Both events form the basis of Jesus core declaration in his ministry

There is a Trinitarian sequence here as God opens a new heavenly dimension, God gives the Holy Spirit, and God discloses Jesus identity as the Son. Or, in more detail, it is not possible to live in this kingdom dimension which God opens, without the Holy Spirit, the power of God which comes gently like a dove, this bearer of the first green twig of Noah's new world, and the bird of sacrifice. Then the voice of the Heavenly Father is heard disclosing Jesus as the beloved Son telling clearly of the nature of this relationship and his identity.

What we discover from the scriptural witness is that for Jesus, the three core matters of his ministry were given to him in his baptism; the message of the kingdom, the power to deliver that message, and the full disclosing of his own identity.

What happens if we take seriously this apocalyptic uncovering of the God who opens heaven here and, in the power of the Spirit, declares who this one is in our midst? It is not only a declaration of the one in our midst, this event discloses what the Lord's Prayer presumes that earth is in fact open to heaven.

With heaven open and the kingdom of God present, the Spirit leads him into the wilderness. There, Jesus demonstrates the power he now has, "by the very act of declining a spectacular moral or political seizure of power, bound to a particular time or a particular people, and by choosing the path of messianic suffering. . . . This demonstration of his power—mediated by the leading of the Holy Spirit—remains unrecognizable and incomprehensible to the world all the way to the cross and resurrection."[23]

In this apocalyptic reality, not only do we have to consider the life of Jesus, his ministry, cross, resurrection and ascension within history, but also the eternal Trinity before whom this history unfolds.

22. It is fascinating to consult commentaries on this phrase. William Placher notes "'What is torn apart cannot easily return to its former state.' In Mark's version the relation of heaven and earth has been permanently changed." (22.) A student's comment is noted that "It's scary. God is loose in the world." (22 & 23). Most earlier commentaries either make no comment on this phrase, compare it with Isaiah 64:1 "O that you would rend the heavens and come down" and other eschatological writings of the time, or claim that it is a literary device to highlight the authority of Jesus. For example, Hooker, *St Mark,* 46. "[an] obvious image for revelation at a time when God was believed to dwell in the top story of a three-decker universe." In this case an Enlightenment world rules out the possibility of a divine intervention.

23. Welker, *God the Spirit,* 187.

RE-EVALUATING EVANGELISM IN THE LIGHT OF AN APOCALYPSE

So far it has become apparent that the view of the self and the world radically affects the way the gospel is not only understood, but shared. The apocalypse of Jesus Christ brings the reality of the kingdom to the universe, the world and every life. Our view of the self is wrapped up in the way we respond or react to the kingdom of God being at hand. Is it primarily a matter of our own believing or convictions, or is the key to the message the way we respond to what happens to us, what breaks in upon us? When the church is having a difficult time in communicating the message, it is vital that we are aware of the way the message that has been presented and heard in the past, and whether it is still effective. That is why it is important to focus on the understanding and practice of evangelism. If the church is not able to communicate the evangel as it once did, serious issues have to be faced.

What follows here is a journey of discovery over a number of years while working first as a consultant for evangelism and then in the field of mission and evangelism. I found that there was, and still is, a widely accepted understanding about what happens in evangelism, conversion and renewal among Protestants and many others who believe in the importance of these matters. It is apparent that there is a particular language for talking and sharing about these life-changing experiences. It is assumed and reinforced by a vast number of popular Christian books. There is a surprisingly wide consensus of opinion that this "common sense" understanding is the "biblical" way of approaching the reality of conversion. It was the dramatic realization of the importance of the "heavens being torn open" that first led me to ask some very basic questions about the nature of this evangelistic message that lies at the heart of the "unchangeable gospel",[24] and later to the relationship with the denominational paradigm. It lead eventually to the discovery of the "apocalyptic self".

The most important question asked in denominational evangelism is summed up in the phrase, "Have you been born again?" It is an important question. It is one way to understand and experience what happens in conversion. In meetings and in conversations how many times have evangelists asked this question of those present. The answer is a decisive "yes" or "no". A "maybe" is really a "no" for the preacher, for it means the listener has not heard or believed what Scripture declares is necessary. "Truly, truly, I say to you, unless one is born anew, one cannot see the kingdom of God."(John 3:3, RSV)

Evangelical churches world wide have majored on this approach, with many minor variations.

But what happens once a person has been born again? The charismatic movement arrived in the 1970s and 1980s and its preachers asked, "Have you been baptized in the Holy Spirit?" Once again, the response expected was a "yes" or a "no". Once

---

24. Drayton, *Understanding Conversion.*

again a "maybe" is really a "no" for the presenter, for it means the listener has not heard or believed what has been shown to be necessary in the Scriptures.

It was a shock to realize that starting with new birth and then moving to the Spirit was actually a reversing of the order of the events in Jesus baptism, that is, the heavens torn open, the spirit given and the identity of the child of God. In the evangelical and charismatic conversions this first category at Jesus baptism, the heavens being torn open, was not addressed. It gave rise to the possibility of a further question that could be asked of those who saw themselves as "born again, Holy Spirit empowered Christians". If the heavens are "torn open" a person finds oneself before God. A rather provocative question took shape concerning the will of God in a similar form to the questioning of the preachers. I began to ask the question, "Do you do the will of God?" "Yes" or "No?"

I was staggered by the response. It was like applying a blow-torch to the spiritual belly of Christians. The best answer from nearly all asked was "maybe". And, of course in this framework a "maybe" is not good enough. How hesitant believers became when this question was asked! [25]

This way of proclaiming gospel raised a fundamental question. Why was the order of events in Jesus baptism (a new dimension, new power and real identity) reversed in the "normal" presentation of the good news?

The question only intensified when the same order of events that happened at Jesus' baptism also occurs at Pentecost. In Peter's speech Jesus was announced as the risen Lord (heaven open), who gave the Holy Spirit (new power), and then received new believers as members of God's community (given a new identity).

It is not hard to realize why this occurs. In the denominational paradigm the key issue for the evangelist is to bring the hearer to a point of commitment. It is the decision of the hearer to opt into faith and opt into the membership of the church that is critical. The message is preached in such a way, that makes it clear that a choice has to be made. Unless one is born again then one is lost in one's sins. This is the crunch point for the individual. Forgiveness for the past and new life for the future depend upon the person's response to Jesus Christ. Will they decide to receive new birth as a child of God? Will they come forward and make their private decision public? The yes or no form of response sets up an individual private subjective decision-making process.

In this denominational era the message has focused on this call to become a child of God. It is effectively a 'Me-God' decision. Without knowing, the realm of the creation, the kingdom of God and the realm of the Holy Spirit are short-circuited out of the event.[26] In Christ God will make me his adopted child. God in His love

---

25. Later I realized it was a question that could have been asked by someone who was concerned for God's justice in society (though I had never heard it asked in this form).

26. Yong, *Evangelical Theology*, 235. In contrast to this reduction Yong, a hybrid Chinese American, shows that the events of Pentecost are not just about individuals receiving the Spirit. "Christian

has sought me and my sins have been taken by Jesus. Now I live in the love of God. This approach has framed the basic message of the church over the last century. In a strange way this message of God's love for the children of God edged both Jesus and the creation out of the picture.

When it comes to the need to be baptized in the Holy Spirit, and be able to know God's will, these are seen as next steps to be made in Christian discipleship. Attention is focused on the need for these particular subjective decisions to be made. Clearly the reference point is that of individual experience. "I have been born again", "I have been baptized in the Spirit", "I do the will of God". The three major groups in the life of the Protestant church, namely, evangelicals, charismatics and those committed to social justice, are each committed to their particular conviction of what is most important for the disciple.

The use of this approach used to work well in the West, but is becoming less effective. Part of the reason is the increasing psychological awareness of the population that suspects that the message in this form can become a form of psychological manipulation. Unless great care is taken, the evangelist, wanting to convince others, whether locally in one to one relationships, or high profile TV ministries, seeks a commitment by this way of questioning. Too easily this becomes a selling of the religious experiences of the evangelist that promises to transform people's lives. "This has happened to me—it can now happen to you." How interesting that Paul was aware of this element among the Corinthians when he states, "For we do not proclaim ourselves; we proclaim Jesus Christ as Lord and ourselves as your slaves for Jesus sake."(2 Cor 4:5) The world of democratic religious individualism has profoundly massaged the way the message is proclaimed. It easily becomes a marketing message, like any commercial designed for the viewer to make a decision to buy a particular product.

This unmasking of the denominational emphasis on the decision the individual is required to make shows how just how much the message has been reframed within and for a democratic culture. Initially this was a helpful release from a previous era in which the church and state restricted the message within a national perspective. But now over two hundred years later the power of individual decision overwhelms and keeps at bay a more foundational message about the kingdom of God.

It renders us deaf to the core of the good news. A good illustration is that of John's famous passage about being born again. Remarkably John 3:3 states that the sign of being born again is to be able to see the kingdom of God, rather than to be able to claim that one is born again by one's decision for Jesus. To be born from above is to be born into the kingdom. Indeed this passage is clear about the apocalyptic nature of the message whereby "one is born from above" by the Spirit, indicating that it is the apocalyptic work of God that enables us to see the kingdom of God.[27]

---

initiation and conversion involves not just turning away from the world and turning to God but also constitutes God's ways of purifying, transforming and redeeming the world in all its complexity."

27. Malina, *Social Science Gospel of John, 81–82.* Malina notes as many other commentators do,

For Moltmann the Spirit is more about being grasped than the individual subjectively deciding what will happen. In his discussion he starts with the Spirit rather than the individual, as important as the individual is.

> According to the Western view—and especially the modern Western view—the human being (which pre-eminently means the man) is the subject of reason and will. His bodily nature plays no part. The life of his senses is subordinate. But we acquire most of our experiences neither through our consciousness, nor through our reason, nor as the result of any deliberate intention. . . . It therefore seems too narrow and too "egocentric" to relate experience merely to "the life of the consciousness" and "the activity of the reason", and to exclude whatever does not belong to these contexts.[28]

The order really matters. Either we start with individual decision or we start with Jesus, the Lord of the universe, as he breaks in upon us with the Holy Spirit, so that we may participate in this Kingdom.

> [i]f the redeeming Spirit is the Spirit of the resurrection and new creation of all things, then to employ Platonic and gnostic conceptions is simply to misunderstand it. To experience the power of the resurrection, and have to do with this divine energy, does not lead to a non-sensuous and inward-turned spirituality, hostile to the body and detached from the world. It brings the new vitality of a love for life.
>
> The new approaches to an 'ecological theology', 'cosmic christology', and the rediscovery of the body, start from the Hebrew understanding of the divine Spirit and presuppose that the Spirit of Christ and the creativity and life-giving Spirit of God are one and the same.[29]

The order of kingdom, Spirit, identity, keeps the creation before us, including the issues of the pale blue dot, all part of a new creation.

TAKING JESUS' MESSAGE SERIOUSLY

At his baptism then, the heavens were torn open, the kingdom of God was at hand. How different it is to start here. Jesus declared the apocalyptic kingdom was at hand,

---

the meaning of the Greek word "anothen" which can be translated "anew" or "from above". They compare it to the English word "from the top" which has at least two meanings depending upon the context. To a conductor the phrase can mean "start again", or to a removalist "from above". So both senses of the word are present in this passage, with the possibility of a second birth, and the possibility of a birth "from the sky". They highlight the importance of birth for a person's life long social status in the Greco-Roman world. To be born again has the possibility within it of a new lifelong status or honor within society as happened with adoption in Roman circles. But as well to be born from above is to be born of the sky or of God, and is to be given the honor of being born a child of God.

28. Moltmann, *Spirit of Life*, 20.

29. Moltmann, *Spirit of Life*, 9.

and invited those who heard the message to repent of not believing the immediate closeness of the kingdom and instead believe in the good news that it was here and available.

In Jesus ministry he announces the coming of the kingdom that impacts on the present and the future precisely because it involves the initiative of God in realizing the kingdom of God on earth. How different this is to the substance era prior to the Enlightenment, when the church made baptism the entrance point for entry into the kingdom of heaven after death. Then after the Enlightenment the church emphasized the 'supernatural work of God' that follows our decisions and prepares us for heaven. In both eras the kingdom of God is located beyond death.

A vital, but usually unacknowledged, feature of the kingdom Jesus preached is important. Given that the core of his message and his teaching in parables and sayings was that the kingdom of God was at hand, or available, is it possible for anyone to enter into this kingdom, here and now, in the midst of life? More directly, did Jesus, in fact, teach that it was possible to enter this kingdom? This is a strange and alien question for most churchgoers, in fact most people. When I have asked that question of churchgoers, as I often have, the usual response is a puzzled frown.

It is strange and alien because it does not fit into the self-world framework of the Enlightenment categories. Not only was Jesus' declaration of the kingdom his core message he also taught specifically about the importance of entering the kingdom in Mark Matthew and Luke, and 'seeing' the kingdom in John. It is really extraordinary that so few know that this is a critical element of the gospel. There are four sayings, most with parallels in the first three gospels, in addition to the John passage already described.

> Mark 10:15. "Truly I tell you, whoever does not receive the kingdom of God as a little child will never enter it".

> Mark 10:24a–27. "Children, how hard it is to enter the Kingdom of God! It is easier for a camel to go through the eye of a needle than for someone who is rich to enter the kingdom of God." They (disciples) were greatly astounded and said to one another, "Then who can be saved?" Jesus looked at them and said, "For mortals it is impossible, but not for God; for God all things are possible."

> Luke 16:16. "The Law and the prophets were in effect until John came; since then the good news of the kingdom of God is proclaimed, and everyone tries to enter it by force."

> Matthew 5:20. "For I tell you, unless your righteousness exceeds that of the scribes and Pharisees, you will not enter the kingdom of heaven."

There are clearly preconditions for entering the Kingdom of God. A person's righteousness has to exceed that of the scribes and Pharisees. In this new era that succeeds the Law and the Prophets, however, everyone tries to enter the kingdom of God by force as though that is the way to enter.

It is helpful to look closely at Mark 10:24a–27. In this case it is easier for a camel to go through the eye of a needle than it is for a rich person to enter the kingdom of God. Then Jesus raises the bar even higher and states it is impossible for a mortal to enter the kingdom. The possibility of entering is there, and Jesus both stresses the importance of it, but not only limits the possibility, but says it is impossible. How can this be when it is the core of the good news? In the Sermon on the Mount two pivotal sayings indicate the entry is restricted and difficult to find.

> Matthew 6:33. "But strive first for the kingdom of God and his righteousness and all these things will be given to you as well. Matthew 7:13a,14. "Enter through the narrow gate; . . . For the gate is narrow and the road is hard that leads to life and few there are that find it.

Jesus is the master teller of stories, the one who hides in his parables the mysterious truth that those who seek may there find. After having closed the possibility for mortals to enter the kingdom of God in Mark 10:27 he adds one more phrase—"for God all things are possible."

That is the key. Of course, if it is to be entry into the kingdom of God, the possibility of such entrance depends on God. To put it simply, the only way it is possible to enter the kingdom of God is if God brings one into the kingdom. This is the narrow gate, this is the way the things of life will be given to us, this is why a child can enter, for a child knows their life depends upon their father.

The logic of the apocalyptic presumes what Jesus discloses: God makes it happen. The initiative comes from God, the good news comes from God and is of God. The logic of Jesus declaration of the Kingdom however, is far more than a mental construct derived from his teaching. As the church later realized, the teacher is involved in the message.

His ministry raises the question as to the way this carpenter from Nazareth is related to this kingdom. That was made plain in his baptism. As the one to whom the heavens were opened, and the Spirit given, and his identity in the kingdom known as the Beloved Son, Jesus displays an amazing freedom for the kingdom. He is not the center of action, the kingdom is. Embedded in the kingdom he is free to bear witness to it. As his ministry proceeds, those offended by what he is saying doggedly pursue him, and those encouraged by his ministry of healing and teaching derived from this kingdom also pursue him. Even when his attackers accuse him of being possessed by Beelzebul it is to the kingdom that he points. He replies that if I am of Satan, then Satan's house is divided and it will not stand. He then tells a parable of the house of a strong man plundered because he was tied up. He does not reference himself but immediately talks of sins against the Holy Spirit. In Matthew and Luke, this is even plainer with the words "But if it is by the Spirit of God (Matt) or the finger of God

(Luke) that I cast out demons, then the kingdom of God has come to you."(Matt 12:27, Lk 11;20). He does not defend himself as a failure or a success, but keeps on breaking open the presence of the kingdom in all that he does.

His teaching makes it plain that the kingdom of God is where the Spirit of God brings liberty, healing, freedom to the people. Here is the promise of the kingdom as *shalom* in society. What we have here is even more than the common good, for it involves the promise of a new divine order. It is good news from God.

It was not until I had to prepare people to witness to their faith that the rather obvious fact became central. Why is it that the heart of the message, as preached today, is in fact bad news? It seems the evangelist's task is to firstly convince the hearer that they are sinners so that secondly, they may then receive the good news that they are forgiven through Jesus's death on the cross. The message is focused on the individual hearer, pushing them back into themselves and the bad news of their past. Jesus' message was so different. He focused on the Good News that the reign of God is close by with its promise for all, offering a new future.

This kingdom message was as divisive as the bad news proclaimed in our time, but it was addressed to the nation not to individuals. The kingdom he proclaimed divided a nation that saw itself as chosen by God. What right did he have to announce "God was on the loose", what qualifications, what presumption and what authority, to bypass the custodians of more than a millennia of tradition and writings? This man was a threat to the existence of the temple and the nation in a time of Roman occupation. Those in power both dismissed him and his understanding of the Messiah, sought to eradicate him and find ways to counter the movement he began. Whereas the poor, the outcasts, those suffering from a Roman occupation, and dismissed by their own leaders for their lack of religious purity, were amazed at what happened as he proclaimed the presence of the kingdom of God, possibilities demonstrated in healing, teaching, in the midst of where they lived and worked.

Jesus finally took his kingdom message to the leaders of the nation in Jerusalem during the Passover week celebrating the nation's founding. After an entrance on a donkey, driving out sellers from the temple, teaching in the temple, his betrayal by one of his disciples led to the sentence of death by a Jewish court, allowed by a Roman Procurator. A crucifixion dealt with a national problem in a way that echoes through the ages. Make an example of those who challenge the system. Show the cost of not keeping the rules. Use the power available as rulers of social institutions to isolate, break, and violently dispose of those who stand in the way of normal operations. And it was done. He was disposed of with the title, The King of the Jews. They had successfully dealt with his dangerous message of the kingdom.[30] Richard Horsley has shown how the message of the kingdom was both a judgement upon the rulers and the promise of renewal to the common people. He has unmasked the traditional view of a 'depoliticised Jesus' and shown the threat he embodied.

30. Horsley, *Jesus and Empire.*

THE RESURRECTION—THE APOCALYPSE PART TWO

The silent divisive kingdom of God to which he bore witness once more irrupted apocalyptically upon the narrative. The dreadful death of an innocent man on a cross culminates with an unexpected conclusion. The three synoptic gospels record that as he died, the curtain in the temple was torn from top to bottom. The same word used at Jesus baptism in Mark when the heavens were torn open is used for this event.[31] Jesus death has the holy of holies in the temple ripped apart by God, opening heaven to earth in a new way. The apocalypse had begun. About 55 hours later a resurrection is witnessed, and the relation between Jesus and the kingdom is disclosed in a new way. Each of the gospels focus on the empty tomb. The earliest account in Mark's gospel ends with the two women fleeing from the tomb in terror and amazement having met there a messenger who tells them the risen Jesus will appear to them in Galilee. "So they went out and fled from the tomb, for terror and amazement had seized them; and they said nothing to anyone, for they were afraid." Mark 16:8. These three words, terror, amazement and afraid give a sense of the existential shock at what had happened. The word terror is from the Greek word, *tremos*,—trembling from fear, terror, agitations of mind- the women reeling in fear. The word amazement is from the Greek word, *ekstasis*,—a displacement of the mind from its ordinary state and self-possession—or amazement astonishment with fear and terror. Afraid from the Greek word, *phobos*—to be fearful, afraid, alarmed. These three words indicated the intensity of what had happened. Beside themselves, their world rocked, shuddering with terror, and yet facing the impossible having become possible.[32] There are two sides to this shock, the mind quaking on the one hand, and filled with amazement on the other. In Luke, Jesus appears incognito to two disciples inquiring and sharing with them on the road to Emmaus, only to show himself to them in the breaking of bread after they invited him into their home. They spoke of how their hearts burned within them as he spoke. And then after they had reported to the disciples Jesus himself stands in their midst. They were terrified, startled and afraid.

It is similar again in Matthew's account. Mary and another woman left the tomb quickly with fear and joy, after hearing words from a messenger and were met by the risen Jesus. He told them to tell the disciples to meet him in Galilee. In Matthew Luke and John the first words of the risen Jesus attempt to dispel fear, and bring peace. The fact of a Risen Christ shook the foundations of their world—and shakes our world and our own lives too, when seen as more than ideas and possibilities, and instead the reality of what God can do in our midst.

---

31. Matt 3:16 and Lk 3:21 use the Greek word to open, whereas Mk 1:9 uses the Greek word to tear open, the same word that Mark, Matthew and Luke use to described the temple curtain being torn from top to bottom.

32. Aernie, "Cruciform Discipleship, 796. The gospel ends with the women rather than the men embodying Markan discipleship. "The named women in Mark 15-16 are narrative examples of the Pauline theme of participation in Christ."

For two hundred years the rational historical mind has tried to come to terms with a resurrection. The resurrection does not fit into the historical world of cause and effect. It cannot, because in it God is acting, disclosing the presence of God, the kingdom of God in the midst of history. It is claimed that it just does not fit into historical categories, nor the rationality of describing this event in terms of other events. It is about time we recognize the shocking intensity of this unexpected happening—the fear and terror that is testimony to the fabric of reality being ripped apart. It is an apocalyptic unveiling with shock and awe. The records that have come to us show this was not a creation of the mind, or a plot by a writer, but the apocalyptic usurping of the world view of the men and women who had seen what had happened in his death and accepted this as the end. The very fact that we have only recently come to recognize the category of the apocalyptic again, gives a new credibility to the way these people responded to the shock of what happened. A resurrection calls into question the very structure of the scientific view of the universe as it is understood in the twenty-first century.

It is not surprising that there are "approximately 3,400 scholarly journal articles and books, written in English, German and French between 1975 and the present, all on the subject of the historicity of Jesus' resurrection.[33] Nearly all of this is the work of biblical scholars, few of whom are practicing historians. In a comprehensive survey of this literature, Michael Licona noted the powerful effect of world-view or horizons of the biblical scholars on the conclusions.

> The powerful presence of horizons has an extraordinary influence on scholars. For some Christians, no amount of disconfirming evidence would ever be sufficient to convince them that Jesus did not rise from the dead. The converse is likewise true: for some no amount of evidence for Jesus' resurrection would convince them that it was an event in the past.[34]

What was unexpected was that the historical perspective of historians provided a basis for carefully evaluating range of conclusions derived from the New Testament record. In a widely acknowledged work of fairness and thoroughness, weighing up the historical evidence and the strongest positions taken about the possibility of Jesus being raised from the dead, the conclusion was that "the resurrection hypothesis is by far the best explanation of the historical bedrock."[35] Such a conclusion is provisional given that further discoveries may bring changes in this cautious assessment which seeks to determine whether this event was a matter of historical fact without attempting to give an explanation or find the cause. Such a conclusion, however, gives weight to further discussion about the world-view involved. "If Jesus was actually raised as a critical historical approach suggests, a limited number of reports about Jesus in the

---

33. Licona, *The Resurrection of Jesus*, 19.

34. Licona, *The Resurrection of Jesus*, 608.

35. Licona, *The Resurrection of Jesus*, 620.

canonical Gospels may gain greater plausibility, such as his miracles, his claims to divinity and his predictions to his imminent and violent death and subsequent resurrection shortly afterward."[36]

The way is open to take seriously the reality of the apocalyptic shaking of the foundations rather than ruling this out on the a priori basis of the Enlightenment view that dead men do not rise from the dead. As Licona points out, John Dominic Crossan "does not see God acting in the manner described in the Gospels and concludes that he did not act that way in the first century."[37] No wonder the possibility of an apocalypse of Jesus Christ is ruled out. It leaves the predominant option for understanding the resurrection of Jesus to be that his crucifixion led to a new self-understanding for the disciples.

In his book *Faith Seeking Understanding* Daniel Migliore created an imaginary robust dialogue between four twentieth century theologians, Karl Barth, Rudolf Bultmann, Jürgen Moltmann, and Wolfhart Pannenberg about the way they understand the resurrection. Toward the end he has his Moltmannian voice sum up the discussion.[38]

> *My* future and *my* hope! That's just the problem with your interpretation of the Easter message, Bultmann. You individualize and privatize the message. Sure, you talk about transformation and new life. But what you mean is transformation of my consciousness. You have split self and world apart. I don't think the early church did that. When they proclaimed the resurrection of Jesus from the dead, they understood this to be the beginning of *world* transformation. . . . To believe in the resurrection of the crucified is not just to have a new *self*-understanding. It is to understand and relate to God differently. It is to understand and act in the social and political world differently. It is to believe in the faithfulness of God in the face of personal and political structures of death. The confession of the crucified one has been raised which always has been and continues to be the expression of a subversive faith with revolutionary implications for our social-political life as well as personal spheres of life.[39]

36. Licona, *The Resurrection of Jesus*, 622.

37. Licona, *The Resurrection of Jesus*, 538

38. Migliore, *Faith Seeking Understanding*, 399.

39. Bultmann with his conviction that it is the existential experience of faith that gives rise to the report of the open tomb is caught within the 'God and Me' framework of the Enlightenment perspective. For him, the scientific framework of the twentieth century calls in question the implicit three level view of the world at the time of Jesus, of heaven, earth and the underworld. If present day science says a resurrection cannot happen, then for Bultmann it cannot happen as an event in itself, only as a subjective event in the person. One can understand this honoring of today's understanding of the world. But it is the apocalyptic that opens up the possibility of God's action in the midst of history being more than a subjective event, a happening in the midst of space and time.

JESUS CHRIST, THE APOCALYPTIC REALITY OF THE KINGDOM

The apocalyptic kingdom of God to which Jesus bore witness had broken in upon them in and through him. The kingdom of God has now to be defined by the one who pointed to it. His message that the kingdom of God is at hand is seen anew. The heavens are opened for all, the Spirit is present and they know him as the Son of the living God. What happened to him in his baptism has now happened to the world in his death and resurrection. They now find themselves brought into the presence of the kingdom.

This is not an individual subjective private experience. The accounts are clear that this is an apocalyptic event that happens in the world; it breaks in upon them. The logic of Jesus' message has now become a fact in and through his life and resurrection. It is God who brings us into the kingdom. Now we know what Paul stated so clearly. We witness "the glory of God in the face of Jesus Christ." (2 Cor 4:6b). What was once a spoken word, an idea, has now become flesh and blood, inviting us into the reality of the open heaven. He himself is the narrow gate that leads into life. The God involved in this kingdom is only really known in Jesus Christ. Beyond all human attempts, longings, projections, God is redefined by God's action in these events.

The whole life of Jesus Christ has become the template of the kingdom present thereby enabling the kingdom to be seen in a fuller light. This is a kingdom where women are accepted as equals, where the outcasts and the rejected are brought into the fold, where leadership is about serving and giving one's life, where hierarchy is dissolved into the profoundest of familial and community relationships, where violence is eschewed, where peace is given, where life overcomes death, where heart mind soul and strength are given to loving God, where the neighbor has a call of mercy upon us.

The apocalyptic message is of a new dimension, a new power and our true identity given in and through the cross and resurrection. The divine logic in Jesus message becomes the human face of a God who brings grace and truth through his Son. The life of Jesus of Nazareth discloses the template for the divine kingdom in our midst: it is now apparent that the kingdom of God is where Jesus Christ is Lord.

This kingdom spelled out in profound teaching both directly, and in parables of events in the life of men and women, speaks of a kingdom that is not spiritual pie in the sky; it is a kingdom to come to the earth, God's dwelling ultimately being with the creation, rather than we going to heaven. The resources of the kingdom of heaven are already available and in the power of the Holy Spirit bringing into being a new creation. It is about community that will be constituted not only with daily bread for all, but a community that knows how to celebrate in an eternal banquet. It is a community constituted not only with divine forgiveness, but this same sort of forgiveness spreading like ripples in a pond, a washing of human lives so that life can be lived in relationship with God. It is a community that does not retreat in the face of evil but stays dependent upon the power of God to deliver them from powers that are greater than themselves.

THE APOCALYPTIC STRANGER ON THE SHORE

It has taken a century for scholarship to come to terms with the apocalyptic Jesus since Schweitzer's critique of the Enlightenment view of Jesus. The great strength of Schweitzer's work was that he exposed how the previous liberal lives of Jesus reflected the best self of the authors. Schweitzer himself, however, was not immune from reading something of his own time and culture into the account of Jesus. He was still a product of the Enlightenment. Schweitzer believed that Jesus was mistaken. The kingdom of God did not come with his confrontation with those controlling the temple, or his arrest and trial. Schweitzer, nevertheless, still believed it was possible to serve this kingdom Jesus proclaimed, because the kingdom is the measure of all moral values. He speaks of a Jesus mysticism expressed in titles like Messiah and Son of God that have become historical parables for us.

> He comes to us as one unknown, without a name, as of old, by the lakeside, he came to those men who did not know who he was. He says the same words, 'Follow me!' and sets us to those tasks which he must fulfil in our time. He commands. And to those who hearken to him, . . . he will reveal himself . . . and as an ineffable mystery they will learn who he is.[40]

Schweitzer was locked into the categories of history of his time, as much as he critiqued those from the previous century. The apocalypse was still to come. The Jesus dream of the kingdom lived on in the history still being written. What is remarkable is that his description of Jesus as the one unknown by the lakeside has removed any hint of the apocalyptic dimension. It reads like a demythologised account of the risen Jesus' appearance to the disciples by the sea of Galilee in the last chapter of John's gospel.

> Just after daybreak, Jesus stood on the beach; but the disciples did not know that it was Jesus. "Children you have no fish, have you?" They answered him "No." He said to them, "Cast the net to the right side of the boat, and you will find some." . . . That disciple whom Jesus loved said to Peter, "It is the Lord." . . . When they had gone ashore, they saw a charcoal fire there with fish on it, and bread. Jesus said to them. "Bring some of the fish that you have just caught." (John 21:4–6a,7a,9–11)

The risen Jesus comes to his disciples by the lakeside. He is not known, until he questions them. With a glorious shout, they cry "It is the Lord." He has come to them, the kingdom of God is broken open to them, and the resurrected son of heaven and

---

40. Schweitzer, *Historical Jesus*, 487.

earth is there with them, unfolding the apocalyptic future of God's activities in their midst in a breakfast on the lakeside.

What Schweitzer did not do was read Jesus apocalyptically. John's account is no mystical event; it is the resurrected Jesus coming in his apocalyptic dimension to open for the disciples a new participation in the way God is at work in the creation. No longer is the self the fundamental reference point. From now on Jesus opens the kingdom of God as a new way for the disciples to see themselves and the world from God's perspective. Each are being opened to becoming an apocalyptic self.

7

Finding the Apocalypse

IN WHAT STORY AM I?

In the mid 1960's *I was involved in the mapping of the Simpson (Munga Thirri) Desert in the center of Australia, south-east of Alice Springs. The preparation of the first 1:250,000 maps needed star sightings to match the latitude and longitude of clearly recognizable geographic features, such as the unique shape of dry salt lakes, to tie them together on overlapping aerial photographs. Using a light plane the procedure was to land near one of those recognizable features late in the day, and at night take the necessary star readings. Eventually the 1100 or so unique longitudinal sand dunes and other features were drawn on paper maps derived from the interlocked photographs. I was proud to have been part of developing the first published maps for this huge desert region.*

Some forty years later, I was in Birdsville, at the eastern end of the famous French line that crossed the desert to the Dalhousie Artesian Lakes on the western side. The Wangkangurru Elder responsible for overseeing Munga-Thirri (the land of sandhills) Desert Reserve had issued us a permit to cross the desert. After, he pointed to a huge map painted on the wall of the office in red, yellow and black, titled 'The Two Boys Dreaming'. Starting from the west at Dalhousie Springs it showed the track of the dreamtime story as the Two Boys Dreaming crossed the desert to Birdsville in the east and then travelled north. The two boys were depicted as kingfishermen near Dalhousie as they followed the serpent (Kunmarri) eastward, leaving waterholes where he surfaced in the desert, with the boys changing their shape as their journeyed. It was an interesting story but such a different perspective to that of a geographic map of the desert.

Leaving the office we started our trip, crossing the parallel sand dunes one by one, grinding west in the low gears of four-wheel drives. On the third day near the western edge of Munga Thirri we camped at about four o'clock in the afternoon. I remember putting up the tent, and with time to spare, went walking between the sand dunes. I heard a bird singing close by and set out to find out what it was. It was elusive. Eventually I positioned myself down wind, and as quietly as I could, crept close to the location of the last song. And there it was. A small kingfisher.

Unheralded the image of the kingfishermen on the wall painting came straight to mind. In that moment I discovered a whole new way to be in Munga Thirri. As a westerner I looked at a map and worked out where I was located. I suddenly knew how Aboriginal people had found their way in and across this desert for thousands of years. For them the dreamtime story was like a hologram in which they found themselves inside the story, living it out as they went from place to place, seeing the features that were part of the story.

Where am I? That is the western question. In what story am I? That is the Aboriginal question. It is a change of reference point from the individual as central (where am I?) to the story as primary (living within the story as the reference point). The aboriginal elders are the custodians of the dreamtime stories handed down to them. Their responsibility is to maintain the holy sites that are part of the story. I wondered then whether we are custodians of anything in our culture, apart from ourselves? It was time to look again at the familiar and perhaps find another way of seeing.

FINDING OURSELVES IN GOD'S STORY

Which story are we in? For nearly two millennia—under the impact of Platonic thought—the Christian expectation of believers was one of going to heaven after death. In the face of the creation, individuals and societies looked beyond their own insignificance to the eternal heavenly world to come.

Then, in the Enlightenment, the human subject slowly became the measure of all things and attention zeroed in on the self and the understanding of this world. This focus upon the self has further intensified since then in the course of an emerging postmodern ethos. How is it possible to escape from always being the observer, the final personal authority in the center, mapping the world about us?

For each person the reality of the self has to be the starting point in finding the self within any world-view. Our culture shapes our inner self to be the observer. The irruption of the apocalyptic from beyond into our midst, however, puts the observer into a radical new setting in which persons have to respond to new and ultimate horizons for life. The story breaks in upon them. The options are limited. Either retreat to the inner self and our view of the world and deny what is happening, or face with others the reality of the apocalyptic story we find ourselves in. That reality now includes the sheer scale of apocalyptic disasters threatening all life on the face of the planet, whether a nuclear holocaust, a pandemic, financial meltdown, global warming, a meteor impact on the planet, or some other scenario. Beyond these apocalyptic tremors lie the deepening mystery of what constitutes life and the nature of planetary existence within the cosmos. The apocalyptic self cannot hide away from the radical step-change that accompanies the vision first glimpsed of the pale blue dot.

The discovery of the apocalyptic kingdom of God requires a re-assessment of the popular traditional Christian message framed in terms of individual conversion as the pathway through life to death and heaven beyond. This message does not reflect the apocalyptic nature of the biblical witness. N. T. Wright argues that "orthodox Christian doctrine affirms 'God's rescue of the created order itself, rather than the rescue of saved souls from the created order.'"[1] "The belief that the creator God will at the last recreate the whole cosmos and that Jesus will be at the center of that new world is firmly and deeply rooted in the New Testament."[2] Writing in *A New Heaven and a New Earth* Richard Middleton underlines how the metanarrative of both Testaments is focused on the restoration of the creation, and the defeat of evil and sin. "In the end, when YHWH comes to judge evil and restore justice on earth, the Old Testament anticipates a grand celebration. Then all the redeemed (human and nonhuman alike) will enjoy the flourishing and blessing God intended; then God's salvation will indeed be as wide as creation itself."[3]

The resurrection of Jesus is an apocalyptic judgement on the existing order of so called-reality. It is the beginning of a radical new order, a new creation that Christ has already initiated for the sake of restoring the creation—and thus bringing in the kingdom to come.

> In the present, as the church lives between the times, those being renewed in the *imago Dei* are called to instantiate an embodied culture or social reality alternative to the violent and deathly formations and practices that dominate the world. By this conformity to Christ—the paradigm image of God—the church manifests God's rule and participates in God's mission to flood the world with the divine presence. In its concrete communal life the church as the body of Christ is called to witness to the promised future of a new heaven and a new earth, in which righteousness dwells. (2 Peter 3; 13)[4]

The implication for this Christian world story and for individual religious experience is far-reaching, but not only for the individual but also for the understanding of the world. Yet it is not easy to let go of one narrative and live into another, especially since this new narrative is not about ideas or concepts, or delayed gratification in terms of a heaven to come, but is about experiencing life as a divine story in which we are all involved in the present moment. The narratives that we inherit are built around a specific script that one imbibes from the culture and includes the church. Finding a new script that is in tension or radically different from our inherited script requires a new experience of what one calls reality.

1. Wright, *God became King*, 17.

2. Wright, *Challenge of Jesus*, 117.

3. Middleton, *A New Heaven and a New Earth*, 154. Middleton carefully documents the holistic salvation of the Old Testament, the vision of cosmic renewal for the New Testament, contested biblical texts, with an historical overview of the recovery of the scope of biblical redemption.

4. Middleton, *A New Heaven and a New Earth*, 175.

In one sense this book documents the struggle in letting go of an inadequate all-encompassing paradigm that is taken for granted, and finding another different way forward. The personal discovery of Jesus Good News as an apocalyptic kingdom in the late seventies and early eighties opened a new way to frame the gospel. This gospel became a vital source of life and energy in the experience of the Christian faith. But with that came a growing awareness of the way the denominational paradigm that I had inherited was making it difficult to communicate this new perspective with the church.

Then in the late nineties came Louis Martyn's lecture on Galatians, which made clear that the Apostle Paul called his confrontation with Jesus Christ, an apocalypse of Jesus Christ. For over two decades I had lived with the fact that the heavens had been torn open at Jesus baptism, and then for the church in the cross and resurrection. Now, for the first time, Martyn showed that they had been torn open for Paul as well. It was clear that the apocalyptic message is at the core of the New Testament. The apocalyptic message brought into being the church. Through Paul this Jewish Christian movement becoming a Gentile church that rapidly spread through the empire. It is one thing to recognize this apocalyptic script of the past, it is another to find an apocalyptic script for now and the future. This was shaking the foundations of my life and world-view. It took time to come to terms with this new story.

I was an Enlightenment geologist/physicist before entering ministry. What became increasingly apparent was that the divorce between self and world, mind and body subsumed in an Enlightenment world was in some way held together in the apocalyptic event of God addressing Paul within history.

There is more than the Enlightenment at work here. The apocalypse of Jesus Christ cannot be entered into fully by limiting it to Enlightenment categories. That was a big step to take. It is clear the power of the denominational paradigm masks the apocalyptic gospel from people in the pews, and nearly all Christian leaders, let alone those in the wider community. As described so far, the category of the apocalypse as God's disclosure, is not easily accessed in the twenty-first century because of the very way the accounts are translated, and the default position that such apocalyptic events can only be heard as cataclysmic events in the future.

It is imperative to take another look at the consequences of Paul's declaration that an apocalypse has already happened within history. An apocalypse calls in question both the individual and the world of that time. What an impact this had on Paul's own life and the growth of the early church. For the past 130 years, the emphasis in Sunday School classes and sermons has been on the change of Saul's name to Paul the missionary, and his missionary journeys, calling people to live by faith instead of the law. There is however a larger story that has to be told that involves both his life and the structures of the society in which he lived. He was born in Tarsus and moved from the synagogue where he grew up as a young Israelite to become a Pharisee worshiping in the temple in Jerusalem. There he lived, faithfully fulfilling the Law, focused on

Herod's temple, continuing the traditions of the Israelite people. In his words, "as to righteousness under the law, blameless."(Phil 3:6). In the name of righteousness he attempted to destroy a movement that initially had gathered in the temple claiming Jesus Christ had risen from the dead. On the Damascus Road the apocalypse of Jesus Christ not only confronted him with what he was doing, it also struck at the heart of all that he had previously practiced, believed, and known.

> The violent persecutor died at the apocalypse of the Son of God, but the biography of Paul took on a new trajectory, one that became increasingly conformed to the portrait of the Son of God. The new creation inaugurated by the advent of the Son set Paul on a new course, empowering him to gather the new-creation assemblies that corporately sought to be conformed to the true lord (Greek *kurios*) of the cosmos who creates and sustains authentic and lasting peace.[5]

The apocalyptic action of God was at work through Jesus cross, resurrection and ascension and the work of the Holy Spirit in the midst of history. Life was to be lived in the new communities of the Holy Spirit, not in the flesh, that is the structures and ways of everyday life. No longer was God limited to the 'holy of holies' in the temple. Since God appeared to Paul on a dusty highway, God in Christ can be known anywhere. No longer is Paul centered on the temple as the center of the universe, now he is announcing the good news, the gospel that God justifies anyone, anywhere, through the death of Christ, as he walks the Roman roads towards Rome. For Paul, Jesus Christ set him on a trajectory that would confront two great power structures of his day, the temple in Jerusalem and the Roman Empire. In writing to the church in Rome he puts it this way. "The gospel concerning his Son, who was descended from David according to the flesh and was declared to be Son of God with power according to the spirit of holiness by resurrection from the dead, Jesus Christ our Lord, through whom we have received grace and apostleship to bring about the obedience of faith among all the Gentiles for the sake of his name." (Rom 1:3–5)

All Gentiles must hear about the Son of God who has come near them if they are to discover the obedience of faith. For Paul everyone in the known world must hear what God has done. No wonder this leads to a series of missionary journeys. Over twenty years (47CE–62AD)[6] his face-to-face proclamation led to the forming of new apocalyptic communities along the roads of the Empire, from Jerusalem and as far round as Illyricum. He had a strategy of starting with the diasporic Jews in their synagogues as the base for addressing Gentiles in the towns wherever he travelled. Some of the synagogues repudiated him, and complained to Jerusalem about his activities,

---

5. Gabrielson, *Non-Violent Gospel*, 137.

6. The period between Paul's Damascus Road happening, and the first epistles depends on which passages in Acts and Galatians are given weight. It is agreed that Paul's epistles to Thessalonica were written in 47 CE and the last to Phillipi from a Roman gaol in about 60-62 CE. Tradition has it that Paul was beheaded in Rome during or after Nero's persecution of the Christians in 64 CE.

and, as well as attacking him, reported to local authorities that he was subverting the emperor. As reported in Thessalonica, "These people who have been turning the world upside down have come here also. . . . They are all acting contrary to the decrees of the emperor, saying that there is another king named Jesus." (Acts 7:6b,7b) It was inevitable that eventually the temple leadership would have to find ways to curtail or repudiate him, and in some way it would lead to a confrontation with the empire as well.

The order of the books in the New Testament is historically misleading. While the gospel accounts of Jesus are placed first in the New Testament, it is the letters of Paul that were written first, before the writing of the gospels.[7] In fact the consequences of this event on the road to Damascus shape the New Testament within an apocalyptic and Gentile perspective. At least two of the writers of the gospels have links to Paul (Luke and Mark)[8]. The author of the book of Acts begins with the twelve disciples called to be witnesses in the power of the Holy Spirit to Jerusalem, Judaea, Samaria, and to the ends of the earth. Acts provides the sequence of places and times for the letters that Paul writes. Most of the book details Paul's missionary journeys and the response to the gospel of God. He calls on his hearers to respond to these life changing events and participate in the overall grand narrative of what God is making known in this invasion of the Holy Spirit into history, so that they too find themselves and their communities 'in the story', already citizens of heaven.

When finally called to give account to the leaders of the temple he tells again the Damascus Road account. This retelling leads to his imprisonment in Caesarea as a way of saving himself from assassination. Once more, after two years of house arrest, he is called to defend himself before a Roman hearing in Caesarea. There he repeats what happened on the Damascus Road as the basis for his ministry. The Roman leaders of the region wash their hands of him and send him to Rome to face the Emperor Nero.

How often western commentators, religious and secular, reduce this Damascus Road event to a private and subjective psychological experience, presented as a resolution of Paul's own guilt from the persecution he had been undertaking. It should not be surprising that twentieth century psychological categories are used to explain away what is happening, leaving it as the personal experience of a troubled person. Recently there was also a scientific attempt to explain away what happened. A scientist studying the effects of the meteor that fragmented over the Russian city of Chelyablinsk in 2013 suggests a first century fireball may well have been the bright light that blinded

7. Some scholars such as Timothy Luke Johnson are convinced that the book of James was written earlier than the Pauline letters, with the author probably James, the brother of Jesus. The overall weight of scholarly opinion, however, is that James was written much later.

8. There is a lot of discussion amongst scholars about whether the 'we' passages of Luke in Acts are genuine (Acts 16:10-16, 20:6-21-18) and about the status of Mark who accompanied Paul and Barnabus as the author of the Gospel of Mark. In any case both writers indicate that they or those they know, write against the background of the Gentile mission.

Saul on the road to Damascus and "helped a small sect become a world faith".[9] He concludes the observational evidence matches with what we see in this first century account, and strains to explain the biblical accounts. He claims "If the spread of a major religion was motivated by the misunderstanding of a fireball, that's something we human beings ought to understand about ourselves."[10] It is as if there has to be another explanation found, either psychologically or by scientific cause and effect, locating the event within the self or within the empirical world. The possibility of God addressing both self and world has to be explained away because of the way self and world are defined! (It is ironic that theologians are critiqued for postulating a God of the gaps in human understanding, while Enlightenment thinkers have to explain away so called experiences of God.)

How much more is happening. The so-called 'explanations' do not take into account the key reason given for why this event was so important. Saul (Paul) is addressed by the Risen Jesus Christ. The apocalypse is the breaking in upon him of the reality of the resurrected Jesus Christ, disclosing the way that the God of Jesus Christ is at work in the creation. What a story he is caught up in. As the writer of Ephesians puts it, the mystery of God's will, "set forth in Christ, as a plan for the fullness of time, to gather up all things in him, things in heaven and earth."(Eph 1:10)

PAUL'S APOCALYPTIC JOURNEY
FROM THE DAMASCUS ROAD TO ROME

Paul's witness to the Damascus Road event is a pivotal event that shapes the mission of the early church, and the growth of the Gentile church in the empire. His apocalypse of Jesus Christ provides an apocalyptic backbone to this witness, that historically flows from the apocalyptic kingdom of God proclaimed by Jesus. It is vital to tell this account from the perspective of the apocalypse he experienced, rather than reduce what happened to his mission and his missionary journeys.

Most are aware of Paul's Damascus Road experience from the book of Acts. The Reformation images of this event have Paul on a horse, but there is no indication that he was other than walking. In an instant the God he worships is disclosed as the enemy he persecutes. The light of this encounter renders him blind for three days. He is shocked to the core of his being. Not only is his intellectual world shattered; the realization of a risen Lord calls into question all the ways death has limited and controlled his life. His whole world implodes in the face of the reality before him, and then in the days and years to come, explodes into its almighty implications. This event surpasses anything he has ever experienced.

9. Aron, "Christianity's meteoric rise," 8.

10. Aron, "Christianity's meteoric rise," 9.

> Now as he was going along and approaching Damascus, suddenly a light from heaven flashed around him. He fell to the ground and heard a voice saying to him. "Saul, Saul, why do you persecute me?" He asked, "Who are you Lord?" The reply came, "I am Jesus, whom you are persecuting. But get up and enter the city, and you will be told what you are to do." The men who were travelling with him stood speechless because they heard the voice but saw no one. Saul got up from the ground, and though his eyes were open he could see nothing, so they led him by the hand and brought him into Damascus. For three days he was without sight, and neither ate nor drank. (Acts 9:5-9)[11] (Note, companions heard the voice but saw no one.)

As this happened unbidden, so his healing happens to him unbidden through Ananias who finds himself part of God's story for Paul and the kingdom. Healed, baptized and filled with the Holy Spirit, he immediately begins to preach in the synagogues that Jesus is the Son of God. (Acts 9: 20) No wonder he describes this event in Galatians as an "apocalypse of Jesus Christ"; it is the overwhelming un-nameability of the ineffable powerful and mysterious God of Hebrew history, known in the light of a specific event of meeting the Risen Jesus Christ. In his own writings everything is brought before the reality of Christ Jesus. For the rest of his life, every event is considered in the light of Jesus Christ crucified, risen and ascended. This pivotal event is the apocalyptic bridge between Jesus declaration of the apocalyptic kingdom and the role of apocalyptic events in the founding of the church in the empire.

The gospel of Luke and the writer of Acts show this apocalyptic continuity in their presentation of these events as book one and book two, written as an ordered account for the Greek named Theophilus. Firstly the gospel of Luke gives the account of Jesus ministry, beginning and finishing in the temple. It starts with the priest Hezekiah and his wife Elizabeth, righteous before God and living blamelessly according to the commandments and regulations of the Lord. Luke's gospel has the temple there

---

11. There are three accounts of this event in Acts. The second is Acts 22:6-11. "While I was on my way and approaching Damascus, about noon a great light from heaven suddenly shone about me. I fell to the ground and heard a voice saying to me, "Saul, Saul, why are you persecuting me?" I answered "Who are you Lord?" Then he said to me, "I am Jesus of Nazareth whom you are persecuting." Now those who were with me saw the light but did not hear the voice of the one who was speaking to me. I asked, "What am I to do, Lord?" The Lord said to me, "Get up and go to Damascus; there you well be told everything that has been assigned to you to do." Since I could not see because of the brightness of that light, those who were with me took my hand and led me to Damascus."(Companions saw light but did not hear the voice)

The third account Acts 26:12-19. "I was travelling to Damascus with the authority and commission of the chief priests, when at midday along the road, your Excellency, I saw a light from heaven, brighter than the sun, shining around me and my companions. When we had all fallen to the ground, I heard a voice saying to me in the Hebrew language, "Saul, Saul, why are you persecuting me? It hurts you to kick against the goads." I asked, "Who are you, Lord?" The Lord answered, "I am Jesus whom you are persecuting. But get up and stand on your feet; for I have appeared to you for this purpose, to appoint you to serve and testify to the things in which you have seen me and to those in which I will appear to you. . . . After that King Agrippa, I was not disobedient to the heavenly vision."(Companions all fall to the ground so must have seen the light)

as the reference point, especially in the last weeks of Jesus ministry. It is the temple police who arrest him. The chief priests help orchestrate his death. The last teaching that Jesus gives, immediately prior to the Passover meal, is the prophecy concerning the future destruction of Jerusalem. The temple will be torn down in this apocalyptic horror. Then after the meal he is betrayed, sentenced and crucified.

Nothing prepares the reader for what happens as Jesus dies.

> At three in the afternoon, "while the sun's light failed, the curtain of the temple was torn in two. Then Jesus, crying with a loud voice, said, 'Father, into your hands I commend my spirit.' Having said this, he breathed his last." (Luke 23:45b,46)

The holy of holies in the temple is breached! Heaven is torn open! After his resurrection the gospel ends with Jesus ascension, and "they worshiped him, and returned to Jerusalem with great joy; and they were continually in the temple blessing God."(Luke 24:52,53). God's place on Earth, the kingdom of heaven, constrained to the holy of holies is now let loose upon the Earth. With the curtain torn they can approach God, and God can approach them, the kingdom of God let loose on the face of the earth through the life death, resurrection, and ascension of Jesus Christ.

Secondly the book of Acts follows immediately with the empowering of the disciples by the Holy Spirit—"you will be my witnesses in Jerusalem, in all Judea and Samaria, and to the ends of the earth."(Acts 1:8b) The disciples presume the kingdom of God will be restored in Israel. They are told to go to the ends of the Earth, and they presume they will go to the Jewish diaspora. They are not prepared for what happens. The story of which they are a part is about to become far bigger than their religious tradition and culture. While it is Peter who is the first to bring the message to Gentiles, it is Paul who is the apostle to the Gentiles.

Five weeks after Jesus death, resurrection and ascension a series of events invigorate and threaten this early community that continues to meet in the temple. Without warning persecution breaks out when Stephen, a leader from the Jewish diaspora, is killed. Brought before a Jewish Council, Stephen accuses the nation of betraying Moses by building a temple, resisting the Holy Spirit, murdering God's holy one, and not keeping the law. He finishes by saying "Look, I see the heavens opened and the Son of Man standing at the right hand of God!"(Acts 7:56) He is dragged out of the city and stoned. Saul who is present, not only abets the killing, he takes a leading role in the ensuring persecution of the movement. In Acts 9 Saul has the apocalypse of the risen Lord. From Acts 13 to the last chapter 28, the account is focused on Saul/Paul. By the end of the book of Acts Paul is in gaol in Rome, waiting for the chance to bring the gospel to Nero, the Emperor of the Roman Empire who rules the known world.

In each critical missional step Paul refers back to what happened on the Damascus road.

From Antioch he starts on the first of three missionary journeys declaring that Jesus forgives sins, and offers eternal life to those who believe in him. The first trip is focused on Galatia, the second on Corinth, and the third on Ephesus. Opposition from Jews in the synagogues increases trip by trip. When Paul is convinced by the Holy Spirit that he must return to Jerusalema gain, the apostle James, and the elders of the church in Jerusalem warn him: "You see how many thousands of believers there are among the Jews, and they are all zealous for the Law. They have been told about you that you teach all the Jews living among the Gentiles to forsake Moses, and that you tell them not to circumcise their children or observe the customs."(Acts 21:20,21)

At the suggestion of the apostles, Paul attends the temple, and offers a series of sacrifices for purification as a demonstration that he is a Jew and observes the Law. While he is in the temple a major riot ensues. Jews from Ephesus accuse him of bringing a Gentile into the inner Temple. In the ensuring uproar he is rescued by a detachment of Roman soldiers. He requests an opportunity to speak to the Jewish crowd in the temple who were trying to kill him. He relates how he persecuted the people of the Way, what happened on the road to Damascus, how Jesus instructed him to go into the city and await instruction, and of Ananias and his (Paul's) healing and baptism. All is quiet. Paul then adds that having returned to the temple after Damascus, while praying he fell into a trance and saw Jesus saying to him, "Leave quickly 'for they will not accept your testimony about me.' 'Go, for I will send you far away to the Gentiles.'" The crowd erupted again, and attempt once more to kill him. They did not protest at Jesus appearing to Paul, after all he was a Jew. It was his report of Jesus sending Paul to the Gentiles that sparked the outburst.[12]

It was inconceivable to the crowd in the temple that Jesus, from the temple, instructs Paul to go to the Gentiles. The holy righteousness derived from sacrifice in the temple, meets head on the redemptive holiness in Jesus. This is the boundary Paul was led to cross in his apocalyptic confrontation with Jesus Christ on the Damascus Road. It was this redemptive holiness that led to the missionary journeys, provided the basis for the Gentiles to receive the gospel, and for the church to be transformed from a Jewish sect into an Empire wide body. The difference between redemptive holiness and sacrificial holiness lies at the heart of the gospel, and the difference between Jesus and Moses.

In the wilderness at Meribah, Moses leadership was judged by God in a decisive event the psalmists and prophets never forgot. Once more the people had quarreled with Moses and Aaron. There was no water for livestock let alone for the people to drink. Moses and Aaron came before the Lord in the tent of meeting and were given

12. Wright, *Son of God,* 390. "Luke was not concerned to imitate Paul's language or to pursue his agendas." There are doubts that Luke, the seeming author of the 'we' passages in Acts during this period of the account, is the author of Acts. It is said that Acts does not reflect the doctrinal and theological accounts of Paul's writings. In this case in the temple, the doctrine of grace is spelled out by the events themselves, rather than in the form of teaching. In Galatians and Romans, Paul writes of 'the curse of the law,' here clearly demonstrated by the event."

instructions as to what to say and command to the rock. Instead Moses calls the people together and says to them. "'Listen, you rebels, shall we bring water for you out of this rock?' He struck the rock twice and water came out abundantly"(Num 20:10b).

> But the Lord said to Moses and Aaron, "Because you did not trust in me, to show my holiness before the eyes of the Israelites, therefore you shall not bring this assembly into the land that I have given them. These are the waters of Meribah, where the people of Israel quarrelled with the Lord, and by which he showed his holiness. (Numbers 20:12,13)

Moses and Aaron here disobeyed the Lord's directions to bring the gift of life-bringing water. Moses brought his own judgement of righteous holiness upon the people, instead of giving the redemptive life giving holiness of the water supplied by the Lord for this quarrelling people.

Paul was taken into the custody of the Roman soldiers and kept in Jerusalem and Caesarea as a result of a series of threats and plots to kill him by supporters of the temple and the Law. After being detained for two years he was given the opportunity to speak to Felix the new governor and King Agrippa. Once more he tells of his persecution of the church and what happened on the road to Damascus. He reports more of what the Risen Jesus said.

> I will rescue you from your people and from the Gentiles—to whom I am sending you to open their eyes so that they may turn from darkness to light and from the power of Satan to God, so that they may receive forgiveness of sins and a place among those who are sanctified by faith in me. (Acts 26:17,18).

Paul informs King Agrippa that he "was not disobedient to the heavenly vision," and presses home with his message. Festus exclaims he is mad.

To escape the power of the temple and the attempts on his life, Paul appeals to the emperor, and to the emperor he is sent. The book closes with these words from his custody in Rome. "He lived there two whole years at his own expense and welcomes all who came to him, proclaiming the kingdom of God and teaching about the Lord Jesus Christ with all boldness and without hindrance."(Acts 28:30)

PAUL AND APOCALYPSE

It is Paul, the apostle to the Gentiles, more than any other apostle in the New Testament, whose life and journeys shape our understanding of the early Gospel and the early church. That is why it is so important to come to terms with the reality of the apocalypse of Jesus Christ that he experienced.

His authority as an apostle is derived from the gospel happening to him as an 'apocalypse' of Jesus Christ'.(Gal 1:12) In 1 Corinthians 15:1–9 he lists the post-Resurrection appearances of Jesus to groups and the apostles. "Last of all, as one untimely born, he appeared also to me. For I am the least of the apostles, unfit to be called an apostle, because I persecuted the church of God. But by the grace of God, I am what I am, and his grace toward me has not been in vain."(1 Cor 15: 7–10a). And again, when Paul is criticized as an apostle, he asks the question of his accusers, "Have I not seen the Lord?" (1Cor 9:1) [13]

More importantly, in the apocalypse of Jesus Christ, God is creating the new, not destroying the old, known in the naming and meeting of evil and the defeat of death. This apocalypse makes all things new, in fact, a new creation. As Martyn puts it: "Paul sees the execution of Christ by crucifixion as apocalypse, as the divine, revealing invasion that changes not only the cosmos but also one's way of perceiving it."[14] It was a "powerful explosion that rearranged the whole of reality."[15] It was Käsemann who saw that Christ burst open the apocalyptic doctrine of succeeding aeons.

> The old aeon has not simply vanished with the inauguration of the new. It still radiates temptation and mortal peril. But this precisely is the sphere that the new aeon invades. In the time ushered in with Christ the two aeons are no longer separated chronologically and spatially as in Jewish apocalyptic. The earth has become their battleground. Assailed faith and the vanquishing of the powers mark the place where Christian boasting paradoxically proclaims that peace and freedom are already secured even in the midst of the ongoing conflict.[16]

This is apocalyptic good news, for God in Christ has already acted making clear God's purpose for the creation. "All this is from God, who reconciled himself to us through Christ, and has given us the message of reconciliation; that is, in Christ God was reconciling the world to himself, not counting their trespasses against them, and entrusting the message of reconciliation to us." (2 Cor 5:18,19)

Paul saw the whole world in and through the 'word of the cross'. Studies of the Greek word for good news—*euangelion*—have shown that in Paul's world the word was commonly used throughout the Empire to describe the birth of a divine one. Some scholars are exploring the degree to which the message of kingdom of God contrasted with the hegemony of Rome.[17] Certainly, using this word, Paul in the course of his missionary journeys, travels toward the center of the empire; implicitly if not

---

13. Wright, *Son of God*, 378–388. This section provides an extended discussion of Paul's statements that Jesus Christ appeared to him; three direct references (Gal 1:11–17, 1 Corinthians 15;8–11, 1 Cor 9:1) and two indirect references.

14. Martyn, *Galatians*, 132.

15. Martyn, *Galatians*, 132.

16. Käsemann, *Romans*, 134.

17. Horsley, *Jesus and Empire*. Since 9/11 some exegetes, like Horsley, have become aware of the way the search for the historical Jesus in the nineteenth and twentieth century gave rise to a depoliticized Jesus. This reflects modern day political contexts of a separation of state and church, whereas there was no such separation in the Roman Empire. The role of Paul and Jesus message in terms of the Empire is an important and highly contested area of study.

explicitly he was making a contrast between the good news of the birth of a divine Emperor with the good news of a crucified Christ as a criminal. This contrast radically turns upside down the values of the empire. Toward the end of his life, he wrote to the saints in Philippi, from a place of detention in Rome. It is a remarkable letter usually read in an individualistic way: Paul urges the Philippians to continue in the same struggle that he continues in, "standing firm in one spirit, striving side by side with one mind for the faith of the gospel."(Phil 2:27b) They are, he declares citizens of heaven, not citizens of Rome.

> [a]ccording to Paul's gospel it is because of the resurrection that Jesus is Lord and Caesar is not. The future resurrection and glorification of Jesus' followers will vindicate them as the true people of the one true God, despite their present suffering and humiliation, and herald the victory of the gospel over the powers of the world through the final act of new creation. [18]

The work of the invading Holy Spirit brings the resources of an open heaven let loose in the cross, resurrection and ascension of Jesus into this apocalyptic confrontation with the power of human empires. This subversion takes place within the structures of power by the Spirit of life, bringing the promise of a final resolution in God's time.

Paul concludes his letter to Philippi with these remarkable words. "All the saints greet you, especially those of the emperor's household."(Phil 4: 22) In the power of the Holy Spirit the *Pax Christi* had permeated to the household of the Emperor of the *Pax Romana*. But it is the days of the *Pax Romana* that were numbered.

This reading of Paul presents a contrary view to the denominational paradigm's collapsing of the kingdom into the 'kingdom of God within', thereby collapsing the apocalyptic reality into a private religious world. The result is a limited encounter with the Lord who is here in our midst. Moltmann insists that, "The Spirit of God is called *the Holy Spirit* because it makes life here something living, not because it is alien and estranged from life. The Spirit sets this life in the presence of the living God and in the great river of eternal love."[19]

The call is to acknowledge the Lord, receive the spirit and become part of this new community caught up in the kingdom coming on earth. It is to enter into the new dimension of God's story, receive the power and become a new person with a new purpose. This kingdom is another script, another story in which we are to find ourself and our world.

THE APOCALYPSE REPLACED BY REVELATION

The call to live in the apocalyptic kingdom before an open heaven runs counter to religious culture as well as the wider society. Indeed, there is a widespread religious

18. Wright, *Son of God,* 233.

19. Moltmann, *Spirit of Life,* x.

amnesia abroad now that the basic New Testament story is not really known. In the West most religious words are discarded by an enlightened society, that may still believe in some form of residual God, but is rather vague as to further specifics. Many of the words of Jesus are lost and referred to more recent sources. Peter Jensen cites a recent book *Imagining Australia: Ideas for our Future,* in which Abraham Lincoln is cited as the source for the saying, 'a house divided against itself cannot stand.' The authors failed to recognize that Lincoln was quoting Jesus. "Jesus is there but he's been rendered invisible. He is an anonymous Jesus; he makes his contribution without acknowledgement."[20] There are still active and alive churches, and people are still coming to faith, but in terms of the gospel being heard in the wider community there is a widespread disenchantment with the church. And even in the church in so many places it is as though God has evaporated into words, and faith has become an empty word that means whatever the person wants it to mean.

The church has not really dealt with the mid-twentieth century of whether indeed "God Is Dead?" and what that might mean. It was Paul's experience of the apocalypse that kept on opening new doors into Christian life. It was then that I realized that few could open those doors because the commonly accepted meaning of key words like, kingdom, apocalypse, have changed, and instead of opening up the key passages, effectively hide them from being discovered. The hardest of matters to resolve are those that are hidden or not directly apparent. Hence it was important to show how Paul's world is an apocalyptic world.

Three different but related questions stand in the way of an apocalyptic reading of scripture. It is only when these questions are faced that it is possible to face the implications for the church to witness to what it means to live in the kingdom of God. There needs to be a clearing away of the obstructions that stand in the way of the church becoming an apocalyptic church. Firstly, we need to visit again why the word apocalypse disappeared from the language of New Testament translations. Secondly, why has theological discussion historically revolved around the issue of revelation and reason and not the apocalyptic? And thirdly, how has the kingdom of God and the apocalyptic been interpreted since the scholarly rediscovery of the kingdom of God at the beginning of the twentieth century?

Firstly, after Paul's apocalyptic confrontation focused attention on the word, it is remarkable that the word apocalypse is not used in any of the contemporary New Testament translations of the Greek. The word disappeared from the English text. As noted earlier, in each case the Latin word for revelation is used to translate the Greek for apocalypse, and in the Johannine letters the word manifest. As shown earlier, the words manifest and apocalypse are about events that happen, rather than the more particular definition of revelation as communication of knowledge by God to humans. The Greek word apocalypse could have, and usually did have, a different meaning to that of the Latin revelation.

20. Jensen, *Future of Jesus,* 8.

This replacing of the Greek "apocalypse" with the Latin "revelation" can be observed twenty seven times in Paul's letters, in Matthew twice and Luke five times. In the Johannine literature, the word "manifest" is translated by the word revealed or revelation in 1 John eight times.

Certainly, by the time of Origen, at the end of the third century, an allegorical form of translation of the scriptural events was becoming widely accepted. Events like the exodus and the cross were reinterpreted, as types of the passage of the internal soul from darkness to light. The scriptural events were related back to the soul within. It was a function of the Platonic world-view that regarded the soul as being on a journey from a decaying passing world to the transcendent eternal world of the divine. Elements of key scriptural accounts were seen as providing the parameters for the soul's journey.

By the fourth century portions of the Greek were translated into Latin. In the last decade of that century Jerome produced the Latin Vulgate by re-translating existing portions of text, and translating the rest of the Bible into Latin. By the beginning of the fifth century these active words had disappeared, and were replaced by the thought word, revelation. This was not a deliberate suppression but a casualty of the church's missionary engagement with the Greco-Roman society. A Latin Bible was a vital resource for the Church in the new missionary context in the post Constantine era of the Roman Empire.[21] How ironic, that words about disclosing what which is hidden, are then masked in the process of translation.

It was then that Augustine's life of reflective thought led to a working through of the implications of the revelation of Jesus Christ. Revelation in the inner self made sense in this culture of the Empire heavily influenced by Platonic thought. But in so doing revelation collapses the irruption of God into history into an internal subjective experience of the individual.

Secondly, as outlined, the early apologetic writers within a hundred years of Jesus death and resurrection, started to present the revelation of God in Christ through the scriptures using allegory and reason. The stress on belief was inevitable because of the Platonic stress on reason as the God-given gift that enabled humans to know what God had done in Christ Jesus. The core of Jesus' message of the coming Kingdom of God was replaced by a focus on the resurrection and the call of believers to become Christ-like. At death, the resurrection of the believer to a transcendent heavenly world highlighted the vertical relationship from Earth to heaven. This synthesis between scriptures and the Platonic world-view began to break down by the time of the

---

21. The difficulty with translating from one language to another is that it can never be a 1:1 equivalence. Each language is a means of communicating key interests and concerns within a particular culture. The translation of words from Aramaic to Greek and from Greek to Latin involved in the Latin form of the New Testament lose some nuances in the process. In the case of the fourth century translation of the Greek 'apocalypse' as 'revelation' in Latin, there are important background issues in the world view of the two languages that turn out to be critical in the centuries after the writing of the New Testament. Words like catholic and universal have similar issues.

Reformation. From then on reason and faith assumed a more dominant role with the Reformers insistence on applying reason to the scriptures and insisting that scripture must be interpreted in terms of scripture. Two centuries later in the Enlightenment through Descartes, Locke and Kant, reason led to the deduction that the self was the source of perception, and that it was impossible to reason to the existence of that which is beyond time and space. When the transcendent perspective was replaced by the historical, reason was used to deduce where it was that the self found itself in relation to others and the wider world in which we live.

In the Enlightenment world theologians presented two primary ways that revelation from God could be known, either in the self or in the world. Schleiermacher (1768-1834) turned within to the self, to reason that the feeling of absolute dependence was the way God was experienced by the person. Hegel (1770-1831) sought the other way, taking the truth represented in finite spiritual experience and transforming it into philosophy. Barth (1886-1968) later provided a radical alternative to these person and reason centered approaches, declaring that God revealed God-self through the Son from beyond the limits that Kant had placed on thought. From this perspective God breaks in upon the self by revelation and provides a new framework for human reason. "It was not that theologians of previous ages were uninterested in the relationship between revelation and reason: Iranaeus, Origen and Thomas all appear to make that point; but they lived in a context where the fact of revelation could be assumed. It is the modern doubt about revelation that makes the contrast with reason vital." [22] For nearly two millennia, reason and revelation have at various times and in various ways been the categories used to describe who Jesus Christ is.

Thirdly it was within this setting that two simple but important observations from earlier discussion need to be reinforced. They show the power of how both the Platonic, and the historical world-views, provide the lens for the interpretation of scripture that powerfully influence the reading of scripture. Either by consulting dictionaries or a search on the internet for the word apocalypse, one finds the word equated with references to the extraordinary prophetic narratives about the end of the age, as in the book of Revelation, or contemporary descriptions of terrible world threatening disasters. From early on in the church's mission, the Latin Vulgate translates 'Apocalypse' as 'Revelation'.[23] It is not surprising that throughout church history references to an apocalypse are immediately related to coming cataclysmic events that threaten the planet.

Martyn's translation of the key verse in his Commentary on Galatians, that it was "an apocalyptic revelation of Jesus Christ" runs counter to more than fifteen hundred

---

22. Gunton, *Revelation and Reason*, 4. This comment by Stephen Holmes in the preface highlights the importance of addressing revelation and reason in the theological task.

23. See the Roman Vulgate translation of the Bible. By 400 AD Jerome in his complete Roman translation of the Bible reflected the accepted translation of the Greek word 'apocalypse' as revelation from at least as early as Origen (184/5-253/4AD).

years of translation of this verse! "For I did not receive it from another human being nor was I taught it, it came to me by God's apocalyptic revelation of Jesus Christ."(Gal 1:12)[24] Compare this verse with the New Revised Standard Version, which reflects all other translations. "for I did not receive it from a human source, nor was I taught it, but I received it through a revelation of Jesus Christ." The Greek is plain, it directly states in one word that it is an apocalypse. In doing Martyn he opens up the apocalyptic dimension of Paul's letters as he shows in the rest of the Commentary. Not only Jesus proclaims an apocalyptic kingdom, Paul proclaims God's apocalyptic Jesus Christ.

As Martyn states, "The precise contours of the apocalypse of Christ, the crucified Messiah, cause Paul to employ certain aspects of the Jewish apocalyptic while suppressing others. Thinking of the event in which God first made Christ present to him, Paul says nothing about receiving a vision from heaven, or of angels, or of a future judgement . . . In Galatians the content of God's revelation proves to be in the first instance the Son whom God has sent invasively into the world."[25][

For here God presents not knowledge, but Jesus Christ to Paul. In the moment of the apocalypse, God in Christ, the world in which the event is happening, and the mind and body of Paul are all brought together in the one event. In this happening the categories of self and world are not separated but held together in the moment of apocalypse. For Paul this moment reconfigured reality for him and changed the very way he saw the world. He found himself caught up in the divine narrative that included him and his times and the world before God.

As Barclay states,

> Throughout, I have emphasized *the incongruity* (and not just the priority) *of grace* enacted in the Christ-event and experienced in the Spirit, since this contributes powerfully to the reconfiguration of reality on the Pauline map. Because the Christ-gift neither recognized nor rewarded the worth of Paul's life "in Judaism," and equally was given irrespective of the worth (or worthlessness) of Gentiles, it jolts its recipients into a new construal of the cosmos.[26]

How extraordinary, "a new construal of the cosmos." The fact of the matter is Paul was shocked to the core by what confronted him. The apocalypse of Jesus Christ was alien and strange, a radical disjuncture in this life, creating new selves for a new world before God.

Thus these two major elements of the gospel message of the New Testament, namely the kingdom of God being at hand, and the apocalypse of Jesus Christ, previously eclipsed by other missional and societal agendas can now be given their full significance. It is of fundamental importance that this Pauline understanding of the apocalypse is recaptured so that an apocalypse is not only limited to the sense that is

24. Martyn, *Galatians*, 3.

25. Martyn, *Galatians*, 158.

26. Barclay, *The Gift*, 443.

normally understood as an event bringing the threat of, if not the actual end of history. It makes it possible to disengage from a Platonic world-view that has run its course, and discover the sheer vitality and reality of the event to which the Scriptures provide a witness. There is a new opportunity for the church to discover "the story that it is in."

THE APOCALYPTIC STORY

Seeing all human history and life in terms of a pale blue dot in an almost infinite universe keeps the crunch question before the world religions. In this long evolutionary history of the human race there are a number of explanations usually given for the emergence of religion. Religion is a result of prior superstitious eras, or the means by which early societies developed morality, or a projection of the human brain in search of meaning. What, though, if religion is the result of profound apocalyptic events experienced in the history of the race that calls the rational historical world view with all its explanations into question? It is outside the framework of such a world-view. What if these events in one nation have culminated in an apocalyptic event that shows how God is at work on this planet, and beyond?

At the end of the era of the denominational paradigm it seems as if the church has lost confidence in its own message. Could the reason be the inadequacy of a Christology that is so implicitly focused upon the self that the only option in the face of the scientific challenge of the Enlightenment is to retreat into the subjective self, and dream of a personal heavenly future. It reveals a modern sort of Gnosticism that cannot address the world as the place of the incarnation. It is as though the debates of the first four hundred years in the life of the church have been undone, and once again it is no longer possible for people to believe in the Christ, who is both human and divine.

The Enlightenment scientific and industrial revolution has meant that the historical world is now the given, and a transcendent up there is nothing more than a creation of the mind. In what way can Jesus be divine in this world now? Divinity is but a state of mind, a rational belief, and the claim that there is a kingdom of God can only be seen as a kingdom within, a state of mind, a personal conviction. Even in scholarship the emphasis is on the human nature, with Jesus the teacher, and the Church describing his impact in terms of titles such as Son of Man, and Lord. Or else he becomes a prophetic social activist often engaged in issues that were unknown in the life of Jesus. The divine nature has become a problem, and the resurrection an impossible conundrum, because it does not fit with the categories of self and world. What has become almost self evident is that the kingdom of God is not found in the arena of suns, seas, and society. Religion is bound up with belief, morality and human values, all internal and in terms of our social being, states within.

It is the apocalyptic that breaks in upon the world so that the action of God takes place in the creation, not just in the human mind. It is the apocalyptic that calls forth the bold statements that what has happened in the resurrection and ascension of Jesus of Nazareth shakes the very frameworks and categories that we live by. He provides another perspective on creation that is not just mind and matter, self and world, but both the self and the world included within the realm of God's action. It is this fact that impelled the church in the first four centuries of its life to face the division of the divine and human and hold them together in Jesus Christ. It is the apocalyptic that provides the basis for the church to re-address the world of mind and matter, and again see them within the compass of the action of God. Only then can the history of the human story be caught up within the mystery of the divine story.

The church as the bearer of this apocalyptic message will always be impelled by the Holy Spirit to witness to the kingdom future that is envisaged. It is the world, not the church, or the nation even, but the planet and the universe to which the message is addressed. It cannot be otherwise if it is an apocalypse of Jesus. The apocalypse challenges all categories that we bring to the gospel. The apocalypse puts us in a new world. As Paul discovered, once the resurrection and ascension of a crucified Lord happens it needs to be heard by the geographical world, the social world, the political world, and especially the global world. The message addresses the issues in terms of the coming kingdom, the future dream of God that those addressed find themselves caught up in, involving the universe, the planet, regions, nations, the family as well as the individual.

We are caught up in a story that is so much bigger than ourselves. We are called into an unfolding kingdom of incredible scope and future, which goes well beyond the pale blue dot to be caught up into the purposes of the God of the universe. This is not a private journey, but the discovery of the way the Spirit of God catches us up into the purposes of God in redeeming and fulfilling the creation itself. This story is a public journey made with all who have heard the call of God in Jesus Christ, all who belong to a church that started with an apocalypse that opens to us the kingdom of God underway in our midst on the way to other subsidiary apocalypses.

8

The Apocalyptic World

THE RIVER FLOWED

YEARS AGO NOW, WHILE *working in Central Australia, four of us set out from Oodnadatta in Central Australia in 2 Landrovers on a clear cloudless day driving north. One hundred and sixty kilometres into our journey we came to one of the world's oldest rivers, the ancient Alberga that flows into the Finke on the edge of the Simpson Desert. It is a river of sand, two hundred metres wide, marked out by a thick line of trees that find water beneath the sand. We drove across the graded track through the river bed. Half way along, an arm suddenly appeared from the left of the cabin of the Landrover ahead, and pointed upstream. We stopped, got out, and then heard a strange rustling. Walking a hundred metres upstream we saw a small tongue of dirty water snaking its way downstream. We ran back to the landrovers, drove to the northern bank and parked there. We watched the tongue of water reach the track, pool, then break through. Within fifteen minutes the Alberga was running a banker, two hundred metres wide, the noise incredible, with the sound of grinding rocks, and huge tree trunks tossed along by the raging torrent. We watched amazed. There was not a cloud in the sky. Where did this awesome river come from? Perhaps a huge storm hundreds of kilometres upstream? We arrived at the right moment to see the river flow. A parched land watered.*

I have never forgotten, standing there in the bush, as a mighty river flowed with extraordinary power and energy. It was totally unexpected. The wonder of being there at that moment. I had crossed the dry Alberga many times before, but from then on it became a sign—that what we take for granted can be transformed in minutes, and a warning never to camp and sleep in a dry river bed.

THE WIDER PICTURE

Paul makes starkly clear that this apocalypse of Jesus Christ was a totally unexpected event. It is important to place Paul's account of this event inside the context of the apocalyptic writings of his day. That context is inter-testamental Judaism The Jewish apocalyptic writings appeared in the time of the second Jerusalem temple after the Seleucid emperor Antiochus IV Epiphanes desecrated the temple in 167 BC. Elements of the apocalyptic had already been a part of the prophetic tradition in Israel as seen in the writings of the prophet Isaiah. But now it became a far more explicit form of resistance to the brutal and systematic attempt to eradicate Jewish religious practices. "For during this period emerged a new literary genre, the historical apocalypse, and with it an apocalyptic world view and consciousness that would become enormously influential in the history of Judaism and Christianity alike."[1] Freedom was restored in 160 BC after the Maccabean revolt finally liberated Jerusalem and the High Priest was able to conduct worship in a purified temple. Over a century later in 40 BC the Roman juggernaut swept through and again the land was subjugated and was still under Roman power in Paul's time, though worship was allowed in the temple. No wonder apocalyptic writings continued to flourish announcing "the transience and finitude of temporal powers, God's governance of time and the outworking of God's plan in history."[2] "For Jewish apocalyptic eschatology, that divine intervention was an imminently future event whereby 'God puts an end to this old age and ushers in the new one through God's sending of the Messiah.'"[3] The writers are future oriented, giving narratives of the coming rise and fall of powers, and timelines for the coming confrontation between God's power, and the defeat of the human and evil powers of the present age. Evil—persecuting powers and empires—will be overcome and God will bring shalom to the earth.

For Paul this apocalypse was not in the future. It had already occurred in Jesus Christ! It was not a series of cataclysmic events in the future; there are no timelines, or narratives, for this event has already broken into human history and is underway in and through the power of the Holy Spirit. Once that happened everything was to be seen through the way God in Jesus Christ was ushering in God's new creation.

Paul as a Pharisee had lived and worshipped a God of grace. At the heart of Jewish worship during this second temple time was the understanding of the God who was abundantly gracious and caring for the people of Israel.[4] Yet, in this apocalyptic confrontation, the grace he discovered in Jesus Christ was radical and incongruous.

---

1. Portier-Young, *Apocalypse Against Empire*, xxi. Both Portier-Young and Horsely find the roots of the apocalyptic genre in the resistance to the Seleucid empire of Antiochus IV.

2. Portier-Young, *Apocalypse Against Empire*, 27.

3. Boer, "Paul's Mythologizing program in Romans 5–8," 4,

4. Barclay, *The Gift*. In this wide ranging summary Barclay shows the various streams of second temple Jewish life and the way they understood grace in a number of different ways; beneficence, reward, security for Israel.

Christ's gift of grace "has subverted every other regime of value;" it has "upstaged every system of worth established on other grounds;" "gives rise to a transformation of values effected by incorporation into the act of God in Christ."[5]

> The emphasis, . . . lies on the *incongruity* of grace—its shocking lack of match with the worth of its beneficiaries, in ethnic, cognitive, moral, or other terms . . . its ability to define new taxonomies of reality, new configurations of history, and new patterns of social life. It is important to Paul that this new creation has already been enacted by God in the form of the Christ-gift; it is not a goal yet to be attained or a favor yet to be gained from God. In that sense the *priority* of grace is presupposed behind the call of believers, though this is not developed in the language of predestination.[6]

These two separate streams of second temple expectation, apocalyptic expectation and grace, fuse together to burst through for Paul into the Christ-event of cross and resurrection and ascension. They have become the source of grace incongruous. This irruptive event has become the proleptic key to the present and the future, relativizing all previous systems of worth, whether in the Torah, or in any other symbolic system. The witness to Jesus Christ is then a radical re-reading of the Hebrew Bible. It furnishes a basis not only for 'theological and social innovation' on a remarkable scale, but the expectation that God will restore the creation to fulfill the purposes of the Creator.

Martyn sees this as an apocalyptic struggle in which God has declared war,

> [w]hen he sent his Son and the Spirit of his Son into the territory of the flesh. This war is, then, the new creational struggle, the apocalyptic war of the end-time begun in the Christ-event and now continues in the power of the Holy Spirit. There is no narrative of what will come, instead the realization that the Galatians are caught up in a war in which God's forces are the ones on the march. The Spirit's weapons, however, are strange indeed. For example, the Spirit bears the fruit of communal *peace*, in order to overcome the *violence* engendered by the Flesh.[7]

It is a creational struggle that seeks to overturn the violence of the old order which Paul code names as the flesh.[8] The means of doing so are indeed quite different

---

5. Barclay, *The Gift*, 444–445. In listing these five effects of this grace, Barclay incorporates and extends the work of earlier scholars such as Dunn, Kahl, and Martyn by showing how their insights are caught up into this understanding of 'incongruous grace'

6. Barclay, *The Gift*, 446.

7. Martyn, Galatians, 530.

8. The word sarx, flesh, is used in a number of ways in the New Testament. In John's gospel, 'the word was made flesh' is a statement of the word becoming incarnate in life. The Flesh in John is not such a supra-human reality as it is in Paul in the passages that have been explored. But Paul too can also use this word in this more descriptive creational sense of our fleshly contingency. It is important to check the context in which this word is placed to see the various ways it is used.

to the *modus operandi* of the flesh; they are the ways of this Kingdom of God, the way of the Son, and the way of the Holy Spirit.

For Paul, the flesh here is not sex, or the body, but the alien power of sin that rules the human orb that was unmasked in and through the Word of the cross. This is an extraordinary claim. It is sin that blinds us to the kingdom of God, the presence of God, the unfolding of the divine human story in the creation.

> Viewed from the perspective of the Christ-event, all history, even Israel's history "under the law," has been subject to the power of sin and propelled toward death. But in Christ, and because of Christ, a new reality has emerged, powerful enough to reverse the tendency toward death, and to propel its recipients, contrariwise, towards "eternal life."[9]

"One who has been on the other side rips the curtain apart, steps through to our side, altering irrevocably our time and space."[10]

How then are we to understand the flesh that blinds us all to the Spirit of God?

Here it is helpful to follow Bonhoeffer in his description and comments about the tree of the knowledge of Good and Evil in Genesis chapter 2 and 3. The original couple are able to live from the "Tree of Life" in the garden, or die if they eat from the tree of the "Knowledge of Good and Evil". When tempted they eat from this second tree, and are expelled from the garden.

> Attaining to the knowledge of good and evil, is thus, in the story, interdependent with falling away from an original communion with God and, indeed, with each other. The "knowledge" that is thereby gained is fundamentally distorted, because it is knowledge apart from God, knowledge whose possession cuts them off from the source of life. (Gen 3.22, 24) . . . Bonhoeffer's basic insight is that the Goodness of God is beyond the dualism of good and evil. Any conception of 'good' that can be opposed to 'evil' is itself already outside of God, which means it cannot be truly good. It is a simulacrum whose origin and judge is not God but human beings seeking to possess themselves independently of their relationship to God. And says Bonhoeffer, it is this Good beyond good and evil that becomes accessible again because of the reconciliation wrought by Jesus Christ.[11]

What is easily dismissed as a mythical story is shown by the resurrection of Christ to be a profound description of the human situation.

No wonder Paul was blinded by the light of God, the reality of the resurrected Christ, finding himself beyond good and evil, beyond what he came to call the flesh. All the categories of Law, whether religious or social or individual feed the flesh, for they divide life into narratives of good and evil, right and wrong. Paul was able to see

9. Barclay, *The Gift*, 59.

10. Martyn, "The Power of Grace," 282.

11. Bachelard, *Resurrection and Moral Imagination*, 60.

that only in the new creation of the gospel is it possible to see beyond good and evil to the righteousness that is given in faith. Even then, if we think we have the power to choose between these alternatives, we make a fundamental mistake.

The apocalyptic breaking into human experience requires a re-evaluation and a re-experiencing of the self. No longer am I the fundamental reference point in the center of all that happens, evaluating my motivation, my commitment, deciding whether I succeed or fail in my eyes or other's eyes. What now are good works? How is the law to be experienced? How does the scandal of the cross provide a new framework for living? How am I caught up in the vast purposes of God on the pale blue dot, and indeed the cosmos itself?

THE PROBLEM WITH GOOD WORKS

For Christians and nominal Christians alike the scriptural framework of right and wrong is accepted as obvious, and not questioned. The Christian life pushes one to choose the good rather than the bad. The law makes clear what is right and what is wrong, and to be Christian is to be committed to, and keep on, choosing the right, depending upon the forgiveness of God when a mistake is made. This individual framework of the role of the self as the choosing agent is written into the denominational paradigm. There is however a dilemma—our inability to do the right. The passage most referred to about this matter is Romans chapter 7.

Nearly every commentator on this passage of Paul claims that it shows there is a profound split within the human individual. "I do not understand my own actions. For I do not do the good I want, but the evil I do not want is what I do. "(Rom 7:19). From this perspective, the human self is actually impotent to do the right. It is taken as a given, that Paul himself is concerned by his inability to keep the commandments. God becomes an impossible taskmaster who demands perfection. Jesus' words on the Sermon on the Mount come to haunt us. "Be perfect, therefore, as your heavenly Father is perfect." (Mat 5:49)

Is it surprising that people give up on trying to do what is right? Is it surprising that they go with the flow of not worrying about pleasing such a demanding God? What is accepted is that for the Christian it is not easy to live a virtuous life, and requires much discipline and moral commitment. This fact is taken for granted in common understanding. What, though, if this interpretation of the passage is not right, and needs to be re-evaluated in the light of the apocalypse of Christ?

Paul W Meyer, has provided a most careful analysis of the text of Romans 7. He shows that for Paul, it is not about a cleavage in the will of the individual, but a cleavage that is in the Law. What Meyer shows, is that even when I do the best that I can, I am deceived by the Law.

Sin has wrested the Law out of the hands of God. That is to say, rather than speaking of two parts to the self, Paul refers to *two Laws* (7:22–23, 25, 8:2), which prove to be the Mosaic Law functioning as the Law of God and the Mosaic Law as it has fallen into the hands of Sin. The terrifying *fundamentum* to the whole of Paul's argument is the fact that the Mosaic Law is not only God's law but also Sin's Law, a tool of Sin. One can see, then, that Romans 7 culminates in a cleavage, but that cleavage "is in the Law and not in the self" (Meyer, "Worm," 78).[12]

What are the consequences for Paul? Paul says in words that are awkward for modern exegetes to read that, he as a Pharisee, claimed to be "as to righteousness under the law, blameless."(Phil 3: 6b) Surely he is exaggerating the past to emphasise his present state. Or does he see from a different perspective what we seem to have lost? He regards all this past achievement as "rubbish" "and instead seeks to "be found in him, not having a righteousness of my own, but one that comes through faith in Jesus Christ."(Phil 3:9) His keeping of the Law fooled him into thinking that doing the right would issue in right. He discovered in his campaign against the followers of Jesus "doing the right," just how much keeping the law issued in evil. He speaks of sin's power to deceive him via the law, the result being that he *accomplishes* the *opposite* of what he intended.

> The subject of the discourse in Romans 7, then, "is not simple frustration of good intent, but good intention carried out and then surprised and dumb-founded by the evil it has produced'"(Meyer, "Worm,"76). And the form in which this good intention is carried out is precisely that of the observance of the Law. Thinking of the Law as God's Law, and of his own clearly willed, altogether admirable and blameless observance of it (Rom 7:12, Phil 3:6), Paul takes as his subject the power of Sin to corrupt the highest good. For in Christ he now looks back on the demonic power of Sin "to use the Mosaic Law to effect the opposite of what its devoted adherents expect, even and especially when it is obeyed." (Meyer, "Worm."80). In short, Paul's argument attaches impotence not to the human will, but rather to the Law. The Law itself is the actor who proves to be disabled vis-à-vis the sinister power of Sin. Indeed it is for that reason that God sent his own Son in behalf of all, "to deal with Sin as the Law could not (Rom 8:3–4)[13]

This is a terrifying realization that sees the outcome of our best actions distorted and morally twisted. It is a world subject to sin, for the good is the good of the 'knowl-edge of good and evil' in a dualistic world of good and bad, and not the goodness of God beyond all of our goodness. What a shock for a twenty-first century world to find that the positive human perspective of us choosing what is good and maintaining it

12. Martyn, Galatians, 538.

13. Martyn, *Galatians*, 538.

through discipline and commitment only adds to the evil in the world. Note it is sin, a paradigmatic experience of the world, the water in which we swim, that gives rise to individual sins. As Dorothee Sölle discovered, "Sin is certainly also my decision, my free will, my 'no' to God, but it is also the destiny into which I was born. I am entangled in it through my parents, my teachers and my tradition. . . . We do not seek out for ourselves the society in which we live and the place we have in it, but are born into something which is already determined by the structures of sin, of separation from God."[14]

We are blind to the Word that forms the fabric of the cosmos, unable to realize that we live in a world that is not able to see the world of the creator. The human perspective is deceived by the Law in trying to do the best but enmeshed in this universe of the flesh.

Attention is focused on the Law, the Israelite Law, but the division that Law brings between Jew and Gentile, is reflected in the duality of all other systems of law that bring division. It is the defining of the other as alien through the law, whatever law, that lies at the heart of the divisions that give rise to the violence of victor over victim, the violence of power, and wealth and advantage. Competition can be good, but this is still the goodness of the tree of the knowledge of good and evil, that holds within itself the violence of evil despite the best of intentions. As clearly demonstrated in our political and business systems of choice, competition can lead to growth and innovation, but can also result in a ruthless exercise of destroying the threatening other.

We are aware of just how often we make mistakes and others bear the brunt of them, but to find that the best things that we do turn sour, and curdle what we wanted to be best, is soul destroying. How then do we escape the "Tree of the Knowledge of Good and Evil", here described as the world of the flesh? The whole story is about the way the Cross of Christ becomes the "Tree of Life", the source of all life as it is portrayed in the Garden of Eden account, but now is seen and experienced in the resurrection of Jesus Christ as Lord. "For God has done what the law, weakened by the flesh could not do: by sending his own son in the likeness of sinful flesh, and to deal with sin, he condemned sin in the flesh, so that the just requirement of the law might be fulfilled in us, who walk not according to the flesh, but according to the Spirit. (Rom 8:3,4)"

There are two wonderful consequences that follow. Through the work of the Spirit we see the cross in this new light, and know and discover the way we are rescued from the "Tree of the Knowledge of Good and Evil". Paul frames this new reality directly in terms of God's act in the cross opening the possibility of the radical gift of faith.

> Therefore since we are justified by faith, we have peace with God through our Lord Jesus Christ, through whom we have obtained access to this grace in which we stand. (Rom 5:1,2a)

14. Sölle, *Thinking about God*, 55. Sölle points out that the very definition of what constitutes sin, differs for male and female due to the role expectations of each within the culture of society.

This is not an internal experience of grace, this is the reality in which we find ourselves. We stand in this new dimension with others, in time and space, the kingdom of God, the realm opened through the cross of Christ. In this place our minds are set on the Spirit, so that we may be communities of the Holy Spirit through which God's redemption is realized in the world. This self is an apocalyptic self, part of a new creation, in which the self and the world depend upon the Holy Spirit. This cannot be restricted to an individual subjective internal experience, of a person touched by or called by God at particular moments and times, but places the individual within the cosmic realm of God's world.

THE COSMIC CROSS

It is not surprising that this claim created problems for Jews and Gentiles in the early church. That all history and tradition and values should be called in question by one event is too much. The scandal of particularity has always been a difficulty for religionists and thinkers alike. Why this event, and not others—because this event is God's act in Jesus Christ. As God's apocalyptic act it supersedes all categories, breaks all frameworks, brings an ultimate purpose that encompasses all that is.

> We proclaim Christ crucified, a stumbling block to the Jews and foolishness
> to the Gentiles, but to those who are called both Jews and Greeks, Christ the
> power of God and the wisdom of God.(1Cor 1:23–25)

It still is a problem for an Enlightenment world and a denominational church that reduces the cross to the forgiveness of sins, and the call for us to be moral, and has difficulty making sense of the need for someone to die. How remarkable is the following account of the cross in Galatians 3:13.14

> Christ redeemed us from the curse of the law by becoming a curse for us—for
> it is written 'Cursed is everyone who hangs on a tree'—in order that in Christ
> Jesus the blessing of Abraham might come to the Gentiles, so that we might
> receive the promise of the Spirit through faith.

This text is widely understood as a statement of the substitutionary form of the atonement. Jesus becomes a curse for us before God—there, in our place, he suffers the wrath of God for our sin, so that we may go free. Beloved by hymn writers of the nineteenth and twentieth century, we see that but for the suffering of Christ we will receive the punishment due to us for our sin. In the following quotation Martyn places Christ's substitution for us on the cross in a much wider framework.

> Galatians 3:13 involves, therefore, more than the standard formulation of
> the doctrine of substitutionary atonement. To be sure, Christ becomes the
> Law's curse *in our behalf*. But he did that not simply taking into himself a
> punishment due to us but by embodying the curse, in such a way as to be, in

his crucifixion, *victorious* over its enslaving power. Paul places the thought of apocalyptic warfare in the foreground. There are not three actors—the guilty human being, Christ as the substitutionary sacrifice for that person's guilt, and God, who, accepting that sacrifice, forgives the guilty human being. There are four actors: the powerful, enslaving curse of the Law, human beings enslaved under the power of that curse, Christ, who comes to embody the enslaving curse, and God, who in this Christ powerfully defeats the Law's curse, thus liberating human beings from their state of enslavement. Central to the action in this apocalyptic struggle is, therefore, not forgiveness, but rather victory, God's victory in Christ and the resultant emancipation of human beings.[15]

With only three actors we are caught up in a 'God and Me' relationship that results in the forgiveness of my sin—sin that is seen in individual terms, and usually in the forms of sexual and personal matters of dishonesty and drunkenness and smoking, the addictions of our age. In this language of previous paradigms the deep religious appropriation of the cross is internal within the subjective self of individual awareness. The creation is ruled out of the picture, and left as the background for the divine drama of Christ's substitution for me.

When the curse of the Law, under the power of sin, is seen as the fourth actor this atonement is properly seen as a cosmic battle. The law is found to enslave all, not only those who seek to disobey it, and those who want to be true to it, but the relationships with each other, society, and the world in which we live. We find ourselves in a distorted and broken world, yet beautiful and inspiring at the same time. For Paul the cross became the place where death derived from the flesh was defeated as Christ took upon himself the curse of the Law for us all. He showed how it was the Law, that was seen to be from God, became in fact the agent that rejected Christ and led to the crucifixion of the holy one of God. The cross disclosed the nature of the Law itself, the curse of the Law which killed the holy one of God. It is Jesus who shows the true nature of the law in operation. It is this law that lies at the heart of human society and the nature of the creation.[16] It is in the resurrection that Jesus is seen as the cosmic Christ, placing the law in a cosmic perspective. Paul declares, "There is one God, the Father, *from whom* are all things and *for whom* we exist, and one Lord, Jesus Christ, *through whom* are all things *and through whom* we exist."(1 Cor 8:6—italics added)

For Moltmann the Easter Event discloses the threefold role of the cosmic Christ;

"Christ as the ground of the creation of all things (creation-in-the- beginning); Christ as the driving power in the evolution of creation (continuous

15. Martyn, *Galatians*, 318, n 110.

16. In Galatians Paul speaks of the curse of the law. In Romans he unpacks the way the curse operates. The law is good and holy, but it is sin that uses the law to curse us. Sin destroyed our reception of the goodness of God and left us with the polarity of goodness and badness that results from living from the Tree of the Knowledge of Good and Evil.

creation); and Christ as the redeemer of the whole creation process (the new creation)."[17]

The providential work of God sustained the creation in its distortion and death from sin. This God radically disclosed in the cross and resurrection is also about the redeeming of the evolutionary process.

> Eschatology is not the end of the evolutionary process. What is eschatological is the new creation of all things which were, and which are, and which will be. What is eschatological is the bringing back of all things out of their past, and the gathering of them into the kingdom of glory. What is eschatological is raising of the body and the whole of nature. What is eschatological is that eternity of the new creation which all things in time will simultaneously experience when time ends. To put it simply: God forgets nothing that he has created. Nothing is lost to him. He will restore it all.[18]

It is only in the last century that the finely tuned laws of this universe have been discovered that enabled the cosmos itself to grow from a first moment through the subsequent birth and death of stars that gave birth to elements and the resultant evolutionary development of life through a vast seemingly inexorable chain of life and death.[19] What remains clear is that the universe has been subject to decay and death since its origin. This act of God discloses God's wider purposes beyond these processes that apply every-where to this universe in which the pale blue dot is found. Whether for an individual or for the cosmos, Paul's language strains to state what it is that has happened.

> For if we are beside ourselves, it is for God; if we are in our right mind, it is for you. For the love of Christ urges us on, because we are convinced that one has died for all, therefore all have died. And he died for all, so that those who live might live no longer for themselves, but for him who died and was raised for them. From now on, therefore, we regard no one from a human point of view; even though we once knew Christ from a human point of view, we know him no longer in that way. So if anyone is in Christ, there is a new creation; everything old has passed away; see, everything has become new. (2 Cor 5:13–17)

He rules as the cosmic Christ. For Paul, death no longer rules. This blinding apocalypse of the resurrection lets loose the law of Christ, the promise of Abraham, the love of neighbour and other, through this one point in time and space, that is

---

17. Moltmann, *Jesus Christ to Today's World*, 94.

18. Moltmann, *Jesus Christ to Today's World*, 103.

19. And not only our own universe, but according to some, billions of parallel universes as well. It is said, as we make each decision in our lives new universes split off to fulfill all the possibilities inherent in the decision. If I just escape an accident, in another universe the accident happens according to some interpreters of quantum physics.

about the recreation of all time and space. No longer does death enslave the universe and the individual.

The other disciples had lived for three years through the events of Jesus' life toward the cross and through the resurrection, to the shock of the Risen One being present in their midst. For Paul all this was concentrated in this one event. Jesus was appearing to him as he was plotting the persecution of those who followed Jesus. The foundational fact of God's victory over the power of death shook him to the core of his life, beliefs and convictions. It is clear that it took some time before he was able to see that it was sin that distorted the good gift of the law into the knowledge of good and evil.

Paul was struggling with the scope of the victory that God had given us in Christ Jesus, reconciling the world to God and making Paul and the church an ambassador of this reconciliation of all things in Christ. The apocalypse of Christ was the realization that God was catching him up in the victory God intended for the creation, to be set free from the powers that enslave the human race. The light of the Risen Christ was the pinpoint source of the new dimension of the creative presence of the living God, the promise of God to Abraham, the source of blessing for all in the one commandment that summed up all others, 'love your neighbour as yourself.' What a story he now found himself in.

Here is found the fount of divine love, knowing and beauty that is the source of light, love and relationship within the story of God's purposes for the creation. The cross is the one place and time when the veil that hides our view of the Creator is ripped away. From then on for Paul every issue is brought back to the risen crucified Christ. In Galatians this was the touchstone that enabled him to unmask those that would destroy the Galatian community created by the Holy Spirit. In baptism Jew and Gentile, by God's act, have been co-crucified with Jesus Christ. A person is given a new identity in Christ as an individual and a member of the family of God.

> Therefore we have been buried with him by baptism into death, so that, just as Christ was raised from the dead by the glory of the father, so we too might walk in newness of life. . . . So you also must consider yourselves dead to sin and alive to God in Jesus Christ. (Rom 6:4 &11)

> There is no longer Jew or Greek, there is no longer slave or free, there is no longer male nor female; for all of you are one in Christ Jesus. (Gal 3:28)

The apocalyptic self is baptized into the cross. This is the way through Christ that access is obtained into the grace in which we stand as a reconciled community. This Christ community is CROSS-cultural, it is CROSS-gender, it is CROSS-righteousness, it is CROSS-life because of our joint baptismal death into Christ.

Was he mad? It surely cannot be that big. When God acts, however, the whole creation is involved. That in Christ, death is destroyed, gives a new perspective on all of life. While it was such an incredulous fact for Paul's time, it is an even more amazing reality now in this universe.

Paul can only say this because he sees that it is the work of God reconciling the creation to God. This apocalyptic event then is the source of what the creation is to become. This seemingly impossible possibility leaves the other apocalyptic narratives of his time relegated to the future as possible future events, contrasted with the sheer divine scope of the reality of the apocalypse that has already happened in Christ.

In this apocalypse there are three distinct expressions, forms and outcomes. The first, the apocalyptic cross and resurrection that discloses the activity of God at a specific event in time; the second, the apocalyptic reframing of the life of Jesus as an apocalyptic life; and third the apocalyptic pointing to the fulfilment of Jesus prayer in the coming of God's kingdom. In the book of Revelation we have a narrative about the apocalyptic consequences of the Christ finally bringing into being a new heaven and a new earth, after the last enemy of life, death is destroyed. God's purpose is to be fulfilled in a new Jerusalem in a new heaven and earth where human beings are to be partners with God and share with God in the fulfilment of God's initial dream.

But is this big enough, now, with the distinct likelihood of discovering other forms of life around other suns? How will the heavenly Jerusalem be envisaged in the setting of the universe rather than just the Earth? A heavenly Jerusalem on Earth is too anthropomorphic. What is essential to see is that the fulfilment of the apocalypse in Jesus Christ is the fulfilment of Jesus prayer that the kingdom of God come on the Earth or, as seems more appropriate, God with us in the creation.

How different this cosmic view is to the accepted view of most in the denominational framework. The New Testament scholar, N.T. Wright, has clearly and publicly denied the ultimate symbol of a "God and Me" universe, the rapture of the saints. The early Christians, "were extremely interested in a topic many Western Christians in the last few hundred years have forgotten about altogether, namely the final new creation, new heavens and new earth joined together, and the resurrection of the body that will create new human beings to live in that new world."[20] How different is one recent scenario, in which in the twinkling of an eye, God takes people up to heaven in the end time, leaving the chaos and threat of cars careening, and planes pilotless, for those who are not the chosen ones. This scenario is a modern form that presumes a vertical division between the supernatural substance of heaven and the ordinary substance of the Earth, with Christianity about the salvation of the individual for heaven. Wright starts with God's covenant with Israel and follows through with the tabernacle and the temple as the places where God dwells with his people. He dismisses the rapture interpretation of scripture and its projections as a fantasy, and keeps underlining the purpose of God is to fulfil the covenant and to bring about a new heaven and a new earth.

---

20. Wright, "Jesus is Coming," 84.

What a story we find ourselves in. The cross is not a personal talisman, our ultimate personal trophy, but the way to discover the purpose of God on the pale blue dot—to live in the possibility of a new creation remaking the old, the great story of the redemption of the creation.

It is not surprising that some thought Paul mad. Governor Festus declared, "You are out of your mind, Paul, too much learning is driving you insane." (Acts 26:24). Festus was wrong. It was not learning, it was an apocalypse that disclosed the kingdom of heaven, the world of the living God.

Now in the self-world universe of the twenty-first century this assertion is more simply dismissed with a relativistic comment like 'It is your opinion. You can believe it if you want.' What is missed is the fact that this apocalyptic event is the work of the Creator Redeemer God. The apocalyptic God who is the source of creation itself acts specifically in the creation. Immanuel, God with us, known in the centrality of the risen crucified Son of God, and the Holy Spirit at work in our worlds, our lives and our cultures.

LIVING IN THE SPIRIT

So in Paul's language, the resurrection catches us up in the story of the God who is at work to redeem the world through enclaves of the Spirit. The apocalyptic self finds itself in the apocalyptic world or dimension of the Spirit. The disciples are called to be free, not to decide, but to live by the Spirit, and not gratify the desires of the flesh.

"Through the invasive Spirit, then, God has created and continues to create the Galatian churches as *addressable communities*, communities that are able to hear God's imperatives *because* of the indwelling Spirit."[21]

These are the communities that live from the Spirit, given in the presence of the "Tree of Life", over and against the Flesh derived from living by the "Tree of the Knowledge of Good and Evil". Here the Spirit of Christ is the primary actor, the one whose battle this is, so what a community does is both an act of the Spirit and their own act, as people who are living the creative communities that the Spirit makes possible. These communities are each the fissionable core of the apocalyptic reality. The Spirit brings a new way to live in a new cosmos. In Galatians the Abrahamic pre-Sinaitic Law is brought to fullness and completeness in the command to love your neighbour. In Romans the circle is complete with the Law completed in the love of neighbour. Underlying this is the remarkable statement in Galatians 5:14. The whole law is summed up in a single commandment, "You shall love your neighbour as yourself." This loving inter-relationship between each person and their neighbour becomes the law of Christ. What is remarkable and indispensably the result of the Spirit's presence, when Paul gives guidance for the everyday life of the Church, these bases of the Spirit, he does not turn to the Law.

21. Martyn Galatians, 535.

In Galatians 5:16–24 one sees that Paul takes four major steps. First he issues a promise explicitly focused on the Spirit, rather than the Law. (v16) Second, referring to one of the presuppositions of that promise, he speaks of the Spirit and the Flesh as two combatants, engaged in a war with one another. (v17) Third, certain that that war is the determinative context for the Galatians daily life—that war being the scene of the Spirit's victory and thus of the Galatians real life (5:25)—Paul gives the Galatians a description of the war. He provides specific guidance, that is, by transforming traditional lists of vices and virtues into community characteristics in the midst of war. On the one hand, there are marks of a community under the influence of the Flesh and, on the other hand, there are marks of a community in which the Spirit is fruitfully active (vv 19-24). Fourth, centrally concerned with the Spirit's apocalyptic war against the Flesh, Paul employs the language of exhortation in the promise itself (v16), thus giving to hortatory expressions a very peculiar stamp.[22]

The Spirit's weapons are most strange for this end time apocalyptic war. "The Spirit bears its fruit of love, joy, and peace in the community of God's church."[23] "There is no law against such things," Paul declares. (Gal 5:23) The Spirit also gives gifts to each of the members of the church. It does this in the face of the violence engendered by the flesh. He adjures the disciples to keep in step with the Spirit and then spells out in language that is the fulfilling of the law of love, released in the cross as the fulfilling of the promise to Abraham, the law of Christ.

It is, then, a serious mistake to read Paul's descriptions of the activities of the Flesh and the Spirit in Gal 5:19-23 as an example of nomistic, moral discourse focused on "vices" and "virtues". By concentrating on the matter of community life, and by speaking of the Flesh and the Spirit as supra-human apocalyptic powers, Paul transforms what had traditionally been a form of moral discourse—vices and virtues attributable to individuals—into marks left on communities by these two apocalyptic powers. In sum, then, at its core, 5:13–24 is not a prescription of the way the Galatians ought to behave, a series of exhortations focused on the demands laid on human beings by the Law or some other system of moral norms. On the contrary, this paragraph is fundamentally a description of the way things are, given the advent of the Spirit, its declaration of war against the Flesh, and its community-building power, already evident in the Galatian churches.[24]

What, then, is the basis of the life of the Galatians as an active base of the Holy Spirit? If we leave out the descriptions of the flesh and the Spirit, we can hear that Paul is not spelling out a new set of laws to live by, but a new way of life to be lived in the Spirit.

22. Martyn, *Galatians*, 525.

23. Martyn, *Galatians*, 530.

24. Martyn, *Galatians*, 486.

For you were called to freedom, brothers and sisters; only do not use your freedom as an opportunity for self-indulgence, but through love becomes slaves to one another (13). For the whole law is summed up in a single commandment, "You shall love your neighbor as yourself" (14). But if you are led by the Spirit, you are not subject to the law (18). And those who belong to Christ Jesus have crucified the flesh with its passions and desires. (25). If we live by the Spirit, let us also be guided by the Spirit. My friends, if anyone is detected in a transgression, you who have received the Spirit should restore such a one in a spirit of gentleness (6:1). If you sow to the Spirit, you will reap eternal life in the Spirit (9b). So let us not grow weary in doing what is right, for we will reap at harvest time, if we do not give up (9). So then whenever we have an opportunity, let us work for the good of all, and especially for those of the family of faith (10).

This way of living in the light, or in the Spirit is clearly spelled out as a community way of living together led by the Spirit.

For too long the writing of Paul in the epistles has been understood to be focused on the importance of justification by faith of the individual, and contrasted with the gospels, seen to provide a basis for just and loving acts in the world. This contrast is partly the result of the way the Enlightenment categories of self and world have played themselves out in terms of the scriptures. The discovery of the apocalyptic dimension enables us to see how Paul's profound experience of the apocalypse of Christ is paralleled in the message of Jesus apocalyptic kingdom of God.

Paul speaks about the divine invasion of the Spirit, warring with the flesh, through the life of the Spirit in Christian communities. Jesus states this dynamic in a different way. In his message he points to the kingdom of God that is hidden but available. As we have seen in Mark 10:27 Jesus states that only God can bring people into the kingdom he proclaimed. Jesus life in the disclosing of the kingdom of God becomes a description of what it means to love one's neighbour, for his life is lived in the dimension of the kingdom by the power of the Spirit, and his teaching is to prepare his disciples to live in the realm of the Spirit.

Given the widespread belief that the need for morality to order early societies gave rise to religion, it is not surprising that so much of the Scriptures are interpreted in terms of choosing to live a moral life. That is what happens when the culture and the church reward the life lived for others on the basis of keeping the Law. There is however, a sickness in morality that was exposed by the cross of Jesus Christ. Living in the Spirit has different boundaries, different attitudes, an otherness to life that is given in the Spirit. No longer is the self, or even the Church, in the center. The people of God become a sent community, on the way to God's promised end in the mission of God, caught up in living in God's story before an open heaven in the kingdom of God. The mighty river of God's grace flows with divine energy, power and life. The horizon is cosmic.

9

The Apocalyptic I

ABORIGINAL GOSPEL

MY FIRST VISIT AS *National President of the Uniting Church in Australia was with Aboriginal Elders in the far north of the continent in Arnhem Land. I was to spend time listening in their meetings after decisions about sexuality in the National Assembly meeting had disturbed some Aboriginal leaders.*

I was sitting cross legged on a mat in the sand with some of these leaders as the Millingimbi Aboriginal community met in grief at the death of one of their most respected members who was there in 1923 when the Methodist Mission had first started. I had just met the members of the grieving family. A ceremonial dance called 'The Tower of Babel' was underway. It had been created in the area after the great charismatic renewal in 1979. Many dancers were milling about in the open area on the sand. Then, as they formed up into two columns of dancers in the shape of a cross, the Elder in Millingimbi took my hand and helped me stand. "Don't worry, just stand here. Nothing will happen to you." he mouthed quietly as he led me ten or so spaces to stand at the head of one of those columns. "What did he mean, nothing would happen to me," I wondered.

The energetic dance went on and I began to move with the music. Then suddenly in a heart beat every dancer stopped. After a brief intense silence, two warriors, one from each end of the arm of the cross, rushed at me shouting, waving spears, which as they ran, they jabbed toward me again and again. Then they stepped back, and the dance had ended.

In a daze I walked back and sat in the sand, my mind reeling. What had just happened? As the leader of the Uniting Church had I just been ritually killed on the cross? I sat trying to come to terms with what had just occurred, hardly present to what followed, as the funeral ceremony continued.

Then a second Aboriginal dance to an Old Testament theme began. This one was called "Noah's Ark". Just after the dance had started the Elder leaned across again and

*whispered, "In a little while, will you come with me, and together we will stand and be-
come the door into the ark?" Cautiously I nodded assent. The dancers gradually formed
into a circle. We stood, walked together into the line of the circle, then stepped apart and
faced each other. I followed his lead and held up my hand over my head. We formed a
door into the enclosed circle. I am not sure who said it, but the announcement was made,
"All in the community and the land are invited into the ark." And that is what happened.
Those who had been standing or sitting under the huge Tamarind trees and on the edge
of the sandy open area, came dancing, walking and running toward this human door of
the Ark, passed between us, and into the inside of the circle. When all had entered the
dance ended.*

*Apart from the directions given me that night, no other words were ever offered in
explanation of what happened or questions asked re the sexual issues. What was clear
was that in less than a quarter of an hour, I had first been identified with Christ, then
called to be part of the doorway into the life God offers. The more I thought about these
events, it seemed to me as if this was the way another culture acknowledged we were one
in Christ in the Church, even if we did not agree with each other all the time.*

*I still tremble when I think about that night. Here in the oldest continuous cul-
ture on the face of the planet, our aboriginal Christian brothers and sisters had in the
language of dance, brought the gospel to life, in the midst of grief and difference on a
northern Australian beach.*

APOCALYPTIC REFRAMING

The recovery of the apocalyptic dimension brings a disruption to the experience of
the self in the radical new setting of the kingdom of God. The apocalyptic gospel leads
to a reframing of who I am/we are. The apocalyptic self that emerges reminds us how
malleable the self is in history. The way we understand self/I changes across time and
cultures and place, and is articulated in different ways.

As indicated, the common conviction I have heard over the past four decades—
and continue to hear—read across many different theological and church traditions,
is that the 'Kingdom of God is within'. What a dramatic reduction and refashioning
of the good news of the kingdom of God has taken place to fit within the subjective
experience of individuals and the expectations of a democratic community. Jesus declaration of the gospel as the good news from or of God was a public declaration to the
nation, not a private message for individuals. "The time is fulfilled, and the Kingdom
of God has come near, repent and believe in the good news." (Mark 1:15)

Now, in the twenty-first century the expectation that God can act beyond our
inner life is not a part of the religious experience of most in the life of the church, let
alone the wider population. We are left with personal life as the actual center of lived
religious experience. We are called to be tolerant of the wide variety of views that are
held in the private and public realms, even if the common retort to a person pushing

a particular point of view, is well, that is only *your* opinion. Certainly as a result of the Enlightenment the realm of religious and subjective values is located in the inner self over and against the face of a secular world of facts and circumstances. Initially the withdrawal into the self gave a freedom for believers to choose for themselves between a range of relatively different points of view and grow to tolerate those they did not agree with. The emergence of many faiths and cultures in the West has complicated this perspective. Discordant religious views about what is true and a plurality of cultural norms has complicated the possibility of toleration. A world fragmented into nations, religions and cultures provides a broad range of particular backgrounds, a series of distinct mosaics into which a person is located by birth. In any nation there will be a diverse range of cultures and religious groups that the self has to process. This diversity gives rise to a huge number of possible options for a person. Most attention is focused on the enormous freedom this gives an individual to be the master of their own life. But not only is society fragmented, the self can be too—fractured in trying to come to terms with so many dissimilar options, stressed in attempting to find a degree of integration, or simply withdrawing in the face of a diversity of 'exclusive' points of view. In this changing and confusing situation it is difficult for the private subjective self to find certainty and focus. "Today more people die by suicide than in all wars, terrorist attacks, murders and government executions combined."[1] And many more attempt suicide. Is this an unintended consequence of the hierarchies of the past being internalised, making the self the judge, jury and executioner? How can a self within, escape perceptions of ultimate failure, betrayal of others expectations, without any means of giving weight to other points of view, when caught with endless internalised judgements and self-accusation? How important it is that others can provide a bridge to a community greater than one. In a confusing and demanding world it is not surprising that many find it hard to make up their mind and have the motivation to seek a way out. Easier to claim my view is the only view, or give up and listen to others. Belief so easily becomes a matter of opinion, or morphs into dogmatism, in the face of a rapidly changing world of facts, claims and options.

The consequence for most believers is that the classic task of 'faith seeking understanding' has been inverted. The individual is left instead first needing understanding to find faith. This approach in the intellectual world gives rise to the triumph of a hermeneutics of suspicion that risks making the researcher the ultimate arbiter of their own truth.

It is not at all surprising that decisions, commitments, and uncertainty in my inner self have replaced waiting upon God to act in the midst of human life. Such decisions and commitments focus on the immediate present and deliver the life of faith to the 'imperialism of the present'. There is little sense of the eschatological dimension of a faith that calls the Christian to live between the times of a resurrected Lord and the coming of a new heaven and a new earth. Of course there are particular movements

1. Storr, Selfie, 7.

of meditation, prayer, and social justice that emerge from the life of the church, but overall it is their absence that is noted rather than their presence and implementation.

There has been a deep wrestling with what are the options for faith in a modern and post-modern world. A century of distinguished theologians has explored the dynamics and the forms of faith for this diverse and changing world. Unfortunately most members of congregations have a very limited awareness of this intellectual history of the faith. For the most it is as though this work has never occurred. The church and its members mostly seem insulated from the theological discussion of matters they have already made their own mind up about. The feature of this time is the individualizing and subjectivising nature of the way any message is received. It is the very power of a paradigm, that what does not reinforce the paradigm is not seen as significant. While there is a large community of scholars and thinkers, they are overall an insignificant percentage of the vast denominational religious movement. For believers the local church is the center of religious life and belonging. It is rare for congregations to grapple with the insights of scholarship. It is amply illustrated by the way a university trained ministry has found it very difficult to raise questions about the historicity of the scriptures in the routine of the weekly life of the people.

We are trapped by the way the gospel, conversion and scripture, derived from the Wesleys, Finney and the Charismatic movement, has come to be understood. The initial freeing of faith in Christ for the individual that happened in the Enlightenment has run its course. It is now reduced to a positive view of the self, locked into the inner self of the religious democratic individual, who finds himself or herself spiritually alone. A seminal core text lies at the heart of the gospel for that revolutionary Enlightenment time, that of Galatians 2:19,20. It is a text that focuses on the 'me' and 'my' in Christian experience. This Galatians text, so important to Luther and subsequent Lutherans, was also vital for the Pietist movement that grew in Europe in the seventeenth century, and as well provided the seed bed for the Wesleys and those who followed them.

> [t]he prime target of this gospel is 'the conscience' or the 'inner man.' This is the site where Galatians is seen to locate freedom: 'Christ has set us free, not for a political freedom or a freedom of the flesh but for a theological or spiritual freedom, that is, to make our conscience free and joyful, unafraid of the wrath to come.'"[2]

The end result in the denominational church was a radical re-evaluation of the message as a gospel of conversion. First the individual waited for the work of God in their life until it happened, then later came the reasoned decision to follow Jesus, and later again an entering into the experience of the Holy Spirit. With each development, the work of God in the individual withdrew further and further into the inner subjective self. What is clear is that for millions it has given rise to a religious experience that is primarily caught up in a relation between themselves and God.

---

2. Barclay, *The Gift*, 341.

This experience of faith is so different to what were the key marks of faith prior to the Enlightenment. On either a confession of faith, or through baptism as a child, the person became a member of the church. In baptism a person was placed within God's ordered creation and also made subject to the expectations of the church. The church was part of the divinely ordered world; through initiation into the church a person was entering into God's world and order in a very particular way.

Early in 1738 John Wesley became convinced by the witness of Moravians, and the emphasis of key scriptural texts, that an instantaneous conversion within, was not only possible, but it was the result of discovering or having faith. Wesley accepted the Moravian logic and was preaching and teaching the need for such an immediate instantaneous conversion while still searching for this experience of 'faith' himself. His younger ordained brother Charles Wesley was offended by "this worse than unedifying discourse."[3] It did not fit with the traditional interpretation of faith that he, as a Church of England minister, believed was consistent with the teaching of the church to which he was ordained.

Surprisingly it was Charles Wesley himself who was the first to have such an experience. He had been reading Luther's commentary on *Galatians* on the Wednesday evening in the week prior to Pentecost in 1738. "I spent some hours this evening in private with Martin Luther, who was greatly blessed to me, especially his conclusion of the second chapter. I labored, waited, and prayed to see 'who loved *me* and gave himself for *me*.'"[4] referring to Galatians 2: 19,20.

> I have been crucified with Christ; and it is no longer I who live, but it is Christ who lives in me. And the life I now live in the flesh, I live by the faith of the Son of God, who loved me and gave himself for me. EXT]

The radical experience of faith finally happened on Pentecost Sunday. It had been an extraordinary day of hearing scripture, personal expectation, a word of healing, and finally, peace with God through faith. He writes in his *Journal* "I now found myself at peace with God. . . . I saw that by faith I stood; by the continual support of faith, which kept me from falling, though of myself I am ever sinking into sin."[5]

This was three days before John Wesley's famous experience of a "strangely warmed heart" during the reading of Luther's *Preface to the Epistle of the Romans* at Aldersgate on the 24th May 1738.

> At a quarter past nine, while he was describing the change which God works in the heart through faith in Christ, I felt my heart strangely warmed. I felt I did trust in Christ, Christ alone for my salvation, and an assurance was given

---

3. Kimbrough et al, *Journal of Charles Wesley*, 100.

4. Kimbrough et al, *Journal of Charles Wesley*, 104.

5. Kimbrough et al, *Journal of Charles Wesley*, 108.

me that he had taken away *my* sins, even *mine*, and saved *me* from the law of sin and death."[6]

The italics in both of the brothers' *Journals* is highly significant. It was the personal experience of salvation that was at the heart of this immediate experience of conversion for both Wesleys.

John Wesley's experience was not related to a particular passage of scripture, as it was for Charles, for whom Galatians 2:19,20 highlighted the "*me*". But John's experience was also focused on the *me* and added the *my* and the *mine* as well.

The historic sequence is vital. Here is the 'red line' of conversion from Augustine to Luther and on to the Wesleys, that continues to have enormous consequences for the West. Augustine's conversion to the church happened in a threatened Rome, Luther experienced faith and helped give birth to a patchwork of nations in Europe, and the Wesleys found a God who addresses the individual "me" in a human centred Enlightenment world. As Bosch points out, "The ordinary people now saw themselves as being, in some measure, related to God directly, no longer by way of king or nobility and church."[7] The Pietist emphasis on the individual experience of salvation had prepared Europe for this direct dealing with God in Christ, rather than through the mediating role the church had claimed to have. The Wesleys' preaching on instantaneous salvation opened powerful new religious possibilities for the "ordinary people" of their time and in the Protestant proclamation to subsequent generations

THE ENLIGHTENMENT READING OF GAL 2:19,20

What incredible consequences have come from this core passage of Galatians 2:19,20 read during this time?

> For through the law I died to the law, so that I might live to God. I have been crucified with Christ; and it is no longer I who live, but it is Christ who lives in me. And the life I now live in the flesh I live by the faith of the Son of God, who loved me and gave himself for me. (Gal 2:19,20)

Here attention was focused on the loved 'me', known as a result of faith. The possibility of faith in Jesus Christ opened a person to the possibility that God could act in them in a moment, instantaneously. By faith in what God, did a person could realize that they had been crucified with Christ. A remarkable act of God allowed the one who took them into his own death on the cross to now live in their own life—'it is Christ who lives in me'. The person was co-crucified, died, and was raised by Christ who took over their life. This "I" became the place where Christ lives! This is the reality that the believer waited to experience. The expectation was that the divine reality

---

6. Ward et al, *The Works of John Wesley,* 249.

7. Bosch, *Transforming Mission,* 263.

comes to 'me'. 'The life I now live in the flesh, I live by the faith of the Son of God, who loved *me* and gave himself for *me*.

For the Wesleys the moment of that experience of faith could not be predicted. It could happen instantaneously, or it could depend upon waiting upon the Lord, aware of one's own sins and helplessness, until there came an actual experience that issued in Charles being at peace, and John experiencing a warmed heart. It was not only a rational decision to believe, but also a waiting for the moment that the Holy Spirit brought an emotional spiritual integration in the inner "I". When that happened lives were transformed and communities were changed.

It should be pointed out that in Paul's writings there are only three places where he states that 'Christ is in us'. There are over a hundred and fifty places where the person or community is to be found 'in Christ.' There is a profound emphasis in the Wesleys and in all that follows on the self as being the location in which salvation is experienced. There has been a profound change of emphasis from 'in Christ' to 'Christ in us'.

Within two years John Wesley had fallen out with the Moravians who counseled that a person had to wait quietly, doing nothing, simply trusting in Christ and waiting for the moment of instantaneous conversion to come. Wesley insisted that a person should use the means of grace (services of worship, sacraments, and serving others) as part of the process of waiting for this consciously given moment of redemption, entering into the new life given by God in Christ. The mystery was in the moment when this became true in "my" own experience. And then, once God's grace had been experienced, a person could live with the means of grace in the perfecting power of the Holy Spirit. For the inquirer there were beliefs to be studied and religious practices put in place prior to this personal experience of forgiveness and salvation; and, then, afterwards beliefs to be studied and religious practices put in place in the power of the Holy Spirit. The believer died to himself and discovered Christ at work in his own self, loving him and giving himself for him. The self may have died, but in the flesh, the focus was on the self as the location for experiencing God's grace at work.

We have seen how a hundred years later the Presbyterian Charles Grandison Finney, preached that a person did not have to wait for this moment of conversion. Finney called for people to make a rational decision to place Jesus Christ as Lord of their hearts. They were to choose who their Lord was in this new republic in which citizens chose their leaders in the ballot box. In a similar way they were to choose to make Jesus Lord of their life. The moment of conversion was the moment of commitment. This decision is a rational and emotive giving of oneself into the hands of Jesus Christ. Rather than waiting for God to act in us, it is up to us to make the decision. This fundamental change places even more emphasis on the self as the locus of faith. I must turn to Christ, rather than look to Christ for God's divine act. The mystery of God's act has receded into the background and it all depends on what I do in the foreground. The evangelist's task was to get the person to acknowledge they had made a decision within, in their inner self. Having made that decision they were urged to come forward in a prayer meeting or revival service and in some way make an inner moment a public moment. This shift opens the process of conversion to the dynamics of persuasion and the effects of pressure and indoctrination. In the twentieth century psychologists and films have made the process look contrived and suspicious, and an object of fun. Sinclair Lewis's 1927 novel *Elmer Gantry* satirically portrayed the fanatical religiosity and hypocrisy of a preacher who preached against all that he did in private. It was made into a famous film of that name in 1960. Despite the abuses millions came to a life giving faith through preachers who brought this approach.

Seventy years after Finney, at Azusa St there came a new experience in the inner self, the baptism of the Holy Spirit. The emphasis was now placed on the work of the Holy Spirit in the person, giving rise to a focus on the gifts of the Spirit, especially speaking in tongues and healing services. The Pentecostal churches that emerged were a slow fuse burning through until the last third of the twentieth century when the experience of the Spirit caught fire across many churches and denominations in the charismatic movement. It was the individual experience of the baptism of the Holy Spirit that was at the heart of this phenomenon.

ORDINARY BELIEVING

It is not surprising this inward understanding of faith triumphed in the democratic age to which it helped give rise. At the beginning of the 21st century few make a public witness to what they have decided, apart from those in leadership, and those who advocate or defend the public content of particular positions within the broad church of the Christian church. Most who attend worship do not speak about their faith, but hold to their inner decision and convictions about what is entailed in the life of being a Christian. Faith is reduced to a personal trust that is made in terms of a person's belief about God and what Christ has accomplished for them. With faith compartmentalized into the 'I' within, it becomes increasingly difficult to determine what the form of this faith is for people who attend church as well as those who do not.

> The gospel is good news for individuals, but it is also much more than that. It is good news for societies—indeed for the whole creation. Isaac Watts put it well in his ever-popular Christmas carol: the power of the gospel is meant to reach "far as the curse is found."[8]

A small percentage of people break through this constraining framework and give their lives and energy for the sake of others in the name of Christ. It is a far, far larger number who sit in the pews and never escape from this so-called biblical world of personal sin, personal forgiveness and a personal heaven, or are left with convictions and beliefs about God, Jesus and the human race that seem to have little effect on their public and social life.

8. Mouw, *Uncommon Decency,* 33.

I know of two careful studies of church members and their understanding of what it is to be Christian. The first was by John Finney in 1991 in Scotland. He surveyed 500 people over the age of 16 who had recently made a profession of faith when they joined their church. A wide number of new members of Catholic, protestant, evangelical and charismatic Churches were included. What surprised the researcher was that while words like forgiveness and the love of God were the general terms most used, there was little awareness of personal guilt. What was expressed in hundreds of statements were "'I feel much better about myself.' The sense of improved self-worth and self-image is impressive." [9] "Only a quarter mentioned that being a Christian was about believing in God, and only 4% spoke of the cross of Christ. Nobody said that baptism had made them a Christian and hardly anybody used the word converted—extraordinary in view of the denominational spread of those participating in the survey."[10]

The second is a study by Ann Christie of 45 Anglican churchgoers in rural north Yorkshire using in-depth interviews about Jesus and his significance for them. With the exception of some evangelicals, she states, "One thing we learn is that in matters Christological, ordinary believers only take what they need. That they do not need much conceptual theology is perhaps not surprising. What is surprising is that they do not need Jesus to be God or have saved the world through his atoning death."[11] And, "Most of this sample appear to have selected a fragmented synoptic Christology. They do not appear to have a Christology that has been shaped in any substantial way by either the gospel of John or the Pauline corpus."[12]

Christie points out that some evangelicals did not fit this profile; they were more aware of doctrinal issues and the importance of Jesus, especially in the Pauline letters. Yet even in these groups the number of articulate believers are outweighed by those who are far more reticent to speak of their faith.

More recently Preston Sprinkle writes

> One survey asked 450 self-proclaimed born again Christians "What is the single most important thing you would like to accomplish in your life?" (Barna, *Growing True Disciples*, 39). The response was both frightening and comical.
> 29% said "being a good parent, raising good kids, having happy kids"
> 14% said "financial security, comfort, retirement funds, wealth"
> 7% said "completing/furthering my education"
> 6% said "having good health"
> I laughed and cried all at once. None of these made it on Jesus's value scale and some of them, like "comfort, financial security, and wealth" directly

9. Finney, *Finding Faith*, 89.

10. Finney, *Finding Faith*, 19.

11. Christie, *Ordinary Christology*, 189.

12. Christie, *Ordinary Christology*, 191.

contradict it. Our ideal of "becoming more like Jesus" needs to be reshaped by looking at who Jesus actually was and what He actually taught.[13]

These three surveys involves small samples of respondents, but the results echo what seems to be the case for many who worship on Sunday. These surveys indicate that in the world of the denominational "I" there is little discussion about the fundamentals of faith. Parishioners are happy to let ordained ministers speak the doctrine and state what the gospel is, but they themselves keep silent about what they really think and let the religious leaders talk on. Even amongst leaders I have found the key words are often left without content. As leaders grapple with a declining response to the gospel from younger generations, the one thing that is assumed is that the word 'gospel' sums up Jesus message. As church structures are remodeled, and new programmes are introduced, the one constant not evaluated is the gospel. The gospel, the Greek word for 'good news' does not actually have any specific content. What then is the content of this good news? These few surveys point up the need to actually ask questions as to what those in churches really believe, and find out what the members in the wider community understand to be the church's message.

Why is it that such basic theological work is not done in and for the life of congregations? There is a deeply held belief that God does not change, and the gospel does not change. The preacher and leaders are focused on declaring the message from the scriptures, rather than considering what the members in the pews actually are hearing and believe the gospel to be. The fact that both leaders and members may not be hearing or interpreting the scriptures because of cultural blocks to their understanding does not ever seem to be considered.

The understanding of gospel and conversion has been trapped within the subjective world of the Enlightenment. It is time to bring a reading that takes seriously the apocalyptic kingdom of God as proclaimed by Jesus. What happens when such an apocalyptic reading is applied to the formative passage of Galatians 2: 19,20, placing it in the wider context of Galatians 2:18—3:5.

AN APOCALYPTIC READING OF GALATIANS 2:19-3:5

In his letter to the churches in Galatia, Paul probably gives the first and earliest written account of the gospel reported in the canon of the New Testament. The letter predates the writing of the four Gospels. It is in this letter that Paul states he received the gospel as an "apocalypse of Jesus Christ". In the book of Acts this apocalypse was a public event that did not happen in his "inner self". He was confronted by the Risen Christ in an event that left him shocked and dependent upon those with him.

When he wrote Galatians he was caught up in a battle for the hearts and minds of a new congregation of Jews and Gentiles in Galatia, somewhere in Asia Minor. (modern

13. Sprinkle, "More Like Jesus."

day Turkey) In the letter he draws upon his credentials as the one who brought the gospel of Christ to them. His task was to confront those who called in question the community Christ had brought into being. Teachers came after Paul had left them. They claimed Paul's understanding of Christ was a betrayal of the Jewish Law and had proceeded to teach this law as an alternative basis for the life of the community. In the first two chapters of Galatians he laid out the basis of his apostleship and then focused on the divisive actions of Peter when visiting Galatia. Peter had eaten with the Gentiles until Jewish-Christian teachers arrived and then would only eat with the newcomers. Rather than a denunciation of Peter, Paul focuses on the implications of the death and resurrection of Jesus Christ. It leads to him giving a testimony as to who Christ is before challenging his readers. Yet it is not like many testimonies we have heard. The testimony begins in verse 19 and flows through into the more familiar words of verse 20 and a declaration in verse 21 before challenging the members of the community in 3:1–5 in terms of who Jesus Christ is for them.

> 19. For through the law, I died to the law, so that I might live to God. I have been (co)crucified with Christ;
>
> 20. and it is no longer I who live, but it is Christ who lives in me. And the life I now live in the flesh I live by faith in the Son of God (or through the faith of Jesus Christ) who loved me and gave himself for me.
>
> 21. I do not nullify the grace of God; for if justification (or righteousness) comes through the law, then Christ died for nothing.
>
> 3:1. You foolish Galatians! Who has bewitched you? It was before your eyes that Jesus Christ was publicly exhibited as crucified.
>
> 2. The only thing I want to learn from you is this: Did you receive the Spirit by doing the works of the law or by believing what you heard?
>
> 3. Are you so foolish? Having started with the Spirit, are you now ending with the flesh?
>
> 4. Did you experience so much for nothing?—if it really was for nothing.
>
> 5. Well then does God supply you with the Spirit and work miracles among you by your doing the works of the law, or by your believing what you heard?

In the first verse the testimony begins with "I" statements in which he unpacks what happened to him. The "I" in this passage is not the "I" of the Enlightenment personal pronoun 'I' as it used in the denominational paradigm.

This is more than a personal witness. Paul does not start with himself. He does not make his experience or his decision the fulcrum for what is happening. In Gal 2:16 he cites how a person, "human being" (Greek *anthropos*) comes to be justified, indicating that, "he is dealing throughout with the deed of God in which the old human being suffers death and the eschatological human being is made alive. Using the first person, then, Paul presents himself as the paradigm of this human being."[14]

14. Martyn, *Galatians*, 258.

It is the experience of the apocalyptic "I." He is describing what happens in and through this act of God, that brings a new creation and an eschatological person into being. Paul makes himself an illustration of what happens in the Second Adam that Christ has brought into being. If it happened to him, it can also happen for anyone.

1. *For through the law, I died to the law, so that I might live to God.*

Through Christ Paul came to see that it was the enslaving curse of the law that stood between him and God, and that as the law[15] was used to kill Christ so it also killed him. Once the curse of the law was destroyed, there was then the possibility for all people to live to God rather than the law.

It is the stark division within the law itself, the result of sin, which distorts the law and the worldview of all who see the law as the way to be faithful to God. Instead the law is caught with the consequences of what the Jewish Torah refers to, as eating from the tree of the knowledge of good and evil. We take the law as good but find it cannot deliver what it promises for our own lives. The law of the promise of the Spirit in the blessing of Abraham is replaced with a law that becomes a curse when pursued with human effort—whether it is the law for the Jews, or what Paul calls the enslaving elemental spirits of the Greco-Roman religion and culture that provided the basis of law for Romans. It is this law that gives power to the society to judge the person who has been deemed to have trespassed the law, whether given by God or elemental spirits or decided by a nation.

The rule of law is now defined by the legislative decisions of parliament. This law finds its basis in common law, as interpreted through a series of legal precedents in the democratic context in terms of crimes against people, social order and property. There are many different types of law involved in the attempt to seek justice and recognize human rights. The law, as a product of one of the three arms of government, is framed within the power structures and relationships of society for the beneficial order of society and its members. In practice it can also be used as a means of control over others. Almost every day the newspapers show how the best lawyers can be paid for by big business, or by criminals, with people's lives destroyed by false accusations and individuals without resources dragged through courts. As indigenous people in Australia have discovered, the law was used to deny them the rights to their land, based on a European legal system that did not recognize the way 'country' was part of aboriginal society. Those with power and/or money and greed can abuse any legal system for their own purposes, and enslave the powerless, the poor and the generous.

In the killing of Christ, Paul saw that the Law was fractured, and divided in two. There was the enslaving law that sent Jesus to the cross, and in doing so killed the Christ by hanging him on this accursed tree. This law is starkly different to the freeing

---

15. Paul's statement that the curse of the law killed Christ in Galatians, is further shown in the Book of Romans to be sin that uses the law to kill Christ.

law of God's promise given through Abraham that is embodied in the spirit of loving one's neighbor.

But then this staggering new possibility emerges. Paul states in verse 19, that through the law, he died to the enslaving law made known in the cross of Christ. "For through the law, I died to the law, that I might live to God." Here is a new way to find oneself before God. But is it possible to 'live to God'? Is this an actual possibility?

It is, in and through the one crucified by the curse of the law. In the crucified Christ, God opens us all to a deeper more fundamental reality, the possibility of being able to live alive to God in and through what Paul calls the law of the promise of the Spirit. This is the blessed non-enslaving law given through Abraham for both Jew and Gentiles so that all might live to God.

2. *I have been co-crucified with Christ.*

How is it that we are caught up into the cross, co-crucified with Christ so that as he lived to God we may also live to God. What is Paul declaring when he immediately states, *I have been co-crucified with Christ?*

So much is freighted into this Greek statement that to western ears is not obvious. In the Greek the word co-crucified is in the *first person singular, perfect, indicative and passive tense.* It is vital to unpack this technical language. Since it is indicative it places Paul on the cross in the crucifixion event; secondly it is in the perfect tense which in the Greek means Paul is still caught up in this key cross event, held in it as it were, and finally in this event he is there as a passive participant. Paul is saying that he is there co-crucified with Christ on the cross as a passive participant.

How can this be? Paul did not see Jesus of Nazareth crucified. Who can place Paul there on the cross, co-crucified with Christ? It is not Paul's act because he is there as a passive participant. The only answer is that it is God who puts him there. In the cross God has acted and placed Paul there with Christ. This is not a decision by Paul, but a realization of what God has done in Christ in catching him up into the event of the cross. This is why Paul declares he learnt of the gospel from an apocalypse of Jesus Christ. This goes beyond psychology and world events for it is the uncovering, the disclosing of what God has done in the cross. This cross of Christ is the place where God has acted, but Paul realizes that because it is the place where God acts that this is not only for Paul. In an extraordinary statement he declares that God has co-crucified all humanity with Christ! "For the love of Christ urges us on, because we are convinced that one has died for all, therefore all have died. And he died for all so that those who live might live no longer for themselves, but for him who died and was raised for them.(2 Cor 5:14,15)"

As if that were not enough, if anyone is in Christ there is a new creation. A new creation happens there in the crucifixion of Christ. "So if anyone is in Christ, there is a new creation; everything old has passed away; see everything has become new" (2 Cor

5:17) and in "in Christ God was reconciling the world to himself, not counting their trespasses against them." (2 Cor 5:18) This is the apocalypse of Jesus Christ.

In Christ God has acted in the midst of history to redeem the universe! Paul and all others can now live to God. It is the grace of God that has caught up the whole universe of sin and death, and in the cross shown how God enables us to live to God, in the righteousness of God, God's gift to us in Christ Jesus, the relationship that is the foretaste of God's ultimate purpose, a new heaven and a new earth. And God has made all this possible in the death and resurrection and ascension of Jesus Christ.

The cross has become the key to God, life, and history, this apocalypse in the midst of history, not at the end of history. God has acted, and now all can be seen anew in the light of the cross and resurrection of Jesus Christ. Here in Jesus Christ 'the heavens are torn open'. This is a new creation in which all is seen to be new in and through our co-crucifixion in Jesus Christ.

Talk about kingdom of heaven, and new creation, eyes opened, and second Adam—such terms are all trying to come to grips with the centrality of the liberation, release and recovery of what happens here. All time and place is seen in a new way through the image of the invisible God making peace through the blood of his cross. The very name given to Jesus, the Christ, the Anointed one and the Anointing One makes him the source of this divine disclosure. Here is Jesus as the Christ in the profound relationship the Son has with the Father, as the healer of creation in a way that excludes no one and is offered to all.

3. *And it is no longer I who live, but Christ who lives in me.*

"*He died for all so that those who live might no longer live for themselves, but for him who died and was raised for them.*" (2Cor 5: 15). Once more these words seem so strange to western ears and eyes. The world is no longer created by the self, or from the self, where law is the arbiter of truth and reality, and life is lived from the tree of the knowledge of good and evil. Now the world is lived in dependence upon the new tree of life, the cross, from which our new world is given, the new creation in which we find ourselves. The apocalyptic Christ is not just the reference point for my life, but the one in whom I am held and hid; the Son is the source of life in which everything holds together. It is not only the person, but the whole creation that is caught up into him. *For in him the fullness of God was pleased to dwell, and through him God was pleased to reconcile all things, whether in earth or heaven, by making peace through the blood of the cross.* (Col 1: 19,20) Christ lives in all and through all. As the Gospel of John asserts we abide in him.

So who is Paul then? It is the Spirit of Christ who dwells, one could say abides, in him, but that does not mean there is no longer an "I". His identity, while he lives in the flesh, is given by the faith of Jesus Christ, who tears open this englobing perspective of the world as an independent cosmos apart from God, to make known the reality of the kingdom of Heaven, the Spirit cosmos in which he now lives.

"It is Christ who now lives in Paul, but that does not mean that there is no longer an I. The I has been crucified and re-created by forces other than the self."[16]

This apocalyptic I is not an "other-worldly" "solution" to the "problem" of death, but a life lived in step with the Holy Spirit in the midst of everyday human existence before God. The Holy Spirit has created a new humanity, a community of peace, which is the body of Christ.

All of this comes alive in and through the apocalypse that is the Cross. Not only is this a new creation and an indwelling Spirit, but it is an experience of being known. For now I am an apocalyptic "I". The "I" is not destroyed, but known in a new way in relation to Jesus Christ. *And the life I now live in the flesh I live by the faith of the Son of God who loved me and gave himself for me.* (Gal 2: 20) This life is lived in dependence upon God, by the faith of the Son of God, for whom I am not just a number or an object but one who is known, loved, and for whom he gave himself.

What is incredible, though it should not be surprising, is that Paul's testimony provides a parallel to the description given previously about what happened at Jesus's baptism. In this apocalyptic event the heavens were ripped open, the Spirit descends like a dove, and the voice of God names the Son. And here it is similar. Firstly, the heavens are ripped open—Paul sees himself co-crucified with the Son of God as God's act. Secondly, the Spirit comes down—Paul now receives the Spirit of Christ who lives in him. Thirdly, God names the Son—Paul lives in the flesh by the faith of the Son of God, as a Son known by Christ.

It issues in a different sort of testimony to that made by those in the denominational paradigm. Their testimony focuses on what I have done in my commitment to Jesus Christ as Savior and Lord of my life. Here the testimony is about what God does in gathering us up into the apocalyptic event of the cross. It is the difference between a personal trajectory for my life and a divine trajectory that includes humanity in what God is about in the whole creation.

PAUL CONFRONTS THE GALATIANS

After this celebration of what God's grace has accomplished, Paul turns to the Galatians and directly confronts them with the question as to whether the power of Christ is manifest, made real in their midst or not. It is also a message for the denominational church as well. Firstly, the heavens are ripped open—Jesus was publicly exhibited as crucified to the Galatians. Secondly, the Spirit comes down—the Galatians receive the Spirit, and there are miracles in their midst. Thirdly, is God still working in power in your midst through the Spirit given in the Son or by the Law?

This is about public ministry in the power of the Holy Spirit that the realization of the apocalyptic cross set free in their midst. In Jesus' death it is about what God

16. Martyn, Galatians, 258.

does in raising the crucified Christ as the beginning of a new age of the Spirit in the midst of a world of elemental spirits and the law. It is a breaking in at one point in time and space to invade the universe along its created song lines. It is a living community that sees the world through the reality of the Spirit, beyond the previously imprisoning world of the Law. It is about the reality of islands of Spirit in the midst of an ocean of fleshly human perspective. It is a new place and a new space over and against the world of the flesh, either derived from the law, or as the result of gods and beings and elemental spirits, or human decision. Such law divides the world, through the knowledge of good and evil, and is not aware of the goodness of God, beyond good.

The Galatians are then reminded that when Jesus was publicly exhibited as crucified in their midst, they received the Spirit, as the community of faith. Then comes Paul's question. Which universe are you in? As Abraham was reckoned as righteous and able to walk with God, so having seen what God did through the cross, tearing open the heavens, and bringing the Spirit to you, are you going to walk away from the identity that you have been given, as children of God through faith? Which story are you in? The universe of the flesh, or the universe of God in Christ? Paul's perspective here is a testimony to God's action in a world context of divisive and violent forces. Remarkably he draws on Abraham's discovery of the God who gives descendants numbered with the stars and the grains of sand on the seashore.

INCONGRUOUS GRACE

The cross was there for all including Jew and Gentile. In the Christ event, "Both Jews and non-Jews are 'called' by an incongruous grace into common belonging to Christ. Their previous evaluations of one another and of their traditions, based on the cultural norms of ethnic distinction, are subverted by an event that has paid no regard to pre-constituted criteria of value".[17] "The connotations of a 'new creation' stretch well beyond individual conversion, gesturing to a cosmic refashioning awaited in the future. But in context the primary focus is the social novelty of communities that disregard boundaries by discounting old systems of worth."[18]

The world has been re-sourced in the light of the cross, and a new creation found to be in place. In a remarkable way in Romans 9–11, Paul's view of the past and future of Israel and Gentile has been recast in terms of the incongruous grace of God. The cross becomes the definitive apocalyptic act of God, making sense of Israel's past, and preparing for the salvation of Gentile and Israel (Rom 11:26) as the future of the creation. The source of this apocalyptic incongruous grace is shown to be the holy tap-root of God's mercy in Israel's history, now fulfilled in Christ, "the moment that gives meaning to the whole."[19]

17. Barclay, *The Gift,* 369
18. Barclay, *The Gift,* 395.
19. Barclay, *The Gift,* 561.

On Paul's reading, by believing in Christ Israel draws again—in consummate fashion—on the sustenance of grace, thereby becoming *not less but more like itself.* Faith is a mode of eccentric existence, a life dependent upon the gift of God. Since this is the essence of Israel's identity from Abraham onwards, what Paul expects is not the eradication but the realization of everything that Israel was destined to be, precisely by faith in the risen Christ.[20]

THE APOCALYPTIC CROSS

Paul comes to his experience and understanding of the apocalyptic cross in the midst of his contemporary culture and religious pluralism. He saw how the apocalyptic act of God in the cross relativized all other values, and all other gods, that demanded attention. It is such an irony that in terms of history it was Paul's use of the "I," that drew the Wesleys and others to these passages as the basis for a personal owning of faith. Yet from this apocalyptic perspective, Paul is describing the universe which he once inhabited in the light of the new order God has made possible. Here the gospel is not an experience in the inner self, but the declaration of the way God was at work in the cross for the creation, the society and the individual.

Paul discovered in the confrontation with the risen Jesus on the Damascus Road that his crucifixion was not just the death of a man, but the death and resurrection of the Son of God. This death and resurrection, destroys not only the power of death, but the power of the elemental powers of the cosmos, such as the law, that hold the universe in the thrall of death. In it God takes up into this crucifixion the death of the cosmos and the death of all people. Martyn writes, "the crucifixion is the apocalyptic, cosmic event in which God confronts the powers that hold all of humanity in subjection." [21] In him the cosmos is crucified, the flesh is crucified, Paul is crucified. And again, "In this event Paul was torn away from the cosmos in which he had lived, and it was torn away from him."[22] No longer does this new human being have an identity as that of a Jew or Gentile given by the law. The second Adam is bringing a new order into existence within existence. "Thus it is written, 'The first man, Adam, became a living being'; the last Adam became a life-giving spirit.'"(1 Cor 15:45). Paul then spells out this new world, this new cosmos.

Paul used spatial language not personal subjective language. In Galatians1:22 when speaking of the churches "He thinks of Christ as the new realm God is now establishing in the world. Thus, while the churches are located in Judea, they are more importantly located in Christ."[23] He sees this new realm when he speaks of his co-crucifixion with Christ. "First he says that Christ now lives in him. Then he adds that

---

20. Barclay,*The Gift,* 553.

21. Martyn, Galatians, 279.

22. Martyn, Galatians, 280.

23. Martyn, Galatians, 258.

he, nevertheless, remains a human being who lives *in* the flesh. Finally, he concludes that he lives his present life not only in the human orb but also and fundamentally *in* a certain faith, namely the faith of Christ."[24]

Having been conformed to Christ's death (cf. Phil 3:10), Paul continues to share Christ's path, finding that the event in which the Risen Christ has seized him is in fact his being brought to life. (cf. Rom 8:1) The dominant motif, then, is not a mystical union with divine nature, but rather the resurrected Christ's powerful world invasion, in which he participates. Thus in 1 Cor 15:45 Paul can say that, at his resurrection, Christ, the eschatological Adam, became an alive-making Spirit. (cf. 2 Cor 5:20)[25] "Believers live to God as walking miracles (Rom 6:11), all the more evidently miraculous because this new creation life begins, in their case, not on the other side, but on this side of death. . . . Paul emphasizes several times in these chapters the mortality of the body: let not sin reign in your mortal bodies." [26]

It is of vital importance to note that the battle with sin occurs also in the body and its organs, not just the self or the mind. The self should not be read "in an idealist or dualist fashion, as if 'the self' is something anterior to, or separable from, the body."[27]

Christian life in this new creation is in the body, where both the self and the world, the mind and the body, are involved in allowing the miracle of the resurrection life to bring the redemption of the body—"the believer is both visibly on the path to death and is required to, visibly and demonstrably, to display the resurrection of Christ, in the service of holiness and righteousness."[28] Here the tension between flesh and spirit is played out in action, not just thought or some sort of 'spirituality'. It is the Spirit that rescues the body from the 'mind set' of the flesh. This mind set is described by Barclay as the habitus, 'the structuring structure' that goes "beyond the sterile dualisms of "structure" and "free agency," of "objective" and "subjective" forces in human action." It is "capable of instilling a whole cosmology, an ethic, a metaphysic, a political philosophy, through injunctions as insignificant as 'stand up straight' or 'don't hold your knife in your left hand.'"[29]

We who live with an embodied habitus of sin and law in the flesh are called to allow our bodies to be baptized. "No longer present your members to sin as instruments (weapons) of wickedness, but present yourselves to God as those who have been brought from death to life and present your members to God as instruments (weapons) of righteousness. For sin will have no dominion over you, since you are not under law, but under grace."(Rom 6:13,14)

---

24. Martyn, Galatians, 258.

25. Martyn, Galatians, 258.

26. Barclay, The Gift, 501.

27. Barclay, The Gift, 504.

28. Barclay, The Gift, 505.

29. Barclay, The Gift, 506.

Put on Christ, that is embody the habitus of Christ, by the power of the Spirit in the unfolding cosmology of God's restoration of creation in space and time.

When religious experience has only the language of the inner self, then this language has to be reduced to the language of the mystic, describing personal experiences. Paul in addressing the law is not describing the world in terms of personal experience, but describing the actual world in which he finds himself. The crucifixion is not a matter of introspection but the description of the way the world is. The cross, this one eschatological time and one eschatological place is the window into the new creation of the life giving and alive making Holy Spirit. The resurrection takes this time and place and in the creative power of the Holy Spirit lets this be the point from which the time and place of the new creation begins. That is why it is an apocalypse, an uncovering or a disclosing of what God has done and is doing. And so we discover Paul's insistence of this invasion of the Holy Spirit, from bases where Christ rules, in this new realm, God is establishing in the world.

For Paul the issue is how one lives by the Spirit in the midst of God's breaking into the midst of human history. It is the interface between the apocalyptic world discovered in the cross, and the work of the Spirit in creating new communities of the Spirit, that are in Christ as spatial local communities, which live in step with the Spirit's presence in their midst.

The experience of the Holy Spirit is not just then about my subjective life, but the experience of the way we are introduced into a new community, in which our new identity as apocalyptic selves is to be in Christ in space and time, not withdrawn within. We are then 'in Christ' and part of the continuing incarnation of the body of Christ in the world. This is the way the kingdom of heaven is invading the world.

How many ways has that gospel found expression in the life of people—the public dancing of the gospel by Aboriginal Australians in Arnhem Land, the witness of martyrs, the creation of Christendom and then later feudal ordesr, national churches, and denominational chapels. Changing settings give rise to different ways this gospel has been lived.

In the twentyfirst century we look forward as the human race into a new future of grace and a new future for this Earth even as it is enveloped in an almost infinite universe. All the old views of time and space now seem so limiting. Indeed the comments from the New Testament take on a new significance.

> But do not ignore this one fact, beloved, that with the Lord one day is like a thousand years, and thousand years are like one day. The Lord is not slow about this promise, as some think of slowness, but is patient with you, not wanting any to perish, but all to come to repentance."(2 Pet 3:8,9)

The human race has stepped out from Locke's single room into an almost infinite world. We stand on the cusp of thousands of thousand years now, and find ourselves quite close in time to the awe-inspiring cross given the possible aeons to come.

Actually the realization comes that so little time has passed since this cosmic shaping event. God has given great significance to those who live on a mote of dust suspended in a sunbeam. The sun of life is shining and through the 'word of the cross' the 'subjective I' has become by God's gift an 'apocalyptic I' in community, ready for life on the pale blue dot and God's future.

10

The Apocalyptic Message

THE ANTHROPOCENE

MY SEVENTY-FIFTH BIRTHDAY WAS *celebrated in the middle of three highly signifi-*
cant events. Two days before, 30 of 35 scientists at the International Geological Congress
in Cape Town discussed a radical proposal. They eventually recommended that the
Anthropocene, be a new geological epoch, which began about 1950. If finally agreed,
it will succeed the 12,000 years of the Holocene on the condition that the expected evi-
dence is found in the rock strata. It is predicted that the Earth has been so profoundly
changed by radioactive fallout, soot, plastics, and even the bones of chickens, that these
signals of human presence will be found in layers of rocks marking this new boundary.
Martin Rees, the astronomer royal and former president of the Royal Society, said of this
announcement

> *The dawn of the Anthropocene was a significant moment. The darkest prognosis*
> *for the next millennium is that bio, cyber or environmental catastrophes could*
> *foreclose humanity's immense potential, leaving a depleted biosphere. . . . Hu-*
> *man societies could navigate these threats, achieve a sustainable future, and*
> *inaugurate eras of post-human evolution even more marvellous than what's led*
> *to us. The dawn of the Anthropocene epoch would then mark a one-off transfor-*
> *mation from a natural world to one where humans jumpstart the transition to*
> *electronic (and potentially immortal) entities, that transcend our limitations and*
> *eventually spread their influence far beyond the Earth."*[1]

Here was scientific prediction of the next millenium against the geologic background
of deep time confidently predicting a positive future if catastrophes can be averted.

Then on my birthday the weekly journal New Scientist *arrived with the head-*
line "WE HAVE FOUND AN EARTH-LIKE PLANET AROUND OUR NEAREST

---

1. Carrington, "Anthropocene Epoch," 30/8/2016.

STAR.—Should we go there?" An astronomy project called The Pale Red Dot had discovered the rocky planet Proxima b circling within the habitable zone around a small red dwarf star, though much more needs to be determined if it is to be shown comparable to the earth.[2] What took my breath away was the editorial entitled 'Hello Neighbour'. The writer describes this is as a new frontier, outlines the facts that are known, dismisses a probe as too soon, for more observations are required, but calls for a new look at what could be done if we end up seeing a habitable solar system nearby. The editor finishes,

> *Curiosity aside, spending big money on Proxima b may eventually become an existential requirement. In 5 billion years the sun will begin to expand, eventually engulfing Earth. But Proxima b's host Proxima Centauri will shine on for a trillion years, basking the planet in its warm inviting glow. If humans or our descendants are still around, we will need somewhere to move to. The discovery of Proxima b may be our first glimpse of an out-of-this- world future.[3]*

One day the inhabitants of the Pale Blue Dot may be on their way to the Pale Red Dot 4.25 light years away.

I was content to have had such a significant birthday, but then the day after, a newspaper report on the Eureka Science Awards in Australia highlighted the comments of one recipient. "There are no bigger questions than the ones being asked by astronomers. Where do we come from, where are we going and are we alone."[4] Of course these questions are the questions of everyone who lives in an Enlightenment world. And in this Enlightenment world there are no answers to the first two of these questions and as yet no one can be sure about the last.

AN APOCALYPTIC AGE

How do we proclaim the good news about Jesus Christ in a new humanly impacted geologic age, when proposals are tentatively suggested about the possibility of travelling to other planets in the solar system and even a planet in another star system? Such long journeys presume the human race on planet Earth can survive the crises of feeding an increased population, adapting to climate change, the use of new forms of technology, and biological modifications to the human mind and body. If there are to be resources for such a massive project there will also need to be a stable ongoing sustainable way of life that values each person socially and politically, and governments that respect the environment. Martin Rees had to temper his remarks about humanity transcending the Earth with "the darkest prognosis for the next millennium

2. Article, "Flares doom life", New Scientist, 19. "Big Flares doom life on nearby world." The pale red dot has been subject to 24 flares from Proxima Centauri in the two years since it was found, including the last a super flare, one of five such flares per year. Not much hope of life there. The search goes on.

3. Editorial, "Hello Neighbor," New Scientist, 5.

4. Strom, "Stargazer's Eureka moment." 9.

is that bio, cyber or environmental catastrophes could foreclose humanity's immense potential, leaving a depleted biosphere."

From the dawn of human civilization meaning and direction have been located in the experience or belief in being, gods or one God. In this last three hundred years of the scientific age the scientific and historical view of the world has seen no need for such explanations. Indeed it has been shown from a philosophical perspective that it is impossible for the human species to think and live beyond the framework of space and time in which life is found. As we have seen, the sphere of religious belief adapted to this new description of world and self by limiting belief and religious experience to the subjective self. This new view of the world has led to a vast historical and scientific project to explore and describe the world and the self as well. And what a story has unfolded. A universe in which space and time have multiplied almost beyond human comprehension, and the human self exhaustively described sociologically, psychologically and historically. We are what we know of our self and our universe.

With this has come the growing realization that it is the human species itself that is the greatest threat to the future of the planet. The spread of homo-sapiens to every part of the continents is bringing about the sixth catastrophic extinction of species from the face of the planet. The creation of nuclear weapons has unleashed the threat of global annihilation. The inventive uses of fossil fuels has initiated rapid climate change that endangers future generations, and the pollution of the land and seas with plastic and rubbish is and will have harmful and unintended consequences. Global travel now allows diseases rapidly to become pandemics. And communications makes obvious the limited access to resources of the poor compared to the rich, with potentially disastrous consequences for the social stability of nations and the global community.

In a profoundly new way each person is part of the problem. In the Anthropocene, the human race has become a geological factor. Anyone who drives a car, or switches on an air-conditioner, or uses fossil fuel produced electricity, is both culpable and complicit in what is happening. Now every issue can become an apocalyptic threat, for there are global consequences to most importantm atters. Just living is sufficient to exterminate and threaten other species, and further climate change. At the same time we have found our place in the universe has made us feel even more puny and insignificant. We find ourselves embedded in menacing actions that threaten the future of the pale blue dot. Is it any wonder, as Robert Jay Lifton points out that our response to the apocalyptic twins of nuclear and climate threats is often one of psychic numbing, continuing to live as if nothing was happening with a 'malignant normality', because of the scale of these events.[5]

Add to this reality that in this setting it is generally accepted there can be no answer to the big questions as to who we are and why we are here.

5. Lifton, *Climate Swerve*. For Lifton the attraction of the end of time apocalypse for the religious self is that it 'takes its place within the pervasive mythological theme of death and rebirth.'

It is not surprising that in this time there is a pervasive attraction to 'end of the world' apocalyptic scenarios in media, books, and especially among some religious groups. In an apocalyptic time, the fascination with end-time biblical scenarios continues to grow. "We can say that the Bible begins (Genesis) and ends (Revelation) with assaults on the human habitat. That is the way God destroys all sinners, along with their sins. Biblically speaking, the human habitat is the essential apocalyptic target. . . . Climate change furthers the temptation to replace history with eschatology."[6] "Both nuclear and climate threat, then, are readily joined with biblical apocalypse. The climate version, though slower to unfold finds more biblical models."[7]

The human race now lives more aware of the threat along with the promise of the future. In this cosmic and planetary setting the religious self is caught up in the creation in new ways that require a reassessment of our human experience in this setting predisposed to apocalyptic scenarios. What does salvation and conversion mean in the Anthropocene when our experience of sin and guilt is now so obviously planetary as well as personal?

> In an epoch we can now recognize as an era of planet-changing anthropogenic power, "claiming for Christ" for "a world-come-of-age," or answering the question, "Who is Jesus Christ, for us, today," will need to take some other course. It will confront human power and knowledge so as to find God in what we do know, rather that in what we don't, and in problems that are solved, rather than only when and where we are vexed. Moral accountability and confession of sins will address the sins of our strengths and powers, rather than our weaknesses only. If God and standing before God in the Anthropocene cannot be located at the heart *of* human power, accountability, accomplishment and failure, then God and morality are pushed to the far margins of what counts for the life of the world.[8]

So far the apocalyptic threats have resulted in a focus on finding solutions for cataclysmic long term threats to the planet, or led to a further withdrawal from participation through some sort of psychic numbing. The responses disclose the limitations are derived from the scientific divorce between self and world and point to the need for a more holistic approach that has to address self and world together before God. From the Christian perspective no tinkering at the edges will do. Radical thinking and experience is required.

---

6. Lifton, *Climate Swerve*, 42.

7. Lifton, *Climate Swerve*, 43.

8. Rasmussen, Larry, "Bonhoeffer and the Anthropocene," 941.

THE APOCALYPTIC MESSAGE

It is time for a re-assessment of the first century experience of apocalyptic message, the good news from God, and the good news of God. The rediscovery of the apocalyptic kingdom of God in the message of Jesus at the beginning of the twentieth century provides a startling new reality in the face an apocalyptic age. The good news is that in this world of end time or crisis scenarios of apocalyptic threats and horrors, the most decisive apocalypse is not waiting there in the future, but has already happened.

In this inter-related, interconnected, global and cosmic world of the Anthropocene, we dare to proclaim the apocalyptic kingdom of God is at hand, or as Jesus is more likely to have said, the kingdom of Heaven is at hand.[9] That presumes heaven and eternity are at least in some way and co-extensive with the finitude of creation. This is evident also for Paul. He experienced the risen Jesus Christ as an apocalypse as the heavens were torn open. In Athens Paul is reported to have said of God to the Greeks, "For in him we live and move and have our being."(Acts 17:28) To the church in Rome he speaks of a quite specific word of faith that is proclaimed—the faith that God's righteousness is given to a person wherever they are.

> But the righteousness that comes from faith says, "Do not say in your heart, 'Who will ascend to heaven?'" (that is to bring Christ down) "or 'Who will descend into the abyss?'" (that is to bring Christ up from the dead). But what does it say? "the word is near you , on your lips and in your heart" (that is the word of faith that we proclaim); because if you confess with your lips and believe in your heart that God raised him from the dead, you will be saved. (Rom 10:6–9)

Paul knew that wherever a person was located, if the Word of Christ was heard they could find themselves in faith. For him it was the profound experience of an apocalypse that was the event that led to his faith. Did this mean that to find faith everyone had to have an apocalypse of Jesus Christ? No, through this apocalypse he discovered the role of God in the creation of faith. The breakthrough was found in Abraham's critical moment in Gen 15:6, when faced with the dead end of his response to the call of God, he confronts God with his own lack of a future. God opens a dramatic new possibility for him by asking him to number the stars, for this would be the number of his descendants. Abraham believed, and God reckoned it to him as righteousness. Abraham's response led to God's action in declaring him righteous and as a result now in communion with God as described in chapter 2. Paul cites

---

9. The writers of the Gospel of Mark and Luke, wrote principally for a Gentile audience, and of course God is the generic term for the divine in the Roman Empire with its myriad of gods. In nearly every occasion, however, in the Gospel of Matthew Jesus speaks of the kingdom of Heaven. It is most unlikely that Jesus used the word God, and far more likely that he used the term, the kingdom of Heaven.

this breakthrough when he presents the critical moment when God acts in us, in and through the cross and resurrection of Jesus.

> Now the words, "it was reckoned to him (Abraham) were written not for his sake alone, but for ours also. It will be reckoned to us who believe in him (God) who raised Jesus our Lord from the dead, who was handed over to death for our trespasses and was raised for our justification. (Rom 4:22–25)

This is what faith is, the realization of what God was doing in the death and resurrection of Jesus. As we believe in this fact, then God declares us to be righteous. And this is, in the incongruity of grace, available for everyone, a free gift for all to receive.

> For there is no distinction since all have sinned and fall short of the glory of God; they are now justified by his (God) grace as a gift, through the redemption that is in Christ Jesus. (Rom 4:23,24)

Faith comes then in the hearing that in Christ Jesus, God has dealt with our trespasses, and discovering that God gives us righteousness and thereby brings us into relationship with him. This sequence tracks what happened to Paul in his apocalypse of Jesus Christ. As Paul is persecuting the disciples of Jesus, he is confronted by Jesus and finds he is persecuting the ascended Jesus. Instead of judgement he discovers Christ's gift to him, the call of grace. In this event Paul lived out in a particular way the words of Jesus about entering the kingdom of God. It is impossible for mortals to enter the kingdom of God, but it is possible for God, for God can bring us into the kingdom.(Mark 10:27). Whether the parable or Damascus Road, these are all expressions of what happened in the events culminating in the cross. As Jesus is betrayed and rejected by human trespass, God acts in his resurrection and ascension to bring into being a new creation of peace and grace.

Faith then is finding that it is God who opens the kingdom, brings us in, and holds us there. God makes this possible by God's act. "So faith comes from what is heard, and what is heard comes through the word of Christ"(Rom 10:17). No wonder Paul says "How beautiful are the feet of those who bring good news"(Rom 10:15b).

This God is present by the Holy Spirit everywhere in the creation, interpenetrating the distorted world of finitude, to bring an open heaven into the midst of a darkened world. The limited view we each hold as our right, the limited space and time which we inhabit, the limited life span we take for granted, the human race to which we belong, are all curved in upon themselves. And even as we can consider the requiem of our species, or a bold leap into an unknown future beyond our planet, it is apparent that nothing that we can do can destroy the horizon of death that encloses the universe and our own self. It is God's act in Jesus Christ, however, that has destroyed our trespasses, wiped away our sins, and given us a new horizon to live in, a new creation, the gift of living within the resources of heaven as God unfolds the promised future of the creation.

Faith here is not a personal matter of what I believe, but a discovery of the action of God in Jesus Christ, thereby being caught up in God's grace and purpose for the creation. It is present, spatially present in space and time, deep space and deep time. The old distorted sinful creation into which we are born is invaded by this new creation. "The earth has become their battleground. Assailed faith and the vanquishing of powers mark the place where Christian boasting paradoxically proclaims that peace and freedom are already secured in the midst of ongoing conflict."[10] And not only the Earth, but the universe is contested space as well and peace and freedom are already secured there as well.

Originally when the apocalyptic scenarios emerged it was in times of desperation for the Jewish people.

> The conviction of the apocalyptic end belonged with the experience of God's absence and remoteness. It was because one *believed* that God must vindicate the righteous, that one knew that transformation must come. But for Jesus, the apocalyptic message stemmed from the *awareness* of God's nearness. Hence the kingdom was at hand, and, indeed, at hand in such a way as to be already effectively operative in the moment.[11]

Jesus told a parable about the kingdom of heaven in which an enemy sowed weeds in a wheat field. The householder, after the weeds came up, was asked by the slaves whether they should be rooted out. He replied.

> No, for in gathering the weeds you would uproot the wheat along with them. Let both of them grow together until the harvest; and at harvest time I will tell the reaper, 'Collect the weeds first and bind them in bundles to be burned, but gather the wheat into my barn.' (Matt 13:29,30)

Jesus speaks from the perspective of the present kingdom of heaven. How long before the harvest? We live in a compromised world, but for the seeds of life, wherever they are, the perspective is for the long term rather than short-term. The harvest may well come much later than we have traditionally expected.

This gospel is good news and available anywhere where self-conscious creatures are within the universe. God is disclosed here, as Immanuel, God with us loving this creation subject to finitude and death.

Seven centuries ago within a different perspective of space and time Julian of Norwich (1342-1416) had a vision of the known world. She describes how God,

> [s]hewed me a little thing, the quantity of an hazel-nut, in the palm of my hand; and it was as round as a ball. I looked thereupon with eye of my understanding, and thought: What may this be? And it was answered generally thus: it is all that is made. I marvelled how it might last, for methought it

10. Käsemann, *Romans*, 134.

11. Cobb, *Structure of Existence*, 112.

might suddenly have fallen to naught for little[ness]. And I was answered in my understanding: It lasteth, and ever shall [last] for that God loveth it. And so All-thing hath the Being by the love of God.

In this Little Thing I saw three properties. The first is that God made it, the second is that God loveth it, the third, that God keepeth it.[12]

Today, even though the sheer scope of the universe takes one's breath away, I do not believe Julian of Norwich would be surprised. The God made known to her was always greater than human comprehension.

For wherever there is life, the kingdom of the Father, the Son and the Holy Spirit is there. Heaven as God's dimension includes what we think of as ordinary reality. Wright puts it this way,

> The point is that Jesus is presently in God's dimension, which is heaven; however, heaven is not a place in our space-time continuum, but a different sphere of reality that overlaps and interlocks with our sphere in numerous though mysterious ways. It is as though there were a great invisible curtain hanging across a room, disguising another space than can be integrated with our space; one day the curtain will be pulled back, the two spaces or spheres will be joined forever, and Jesus himself will be the central figure.[13]

In the apocalypse of Jesus Christ, however, the two spaces or spheres have already begun to be joined. Heaven has already invaded the present space-time dimension, Jesus is the central figure and our battle is here in the power of the Holy Spirit.

The primary reality for Jesus Christ is the present kingdom of God/Heaven given us in faith in which we are to live and pray. "But strive first for the Kingdom of God, and its righteousness, and all these things will be given to you as well."(Matt 6:33). The existence of such a parallel realm should not be difficult to make known in a computer age. The twenty-first century west is already dependent upon the internet, a parallel universe in cyberspace into which we plug computers and a myriad of devices. The kingdom of God/Heaven is an immanent parallel universe also, but is accessed in a radically different way. In the kingdom of God/Heaven, God takes the initiative. We gain access because God opens this reality to us, indeed that is what faith is, seeing access has been made possible by a gracious redeeming God rather than accessed by any performance, work, tricks or subterfuge of our own human effort.

The Holy Spirit points us to the life, death resurrection and ascension of the Son as the way God has opened the kingdom of God/Heaven to self-conscious life. Faith is for us this divine operational reality given to humanity that lets God re-configure us into God's purpose through his Son, bringing us into the cosmic redemption released in this divine dimension.

12. Julian of Norwich, *Revelations of Divine Love*, 10.
13. Wright, *Surprised by Scripture*, 96.

Jesus faced the consequences of the primal trespass that gave rise to finitude and death in the creation. The almost endless chain of trespasses that have followed constitute the world of the flesh, that is human nature, that includes our own. The very presence of the kingdom of God/Heaven in him drew to him the violence, anger, hatred and distrust that distorts this creation. As the embodiment of light in the darkness and half darkness of this world of finitude and death, he starkly disclosed the infection of sin that had to get rid of him. In the Lord's Prayer Jesus declared that we need to forgive the trespasses against us, for we are utterly dependent upon the ongoing forgiveness of God. God forgives the trespasses of a creation grown up to heaven without obliterating those who were involved in them, namely, all life. Here on the cross the devastation that trespass has brought is made plain. It is the disowning of the nature of God in the name of the freedom of finitude.

The apocalyptic cross is the decisive divine battlefield, where the eternal victory has been won; a new creation that finally will issue in the destruction of death and the opening of time to eternity. The cross of Christ is for Paul the key to the divine story. "For the message of the cross is foolishness to those who are perishing, but to us who are being saved it is the power of God."(1Cor 1:18)

THE CROSS—HISTORICAL PERSPECTIVE

Powerful currents in the New Testament have been to the fore in the way the cross has been experienced and understood. As a result of the historical perspective, alternative views of how to understand the cross now divide Christians.

Alan Kreider[14] documents how in the time of the early church, before Christianity became the religion of the Roman Empire, the focus was on preparing catechists to walk in the newness of life that followed from baptism into the Christian community. This involved not only changes in belief, but belonging and behavior as well.

> Do you not know that all of us who have been baptized into Christ Jesus were baptized into his death. Therefore we have been buried with him by baptism into death, so that, just as Christ was raised from the dead by the glory of the Father, so we too might walk in newness of life. (Rom 6:3–5).

Baptism was the key for believers, entering into the cross and the newness of resurrection life. There were two principal views of the cross, the ransom theory in which Jesus death was a ransom paid to the Devil to set people free from death, and the Christus Victor theory, in which Christ's death defeated the power of evil. As the church grew in influence and engaged in apologetics with the Greco Roman culture, the church affirmed Jesus was both divine and human. Baptism was baptism into his resurrected life. From late in the fourth century, when Christianity became the religion of the empire the importance of the baptismal catechetical process with its stress on

---

14. Kreider, *The Change of Conversion and the Origin of Christendom.*

belief, behavior and belonging lessened. Gradually preparation for baptism lessened, and it became a rite available for all, even the children of non-Christian parents, and in some cases of conquest, forced on people.

Within Christendom, a different form of question emerged for believers. What did Christ's death on the cross mean for their soul's salvation. At the beginning of the twelfth century Anselm (1033/4-1109) set out to answer this question in his search to understand faith. If baptism could be said to dominate the first millennium of the church's life, then Anselm's answer helped the cross become the focus of the church's life for the next millennium. "For what cause or necessity God became a human being, and by his own death, as we believe and affirm, restored life to the world, when he might have done this by means of some other being, angelic or human, or merely by his will."[15]

"In reasoning about the necessity of the cross, however, Anselm extracts the cross from the ministry of Jesus and interprets it against the background of his own feudal context."[16] Feudal Europe understood sin to be a violation of the divine honor as expressed in the divine order of society. Everyone who sins must be punished or offer some form of satisfaction to God. Unless this satisfaction is offered then evil will undermine God's control of society. The God who becomes human, sinless Jesus, voluntarily chooses to offer himself up to death for God's honor. This presentation touched a deep chord, and became a dominant motif in the life of the church. Yet it is strangely distant from the gospel narratives. Nothing of Jesus ministry of the kingdom is mentioned, and there is nothing about the resurrection. The satisfaction theory is a logical answer to the problem of human evil in the divine hierarchical society of Christendom.

It was not long before Abelard (1079-1142AD) presented the alternative 'moral influence' theory, in which Jesus by the example of his life, ministry and death brings a moral challenge to humanity. By the time of the Reformation with the focus on individual salvation, the two predominant theories of the atonement were that of the moral influence view (the subjective theory) and the penal substitution theory (the objective theory), a modification of Anselm. The penal substitution theory, now happens in a legal setting. Instead of sin being an insult to God's honor, sin incurs a debt to a holy, perfect and just God. Jesus, the sinless one, faces the wrath of God as the substitute for the sinner, and through his death on the cross averts the wrath of God.[17] After the Reformation, the Enlightenment focus on the individual has continued this polarization, with conservatives mostly opting for the penal substitution theory and liberals the moral influence theory.

---

15. Johnson, *Creation and the Cross*, 3.

16. Johnson, *Creation and the Cross*, 6.

17. While there are many views of the atonement, none has ever been incorporated in the formal confessions of faith or creeds. Attention here is focused on the views developed in the western church.

The feudal and Reformation view, while logically objective about God is not concerned with the creation itself. It is focused on addressing the problem of sin for individuals in human society. Likewise the subjective moral influence theory depends for its power on the example of Jesus. Theologically these are God and Me views which do not even consider the creation, and do not address the core good news of Jesus ministry, the apocalyptic kingdom of God/Heaven. They are no longer adequate to address the present time.

It is the rediscovery of the apocalyptic kingdom of God that leads to a view of the atonement closest to that of the early Christus Victor account. There Jesus defeats the power of evil in a ministry that culminates in the cross itself as the inauguration of a new creation. This is a total perspective that has God bringing the resources of heaven into a battle to bring in the kingdom of God/Heaven within time and space. From this perspective the incarnation of Jesus is a deep incarnation to redeem all of history. And not just the history of the pale blue dot, but that of the universe itself.

Since God has brought all life into being through him, the cross is God's way of opening all life to a new creation. This gift is made possible by the unmerited incongruous grace of God. Paul does not and will not fall back from the astounding declaration that when a person is in Christ, "there is a new creation in which everything old has passed away, see, everything has been made new."(2 Cor 5:17) To be in Christ is to know that God is the source and the center of everything, this cosmic justifying and reconciling God.

The cross when seen as God's act opens a person to discover the reality of what God is doing. That this apocalyptic divine action takes place in time and space is integral to the message. It cannot be limited to a private subjective experience and life after death. It is about living in the kingdom open to keeping in step with the Holy Spirit with the reality of the Holy Spirit's power and presence at work in our lives and society now and in the future. As with Buber's call for a duty of care in addressing this precious word God, so we are called to have a duty of care not only for God, but for this creation disclosed as God's creation in our midst. Care not only for the universe, and the Earth itself, but for future generations to come;

> Liberation from inter-generationally transmitted idolatory, from sustained patterns of deathly existence, and from the handing on of 'misery' from generation to generation that Philip Larkin[18] saw, comes about by the grace of God within enfleshed existence, in and through intergenerational communities themselves. Being loved 'before we are here' sustains the kind of hope that makes both costly action and confident expectation possible.[19]

Faith then is not my commitment, it is the acknowledging privately and publicly that God has made me his own, in the raising of Jesus Christ from the dead. Jesus is

---

18. Phillip Larkin (1922-1985), a popular British poet, whose poems are about loss and hypocrisy.
19. Muer, *Living for the Future*, 198.

Lord of a coming restored creation in which the power of death has been destroyed, and death itself will be destroyed so that life is celebrated with God for God's purposes. The sheer scope of this is extraordinary, injecting God back into the discussion about the future once more. It is the cosmos being metamorphosed from the processes of death to the life-restoring field of the Holy Spirit.

APOCALYPTIC SHOCKS

What does this mean for an Enlightenment age obsessed with a world of self and reason? Perhaps it is not surprising that the discovery of God presently at work in the world will come as an apocalyptic shock. For so long humanity has been at the center of our attention, and even religiously there has been a limiting of our God language to the 'humanity of God.' In this cosmic world it is time to rediscover the divinity of God. What is being shared here is not a direct continuity with ordinary history as it is normally presented, but what is at the heart of human history on this planet. God has spoken into the midst of history apocalyptically, to recreate the earth and more, in an en-globing universe of deep space and deep time.

What is becoming more apparent though is that our predisposition to a 'malignant normality' can and will give rise to future cataclysmic apocalyptic scenarios. The Anthropocene puts on notice the critical role of the human species in its long-term future, and the realization that no longer can the role of the self be divorced from the world. What every person does, matters, because it is integrally caught up with the wider habits of a society inter-relating with a specific limited world of resources and opportunities. The Anthropocene is a clear indication of the downstream effects of the Enlightenment and the need to rethink the human relationship to the world.

No longer can theology be limited to confessional statements from the perspective of the believer, but must come to terms with the public reality of the world. A public theology is required. No longer can Jesus be limited to being a personal Savior. Once more he is the cosmic Lord, and hence Lord of the planet. This Lord requires a living into a different understanding and experience of the God we profess. How tantalizing to propose once more that the narrative about God has a place, especially in terms of a radically different experience to the present apocalyptic threats that confront humanity. Instead of apocalyptic bad news for the future, apocalyptic good news providing new ways to conceive what the future could be.

One should not under-estimate the power of this present paradigm that puts the subjective self in the center, even as this view of the self is undermined by a cause and effect world. There has been a profound change in the understanding of the self in the generations born since World War II. The confidence of the "I" in who I am, the irreducible me, the given for my thought and experience, the center of who I am as a person, has been shaken.

Paschal's wager on the existence of God has the longer and longer odds of Barth's puny man hoping against hope in the face of death. The proud shaking of the fist of the rebel against society, the sense of me and the world, or more specifically me and God, is still there in many, but a more subdued and less certain awareness has emerged as more is discovered about the world in which we live. The more discovered about the brain as an electrochemical wonder, the more discovered about the DNA that humans share with the rest of the animal world, and the more discovered about the way we are socially formed in our attitudes and approach to life, then the more the uniqueness of each person recedes into the background. Each of us find ourselves explained within an historical narrative, an inter-related family, a social, cultural, geographical, national, international and planetary web. It is as though each person slowly disappears into the historical story, another unit in the ongoing march of society and the world. The significance of the self as an individual in the society evaporates. Instead of the sharp outline of a person slowly appearing on the wet photo paper, the process has reversed and the clear edged image slowly dissolves away into an Alzheimer like blankness. The cosmic world overwhelms the insignificant individual and intensifies their experience of non-being. Or in frustration and reaction the 'I' demands to be heard just because he or she is a person. This not uncommon reaction tries to deny the overwhelming scope of the world by an intensification of ego strength, as a way of shoring up the ego as number one.

It is perhaps to be expected that there is a more widespread background of depression and anxiety, especially in teenage years, that reflects a deep uncertainty in the twenty-first century. The less sure the person is about themselves, the more the self is pushed toward a search for ways to be recognized by others on the one hand or feels insignificant and less valued and less able to assert themselves on the other. An internet and media world rewards the flamboyant, the unusual, the celebrity. The dream of so many is to see their name up in lights on the world stage, however that happens, as creative genius or destructive rebel. For most that feeling of insignificance leads to a sense of worthlessness and withdrawal of themselves to their own inner world.

It helps to see why that pressure is either towards notoriety or nothingness. It is a result of a commonly accepted understanding of our world with everything in it defined by the laws of nature and the laws of social science. It is a result of the scientific, social and psychological world-view of our time imploding upon the "I".

This happens against the background of apocalyptic events that are seen as threatening the form of society as we know it. Ironically the more the self disengages from the world or is numbed by apocalyptic threats the more likely it is that apocalyptic scenarios are likely to multiply.

The events of 9/11 were an apocalyptic shock to the world, heralding a different sort of twenty first century to follow. Since then militant terrorists with a background in Islam have vowed to destroy the world of the west and the education system that makes it possible. First Al Qaeda, and then ISIS, fill the headlines. In Nigeria, Boko

Haram (which means Western education is forbidden) is such a movement whose proper name is "People committed to the Prophet's teachings for Propagation and Jihad". This group gives absolute priority to a particular interpretation of the Prophet's teaching above any other religion or educational system. To most in the west it is preposterous that a religious group could call in question the scientific historical worldview of the Enlightenment. Francis Fukuyama, had earlier made the claim that the triumph of such societies indicated the end of socio cultural history.[20]

The language of the apocalyptic has gradually been taking hold in the West partly as a consequence of media and films. The world wide threats to end the world as we know it, from a pandemic, a nuclear war, an asteroid, or more gradually through climate change and environmental degradation have slowly intensified in the public imagination. For the young, books and films herald the ending of the world through dystopian views of the future. Films such as hunger games, or about the parallel universe of werewolves, seem to indicate a profound disenchantment with the world as they see it. In television advertising, marketers strive for effect, looking for that extra edge. So often this tactic fosters more extreme scenarios that build on threat and fear, and since many of these products are international products, they add to the general supra-national impact of such attitudes. It is salutary how often the back cover summary of the plots of so many action novels are all about the few who save the world from cataclysmic doom at the very last minute. In the most rationally educated generation of all time, it is extraordinary how the longing for excitement and searching for the unusual, push beyond the boundaries of the reasonable. The move to the extremes provides fertile ground for those who call worlds, civilisations and systems into question.

As the Anthropocene indicates the apocalyptic is in part a result of the move from national perspectives to a planetary perspective. The Earth with its history, discoveries and peoples is now being conceived of as one entity, one pale blue dot. The benefits of this for individuals and groups depend upon where one lives. In the wealthier nations medical advances help most live longer with a better quality of life, offer greater options for a healthy and comfortable lifestyle, have the world beamed into home communication centres, live networked through the internet and phone, expect better travel conditions for commuting to work and popular events, as well as enjoying the possibility of travelling to see the world. The whole context gives time to search for one's own significance in the whole process through family, work, career, fame, spirituality or whatever the person considers important or vital. In the poorer nations most of these possibilities are still dreams not yet available for the overwhelming majority of most people.

One consequence of a networked, interconnected world is that any event that threatens its existence can quickly escalate into an apocalypse. The fact is that the greater the inter-relatedness of society, the greater the impact of that which can

20. Fukuyama, The End of History.

imperil life as we know it. The relatively sudden emergence of digital means of communication in the Facebook and the Twitterati world has created a world of post-fact and post-truth where the danger is that what I or my group or ideology decide is true, has to be true. And, as we have seen in the headlines, terrorist groups have arisen that claim to be the bringers of the apocalypse that bring down the existing order, in this case in the name of religion. But anything that threatens the pale blue dot has the potential to be an apocalyptic event. The chaos depicted in the Revelations account is one more scenario to add to the those that come whenever planetary order is thrown into confusion by disease, war, global warming, nuclear confrontation, rogue satellites, space rocks or whatever unexpected menace imperils the planet. How many times has New York been destroyed in the movies!

The power of the apocalyptic grows with images often threatening the cataclysmic and violent destruction of the planet itself, its surface or society, with the ominous foreboding and fear mongering that goes with this in the public media.

THE IMPOSSIBLE POSSIBILITY

Late in the twentieth century, the focus on the self has been further undermined by postmodern philosophy critiquing the modern view of the self as the center. There has been a noticeable retreat from the rationalism of the modern Enlightenment in the face of philosophical questions as to the role of power and the view of the self in human understanding and experience. The very basis of the Enlightenment separation of self and world has been critiqued and shown to be part of a dualism that has legitimized and protected those in power as well as maintaining the centrality of the individual as the fundamental reference point for thought and action.

Postmodern philosophers, such as Derrida, have asserted that the power structures of various world-views that claim to be legitimated by meta-stories of the world above and beyond history, are actually creations of these same power structures to maintain and legitimate their own authority. He shows such "stories" are projections or explanations that have been created and have no factual basis. He asserts the documents positing such meta-accounts have to be read in the terms of their own arguments. A careful re-reading within the grammar of the text shows that there are either inherent contradictions present or that there are other possibilities and ambiguities that must be taken into account. This method of reading or "deconstructing" the text has become one of the hallmarks of this approach and is now used to critique philosophy, art, literature, economics, architecture, music and indeed any field of thought.

The postmodern view of the world exposes the binary or dual nature of the sources of power in the past. In the feudal view the transcendent was contrasted with the immanent. The Enlightenment called this structure in question. Instead reality was divided into self and world, mind and body in a rational creation. No longer could the human race be saved through the divine structures of the world. Kant claimed that the autonomy of reason would emancipate the human race from the darkness of immature reason over time. From the postmodern perspective the meta-narrative of one binary view of the world was succeeded by another.

The postmodern world focuses on the reality of the "other" beyond this self/world dichotomy. Emmanuel Levinas asked the fundamental question as to the status of the 'other' that confronts both the self and the world who are not part of my text, or our grammar, or our story. In the approach of other cultures, the emancipation of women as the "other", the integrity of the other person beyond my "I" calls out to be explored. Levinas inverts the normal understanding of philosophy. Instead of philosophy understood as the "love of wisdom" where the object is an object to be known, philosophy is understood to be the "wisdom of love" in which the other confronts the self with difference and an infinite moral demand. The radical difference is that "this relationship overflows comprehension."[21] The experience of love is more vital than the knowing of the other.

One of the critiques of postmodernism is that questioning in this way relativises all truth and authority if we have to accept the 'other' perspective alongside our own about the way reality is. Yet even to understand the other, there is a given structure required for communication to be possible between people—that of a sufficiently accepted language, logic, and understanding held in common. Various postmodern writers reflect varying degrees of that accepted framework required for the word to be a means of communication, and as such open the possibility that there is truth implicit in the frameworks. Yet even here there is much discussion about the very understanding of perception, representation, and the role of the individual.

This approach has resulted in a far greater awareness of the role of language in theology, such as the role of metaphor in language about God, and has led to the exploring of models of God that are derived from the images and the thought patterns influenced by social and psychological sources that are implicit in faith. If, as it is claimed, history provides the only framework for life, then language about God either has to claim it is true in itself or be explained in terms of history. Prior to the historical era it was the power of the Platonic elevation of God as transcendent that underlay so much language. The transcendent God of the pure, the eternal and perfect or ideal forms, was used to contrast with the immanence of God at work in a creation that is impure, temporal, sinful and distorted, in a way that transcendence and immanence seem to parallel the biblical heaven and earth. In this understanding transcendence is seen to be the goal for that which is immanent. In a similar way the route for believers to escape the limitations of life, was to escape from the temporal Earth to the eternal heaven.

The apocalyptic however is focused on God's disclosure within history. There is no need to either explain away God in the historical process or invoke a transcendent world over and against this world. Instead the apocalyptic events show the God who

21. Peperzak et al, *Levinas*, 6.

is Immanuel, bringing heaven to earth with the purpose of creating a new heaven and a new earth. Indeed these apocalyptic events disclose God's providential care for the creation from beginning to end.

The extraordinary confession of Paul in identifying the apocalypse as happening in the midst of history in the cross and resurrection, affirmed that the salvation, redemption and healing of the creation occurs within the historical process as the foretaste of the new heaven and the new earth at the end. It brings with it a particular three stage metanarrative, first the big picture of the creation of the heavens and the earth, then second the sin, distortion, alienation in the universe which affects the heavens, issuing in the cross, resurrection and ascension as God's act within history to bring thirdly, the promise of a new heaven and a new earth to come. It is a metanarrative that does not need to borrow from a Platonic or an Enlightenment framework, for it has its own legitimating healing power.

The postmodern world, however, is much more than deconstruction and metanarratives of power. There have been profound intimations of the limits imposed by our world-views. The focus is much more on the perspective and value of the individual and especially the "other", and a far greater awareness that the history that defines us is actually the creation of rational thought. This great achievement of human science and thought turns out to be fraught with ambiguity. History also becomes an ineluctable cocoon of birth and death that enshrouds and encloses us all. Kant's view of rationality has created a prison bounded by time and space. Prior to the twenty-first century, the logic and content of perspectives that were not in tune with the rational meta-narrative of modernity were suppressed, rejected, hidden, kept out of sight.

It is worth taking seriously the "otherness" of life, beyond the permitted view of what can be thought. Slowly there is a growing realization of the importance of first respecting the otherness of another person from another culture, who needs to be listened to and taken seriously, instead of pre-judging from our own familiar perspectives. This attitude to the other is vital in responding to indigenous cultures and cultures that have suffered from long colonial eras of suppression on all the continents. In various ways they embody other perspectives that differ from the metanarrative of history that was brought to their shores. It is not surprising that a hermeneutics of suspicion has developed among those who are evaluating the past story of their lives as a means of challenging the status quo, for the experience of women, the perspective of post colonial societies, and the claims of indigenous cultures. Together this is an area "that is beaconing welcoming signals to scholars, teachers and laypeople from disciplines that are non traditional, and who may not feel that they (want to) belong among mainline critics."[22]

The "other" can also be an apocalyptic irruption into the life of those in the west in surprising ways. As time and space close in around us, elements of language push beyond the limits imposed upon the Pale Blue Dot. For this is what postmodern

22. Havea, "Scriptures from Oceania," 11.

deconstruction is about, 'a thinking of the limit of language and of knowledge'[23] Jennings has shown in his "Reading Derrida / Thinking of Paul" that a postmodern analysis sheds light on aspects of Paul's thought that an Enlightenment world has not seen, indeed has obscured. Derrida in his reflections on justice describes the relationship between Law and laws as necessary attempts to address the issue of Justice. For even when the Law is reflected upon and put into practice as the Law, this Law gives rise to injustice, for the laws of the land are both affirming of order but restrictive and harsh and not always just. For Derrida it is the 'impossible possibility' that it is possible to be just, that stands behind all attempts at justice in the action of Law and the implementation of laws in our society. In a similar extension of this thought to gift, forgiveness, hospitality and love, he shows that in any attempt to make a gift, or forgive, show hospitality or love, the other inevitably falls back into a human economy of exchange that is less than what is possible or hoped for or hinted at in these categories. Indeed all these (justice, gift, forgiveness, hospitality and love) are impossible possibilities that lie at the heart of what we desire to happen but despite our best attempts get caught within the concrete limitations of our acts.

> The question of justice and the impossible possibility that justice comes not through the refinement of the law but by way of a gift that awakens us to a messianic promise and vocation is one that concerns us all, I think, whether or not we call ourselves Christians or deconstructionists or some other term. It concerns us quite simply as human beings who share the doom and the promise, if there is one, of this planet, and who have the obligation to think unflinchingly about our common lot, even if leads us to embrace what may seem foolishness to those who are deemed knowledgeable and weakness to those who think they have and exercise power.[24]

Jenning points out that Paul builds upon Abraham, the one who believed, hoping against hope in God's impossible promise to an old man and his barren ninety-year old wife, that he would become the father of many nations. It was this faith that in the grace of God was reckoned to him as righteousness or justice, and is also reckoned to those who believe in the resurrected crucified Christ

> This will mean, as we shall see, that gift or grace is by no means exhausted by a reference to the past (as forgiveness), but rather it has the structure of promise. This, of course, was true for Paul as well, because the model of grace or gift had been the promise given to Abraham concerning the future, a future of land and progeny, and this promise has expanded, according to Paul, to include the resurrection of the dead and liberation of creation.[25]

---

23. Jennings, *Reading Derrida / Thinking Paul*, 175.

24. Jennings, *Reading Derrida / Thinking Paul*, 176.

25. Jennings, *Reading Derrida / Thinking Paul*, 133.

And again, "The promise promises what is actually impossible. And this promise of (impossible) progeny is formally like creation out of nonbeing or resurrection from the dead."[26] Paul in Christ Jesus sees that the promise has been "widened almost beyond recognition" such that, "Instead of progeny, we hear of the resurrection of (all) the dead, and instead of land, we hear of a new creation."[27]

Paul is not concerned with

> "the blessedness of something like forgiveness, but rather the blessedness of the inclusion in the promise made to Abraham, an inclusion made real through sharing in the same sort of reliance on the word of promise itself. . . . Because Paul is most concerned with precisely that gift or grace, he is not preoccupied with forgiveness. Here, as elsewhere . . . he is pressing ahead, in response to the promise that makes justice possible beyond the law."[28]

The discussion of righteousness or justice, for the word can be translated in either way, illumines the language of the impossible possibility. As John Caputo writes,

> Jesus displays the stunning power of powerlessness—of non-violence, non-resistance, forgiveness, mercy, compassion, generosity. The divinity that shows through Jesus consists not in a demonstration of might but a complete reversal of our expectations culminating in the most stunning reversal of all. It is the centerpiece of this madness, the one that makes as little sense as possible from the point of view of worldly commonsense, the most divine madness of all: love your enemies. The key to the kingdom is to love those who do not love you, who hate you, and whom you, by worldly standards should hate. That is exactly the madness that a deconstructive analysis of love would predict. Loving the lovable is entirely possible, but loving the unlovable, those who are impossible to love, that is when the kingdom reigns.[29]

Here Jennings and Caputo here use the language of Derrida to show how the post-modern era opens up new possibilities at the heart of the language concerning the life of Christ. What is even more extraordinary is the event of the resurrection itself in which the impossible possibility of God's act, opens up an impossible possibility for the human race and its place in the universe on this Pale Blue Dot.

It is the impossible possibility that this justice (or righteousness) has actually happened in one event, the life, the death and resurrection of Jesus Christ, that Paul received as an apocalypse of Jesus Christ. Here is God bringing the impossible possibility of the end of the creation within the history of the creation. What Derrida and Jennings show is that the Enlightenment metanarrative can only read this apocalypse as a rational event that is described in terms of a "revelation" of what is to come, and

---

26. Jennings, *Reading Derrida / Thinking Paul*, 167.

27. Jennings, *Reading Derrida / Thinking Paul*, 167.

28. Jennings, *Reading Derrida / Thinking Paul*, 141.

29. Caputo, *Would Jesus Deconstruct*, 84.

not as the impossible possibility of the apocalypse already begun. In seeing this as a revelation, however, the apocalypse has already been collapsed from an impossible possibility into a form of belief and conviction within the individual. That is, it has been brought into the "rational market" of intellectual and experiential exchange of belief and conviction.

The focus then moves on to the response the individual has to make rather than glorying in the impossible possibility that we have been given. An apocalypse keeps us in the realm of experiencing a new God-given gift, forgiveness, hospitality, and love, in the creation, rather than the limited Enlightenment restriction of this to individual intellectual belief and emotional experience. For most, for whom the apocalypse of Jesus Christ in and through his resurrection and ascension, does not fit into this modern world, the response to the apocalypse is either that of unbelief (it could not have happened), or the holding on to what can be derived from the story mostly in terms of categories of goodness and love (values for the self and society).

THE APOCALYPTIC INVASION

In the Pauline apocalypse, the resurrection of the crucified Messiah was "the invasion of God's power into a world occupied and preoccupied with death",[30] that shook his world to its foundations and let him see a 'new creation' that had dealt with death on the cross. Then all of life is seen as non-life in relation to what God's power has released in this scandalous event. It is Brian Blount, in his sermon, Preaching Apocalypse, who dramatically declares;

> Sin and Death are poised for the most stunning of victories. Unless God can unleash an even greater, opposing power. On the violent and unforgiving battlefield upon which they meet, the evil that is the spawn of Sin and Death—given ruthless expression in the likes of Hitler's Final Solution, Eastern European and African Ethnic Cleansing, American chattel slavery and segregation, South African Apartheid, the economic and political imperialism of the Roman Pax Romana, in examples too legion to number—cannot be absolved, its ruin expiated. One does not atone for Sin and Death; one engages and obliterates them. Resurrection is God's silver bullet. When Jesus of Nazareth is raised from the depths of Hades, it is as though God, manipulating the dirt of the earth like the muzzle of a gun, shot him straight through the heart of an enemy otherwise impervious to every strategic and tactical maneuver against it. Then, and in the future to come, God triggers resurrection. It is resurrection that puts the enemy down. Resurrection's truth, resurrection's

---

30. Long, Thomas. A summary statement about Brian Blount's book "Invasion of the Dead" on the back page.

promise, and resurrection's historical reality must therefore be the primary proclamation of the apocalyptic.[31]

The apocalyptic cross, resurrection and ascension is the way God has invaded this world to reclaim it, and remake it. The kingdom of God/Heaven fills out the understanding of God in terms of an alternative to the Emporer's domain, and fills out the understanding of God in terms of Jewish history and hope. Beker sees to the heart of the issue for this apocalyptic language—"the gospel proclaims the new state of affairs that God has initiated in Christ, one that concerns the nations and the creation."[32] So often it is dismissed as symbolic inner language of the soul that has no place in the 'real world'. It is, however, the issues of the real world that the apocalyptic is seeking to address. "For Paul there is no dualism between the human soul and the external world. He places the human being in the context of the world and its power structures."[33]

As we have seen from Galatians the apocalyptic reality of the cross and resurrection led Paul into a 'radically new view of the cosmos' that does not separate self and world as separate realities, but brings life in a new creation lived before God in God's world and what God is unfolding. His was a new view of the cosmos itself made known in and through the cross of Christ. It is not a re-socialising of the self in a new context, as though the self was able to choose to be different for the sake of God. That would only continue the dualism between the human self and the external world. It is the realization that through one time and place, God is bringing about the death of an old and enslaving cosmos, and the birth of a new life giving creation or cosmos.

Paul's apocalyptic description of this invasive Spirit sees this as a hostile war that is underway. He is clear that there is no negotiation between the flesh and the Spirit. The weapons of the Spirit are in a different category to those of the flesh. Instead of divisions between people leading to violence against others and against oneself, this is the reconciling word of God bringing peace and love into the midst of the world. Martyn heightens this fact so that there is no mistaking the world shaking and creating Spirit at work in and through the Spirit communities. This discovery of what God is about in the world is a new reality rather than a new emphasis on the decisions we are to make. It is the discovery of God's 'what is' in the midst of the world, and not a call to a new ethic, a new 'ought'.

> "What is" proves therefore to be the result of that invasive action of God, the war in which God is calling into existence his new creation, the church, with a view toward ultimately delivering the whole of humanity—indeed the whole of the cosmos (Gal 3:22; Rom 8:21)—from the grip of the powers of the

---

31. Blount, *Preaching Resurrection*, 1.

32. Beker, *Paul's Apocalyptic Gospel*, 8.

33. Bosch, *Transforming Mission*, 169.

present evil age, the curse of the Law, Sin, the elements of the old cosmos, and not least the Flesh.[34]

This Spirit reality is a different way for individuals and communities to live, with the law of Christ as the gift of God that the Spirit enables those justified by faith to keep in obedience and freedom. Calvin described this as the 'third use of the law'. The first use of the law is to convict of sin, the second use of the law to restrain the ungodly, and the third use of the law is the liberty and obedience given by the grace of God. Martyn here notes that the law is divided into the Abrahamic, 'love your neighbor as yourself', and the Mosaic law used by Sin to curse Christ. It is the Holy Spirit who enables the people of God to live in the Abrahamic 'love your neighbor as yourself' through the law of Christ.

THE APOCALYPTIC KINGDOM

It is not, as it is often said, that the kingdom of God/Heaven in Christ is "yet" and "not yet" as though there is a waiting in an intermediate phase between the cross and the 'end'. No, the kingdom of God/heaven already is, and is coming. The apocalypse has begun, the kingdom is already here, the new creation begun, heaven is open to the earth, and earth to the heavens, because of the ascension of Jesus Christ.

> "The stress of Paul's argument rests, therefore, not on the eschatological ten-
> sion between the now and the not yet but on the present tension which exists
> in the divide between pleasing God and pleasing humanity."[35]

Paul in the new creation begun is exhorting the Corinthians to live "not on the basis of human perceptions but according to the shape of Christ's faithfulness."[36]

He who is Son of Man and Son of God rules with the Father while the Spirit is at work preparing for the coming kingdom in its finality. In fact the Spirit makes clear how Christ rules the kingdom of God through the cross, which even now is in the process of destroying rulers and authorities and powers that are alien to the life of God's reality as Jesus displayed it. The God who is light, in whom there is no darkness at all, blazing forth in the Son, forgives and heals all who come to him, all who look upon him, who believe what they hear about him. "And just as Moses lifted up the serpent in the wilderness, so must the Son of Man be lifted up, that whoever believes in him may have eternal life. For God thus loved the world that he gave his only begotten Son, that whoever believes on him shall not perish but have eternal life." (John 3:14–16) For the cross and resurrection and ascension is the ultimate apocalypse of Jesus Christ as the Son of God. It is the public reality, not a private reality. The kingdom of God/

---

34. Martyn, *Galatians*, 536.

35. Aernie, "Life of the Believer," 450.

36. Aernie, "Life of the Believer," 454.

Heaven and of his Christ is underway. Today is a day on the way to a promised end of reconciliation and renewal because of the Lamb slain from the foundation of the world, realized in the events of the apocalypse.

It is because the gospels are witnessing to an apocalyptic event that we have the language to describe what is happening. The language of self and world, subjective feelings and objective cause and effect, limit what can be said about Jesus. The result has been an emphasis on the human Jesus. In this Enlightenment framework it is virtually impossible to name and experience the divine Jesus that the accounts declare. Does that mean the gospels have to be taken at face value, and reason and the need to interpret texts that are two thousand years old, not seen as an important factor? Not at all. It does mean the reality of God disclosed in these accounts should not be ruled out by methodological presumptions in an Enlightenment perspective that limits how to describe or know the presence of God, both then and now. The apocalyptic message confronts us with the kingdom of God/Heaven once more.

11

InChrist

IN THE LORD

I did not look forward to this particular week. I write out by long hand three verses of the Bible a day, six days of the week. It forces me to slow down, and see more that is there, but it takes a long time to work through a book. It has been such a blessing. But when a long genealogy, or list of names appears the heart sinks a little, as it did as I started on the greetings Paul lists in Romans 16. Four days later I was dutifully writing out v12, "Greet those workers in the Lord, Tryphaena and Tryphosa. Greet the beloved Persis, who has worked hard in the Lord." I sat back and thought, I would not write worked hard "in" the Lord, but worked hard "for" the Lord. Then a picture came to mind. It is like the difference between rowing a boat and steering a yacht across a river. Clearly in the first, the one who does the rowing gets the boat across the river, but in the second, the work done in steering lets the power of the wind (Spirit) in the sails get the yacht across. The first can say, "I did it," but the second, "I was involved but it was done in the wind (Spirit)."

I checked back through the preceding verses to find that Paul is utterly consistent in speaking of sharing with others "in Christ Jesus", "in Christ", and "in the Lord". In this profound way, Paul puts into daily practical language the apocalyptic gospel—the message of the letter. This use of the preposition "in" describes what it means to live in the righteousness of God, in Christ, in the power of the Holy Spirit. What we do is done in the Lord who has gifted to us this world of grace in which we stand in and through the apocalypse of his Son.

In this letter to the church in Rome, the first city of a million people, the multicultural focal city of the Empire, the readers hear and receive an ecumenical cross-cultural gospel in which it is the Lord who brings all people together in the Kingdom. This inclusive gospel is clearly expressed here in Romans 16 with the use of the preposition "in".

Paul greets young and old, female and male, Jew and Greek, Asian and Romans all working together "inChrist".

"The capsule dropped down and down past the glare of the lights in the huge exit tube of the space station and out into the blackness below. I sighed with relief to be out in the black velvet backdrop of endless space again."[1] Of course there is no up or down, only the cosmos in all directions, but the spaceship nearby was "beneath" the space station. There "inChrist" I was ready for the next trip in this star system. Anthropocene Earth was but a small blue marble in the blackness, a long, long way away.

INCHRIST

Epistles and gospels in the New Testament are written to particular people or for particular communities, hence their names, e.g., John, Philippians, Romans, James. The gospel of Luke, is unique in that, as outlined previously, the book is written as an orderly account for a Greek dignitary named, Theophilus, (lover of God) to hear and experience. Luke carefully frames the message for anyone in the Roman Empire, setting the account within the world of the empire.[2] The gospel begins in the Temple in Jerusalem (by then destroyed by Rome), the birth of John the Baptist and Jesus, an imperial census, the structure of Roman rule in Judea, and the baptism of Jesus, with a genealogy traced back through 'the son of Adam to the son of God' before starting with Jesus ministry. Then, in the book of Acts, written to this same Theophilus, the apostles in the power of the Holy Spirit are sent from Jerusalem to the ends of the Earth, and ends with Paul in Rome waiting to appear before the Emperor Nero.

Now more than 2,000 years later who is the equivalent to Theophilus for whom we should be writing about Jesus Christ? At a time when the discoveries of science have let us see that Earth is but a pale blue dot in the universe, I believe it is time to frame the message for one, Cosmophilus, a lover of the cosmos, God's created order.

There 'inChrist' I was ready for the next trip in the star system. Anthropocene Earth was but a small blue marble in the blackness, a long, long way away.

For over two hundred years the gospel has been addressed to individuals calling them to make a decision to choose Jesus Christ as the Lord of their life, to commit their lives to him and join the church. The present emphasis upon discipleship has been a result of the Enlightenment focus on the historical life of Jesus. The first five books of the New Testament, namely Matthew, Mark, Luke, John, and Acts reinforce this emphasis on discipleship because they present the life of Jesus in a sort of historical way.

---

1. Drayton, Cosmos, 161. A dream in late 1994.

2. Some scholars question whether Theophilus was an actual person or a representative God-lover, God-fearer.

The language of discipleship is the normal way that following Jesus is understood, for it brings together the focus on personal decision and the teaching and life of Jesus. Each believer is called to make the decisions involved in worshiping, witnessing and serving others. The Christian life then consists of doing what Jesus did and commanded, loving our neighbor and loving God in a world in which Jesus is absent. At its best, discipleship is following Jesus, trying to do what Jesus did, and seeking forgiveness before the cross. Attention is focused on what the believer has to do, and that leads to the stress on working for the Lord.

In a twentyfirst century world of cause and effect it is difficult for many believers to believe in a bodily resurrection, and ascension. It is easier to comprehend the event of the cross and Jesus' crucifixion. Discipleship is limited to following Jesus from his birth to his death, from Christmas to Good Friday. Attention is focused on the cross and the need for forgiveness. What happens after the Friday seems symbolic and metaphorical as in some measure the resurrection and ascension are, disclosing Heaven in the midst of history. The result is a drastic limitation of the language and experience of faith to 'Me and my discipleship', and an inability to comprehend the apocalyptic reality of a risen Christ who is at the right hand of God.

What might the implications be for us, if the way we see the world makes it almost impossible to hear the clear message of the writers of the epistles, that we live our life inChrist and not for Christ![3] Here Paul's framing of life inChrist is starkly at odds with the denominational paradigm, in which the world-view is focused on the autonomy of the individual in which human events are the result of human decision. Readers of the New Testament, however, rarely realize that most of the letters of the New Testament were written before the four gospels and the book of Acts, and the letters do not use the word disciple. In these earlier texts, believers worship and serve the risen, ascended Lord.

It comes as a surprise for most believers to hear that the attention of the early church is fixed on the ascended Lord rather than the life of Jesus. Jesus Christ is Lord, that is the Son of God. He is at the right hand of God. The events post-Easter are not 'symbolic' events but the way that the risen Lord rules over all. "Grace to you and peace from God our Father and the Lord Jesus Christ," Paul writes in his greetings to the churches. Or, to the church in Ephesus, "Blessed be the God and Father of our Lord Jesus Christ, who has blessed us in Christ with every spiritual blessing in the heavenly places." The ascension opened heaven to them in and through Jesus, the Son of God, not as some future place, but as the reality they experience in the present.

There could be no church without the ascension! The epistles are declaring that through the cross, resurrection and ascension, God opens the way for us to receive the Holy Spirit and live alive to God and God's purposes for the creation. The declaration

---

3. For emphasis inChrist is written as one word to draw attention to this way of describing our relationship with Christ.

that we are inChrist involves the disclosure of heavenly realities. In a profound sense these realities are more to be trusted than the rest of the church's experience.

One of the most common terms used in the early Gentile church for being a Christian is that of being inChrist. This Jesus Christ is Lord, all authority in heaven and earth has been given to him; He is the king of the kingdom of God/Heaven; He is seated at the right hand of the Father; He has poured out the Holy Spirit; He is the cosmic Christ of Ephesians and Colossians, and the world and all that is, is found in him, including those who bear his name.

A COSMIC PERSPECTIVE

In the recent past such language was often seen as a human projection. There was a confidence that the universe we live in is vast, but can be described in terms of fundamental laws. There has been a profound change in the understanding of the universe in the last century, however, that questions the past certainty of the Newtonian billiard ball universe. The nature of the universe is now grounded in the weirdness of quantum physics including the fact that atoms and electrons are probabilities, and points a universe apart can exist in entanglement. Millions of universes are postulated as being in parallel to this universe. And in somewhat of an embarrassment for physics, at least 85% of the universe is made up of dark energy and dark matter that cannot yet be described. In terms of ordinary experience the invisibility of the radio world, TV transmissions and mobile telephones are now taken for granted, while the recent emergence of a parallel invisible world in the internet highlights how the invisible is accepted as part of life. Nearly every household is connected to a power grid that provides the source of energy for appliances, lights, communication and air-conditioning that at the flick of a switch is available. Movies have majored on special effects that create magic, powerful marvel characters, and imaginative worlds for children and adults, far beyond the ordinary powers of everyday life.

There is now somewhat more of an openness to seeing beyond what can be seen. As the denominational era comes to an end, it is an important time to hear again the early church's description of what followed on from the cross in Christ's resurrection and ascension. It is time to consider what the epistles of the New Testament share with us about Christ and what it means to be inChrist against the background of the history and the cosmic context of the pale blue dot.

Once more problem which immediately hoves into view is the 'scandal of particularity'. How might the salvific purposes of God be released in and through a particular person living in a particular time and a particular place. The distinctive claims of the Christian faith had found itself increasingly at odds with the Enlightenment emphasis on truth that was conceived in terms of that which is universal, rather than that which is particular. In a post-colonial, post-modern context, the scandal of particularity deepened. How might the salvific claim associated with Christ be reconciled with the claims of other faiths, especially those like Islam and Buddhism that gather around the humanity of their own particular person? Now, in a cosmic setting as the Earth finds itself as one planet bearing self-conscious intelligent life in deep space and deep time, the scandal of particularity further intensifies. The scandal finds itself inextricably bound up with the Incarnation, Jesus of Nazareth, Immanuel God with us, that is played out on one obscure planet in an ever-expanding pluriverse. How can this focus on one person be even considered? The finality of Christ has always depended upon the discovery that in Him the kingdom of God/Heaven has been present within earth bound history. The affirmation that He is Immanuel, God with us, makes this one 'dot' in time infinitely important in the context of an almost infinite universe. The realization of the early church that He is the cosmic Christ can only be so if He is also known as the Word of God, the Son of God through whom the creation came into being. The finality of Christ is disclosed by the Father in the role in which He is given in creation and the completion of that creation in its redemption. It remains a scandal of particularity—that the church's faith has always defended. This scandal is part of the good news that does not originate within the human sphere, but is given as the gospel of God. The church can only bear witness to these originating events.

The church began and continues as a result of the ascension. Through this event, the God-person releases into finitude the new creation brought into being by the cross and resurrection. That is why the ascension is so important, giving us a new location inChrist, over and against the pre-occupation of working for the Lord in the denominational paradigm. The ascension begins on Earth the saving, healing, restoring of the creation in a new creation that was put into place as a result of Jesus announcing of the kingdom of God/Heaven, the apocalypse of Christ.

A NEW REALITY

While the language of this account goes beyond what can be directly seen and described, the writers are sharing a reality that is being experienced. They create a new language to describe the intersection of the divine eternal Incarnation into the finitude of human events in space and time. Paul puts this relationship directly but it is a relationship presumed by the Lord's Prayer, and Jesus' teaching:

> For now we see in a mirror, dimly, but then we will see face to face. Now I know only in part; then I will know fully, even as I have been fully known. And now faith, hope and faith abide, these three; and the greatest of these is love.

"To say I know in part," is knowledge, even if it is not yet possible to know fully what will be. But Paul does know that he has been fully known inChrist! From the experiential side, the heavenly realm that is at work in their midst can not be fully described, but from the heavenly side this world is completely open to the Lord he serves.

The extraordinary reality of what it means to be inChrist is that wherever a person is in space and time, they can find themselves inChrist. It does not matter whether Cosmophilus is in orbit around a planet, or on leave in a space station, (s)he can be inChrist because it is the ascended Christ who is immediately available by faith through the word of Christ.

Cosmophilus's cosmic perspective obviously goes far beyond the world in which the New Testament was written. Even in this first century world the apocalypse of Jesus Christ causes a remarkable reframing of the words and expectation of the early church in who Jesus Christ is, and what God is doing. In a number of different ways the significance of Jesus Christ is amplified and emphasized by reassessing previous events in Israel's history.

Firstly, Paul dramatically changes this declaration by Moses that the commandment of God is present with the people to be fulfilled—"[the] word is very near to you; it is in your mouth and in your heart for you to observe."(Deut 30:14) The word of command, becomes instead the word of faith. "The word is near you, on your lips and in your heart." (that is the word of faith that we proclaim) (Rom 10:8)

Secondly, at Jesus birth, the expectation that the Messiah was to come, is fulfilled. Luke cites Simeon, a righteous and devout man, took the child Jesus in his arms in the temple and praised God saying, "my eyes have seen your salvation which you have prepared in the presence of all peoples, a light for revelation (Greek apocalypse) to the Gentile and for glory to your people Israel."(Lk 2:30-32). This light of salvation in him is there for all peoples.

Thirdly, the promise to the patriarch Abraham that in him all the families of the Earth will be blessed, is linked directly with Jesus Christ—he is the seed or offspring of Abraham. "Now the promises were made to Abraham and to his offspring; it does not say, 'and to offsprings,' as of many; but it says, 'And to your offspring,' that is, to one person, who is Christ."(Gal 3:16) Those who are justified by faith, as Abraham was, receive the promises of God through Jesus Christ.

Fourthly, both Matthew and Luke trace Jesus' genealogy in a way that underlines his significance. In Matthew he is "Jesus the Messiah, the son of David, the son of Abraham."(Matthew 1:1) In Luke he is the "son (as was thought) of Joseph son of . . . son of Adam, son of God."

After the ascension, the early church finds that inChrist their lives and hearts and minds are opened to realize who was present with them.. This is the apocalypse, the divine disclosure that happened in their midst, fulfilling all that Israel had ever hoped for, refashioning and realizing the promises of God to the nation. InChrist Jews, Gentiles, all families of the Earth are blessed. Through the ascension they saw that in him, all that God had promised was available for all.

But it is the gospel of John that takes the almost unimaginable step and rewrites the creation stories of Genesis. Jesus is named the Word of God, and is written into the account of creation with God. The first words of the Hebrew Bible, "In the beginning when God created the heavens and the earth" become, "In the beginning was the Word!"

> In the beginning was the Word, and the Word was with God, and the Word was God. He was in the beginning with God. All things came into being through him, and without him not one thing came into being. (John 1:1)

He is now the means by which the cosmos, the universe that they knew, came into being! Jesus, the Word of God is the agent of creation itself. No wonder the early church came to see Jesus as the cosmic Christ, echoing these words at the beginning of John's Gospel in Colossians, and elsewhere in Ephesians. In this account the creation is not defined as it was in Genesis, as the creation of the heavens and the Earth. Here, attention is focussed on the creating one rather than the extent of creation. "All things came into being through him."

Since that time the scale and scope of the universe has extended almost beyond knowing. In this account the 'all things' is open to include even the cosmos as it now is. This cosmos is still the cosmos that 'God with us', Jesus, the son brought into being. And, in his ascension, we are taken up into him. No wonder Cosmophilus can know wherever (s)he is that (s)he is inChrist; for she is not only in his universe, she has found herself in him, by his actions in the apocalypse of Jesus Christ.

The early church had discovered so much more of the Good News after Jesus had walked the roads of Israel. There is no need to get to heaven, deal with death, go somewhere beyond the sea, go anywhere. The kingdom of God/Heaven, the kingdom of righteousness comes to where we are. No searching is required, no going anywhere. Wherever we are, we are justified by faith, reckoned righteous, because we know that God has raised Jesus from the dead. The ascended cosmic Jesus Christ, unseen beyond time and space, yet bearing the cosmos and the life he created, is open to the whole cosmos. His gift to us is peace with God and access to the grace of God in which we stand, or sit and run. It is the experiencing of the gift of a new identity as a child of God in the kingdom of God/Heaven, with an integration of heart and voice, mind and speech, witnessing to the apocalyptic reality of God at work in the here and now for God's eschatological future. This reality is not 'ideas' or 'thinking'; it is living in the presence of a new creation that comes to us and incorporates the person in this new creation.

After the resurrection, and ascension, the early church found how the Holy Spirit, given to the church by Jesus Christ, gave them the power to bear witness to what had happened in and through Him. The ascension led to a new perspective on the events they had experienced. Critics of the faith may make much of how the gospels and the letters of the New Testament were written by the early church. The inference is that much that was written was a creation of the early church to give meaning to the death of Jesus Christ. That interpretation certainly makes sense to an historian who must evaluate these events from within an immanent view of the universe. For an historian there are no historical categories to describe the way an event such as an apocalypse, an irruption from beyond, can occur. The consequence is that rarely in our time is the importance of the church's experience of the risen ascended Lord given credence.

THE RISEN ASCENDED CHRIST

Those who claim to have experienced the apocalypse of Jesus Christ not only had to find a language to describe what happened, they also had to find answers to vital questions that arise when death itself is breached, and appearances occur. This scandalous event has to be substantiated in some way, and its significance evaluated in terms of the basis of such a declaration. What do the documents of the early church disclose?

After the Easter weekend, it is the risen Christ who takes the initiative in appearing to the disciples.

> If his forty day presence on earth is, for Him, an ascent to the Father, then in its other aspect it represents a new establishment of His connection with the earth, with this world. What we have in mind here is the completion of His prophetic ministry, insofar as he opened His disciples "understanding, that they might understand the Scriptures"(Luke 24:45), "speaking of things pertaining to the kingdom of God"(Acts 1:3). He also manifested Himself to His disciples in His resurrected body, thus attesting to the fact that He had preserved His connection with the world, a connection that included the ability to be touched and partake of food.[4]

The empty tomb has given rise to a resurrected spiritual body. This new spatiality enabled connection with the "ordinary spatiality" of the disciples, although with some different properties, as evidenced by "appearing with a body" behind locked doors retaining his pierced feet and hands.

Then comes his farewell. The four gospels record this event in varying ways. Mark and Luke (both in the gospel and Acts) have his departure from them in the event of the ascension. After his blessing he is lifted up and a cloud takes him from sight. In Matthew, Jesus declares to his disciples that "all authority in heaven and on earth has been given to me," details missionary instructions including discipling nations, baptizing and "teaching them to obey everything that I commanded you," and then "I am with you always, even to the end of the age"(Matt 28:18,20b). John's gospel has no direct narrative about the ascension, although Christ says in various ways in speaking with the disciples, "Nevertheless I tell you the truth: it is to your advantage that I go away, for if I do not go away, the Advocate will not come to you"(John 16:7).

For a long time in the west, the ascension of Jesus has been the Cinderella doctrine, a footnote to the cross and the resurrection. The empty tomb and 'appearances' of a spiritual body were dismissed as an awkward interval that had to be explained

4. Bulgakov, *The Lamb of God*, 386.

away. These events did not fit into the world-view of first century Palestine, nor do they fit into the world-view of the twenty-first century. The present focus on the individual and reluctance to accept the possibility of divine intervention, limits the understanding of what happened, at the best, to visions of the Lord. The empty tomb and a spiritual body appearing to the disciples are a step too far for most. One of the results of this world-view is that in the church, discipleship tends to end at the cross, focusing on the forgiveness of sins. But discipleship does not stop at the cross. Forgiveness of sins opens the door for us to live in the presence of the resurrected and ascended Lord.

The ascension is not only the dramatic next stage in the Incarnation of Jesus Christ, it opens the disciples to be able to live inChrist. Indeed, for most of the epistles in the New Testament this is the description of what it means to be Christian.

The intervening 40 days after the cross and resurrection are a bridge between his continuing abiding in the world and his presence in heaven. Christ is both there and here, both beyond the world as we know it and in the world as it now is. His spiritual body implies a spiritual cosmos, not somewhere "up there" but the kingdom of God/ Heaven coterminous with the world as we know it. This kingdom to which Jesus bore witness in his ministry is a holistic view of the cosmos in which self and world are held together before God in one reality. No longer can finitude hold the resurrected Jesus, for the Son returns to be with the Father. Yet the disconnection entailed only underlines the deeper connection that remains. We see dimly and in part from within finitude, yet from heaven we are fully known by the Son.

> Because of the ascension, elemental notions such as "world," "heaven," "time," and "place" need to be recast. If Christ has ascended, in his humanity into heaven, then humanity and the world in which it is inextricably linked has entered a new mode of existence. It is not as though Christ has left the world. He now relates to it in a new way—our humanity has not been discarded in the ascended Christ. In this sense, heaven, in Christian terms, is not a vague celestial location but communion with God in Christ in a creation transformed.[5]

How important it is that this Christian view of heaven is carefully understood and experienced. To make this clear the whole story of the Incarnation needs to be told, from the birth of a child through to the finality of this child being disclosed as the ascended son of God in communion with the Father. For the early church the apostles participation in the unfolding of what they now knew to be his incarnation, became ever more important, for both his person and the message were key. They were witnesses to the scandal of particularity, a human life, Jesus of Nazareth that disclosed how Immanuel, God with us, had lived with them with his message of the kingdom of God/Heaven.

In the Hebrew scriptures the kingdom of God is understood to be God's reign over heaven and earth. "The Lord has established his throne in the heavens and his

---

5. Kelly, *The Ascension of Christ*, 157.

kingdom rules over all."(Ps 103:19) Jesus' declaration of the kingdom of God/Heaven being at hand signalled that this reign, this dimension of communion with God, could be known as a reality in human life. He was the Son, keeping His own identity on the periphery of the central message of the presence of the apocalyptic kingdom of God/Heaven. At the same time the apocalyptic kingdom was evident wherever He was healing and teaching. He taught the disciples that their task was to proclaim this kingdom. Jesus hidden openness to Heaven's eternal dimension continued through his aw(e)ful humiliation as the crucified Son of Man. It was not until His resurrection the glorious presence of the risen Son of God was disclosed. Then the apocalyptic kingdom of God/Heaven was let loose into human history. The curtain in the temple was torn from top to bottom. In human terms God was no longer unapproachable, limited to the holy of holies. InChrist the eternal immanent Trinitarian God was disclosed, manifest in time and space, at work in the economy of salvation. Then "all authority in heaven and on earth has been given to me." (Matt 28:18) The one who ascends to the Father is known. The finality of Christ is inextricably involved in the scandal of particularity of one life at one time and one place. The Son of God or the Word of God through whom all life came into being, had to assume this life, so that it could be saved, healed, and restored to the divine image.

This divine act is why the apocalyptic world needs to be affirmed and the dualistic world of immanence and transcendence repudiated. Finitude/Heaven, is parallel to temporal/eternal, and not matter/spirit, or immanent/transcendent as is generally understood. For finitude is the creation alienated from the communion of Heaven. This communion is intrinsic to its potential to be restored, healed or saved. The lived kingdom of God/Heaven is the communion with God that is possible when the creation is transformed from within, healed, completed, made whole. It is to experience the gift of a new identity as a child of God in the kingdom of God/Heaven. It is to experience a growing integration of heart and voice, mind and speech, witnessing to the apocalyptic reality of God at work in the here and now of space and time. It is not about thinking certain thoughts, believing certain propositions, or saying certain words, but living in a new creation that comes to us and incorporates the person into their immediate environment more fully than ever before.

This turn to a new creation deserves some critical scrutiny. So often talk of a new creation has been confined to words of assurance following the prayer of confession. It has been seen as something individual and personal. Or, the new creation has sometimes been the preserve of those who look forward to the end of the world, which they wish to hasten, so that a new creation might arrive.

If this kingdom of God/Heaven, the new creation, is assessed from an immanent historical perspective, then as is commonly said, the kingdom is yet and not yet. What the early church discovered is that the apocalypse had already happened within history in Jesus Christ. The apocalypse of Jesus Christ becomes the divine reference point for all that came before and what comes after. Now the eternal resources of a new creation are available within the creation. Either a creature lives in the new creation that is found inChrist, or does not, as this new creation is brought to bear on the whole creation, the final light shining in every penultimate corner of the cosmos. Instead of yet and not yet, it is that the kingdom of God/Heaven has come and is available in the midst of the finitude of sin and death.

It is surprising how often Jesus links heaven and Earth in his teaching and praying. Jesus during his ministry prays, "I thank you Father, Lord of heaven and earth,"(Matt 11: 25) teaches, "whatever you bind on earth will be bound in heaven,"(Matt 18:18) and "where two or three of you are gathered in my name, I am there among you." (Matt 18:20) After the ascension the early church had learnt to live in this relationship between heaven and earth, our lives inChrist, known to him, but known to us only in part, living within finitude, knowing death has been defeated.

"What no eye has seen, or ear heard, nor the human heart conceived, what God has prepared for those who love him—these things God has revealed (Greek: *apocalypsed*) to us through the Spirit; for the Spirit searches everything, even the depths of God." (1 Cor:9,10)

As a result of the ascension, the whole creation, a new creation, is in communion with God inChrist. Jesus the God-man is no longer ministering to a particular time and a particular location, he is now able to minister to the creation and all its life. With the ensuring giving of the Holy Spirit, the economic Trinity further discloses how the divine life is now active in this transformed creation. There is now a process to unfold which will reach its final end point when Christ hands over the kingdom to God the Father. "When all things are subjected to him, then the Son himself will also be subjected to the one who put all things in subjection under him, so that God may be all in all."(1 Cor 15:28)

The time after the ascension provided the disciples of Jesus with a profound new arena for the life of discipleship. They had moved from walking with the Lord from Galilee to Golgotha, to waiting for his appearances to them after his resurrection, to living before the ascended Lord in the power of the Holy Spirit. Life was now to be lived inChrist open to the kingdom of God/Heaven, the new creation, in and through our Lord Jesus Christ. As His Incarnation extended further through resurrection and ascension, the totality of the world is now found within the redemptive reality of Christ's life.

> The continuation and expansion of the humanity of the ascended Christ makes clear that there is no God without the world; and there is no world apart from God. To use a spatial metaphor, the world, owned, claimed, finalized in Christ, is now forever "in God."[6]

Jesus, however, is no longer directly with them, constrained by the world of space and time to the here and now of his followers in Israel in the time of the second

---

6. Kelly, *The Ascension of Christ*, 152.

temple. Christ now inhabits a new space, the boundless field of the creative word. He is now able to relate to those of every time and place, sometimes to appear, but mostly withdrawn from view.

> It is this Jesus who is ascended and glorified, who is now universally accessible, whose person, words, and deeds—all that he did and suffered—are rendered contemporary to the faithful of every age and place.[7]

Amazingly Jesus proclamation about the kingdom of God/Heaven being at hand at the beginning of his ministry, is still true when he is the ascended Christ in the kingdom of God/Heaven. To anyone inChrist the kingdom of God/Heaven remains at hand, though now there is the richness of the presence of the kingdom of God/Heaven known through his ministry, cross, resurrection and ascension. Still so simple a child can receive this kingdom, but now in this new creation inclusive of the cosmos as well.

Cosmophilus is not alone in the capsule as (s)he manoeuvres toward the mother ship nearby; or anybody else, anywhere, inChrist. Only a horizon enlarged by faith in the resurrection and ascension of Jesus can appreciate that Jesus that Christ embodies "a new creation: everything old has passed away" (2 Cor 5:17).[8]

FAITH IS A NOUN

It is the ascension that opens the arena of faith, the possibility of a faith that is available to all. That possibility of faith, however, has been distorted by the Enlightenment focus on the self in such a way that makes it difficult to know what is faith. Generally in conversation, including Christian conversation, the word faith is used as a verb. In a time focused on the individual, faith is used widely in the sense of faith in myself, my abilities, my effort, my potential. Faith then becomes something I do, or we do. In Christian conversation my faith is equated with verbs such as my trust, my conviction, my believing, and used interchangeably with these phrases. There are at least four Christian life books available to be purchased on the internet entitled *Faith is a Verb*.

It was a surprise to find the word faith in the New Testament is not a verb. It is a noun, whether in the Pauline epistles "You are justified by faith" or on the lips of Jesus, "Your faith has made you well." Even when it is known that faith is a noun, it is not uncommon that it is described as a nounal verb, or a noun that acts as a verb. What is the reason for this insistent interpretative pressure? The desire for verbal doing language flows from Christians seeing themselves as the source of action in being disciples of Jesus, trying to do what Jesus commands. Many Christians at one stage wore WWJD (What Would Jesus Do) bracelets. What is not realized is that in doing so, believers become pre-ascension believers, short-circuiting the full incarnation of Jesus. They make their decision for Jesus, and commit their life to him to do what

---

7. Kelly, *The Ascension of Christ*, 61.

8. Kelly, *The Ascension of Christ*, 151.

Jesus wants them to do as forgiven people. They are focused on their 'faith' as they understand it. It is this 'doing' mistranslation of faith that helps mask and confuse the vital New Testament witness to the ascended Lord. The danger of a 'working for the Lord faith', is that this attitude thought to be faith becomes dependent upon what the individual understands to be the way of the Lord. This view of faith can easily reduce faith to religious morality, or Christian human values, rather than finding the good news of being inChrist.

It is important to answer the first question, what is a noun, before the second question as to what this means for the word faith. A noun is a word that functions as the name of some specific thing or set of things and is usually the subject or object in a sentence. If faith then is a noun, faith then functions as a name, not as an action, though faith may well lead to action. Since faith names something, faith involves a subject naming an object. Faith is in the acknowledging or recognizing of the other. Faith then depends upon the naming of the 'other' who is present and in so doing opens the possibility of a relationship with the other. Faith names the man on the highwire, inviting us to let him push us across Niagara Falls in a wheelbarrow, as trustworthy. The modern subjective view of belief finds this puzzling. Trust is taken to be the same as faith, and then likened to other subjective actions like conviction or belief. In this invitation to step into the wheelbarrow it is trust not faith that is involved. Do I trust this person to wheel me across, rather than is this person's word trustworthy. The issue of objective trustworthiness, has been changed into a matter of personal trust. Of course it is vital to know before one gets into the wheelbarrow, that this person has wheeled at least ten or twenty people across before, but getting into the wheelbarrow is the trust that follows the faith.

Faith in the unseen God heightens the importance of this distinction. The book of Hebrews states, "Without faith it is impossible to please God, for whoever would approach him must believe that he exists and that he rewards those who seek him."(Heb 11:6) The ability to name the God who is present is involved in 'believing that he exists and rewards.' It is this recognition of this 'other' that enables God to be approached. When God is known, then "Faith is the assurance of things hoped for, the conviction of things not seen."(Heb 11:1)

It is possible to name Jesus in many ways; teacher, leader, mystic, forgiver, healer, sage. This naming is what humanity does as an expression of our intelligence and awareness that enables us to share a word in society, knowing that it is commonly understood. In the case of these names for Jesus they do not name who he is, but indicate what he did in ministry in terms generally understood in society.[9] Jesus and

---

9. The ability to name things, people, and even God, underlies human freedom and the possibility of human society. The naming of objects and things is to a large extent an agreed exercise within any language; there is a chair, or a rock, or a waterfall. The naming of creatures and people is more involved and more complex because of the inherent freedom of creatures and people. Who a person is, is not fully expressed in a Christian name and surname, but is dependent upon their decisions and life history; she is a scientist, he is an artist). The ability to name is most critical in dealing with that which is

Paul, however, identify faith as the key to discovering the presence of God disclosed in our midst. Faith sees the apocalyptic reality of the kingdom of God/Heaven.

It is being able to name the God who is present. When Jesus says, 'Your faith has made you whole,' his attention is on the person who is asking for healing. He acknowledges that the person has recognized that the healing God of the kingdom of God is present. Because God is present, or the Messiah is present, or the kingdom of God/Heaven is present, then healing can occur. The subject has recognized who can bring this about and has come to his presence. For the woman with an issue of blood, "She had heard about Jesus, and came up behind him in the crowd and touched his cloak, for she said, 'If I but touch his clothes I will be well'"(Mk 5:27,28). Blind Bartimaeus, "When he heard that it was Jesus of Nazareth, began to shout out and say, 'Jesus, Son of David, have mercy on me'"(Mk 10:47). The centurion names Jesus as one under the authority of God, who can command by a word, for healing to occur. "Only speak the word and let my servant be healed."(Lk 7:7). In each of these situations those searching for healing took the initiative to name and recognize who was present—Jesus, the bearer of the kingdom, the one who could change their life.

The dynamics of this naming are even clearer as Paul outlines how a person is justified by faith. "The righteousness of faith is reckoned to those who believe in him (God) who raised Jesus our Lord from the dead, who was handed over to death for our transgressions and raised for our justification. Therefore since we are justified by faith we have peace with God through our Lord Jesus Christ through whom we have obtained this grace in which we stand." (Rom 4:24—5:2a)

Faith is being able to name God as the God who handed Jesus our Lord over to death and raised him from the dead to become our ascended Lord. Faith in the name gives authority to this God who we can believe. It is the named God who reckons us as righteous: we are justified by this faith, knowing what God has done and finding ourselves in the gift of a new creation that is open to us in our ascended Lord. As this God is named as God, it is like inserting the right key into a lock, and hearing the tumblers fall into place, giving us access to an open heaven. When a person is able to name this God, it is to know God has already found them in and through the death, resurrection and ascension of his Son, and placed us in Him.

The consequences follow: we then experience that we are at peace with God by God's act, and have obtained access to God's grace, which opens to us this new creation in which we are found inChrist. It has to be underlined that this faith in a new creation is not only experienced in our heart and mind as it was for Calvin[10], or as

---

not visible such as character and love, or world-views, gods, and spirits. It is in these relationships that the realm of faith becomes especially important. This aspect of faith is clear in the classic description of faith in Hebrews. "By faith we understand that the worlds were prepared by the word of God, so that what is seen was made from things that are not visible."(Heb 11:3)

10. Calvin, *Institutes*, 551. Calvin defined faith as a *firm and certain knowledge of God's benevolence toward us, founded upon the truth of the freely given promise in Christ, both revealed to our minds and sealed upon our hearts through the Holy Spirit.* The revealed truth is named in our minds, and the Holy

grace within our self as it was for Tillich[11], it is to stand in the time and space of a new creation, an open heaven, inChrist. It is because it is an apocalyptic event that we find this reality disclosed and new life flows.

It is the power of God for those who are being saved, healed, restored, for the old creation is taken up into this crucified Christ to bring into being the new creation. As we read, Paul confronts the church in Galatia. "It was before your eyes that Jesus Christ was publicly exhibited as crucified! . . . Does God supply you with the Spirit and work miracles among you by your doing the works of the law, or by your believing what you heard?"(Gal3:1,5) It is the discovery of the light of truth, goodness and grace. It is discovering how the fruit of the Holy Spirit may then grow in our lives, as we let the Spirit guide us into love, joy, peace, patience, kindness, generosity, faithfulness, gentleness and self-control.

No wonder the gospel writers found in the suffering servant a remarkable description of the great transaction that occurred in the cross. This servant enables us to name what happened then, as also happened in Christ Jesus.

> Surely he has borne our infirmities and carried our diseases:
>
> yet we accounted him stricken, struck down by God, and afflicted.
>
> But he was wounded for our transgressions, crushed for our iniquities;
>
> upon him was the punishment that made us whole, and by his bruises we are healed.
>
> All we like sheep have gone astray; we have all turned to our own way,
>
> and the Lord has laid on him the iniquity of us all. (Isaiah 53:4–6)

Faith is able to name that this has happened in and through the ascended Christ. It is not what we do, but what God has objectively done so that we might subjectively discover who we are inChrist and how we are now in a creation in which self and world are held before God.

LIVING IN THE KINGDOM OF GOD/HEAVEN

The recovery of Jesus message of the kingdom of God opens the way for believers to discover this faith of the early church as post-ascension believers. We live as they did, inChrist, in the kingdom of Christ, the kingdom of heaven, which is at hand! Jesus' teaching about entering the kingdom of God/Heaven is now experienced in a new way. We are born from above and can see the kingdom of God/Heaven; we are in the kingdom as a child of the Lord, and we realize that only Christ can bring us into this

---

Spirit confirms this to our hearts.

11. Tillich, "You are Accepted,"163. "Sometimes at that moment a wave of light breaks into our darkness, and it is as though a voice is saying: 'You are accepted. *You are accepted,* accepted by that which is greater than you, and the name of which you do not know. . . . *Simply accept the fact that you are accepted!*' If that happens to us we experience grace." For Tillich grace, the healing of separation from God, may happen as we subjectively accept that we are accepted.

kingdom. The kingdom is the treasure in a field, the leaven in the flour, the mustard seed, growing with the tares, this kingdom at work while we sleep.

How surprising to most Christians it is that the kingdom of God/Heaven not only impinges upon time and space, but also in some measure to be inChrist, is to be operating already from a heavenly dimension. Not only is heaven present in the midst of life, "our citizenship (or commonwealth) is in heaven, and it is from there we are expecting a Savior, the Lord Jesus Christ."(Phil 3:20) The early church "blessed the God and Father of our Lord Jesus, who has blessed us in Christ with every spiritual blessing in the heavenly places."(Eph 1:3) Since the apocalypse has happened, live in this new creation. "So if you have been raised with Christ, seek the things that are above, where Christ is, seated at the right hand of God. Set your mind on the things that are above, not on things of earth, for you have died and your life is hidden with Christ."(Col 3:1,2). Life inChrist is lived from the perspective of the above things of heaven, the new creation. "From now on, therefore, we regard no one from a human point of view, even though we once knew Christ from a human point of view, we know him no longer in that way. So if anyone is in Christ, there is a new creation, everything old has passed away, see everything has become new." (2Cor 5:16-18) Life is lived in the flesh, the human dimension that is finitude, alive to God in and through Christ. This is the context for the Galatians assertion of Paul. "Through the law I died to the law so that I might live to God. I have been crucified with Christ; and it is no longer I who, but it is Christ who lives in me. And the life I now live in the flesh, I live by faith in the Son of God who love me and gave himself for me"(Gal 2:19,20). Heaven is the seedbed of love, life and grace. While still living in finitude, death has lost its controlling power. This faith, which names the God who has been disclosed in the apocalypse of Christ, is caught up at the heart of all human action.

What we name matters. It is the nature of faith that it respects the fundamental importance of the freedom of creatures. Faith enables creatures to name their world, describe their world and create their world, individually, socially and as a species. Faith not only opens us to God, it also undergirds all human imagination and human creation. If God appeared directly in Heavenly power and glory, the freedom of creatures would be obliterated. God so acknowledges the importance of freedom to self-conscious life that God's action is hidden in the life of Jesus of Nazareth. The presence of the kingdom of God/Heaven is announced in such a way that the response both acknowledges freedom of all who hear, while at the same time, invites the discovery of the apocalypse of Jesus Christ, and so name what God has made available. God depends upon the creatures initiative of faith in discerning and naming the divine initiative underway in the creature's world. The apocalyptic disclosure both confronts and invites a free response. In a remarkable way faith both preserves the role of human freedom while confronting the fundamental issues of finitude and death. The nature of faith requires that God be hidden until these issues are faced and found as acts of God in the midst of life.

It was noted earlier that there are parallels between living with the digital world of the internet, and living in the kingdom of God/Heaven. Both require access; both are invisible. Whereas the internet is accessed by device and the necessary passwords, it is the kingdom of God/Heaven that makes the connection through our naming this God. The internet draws users into an invisible worldwide web, while life inChrist opens the person to a new creation of grace in the power of the Holy Spirit, the invisible kingdom of God/Heaven at work in the world. This awareness of God's presence happens in the midst of life, in all the antagonism and hurt that washes through and around people. The apostle Paul knew that this experience of grace is no retreat from the world but an intensification of its issues before God. As he states,

> But thanks be to God, who in Christ always leads us in triumphal procession, and through us spreads in every place the fragrance that comes from knowing him. For we are the aroma of Christ to God among those who are being saved, and among those who are perishing; to the one a fragrance from death to death, to the other a fragrance from life to life. Who is sufficient for these things? For we are not peddlers of God's word like so many; but in Christ we speak as persons of sincerity, as persons sent from God and standing in his presence.(2 Cor 2:14–17)

This life is a life open to God, where we are for God the fragrance of Christ, and pleasing in his sight, and what we do is done as ambassadors for Christ, standing in the presence of God. This passage is usually interpreted in a mystical framework, "to be in Christ is not merely to be within the sphere of his influence, but is to be mystically and really in Him."[12] The apocalyptic perspective reverses the location for being inChrist. Instead of being mystically and really in the ascended Lord, we are persons inChrist sent from God and standing in God's presence in the midst of life. It is the aroma of Christ, the declaration and living out of the kingdom of God/Heaven that is so powerful and dangerous to do in God's presence.

No wonder there is such an emphasis on baptism in the early church, for it is baptism into being alive to God—and the Eucharist is the heavenly food that we eat as we participate in the dimension of the kingdom of heaven.

This view of the ascension helps recast the categories of a tired dualist immanent transcendent framework locating heaven up there at the end of life, to the holistic realization of the present kingdom of heaven open to us in Christ and resourcing the fulfilling of God's purposes in our midst.

It is not surprising that the early church soon knew Christ had to be described in cosmic terms for the ascension relates the risen Son to the whole creation, not just Palestine in the first century. Such a discovery opens the kingdom of heaven to a Cosmophilus as well as Theophilus.

12. Hughes, Corinthians, 78.

THE COSMIC CHRIST

It is only when the church experiences the apocalypse of Jesus Christ that it will be able to escape from the subjective religious world with mystical overtones in which it now finds itself. It is called to rediscover what it is to live before the cosmic Christ who is Lord of the Universe bringing God's purposes for the cosmos to pass in and through the apocalypse that has already happened within history. The "apocalyptic Christ" breaks open the subjective trap within which the contemporary emphasis on revelation has found itself in the pews and frees the church to participate in the mission of God.

It is so easy to forget the radical revolutionary power of the apocalypse in the first century after Jesus Christ. The letter to Colossians composed under the name of Paul shows the way the Christ holds all together.

> **He is the image of the invisible God, the firstborn of all creation; for in him all things in heaven and earth were created, things visible and invisible, whether thrones or dominions or rulers or powers—all things have been created through him and for him. He himself is before all things, and in him all things hold together. He is the head of the body, the church; he is the beginning, the firstborn from the dead, so that he might come to have first place in everything. For in him all the fullness of God was pleased to dwell, and through him God was pleased to reconcile to himself all things, whether on earth or in heaven, by making peace through the blood of his cross.**
>
> And you who were once estranged and hostile in mind, doing evil deeds, he has now reconciled in his fleshly body through death, so as to present you holy and blameless and irreproachable before him—provided you continue securely established and steadfast in the faith, without shifting from the hope promised in the gospel that you heard, which has been proclaimed to every creature under heaven. I, Paul, became a servant of this gospel. (Col 1:11–23)

The words placed in bold make it clear that this description of Jesus Christ could only be written because the apocalypse of Jesus Christ had already occurred within history and not at the end of history as had been expected. The cosmic implications quickly became clear. Phrase after phrase is a devastating realization of who it was that was crucified, resurrected and ascended to God. In this passage considered to be an early hymn, Jesus of Nazareth, Israel's Messiah, is seen in terms of the universe as the Cosmic Christ. James Dunn concludes that

> [t]he vision is vast. The claim is mind-blowing. It says much for the faith of these first Christians that they should see in Christ's death and resurrection quite literally the key to resolving the disharmonies of nature and the inhumanities of humankind, that the character of God's creation and God's concern for the universe in its fullest expression could be so caught and

encapsulated for them in the cross of Christ. In some ways still more striking is the implied vision of the church as the focus and means toward this cosmic reconciliation—the community in which that reconciliation has already taken place (or begun to take place) and whose responsibility it is to live out as well as proclaim its secret.[13]

In the ensuring centuries the cosmic Christ was not forgotten in the life of the church. The famous Christ Pantocrator on the dome of Hagia Sophia in Istanbul and in other cathedrals throughout Europe witness to this belief. Matthew Fox renewed attention on the cosmic Christ in 1988 with his book, *The Coming of The Cosmic Christ: The Healing of the Earth and the Birth of a Global Renaissance*. This approach focuses on a spirituality of the wisdom emerging from Mother Earth through world religions, indigenous religions, artists, and folk movements.[14] The dream is to celebrate God's original blessing in the divine image given to all creatures including humans, and "calling forth the Cosmic Christ traditions from their spiritual heritage and offering them as a gift to redeem Mother Earth"[15] The stress on spirituality locks this approach into a wisdom that is of an anthropocentric perspective. It does not do justice to the evil and destruction involved in the emergence and risk of an evolutionary world and the place of the pale blue dot in this universe. The apocalyptic view is closer to John Zizioulas' view of the cosmic Christ, for the truth experienced there is the truth of being in communion with the Creator, but even there the horizon is limited to the Earth rather than the universe. Christ is the Cosmic Christ in that "The Spirit allows Christ to enter again and again in every culture, and assume it by purifying it, that is placing it in the light—one may say under the judgement—of what is ultimately meaningful as it is revealed in Christ."[16] In the twenty-first century it is time to reframe the Cosmic Christ in terms of this vast universe. While the scale has changed radically, his creation of all things is still congruent with what the early church quickly realized and declared in Colossians.

We are invited to make a step into this apocalyptic reality in which the early church found itself. In Colossians the fact that, "the author was able to think creatively . . . and to lay claim to the universe in the name of Christ, without dissolving the uniqueness of the Christian community, was a remarkable and highly significant achievement."[17]

But this uniqueness is more than thinking or realization, it is an acknowledgement of the good news of what God has done in the midst of the people then, that is now available to be experienced by all.

---

13. Dunn, *Colossians*, 104.

14. Fox, *The Cosmic Christ*.

15. Fox, *The Cosmic Christ*, 245.

16. Zizioulas, *The One and the Many*, 394.

17. Barclay, *Colossians and Philemon*, 94.

The 'apocalyptic' Christ enlivens the task of being 'inChrist' with a gospel of the Spirit's activity in a multicultural and multi-ethnic world finding itself as a pale blue dot in the cosmos.

Without a cosmic faith, the dominant call from believers and the church is to want and expect the end times to come soon. "Come now Lord Jesus; your delay in coming is taking too long." This century, for the first time, the church is getting some idea of the enormity of the creation. Two thousand years in a cosmic perspective is but a moment. To appreciate the magnitude of deep time it is necessary to find a way of describing the story of the presence of humanity on the pale blue dot in terms of the creation of the universe itself starting with the big bang.

> John Haught has worked out a schema for the various stages of evolution that is illuminating. He suggests that we consider having a thirty-volume set of books of 450 pages in each with each page representing one million years. The Big Bang would be in volume one, page one, . . . Earth's story begins in volume 21, but life doesn't appear until volume 22. . . . Modern humans only show up at the bottom of the final page. As Haught sums up, "The entire history of human intelligence, ethics, religious aspiration, and scientific discovery takes up only the last few lines on the last page of the last volume.[18]

It is more likely that the few lines on the last page is the precursor to further pages if not volumes. Now the rediscovery of the kingdom of God and the expectation that the whole creation will be renewed in a new heaven and a new earth radically expands the scope of what God is about in and through the creation. It raises the real possibility that this future may involve far, far longer time scales.

The resurrection and ascension disclose the scope of the Word made flesh. It is the apocalyptic perspective that frees us to see God at work in the evolution of the creation through the cosmic Christ, both beyond and within a human perspective of time and space. The expectations, words, feelings, values and organization, are placed in this much wider context of the planet and the universe. Here, the impossible possibility of grace, love, hospitality, and justice is found.

Cosmophilus, inChrist is set free to be at home with others in a new creation that lets the universe be home wherever (s)he is. (S)he knows (s)he is not only on the next journey to Star X, living in the Lord, but caught up in the ultimate divine trajectory to free the universe for full communion with the Triune God.

---

18. Vincie, *Worship and Cosmology*, 30.

12

The Apocalyptic Image of God

COSMOPHILUS

For Cosmophilus the Earth *is such a beautiful place. The planet shaped over billions of years by almost unimaginable forces, until the continents came to be, risky and exhilarating places for life to emerge. Much later from beginnings, deep in time, human ancestors lived in caves and camps, before building towns, which gave rise to civilisations, which now threaten the future of the pale blue dot. There each person on Earth is born, a unique combination of sperm and egg. They grow and die of natural or unnatural circumstances.*

As Vincie points out, "Our story, the human story, can only be told from this point on within the story of the universe. The Universe story is our story."[1]

WHO NOT HOW

In this story of the universe, humans are not only embedded in life; they are also embedded in death. The processes that gave rise to the universe require both birth and death, whether of stars, or planets, or civilisations or individuals. For Carl Sagan there is no story, death is the ultimate horizon for everything, and the search for meaning in the universe is a meaningless exercise.

There is a remarkable agreement among three of the major world religions on this planet, however, that challenges this narrative of death as a result of particular experiences of a creator God within various cultures. The conviction is that God created the cosmos as a place to dwell and a place to bring into being creatures made in the "image of God" where death is not the last word.[2] The expectation that God would bring a decisive end time to history grew over nearly a millennia from 700 BC on.

1. Vincie, *Worship and Cosmology*, 33.
2. The understanding of the 'image of God' will be developed later in the chapter.

Then, unexpectedly, the apocalypse of Jesus Christ happened within history not at the end of history.

In view of the sheer scope of the universe does this not place too much weight on the apocalypse of Jesus Christ and the emergence of a new creation within history? For Bonhoeffer this is the wrong question. It is not "how" this can be, but "who" is involved. It is the resurrected Christ who has defeated death who gives the answer to the "who".

It is Jesus himself who asked, "Who do people say that I am?" (Mark 8:27b) He who proclaimed that the kingdom of God/Heaven was at hand, now raised from the dead, thereby destroyed the horizon of death for the universe as well as each individual. He has the right to ask of any one—"Who do you creatures say that I am?" As the risen one he challenges those he addresses. 'Who are you, who can still only inquire after me when I restore you, justify you and give you my grace.'[3]

This Christ is the Logos, the Word of God, a Counter-Word over and against the human Logos, human reason. Jesus, Immanuel, said, "You have heard that it was said, . . . but I say to you." His teaching and ministry called in question the nation's view of God, the Messiah, the Sabbath, the Temple, marriage, the place of children, the use of money, and so much more. It was no wonder this Counter-Word would be judged and killed.

> Because the human Logos does not want to die, the Logos of God, who would be the death of it, must die so that it can live on with its unanswered questions of existence and transcendence.
>
> Now what happens if this Counter-Word, though killed, rises living and victorious from the dead as the ultimate Word of God. . . . Here the question 'Who are you?' reaches its sharpest climax. . . . Man can struggle against the Incarnate, but in the face of a Risen One he is powerless. Now he is himself the one who is judged and killed. The question is reversed and rebounds on the human Logos. . . . 'Who are you, who can still only inquire after me when I restore you, justify you and give you my grace.[4]

The early church in its mission to the Roman society had to work through the question as to how Jesus could be both human and divine. From 200 AD to 450 AD there were a series of attempts to find a solution to the Greek understanding of how God is related to life, and the Hebrew understanding of God as separated from human experience.[5] Despite these attempts the Council of Chalcedon (451 AD) could not give a resolution apart from saying who Jesus was. He was both human and divine without affirming how it could be. In fact the creeds jump from Jesus birth, to his death, and omit his life of ministry. And, in doing so, his declaration of who he is as the bearer

---

3. Bonhoeffer, *Christology,* 33.

4. Bonhoeffer, *Christology,* 33.

5. Bonhoeffer, *Christology,* 86.

of the kingdom of God/Heaven being at hand was lost. This removed the apocalyptic reality that is central to his message—He is the one who brings the kingdom of God/Heaven. The "who" eclipses the "how". Jesus asked this fundamental question to his disciples, this question which now faces everyone. "Who do you say that I am?" (Mark 8:29) The Messiah, the anointed One who conquers death, for those who are self-aware and the worlds they bring with them.

For the Logos, through whom all things come into being, the created ones are loved and of inestimable value. That the son of God is injected into the story of the universe, indicates what the major world religions have stated, that self-conscious in-dividuals are precious to God. Jesus teaching about the preciousness of children only highlights the value of the person within the kingdom of God/Heaven. According to Jesus, woe be-tide those who harm children. In a patriarchal society women are given equality and a woman is first to witness the resurrected Lord. Every person is unique and loved by God.

As the early creation stories indicate, humanity is made in the 'image of God'. Those who have been created are then able to be in communion with God.

THE IMAGE OF GOD

In the first half of the twenty-first century the likelihood of self-aware life being dis-covered elsewhere in the universe raised the question once more as to what is the image of God in which self-conscious life is created. For humans, the image of God has been interpreted in varying ways over the centuries as the faculty or property that enables a created being to relate to or be like the creator God. "In western Theology, it has been customary to identify the imago Dei with human intellectual and cognitive capacities."[6] It has been identified in many different ways including reason, intelli-gence, language, creativity, spirituality, morality, awareness of goodness, the ability to be responsible, the ability to relate to others. What is important to note that in the creation stories, it is God who says, "Let us make humankind in our image, according to our likeness."(Gen 1:26) It is God who differentiates the creature created in the im-age of God from all other creatures. God the Creator sees those created in the image of God as sharing in God's goal for creation, yet still part of the creation. In the Garden of Eden picture God walks and talks in the Garden with the primal couple highlighting a shared relationship that they subsequently repudiated and fractured.

In the New Testament the image of God is not presented as a human character-istic, a mystic relationship, but in an event, a manifestation, the apocalypse of Jesus Christ. Jesus Christ lives as 'the image of God', the Son sharing in this relationship with God—"the light of the gospel of Christ, who is the image of God." (2 Cor 4:4) "He is the image of the invisible God." (Col 1:15a) It is an apocalyptic 'image of God'

---

6. Vainio *Cosmology in Theological Perspective*, 143.

within finitude. It is through his resurrection and ascension this image is both given and received InChrist.

The creation, brought into being through the Word of God, is an expression of the overflowing love of a Trinitarian God, a creation in which love gives rise to life, and life to self-conscious intelligent life. "Formed from the dust according to this divine image, we are to be some sort of version or counterpart of the second person—a created one, refracted through the nothingness that distinguishes us from God."[7] Flesh embodied self-consciousness is a specific kind of life that already in some way reflects the life of the son in relation to the Father no matter how marred this awareness is, because it was created in and through the son.

It was Athanasius who provided this fundamental insight into the relation of the Father to the son and thereby into the role of the son in creation, the image of God in creation and the restoration of creation. The Father is always the Father as the son is always the son in the Trinity. The son delights in being the son obedient to the Father,

> [a]s an *expression of his free self-distinction from the Father by which he lets the Father be the one God and by which he became the origin of all that is distinct from God (italics added)*, so that for this reason he could be manifested as the Son of the Father in the form of creaturely distinction, in the finite form of existence as distinct from that of God. . . . It is primarily an expression of the self-giving of the Son to the Father in an obedience that desires nothing for the self but serves totally the glorifying of God and the coming of his kingdom. Precisely thus the way of the Son is also an expression of the love of God for us.[8]

All things came into being through the son, the Word, both heaven as the dwelling place of God and thus a place where creatures embody this same character of free self-distinction, and likewise the Earth (cosmos) where self-conscious, intelligent and sentient life share in some measure this character of free self-distinction. Therefore this self-distinction of the son from the Father is written in to the very fabric of life. There is the potential for this relationship to be experienced by any creature wherever there is self-conscious intelligent life.

This relationship means that instead of the usual approach of trying to identify human characteristics as the image of God, what constitutes the image of God is derived from the apocalypse, the disclosure of Christ, who is the image of God. It is in the good news of the apocalypse of Christ that the creation is taken up into the cosmic Christ as the head of a new creation. In this new creation God makes it possible for the human race to be InChrist, living in Christ, the image of God.

> Emphasis can be placed on God's decision to have a special relationship with humans rather than on the character of human nature that warrants it. . . . Moreover, since the whole human being is made for such a relationship, little

---

7. Tanner, *Christ the Key*, 141.

8. Pannenberg, *Systematic Theology, Vol 2*, 378

interest need be expressed in particular characteristics or dimensions of their nature that distinguish humans from other creatures.[9]

This view of the image of God emphasizes the action of God in creating the relationship with humans, or with any other life form. Since Christ is the cosmic Christ, through whom all things were created, this relationship with God is available to any self-conscious creature, wherever they may be in the cosmos. This relationship is offered as a gift by God through faith to restore the relationship for which self-conscious creatures were originally made. What is important, then, is whether humans and other life forms are open to transformation and open to receive the divine Spirit involved in the divine life relationship that is expressed in Christ the son, the "image of God". These creatures are to be given this image of God as a gift of grace. As children of God they will be open to discover the free self-distinction from the Father that enables them to be fully for other life, fully for the world and fully oriented to God, in spite of the finitude and death into which they were born. "The grace of God in Christ becomes the highest way of addressing the impediment to God's design posed by creation, irrespective of any problem of sin."[10]

For humanity on this pale blue dot, it is not a matter of living a Spirit-filled human life. Rather Christ has given us the gift of his humanity. The image of God is first given us, for the Spirit to then set about conforming us to this divine image. Or more comprehensively the cosmic Christ holds the creation in himself, the creatures within the creation, so that in his death the creatures and the creation itself may be justified, restored. These remarkable passages we have looked at before spell this out so clearly.

> For the love of Christ urges us on, because we are convinced, that one has died for all, therefore all have died. And he died for all, so that those who live might live no longer for themselves, but for him who died and was raised for them. (2 Cor 5:14)

> For you have died, and your life is hidden with Christ in God. When Christ who is you life is revealed (*Greek: manifest, display*) then you also will be revealed (*Greek: manifest, display*) with him in glory. (Col 3:3, 4)

> It is no longer I who live, but it is Christ who lives in me. And the life I now live in the flesh, I live by the faith of the Son of God who loved me and gave himself for me. (Gal 2:20)

The crucified, risen, and ascended cosmic Christ is the God-person at the right hand of God, holding before God the cosmos and all life. The writer of Colossians says of the cosmic Christ, "For in him all the fullness of God was pleased to dwell, and through him God was pleased to reconcile to himself all things, whether on earth (cosmos) or heaven, by making peace through the blood of the cross." (Col 1:19, 20)

9. Tanner, *Christ the Key*, 2.

10. Tanner, *Christ the Key*, 60

All have died in him so that he may give his life to all from eternity to eternity. He has given the gift of righteousness to all things so that self-conscious life can live in this image of God, freed from darkness. In this way the Spirit enables life to be lived in the image of God. Paul calls this the life of sanctification. "In this sense of natural, sin is unnatural, and grace, at the very least, restores us to a natural condition."[11] "In him, we see perfectly achieved what the divine Spirit is to mean for human life when made over into the image of the second person of the Trinity."[12]

In his self-distinction from the Father, the son agreed to destroy the darkness that was let loose in the creation. Through him, the true light that enlightens everyone shines upon all created beings in the cosmos, all self-conscious intelligent life, wherever it may be, including humanity. "Hence the event of the incarnation is no alien thing, even though it may seem alien to sinners who are alienated from God."[13] On this planet the son of God takes human form from his birth to his death and resurrection and into his ascension. In one sense Jesus Christ is the only truly human—the one who gives us his humanity, for us to grow into by faith through love in the power of the Holy Spirit.

In an evolutionary narrative of the creation, the darkness gave rise to an unfolding evolutionary universe that is finite, where all must die, and finally the universe itself will die. Wherever self-conscious intelligent life is found in this universe it will be under conditions of finitude and death, as is the case on this planet in which all creatures are destined for death. The incarnate One seems alien to self-conscious intelligent life, for our lives of self-distinction rebel against these limits that confine us, rather than in an obedient self-giving to God. "We are to seek the root of evil, rather, in revolt against the limit of finitude, in the refusal to accept one's own finitude, and in the related illusion of being like God."[14] Here is the truth from the oldest Genesis creation narrative. "But the serpent said to the woman, 'You will not die; for God knows that when you eat of it your eyes will be opened, and you will be like God, knowing good and evil.'" (Gen 3:5) Intelligent self-conscious life finds that living in the finitude of time and space is to live in sin under the shadow of death, grasping at the dream of being like a god, not only refusing to live a life of free self distinction before the creator, but unable to do so.

> Death is the last enemy of all living things. (1 Cor. 15.26) Fear of death pierces deep into life. On the one hand it motivates us to unrestricted self-affirmation, regardless of our own finitude; on the other hand it robs us of the power to accept life. Either way we see a close link between sin and death. The link is rooted in sin to the extent that only the non-acceptance of our own finitude makes the inescapable end of finite existence a manifestation of the power

11. Tanner, *Christ the Key*, 130.

12. Tanner, *Christ the Key*, 99.

13. Tanner, *Christ the Key*, 386.

14. Pannenberg, *Systematic Theology, Vol 2*, 171.

of death that threatens us with nothingness. The fear of death also pushes us more deeply into sin.[15]

Since life is interdependent, creatures live off and for one another in competition. The threat of others pressures creatures, especially humans, to the point of violence, the denial of inter-relationship, and the pursuit of limited gods that wreak their own vengeance. Death, then is a result of the darkness or evil that gave rise to finitude. While God did not will this, God gave the freedom for this possibility to eventuate. God takes responsibility for this turn of events by then countering what has happened to bring redemption, restoring the creation and defeating the power and horror of death.

In the darkness the cosmos experiences the convulsions of stars, the violent birth of planets, earthquakes, floods, tsunamis, and fires that bring life and death to all who are born. While at the same time the light that enlightens the creation brings to birth emergent order as the constant laws of the universe let events and creatures evolve to include intelligent self-conscious life. As Luther saw, we who have self-conscious intelligent life want to be as God, sense this in others and condemn them for it. The horror of what is done in the human search for power, wealth, control and indifference to others, even in the name of God, shocks to the core.

THE APOCALYPTIC IMAGE OF GOD

The Trinitarian living out of the original intent and plan of God for the creation reaches its climax in the apocalypse of Jesus Christ. He lives in God-given interdependence in contrast to the rest of humanity living in self-independence. "Jesus is not the representative of the Father but the mediator of his presence. Decisive in this regard is his self-distinction from the Father, by which he shows himself to be the Son—even on his way to death."[16] From his birth to his death Jesus mediated the kingdom of God in his self-distinction from the Father.

What can be learnt from his presence in our midst as Jesus of Nazareth? Katherine Tanner concludes that, "Jesus of Nazareth . . . retains on earth those relationships to the Father and the Spirit which are his eternally, but he exercises them under the conditions of human life on earth."[17]

It follows that during the incarnation the eternal relationship with the Father is spread out in time and finitude. Tanner continues, "Although his whole life is his mission and he freely consents to what the Father through the Spirit is telling him what

---

15. Pannenberg, *Systematic Theology, Vol 2.* 273

16. Pannenberg, *Systematic Theology, Vol 2,* 433.

17. Tanner, *Christ the Key,* 180.

to do, he does not completely understand the will of the Father (Mark 13:32) and so must simply have faith and trust in it."[18]

But the relationship of the Word with lived flesh also involves a struggle within the conditions of finitude. Not only a divine encounter with the human race, but the disclosing of how this encounter is also lived out in finitude. In fact the creeds are silent about this in the life and ministry of Jesus, between his baptism and his crucifixion.[19] The Platonic framework unintentionally screens the unique relationship between Jesus and the Father that is disclosed in what he did and taught in his ministry. The life and public ministry of Jesus spell out the human dimension of his life in the kingdom of God. "The perfect return is delayed, hampered by the sin and death in human life that Son and Spirit face in the course of the mission."[20] In taking upon himself a human life he, the son, in relationship with the Father and the Spirit establishes a beachhead of communion that starts with his birth and continues through his baptism, ministry, to his death on the cross, living out the kingdom of God/Heaven in the human condition within time and space. Until his death he faces the predisposition of the human condition to the disobedience of sin, and reclaims, stage by stage of human life, what it is to live in the partnership of the Father and the son.

Throughout, the son of God, the Word made flesh, is hidden in our midst. As Gregersen emphasizes that this 'deep incarnation' includes more than what is accepted as human, but the wider networks of life on which intelligent awareness is dependent.

> The central point he wishes to emphasize is that the carne or flesh of in-carnation refers to all that is material. The term flesh (Greek sarx) connotes every life form and every species in the history of biological evolution. "The New Testament nowhere states that God became human," he writes. "Rather the Logos of God 'became flesh' (John 1: 14a) . . . God's incarnation also reaches into the depths of material existence." One implication of this observation would be that incarnation is not limited to putting on a show for only rational beings to observe. The significance of God becoming flesh stretches to every nook and cranny of the physical universe, including plants and animals who do not actively or consciously share communion with God. God's presence is not restricted to the realm of the mental, the intellectual, the spiritual. It is physical as well.[21]

In this process the son does not draw attention to his role but points to the Father, the Lord of heaven and Earth, the king of the kingdom of God/Heaven that he proclaims. He lives out his unique self-distinction by only doing what he sees the Father doing. What is remarkable is how his teaching, travelling and healing push the

---

18. Tanner, *Christ the Key*, 182.

19. Personal communication from Clive Pearson.

20. Tanner, *Christ the Key*, 180.

21. Peters, "One Incarnation or Many," 293.

boundaries of finitude, as in him the restoration of the creation is happening. Jesus announces the Lord's favor, the presence of the kingdom of God/Heaven through him restoring the creation in and through his presence—the poor hear good news, and those captive to sin, sickness, and death, are set free through his ministry. That claim is powerfully illustrated by the way the gospels state that all who came to him for healing were healed, including three who brought the plight of someone close to them who was at a distance. The kingdom of God/Heaven was a spatial presence where he was, integrating life back into the presence of the Father. And, indeed, it is important to read the parables of the Kingdom in this way. They are not earthly stories of heavenly realities, but the way that heaven torn open in his ministry is discovered in the midst of life. This integration, this restoration is like a mustard seed, a treasure found, a lost coin discovered, each, in the midst of this life, a disclosure, an apocalypse of the kingdom's presence. During his ministry this restoration was limited to his immediate presence, and that of his disciples.

But the kingdom of God/Heaven was not to be limited to his Palestinian ministry. Rejected, he suffers the humiliation of the cross. It is then through his resurrection and ascension that he discloses who he is, the one who rules with God as the son of God, the cosmic Christ. Through his death on the cross, finitude and death were destroyed in his resurrection and ascension, setting free the kingdom of God/Heaven within the creation. Through the cross, the eternal presence of God is made available to the creation. These words keep coming to the fore. "We have peace with God through our Lord Jesus Christ, through whom we have obtained access to this grace in which we stand."(Rom 5:1b-2a) Through his ascension the new reality of the gift of his image to the human race is incorporated into the second person of the Trinity so that we may live our lives inChrist. "Jesus is presently in God's dimension, that is, heaven: however heaven is not a place in our space-time continuum, but a different sphere of reality that overlaps and interlocks with our sphere in numerous though mysterious ways.[22]

The God who has structured the creation for love in spite of all that has happened, has shown in the son the true purpose of life. Paul writes,

> For the creation waits with eager longing for the revealing (Greek: *disclosing*) of the children of God; for the creation was subject to futility, not of its own will but by the will of the one who subjected it, in hope that the creation itself will be set free from its bondage to decay and will obtain the freedom of the glory of the children of God. We know that the whole creation has been groaning in labor pains until now; and not only the creation, but we ourselves, who have the first fruits of the Spirit, groan inwardly as we wait for adoption, the redemption of our bodies. (Rom 8:19–23)

---

22. Wright, *Surprised by Scripture*, 96.

This passage shows the sheer audacity of Paul's description of the apocalypse as an event that unleashes God's life into our cosmic setting and human setting. God is greater than the created cosmos, however. Paul reports on a new creation of grace, life, meaning, and purpose, which Jesus announced as the kingdom of God/Heaven. No longer is the ultimate reference point the horizon of death that consumes all, but the living God whose new creation is available and open to the cosmos. The apocalypse of Jesus Christ embeds all that we know about God in the life, death resurrection and ascension of Jesus Christ. Rather than a transcendent realm elsewhere, heaven is open to the Earth from within history.

THE CREATION NARRATIVE

In the apocalypse of Jesus Christ, not only is the image of God reframed in terms of the son, but the creation narratives are reframed in terms of the Word of God. The creation narrative in John's gospel has a different perspective from the earlier accounts of the creation in Genesis. The New Testament creation account in John's gospel focuses on the creating Word of God rather than the creation of the Earth. "In the beginning was the Word, and the Word was with God, and the Word was God. He was in the beginning with God. All things came into being through him, and without him no one thing came into being. What has come into being in him is life, and the life was the light of all people. The light shines in the darkness and the darkness did not overcome it." (John 1:1–5)[23]

Similar words are found in Pauline writing. "He is the image of the invisible God, the firstborn of all creation; for in him all things in heaven and earth were created, things visible and invisible, whether thrones or dominions or rulers or powers—all things have been created through him." (Col 1:15)

These writers take for granted that all things in heaven and on the Earth refer to the Earth as the centre of creation. But, unbeknown to them, "all things" can also encompass a cosmos or multi-universes. A wider framework is not excluded, because the focus is on the Creator rather than the creation of the Earth as it is in the Genesis accounts.

---

23. McHugh, *John 1-4*. McHugh provides one of the most recent exegetical discussions of this passage. There is an immense exegetical and theological literature to draw on from the early church Fathers to the present. Since the original Greek is in consonants, there are important nuances in the interpretation of the passage that depend at a few points upon the punctuation. A survey of sources discounts the traditional interpretation of a Greek Platonic background to the Word and instead sees it as an expression of the Aramaic word Memra, meaning 'utterance', as in the Holy Ineffable Name of God in Exodus 3:14, "I am what I am." The writer of John's gospel also writes in a way that has a number of levels of interpretation. In this passage the opening words point back to the creation account in Genesis 1, but can also be read as the framework for the saving work of the Word as it unfolds in John's gospel. For readers who want to discover the intricacies in the exegesis, and the theological issues involved see above. This discussion focuses on what can be learnt about the nature of the creation.

All things, have come into being through him including life, and the light of this life shines in the darkness and the darkness did not overcome it. This is the true light, which enlightens everyone." (John 1:9b)

The darkness is passing away and the true light is already shining.(1 John 2:8b)

Giving thanks to the Father who has enabled you to share in the inheritance of the saints in the light. He has rescued us from the power of darkness and transferred us into the kingdom of his beloved Son. (Col 1:12,13)

The darkness is the powerful background opposing the true light. Here there is no attempt to explain the source of death and finitude. It is assumed as a given.

The language of light as both the presence of the Word and, as the energy of the universe, provide parallel forms of language for God as the creative Word, and the scientific view of light as a primary description of energy in the universe. These parallel languages open the possibility to learn from both about the beginning of the creation—a God account derived from apocalyptic moments and a scientific account derived from experiment and logic. Such a story of the universe, a meta-narrative, is a way of synthesizing these two different forms of data.

The early creation accounts are meta-narratives from earliest times, wrestling with the question as to how the world was created, and how sin and death came to be. While there are many creation accounts in various cultures, it is significant that four of the five major world religions[24] have God creating the Earth, and three of those five religions share the accounts of the Hebrew book of Genesis. As scholars have shown, there are two creation stories in the first three chapters of this book. Both accounts focus on the Earth as the center of the creation.

The oldest story echoes the period 8000 to 4000BC, when hunter -gatherers settled, tilled the soil and lived on farms and small villages in Mesopotamia. In this earliest account in Genesis chapter 2:4—3:24, God creates Adam (which means literally 'of earth') from the clay of the earth, to till the soil in a garden that provides all that is needed for Adam. Then Eve is created and they live in a garden of delight with all they need for food, including the fruit of the tree of life. The garden is also the place that God created to dwell with them. There they live in communion with God, never growing old in a place open to living in eternity with God. They are, however, directed never to eat from one tree—that is the tree of the knowledge of good and evil. If they do it is said they will die. When they succumbed to the tempter, who lives in the garden, they ate and were ejected from the garden of Eden into the finitude of a world of pain, toil, sorrow and death.

24. The five world religions cited here are Shamanism, Judaism, Hinduism, Buddhism, Christianity and Islam. In fact most tribal and societal accounts of their origins name some sort of God as the creator. Buddhism is unique in looking beyond the self and the world to discern an ongoing flow of awareness as the fundamental given.

This older account is prefaced by a younger account of creation in Genesis chapter one, derived while Israel was in exile in Babylon. There, in the sixth century BC, Israel was confronted with creation stories from the priests of the first nation states that developed in the middle-east after 4000 BC. While there in exile they write of a God who creates the known world of the day. God creates the heavens and the Earth in seven days from primordial chaos and darkness. The account does not explain the source of this primordial chaos and darkness. The heavens and the stars are created above the earth and the depths of the earth are below the earth in this three-tiered presentation of the creation. Attention is focussed on God's purpose to provide a place where the created persons, live in relationship with God. The creation of the heavens provide a dwelling place for God in the heavens and the creation of the Earth a place where humans dwell with all the life of land and sea. In this account humans are created 'in the image of God', in a creation that God declares good.

A condensed overview of these two accounts has the eternal God, creating an eternal heaven and an Earth that seems to be eternal, for death does not come until the sin of this primal couple in the garden. They leave the eternal garden, sentenced to a life of finitude ending in death, the result of the temptation to become like God and disobey God's orders. The account hinges on the decision of the primal couple to sin as a result of the deceit of the tempter. In their desire to be like God, they reject living from the tree of life, and choose to live from the tree of the knowledge of good and evil, only to end up in the dark separated from the source of light.

There is a similar account in the Qur'an in which Iblis (Satan) challenges God's determination to create humans as a vice-regent over an eternal garden within the heavenly realm. It is at the point of 'slipping' or 'falling' that the human race and Satan are delivered over to death and finitude for a final judgement to come later.

In both accounts finitude and death come about, either by human decision as a result of a tempter on the earth, (Genesis) or as a result of Iblis tempting the human couple in heaven, (Qur'an). Neither finitude nor death are presented as the intent or purpose of God, though God's giving to the created couple the freedom to decide, opens the door to this possibility. Inevitably, God bears some responsibility for this possibility that freedom will be misused when given to creatures. Indeed, in the Qur'an, God is not surprised. And to Adam after he named all things, Allah said, "Did I not tell you that I know the secrets of heaven and earth, and I know what you reveal, and what you conceal."[25] God's final responsibility requires the whole story to be known, and this betrayal is but the beginning.

The question remains—does the disobedience that leads to finitude and death happen before the creation of the Earth or after the creation of the Earth? In these accounts it is not clear. Elements of human decision and temptation from heavenly beings are both seem to be vital, but framed in terms of a limited creation involving only heaven and Earth. It seems that the primal couple were eternal in God's creation

25. Qur'an: Serat 2A:33."

of the Garden of Eden. After their disobedience, they lost eternal life. The Garden was then closed to them, guarded by a heavenly creature, a Cherubim, blocking the way back into the reality that preceded finitude and death. This account has similarities with the Islamic account in which the Garden is created in heaven with temptation and disobedience sentencing them to a creation of finitude and death.

These creation accounts are quite different from the scientific and anthropological account of the emergence of the human race. The scientific discovery that any primal humans were created as a result of a long process of evolution, spanning billions of years, is not only dependent on the existence of a universe to provide the elements for life to appear on at least on one planet around one sun, but also occurs within a universe which is already one of finitude and death. In this case primal humans emerged within a universe of finitude and death. Death and finitude do not flow from human decision, but from the initial conditions of the actual creation.

In the attempt to harmonize the creation accounts with the scientific account, it is often suggested that at the emergence of evolutionary human self-conscious awareness, the primal Adam and Eve were first obedient to God before their act of disobedience led to finitude and death. The difficulty with this approach is that the death of all creatures is already part of the evolutionary story. The discovery of the geological and astronomical time scales preceding the emergence of a primal couple rules out the possibility that finitude and death flowed from their decision in time. The universe is one of finitude and death from its origin. The source of finitude and death lies in what happens in the act of creation itself.

In a way that is what the creation stories are presenting. The initial conditions of the creation were good and Adam and Eve were created in the image of God in an eternal setting, but in the unfolding of the creating this primal couple rebelled, led astray by another in the eternal realm, the tempter, resulting in finitude and death. Trying to equate the truth of the picture language with a scientific account complicates the detail, but does not compromise the key insight. The point of disobedience happens within the eternal realm that precedes the finitude and death involved in the created cosmos.

The accounts are clear that once this disobedience happened, God still continued to be actively involved with the realm of finitude and death. Later the core message of Jesus is framed in terms of the coming kingdom of God/Heaven within the realm of finitude and death.

LIFE IN THE GALAXIES

It was not until the late eighteenth century that James Hutton, the founder of modern geology realized the Earth was millions of years old. It still took nearly a century for James Ussher's assertion to be dismissed, that according to calculations from the Bible, the Earth was created in 4004 BC.

The twentieth century has brought with it the discovery of an almost infinite universe, and with it the possibility of self-consciously aware life on other planets and locations elsewhere among the stars. From 2009 to 2013 the Keppler Space Telescope searched for planets in a region of much less than 1 percent of the arms of the Milky Way Galaxy. With the mission finished and new telescopes soon to take up the task, a total of 3,000 planets were found, including 20 potential Earth-like worlds.[26] When this data is extrapolated to the whole Milky Way it is estimated there are of the order of 50 billion planets,[27] with 16 billion of these around stars like our sun. Extrapolating further for the universe with its billions of galaxies it is estimated there are currently 100 billion billion Earth-like planets, with at least a 1000 billion billion such planets yet to form.[28] As yet there is no real basis for determining what is the probability of life, and intelligent life in particular, developing on a planet or some other way as a life form. If it is a one in a hundred billion chance of a planet giving rise to sentient life, there are still of the order of a billion planets where such life could have formed so far. If it is one in a billion billion, it would be of the order of 100 planets.[29] Until life and intelligent life is found elsewhere, these probabilities remain just that—probabilities. There is, however, a growing realization that the chemistry required for life has been found on meteors and comets and is available to planets during their formation.[30] There are assumptions involved, however, that are most difficult to elucidate. If the evolutionary process is a convergent process that results in features like eyes emerging in different and unconnected branches of life, there is a greater chance of finding intelligent life that in some ways may parallel the evolutionary outcome on Earth. If the process is not convergent, the probability of finding life elsewhere is drastically lessened. Inevitably any Earth based prediction is probably skewed by an anthropocentric, terracentric and carbonocentric perspective. And probably other hopes,

---

26. Wenz, "Earth-like worlds," 7.

27. Borenstein, "Cosmic census." 19/11/2011

28. Aron, "No place like home?" 8.

29. Wilkinson, *Search for Extraterrestrial Intelligence*, 40. Frank Drake, one of the pioneers of the Search for Extraterrestial Intelligence devised a complicated formula of the factors involved in the probability of there being intelligent life on other planets. Much depends on the assumptions factored into the equation, but his estimates were between 1,000 and 100 million civilizations in the Milky Way galaxy. Others put in other numbers and came up with 1! Recent discoveries that indicate meteors and comets are awash with organic compounds involved in the emergence of life, are pushing the figures up rather than down.

30. Drayton, *Pilgrim*, 166. In 1995 I stated my hunch that the evidence then suggested that life would be found on other planets and that "In the next decade the church needs to be ready for the implications of such discoveries." During the twenty years since a series of films such as Star Wars, A Space Odyssey, Aliens, Avatar, Contact and Arrival, amongst many others have dealt with this issue, while little has been said for the churchgoer about what this raises for believers. It is another indication of the way a 'God and me' relation does not have to come to terms with these creation matters. A 2014 NASA grant to the Princeton Centre for Theological Inquiry to study 'the societal implications of astrobiology' is an encouraging sign. This has given rise to a field of theology to study these cosmic issues called 'exotheology.'

myths and projections are involved as well. Still, as the sheer scale of the universe is realized, the likelihood of self-conscious life being found elsewhere continues to rise. Whatever the scale at which one looks at the universe the numbers are staggering.[31] What, though, are the forms that intelligent life might take?

> For Christian faith and theology, the nature of other intelligent creatures is open. For Galaxies with hundreds of millions of solar systems, it is likely that the divine being sets forth a diversity of intelligent creatures. . . . On other planets, thousands of light-years away, a culture might exist that now in the twenty-first century would be unimaginable to us. While the universe increasingly suggests the possibility of varied ways of life, including intelligent life, the field of bio-astronomy seeks patterns amenable to life. Scientists discuss unusual life-forms like plasma life, life in solid hydrogen, radiant life and life in neutron stars.[32]

From the perspective of self-consciousness it is marvellous that the mind's eye can describe these almost unimaginable scenarios of the past and the future. Imagination, rational thought and experimentation now see the possibilities of an infinite series of universes, while at the same time appreciating the constants and patterns involved in this universe that make life possible. And, of course, as Einstein changed the world with a new understanding of the cosmos, there will in the future be new discoveries that, if the past is any guide, will radically change once more the understanding of the universe.

Indeed, Einstein not only changed the perspective of science he also showed that science has an unfolding history. One day the 85 percent of dark energy/matter of the universe, that is invisible to the science of our day will be rendered visible and its significance assessed. The puzzle of how paired electrons can be entangled and respond immediately to each other while separated by nearly infinite distances will bring new perspectives and theories. The relationship between matter and consciousness will continue to be explored more deeply. When science at the beginning of the twenty-first century looks back on science at the beginning of the nineteenth century, the limitations are evident. And, one suspects, when the scientists of the twenty-third century look back, they will consider today's truths similarly limited. The next centuries may bring to light new ways of travelling in space and time that could open up the possibility of galactic Federations and inter-galactic travel that as yet only exist in science fiction. History is by its very nature changing, dependent upon what is

---

31. After all each of us is made up of a staggering number of components. There are 7 billion billion billion atoms in a human body (4.5 billion billion billion Hydrogen atoms and 2.5 billion, billion, billion Oxygen and Carbon atoms, originally created in super novas), 37 thousand billion cells and a thousand billion neurons (greater than the number of stars in the Milky Way Galaxy). What is important are the specific configurations of these elements that give rise to life and consciousness. There are big numbers for atoms or galaxies, whatever the scale chosen for a perspective.

32. O'Meara, *Vast Universe,* 21.

discovered along the way. Science has been historicised, and without fanfare, it has become part of the historical metanarrative that rules our lives. The human perspective of rationality and scientific method has triumphed in our era. History has become its own grand meta-narrative. For most an immanent world is all that exists. But as the years pass, each new world perspective is limited and threatened by the straightjacket derived from the preconceptions of the particular age that precede it.

THE STORY OF THE UNIVERSE—A DIVINE META-NARRATIVE

This radically enlarged universe in which the pale blue dot finds itself also requires us to take seriously the scandal of God's particularity in addressing life on planet Earth in the apocalypse of Jesus Christ. As described, the divine metanarratives of previous creation stories are centered on the Earth. What would it mean for a creation narrative of the universe as it now is understood? The key question concerns who it is that is creating and addressing the creatures that are part of the creation. For too long the practicalities of faith have majored on the internal and subjective individual, rather than a holistic view of the purposes of God for the creation. What follows is a tentative beginning to outline some of the key issues needed in a metanarrative that takes seriously both science and religious insight.

In the eternal light of God's purposes God sought to create a son and a daughter to be eternally with God as a Father. From a Christian perspective Satan sought to bedevil this plan, or from an Islamic perspective Iblis protested and refused to accept being ruled by another creature. As God began to create an eternal garden of Eden in a singularity of loving light and order, a rebellious angel injected into this moment the darkness of chaos. The result was the Big Bang. The original moment of light is shattered into what will emerge as billions of billions of shards of light in an expanding cosmos of deep space and time, itself born to eventually die and be no more. God's initial dream of one garden was shattered into fragments of gardens scattered infinitely.

To the eternal God this consequence was not a surprise, but the multiplication of life from one place into possibly thousands and millions. God's mysterious plan is made plain as the life of the garden is now seeded in the midst of darkness. The light was never extinguished, but instead given a vast cosmic canvas for the purposes of God to unfold through the emergence of life and light in many places over millions and billions of years. The laws of the universe given in the creation slowly bear fruit in the light of truth and grace, in the midst of the darkness of chaos, disorder and deceit. Over billions of years on some planets, and who knows where else, life began and developed, until perhaps in a few places, or many places, conscious intelligent beings came to be who find in themselves the possibility that they were created in relation to God.

On this planet the apocalyptic Word intimates and prepares for God's great restorative mission. The healing of the universe, the restoring of the purpose of God occurs in our midst as 'God with us' through the Word,—starting with leaders, temple, prophets and priests responding to God's disclosures, leading to the apocalypse of Jesus Christ, in which the eternal God defeats death, discloses the eternal present within the temporal, and prepares for the end of finitude.

The relation of the Father to the son provides the key insight into the very nature of the creation with both the heavens and the Earth (cosmos) created by the Word and open to each other.

This view is so different to the common view derived from Greek philosophy. From a Platonic perspective God is pure being who creates in a series of emanations, to keep at a distance the final emanation Earth (cosmos), the place of change and decay beset with finitude and death. The result is a radical difference between the purity of heaven and the sinfulness of the Earth (cosmos). Heaven is seen to be a supernatural spiritual place and the Earth a natural physical place. How different this is to the biblical record in which heaven as an eternal dimension is not only open to temporal reality, but actively involved in this reality.[33] In fact the light that shines in the darkness and shapes the story of the cosmos, is derived from heaven. It is not surprising then that a new heaven and a new cosmos is needed to restore and heal the original creation of heaven and the Earth/cosmos.

With this background it is possible to frame a metanarrative of the creation of this cosmos with a God account derived from apocalyptic moments in history and a scientific account derived from experiment and logic.

As with earlier metanarratives this narrative is a first step, but a necessary next step, to locate ourselves in relation to the God at work on the pale blue dot.

> *The Trinitarian God lovingly created all things through the Word, with the gift of freedom for all who would become aware. Such freedom required that the Word would suffer the consequences for the trespass that this creation made possible if not inevitable. First heaven was created as a dwelling place for God with other eternal creatures. When God, the mother, father, shared a dream to create an eternal garden to share with a son and daughter created in the image of God, this was repudiated by some heavenly creatures, who, in rejecting the wisdom of God's love, let loose the terror and chaos of un-creation. As God uttered the garden into being the light of creation was shattered into billions of shards of light in a primal cataclysm throwing the cosmos into the darkness of finitude and death that gave rise to galaxies, star systems, and planets in an evolutionary cosmos. Undeterred God, now the cosmic gardener through the creator Spirit,*

---

33. The common link between heaven and earth is the Word and the Holy Spirit. It is important to note that the word supernatural only occurs once in the biblical record. It is used in 1 Cor 10:3,4 in the Revised Standard Version and the New English Bible to translate spiritual food and drink as supernatural food and drink as a way of avoiding using the word 'spiritual' twice in the same passage. The eternal/temporal of the Platonic background of the middle ages became the supernatural/natural for religion as a means to have another dimensions other than that of the immanent world in the Enlightenment world.

nurtured these points of light into life over billions of years in this cosmos of law and love, for with God "a thousand years are like one day". What was meant to destroy God's dream, God used to spread creatures open to the image of God throughout this expanding cosmos. In the darkness when light and life emerged it was isolated, awareness limited to local perspectives, that turned the law into a curse, and restricted attention to immediate needs and desires within the horizon of death. The darkness bred violence and distortion, alienating creatures from each other into ghettos of fear with twisted views of the God whom some sensed. Yet God spoke into these settings in the Word through whom the cosmos was created and sustained by the Holy Spirit announcing the presence of the eternal kingdom of Heaven to restore the Father's dream of knowing and working with his sons and daughters. The son gave himself up to the trespasses claimed in the process of life, to reconcile the cosmos to God, facing the darkness, destroying death and opening finitude directly to the eternal. In every place this came as a gift of grace and truth from the Cosmic Christ through the Holy Spirit reconciling self-conscious life to God and each other. In this way God called all his sons and daughters throughout the cosmos into God's purpose of reconstituting all things together in a new creation of an eternal network in a new eternal heaven and eternal cosmos. Through his son and his Holy Spirit the powers of darkness in heaven and the powers of darkness in the cosmos were faced, judged and removed in this culmination of heaven and the cosmos. God the Father the son and the Holy Spirit invite all into this divine eternal dance, the celebration of God's gracious everlasting being.

In 1995, just prior to the search getting underway for planets around other stars, Pannenberg considered the question of whether human beings can be called the crown of creation, because the son of God comes as a man to fulfil the fellowship of the race with God. Pannenberg asks;

[w]ould intelligent beings in other galaxies need no redemption, or would there be other plans of salvation specifically designed for other worlds? In reply we may say first that though some authors support the possibility of non-terrestrial forms of life and intelligence, other researchers have good reasons for rejecting it. Second, traditional Christian teaching does make mention of other intelligent beings apart from humans, namely, angels, of whom some need no redemption, while others, having turned against God, are incapable of it.

Hence Christian teaching traditionally developed the incarnation-related thesis of our central position in the universe in spite of the acceptance of other intelligent beings superior to us. It is hard to see, then, why the discovery of non-terrestrial intelligent beings should be shattering to Christian teaching. *If there were such discoveries, they would, of course, pose the task of defining theologically the relation of such beings to the Logos incarnate in Jesus of Nazareth, and therefore to us.(my italics)* But the as yet problematic and vague possibility of their existence in no way affects the credibility of the Christian teaching that in Jesus of Nazareth the Logos who works throughout the universe became a man and thus gave humanity and its history a key function in giving to all creation its unity and diversity.[34]

Rather surprisingly Aquinas contemplated this dilemma in the thirteenth century. If there were others worlds or intelligences, would Jesus need to be incarnate in each world or intelligence? Aquinas did not believe that the one incarnation of Jesus here curtailed the divine word to this one earth. He concluded that "[t]he power of a divine person is infinite and cannot be limited to anything created."[35]

Not all agree with Aquinas. In the last century both options have been canvassed by theologians.

> [a] single, universally efficacious incarnation is supported by Protestants Ted Peters and Wolfhart Pannenberg along with Roman Catholics L. C. McHugh and J. Edgar Bruns, while multiple incarnations have been advocated by Protestants such as Paul Tillich and Lewis Ford along with Roman Catholics such as Karl Rahner, E. L. Mascall, and Ernan McMullin. David Wilkinson, in his masterful survey and assessment of this and related questions, points to Teilhard de Chardin, Yves Congar, Norman Pittenger, Bishop Frank Weston, John Polkinghorne, and even Thomas Aquinas as open to, even supportive of, multiple incarnations.[36]

In the wider culture, Thomas Paine presumed in the late 18th century there was some sort of life on millions of worlds in his book *Age of Reason* (1794). At that time it was generally believed[37] all stars were held together by gravity in the Milky Way galaxy. Paine's purpose was to ridicule Christian doctrines about sin and redemption. Paine contemplated how "[t]he person who is irreverently called the Son of God, and sometimes God himself, would have nothing else to do than to travel from world to world, in an endless succession of death, with scarcely a momentary interval of life."[38]

In the 20th century Alice Meynell (1847–1922) gave another possible response in her poem 'Christ in the Universe.'[39]

> With this ambiguous earth
>
> His dealings have been told us. These abide:
>
> The signal to a maid, the human birth,

34. Pannenberg, *Systematic Theology*, Vol 2, 75.

35. Aquinas, *Summa Theologiae III*, 7,3.

36. Russell, "Many Incarnations or One," 305.

37. Immanuel Kant considered there may be many "island universes" (equivalent to galaxies) as well as the Milky Way, but his was an exception to the general view.

38. Paine, *The Age of Reason*, 44.

39. Meynell, "Christ in the Universe." 92.

The lesson, and the young Man crucified.

But not a star of all
The innumerable host of stars has heard
How he administered this terrestrial ball.
Our race have kept their Lord's entrusted Word.

Of his earth-visiting feet
None knows the secret, cherished, perilous
The terrible, shamefast, frightened, whispered, sweet,
Heart-shattering secret of His way with us.

No planet knows that this
Our wayside planet, carrying land and wave,
Love and life multiplied, and pain and bliss,
Bears, as chief treasure, one forsaken grave.

Nor, in our little day,
May His devices with the heavens be guessed,
His pilgrimage to thread the Milky Way
Or his bestowals there be manifest.

But in the eternities,
Doubtless we shall compare together, hear
A million alien Gospels, in what guise
He trod the Pleiades, the Lyre, the Bear.

O, be prepared, my soul!
To read the inconceivable, to scan
The myriad forms of God those stars unroll
When, in our turn, we show to them a Man.

Meynell shares with the nineteenth century the belief that Earth, and every other planet are but the forerunner of heaven. She does not consider how the Incarnate One is part of God's mysterious purpose to create a new heaven and a new cosmos—that these many gospels are not alien gospels, but all integral to God's intent to bring together the completion and fulfilment of a divine network of relationship in a new heaven and a new cosmos. In this perspective, the purpose of heaven is to re- unite all the separate pieces into the one new Heaven and cosmos. What was intended to produce harm God intended for good.[40]

---

40. Gen 50:20. Joseph's comments to his brothers who sold him into slavery.

Celia Deane-Drummond sounds a cautionary note, however. She warns against the redemption of all evolutionary history as somewhat far-fetched. "Is it necessary, therefore . . . or even helpful for that matter . . . to envisage such a grand restoration."[41] She affirms the need for a "sense of awareness of the created world as having supreme worth for God, that violation of the earth amounts to an affront to God's holiness."[42] Here she is thinking in terms of the Earth rather than the universe! But that is the point. That is why resurrection is such a problem for the Enlightenment. Resurrection in a world of finitude and death requires a new creation, and eventually a new heaven and a new cosmos.

It is the resurrection of Jesus Christ that rips open the straitjacket of finitude and death, the final horizon of an immanent world. The apocalypse of Jesus Christ requires a metanarrative to make plain the sheer scope of God's 'grand restoration' of the original creation and its evolutionary history into, a new heaven and a new cosmos. The God who created the cosmos is the only one who can restore the universe so that God's purposes are fulfilled. In this way self-conscious life, human and otherwise, will be brought into the communion with God that God intended. God brings this new creation into being, not by the destruction of the universe, and reconstituting it again,[43] but by entering into the creation and restoring or re-constituting it from within, both affirming the creation, redeeming the creation and judging the creation at the same time. The metanarrative states that heaven is the source of God's initiatives in bringing the kingdom of God into fulfilment in the creation—your will be done on Earth (in the cosmos) as it is in heaven.

It is clear how this happened on the Earth. The Logos, the uttered Word of God, the source of all things is made flesh within the evolutionary process.[44] How a project of restoration is implemented in other places where there is self-conscious intelligent life is not yet known, but depending upon our experience of the image of Christ, some basic affirmations may tentatively be made.

41. Deane-Drummond, *Christ and Evolution*, 48.

42. Deane-Drummond, *Biblical eco-theology*, 97.

43. This is the first option in beginning again. It is what is declared in Gen chapters 6–8. God decrees to blot out humankind from the face of the earth for their wickedness. This is the Noah option.

44. Deane-Drummond, *Biblical eco-theology*, 58. This discussion re Christ and the evolutionary process is focused on the Earth, and does not raise the matter of other forms of conscious intelligent life. Other theologians such as Teilhard de Chardin, Karl Rahner, and Jurgen Moltmann address the evolutionary process focused on the Earth. For Teilhard de Chardin, the increasing complexity of the evolutionary process leads to an increasing emergence of the Christ as its culmination in inter-communication and a planetary end point. Rahner sees that Jesus' divinity emerges from the self transcendence of the grace all humans know, with God accepting this offering of himself in making him divine. Moltmann aligns Jesus with the victims of evolution and the Spirit's role in the process of novelty and complexity bringing about a redemption of evolution itself with all its ambiguities. Drummond presents the humiliation involved in a kenotic Christology in the drama of God's involvement that leads to redemption.

Pannenberg first poses the question as to whether such beings would be in need of redemption. He asks whether there would 'be other plans of salvation specifically designed for other worlds'. The metanarrative indicates that darkness, finitude and death inevitably leads to rebellion against the Creator with the light of law distorted into a curse for all forms of life. In this universe all would need redemption. Would such redemption need to be specifically designed for each form of self-conscious intelligent life? The beings Pannenberg cites are, in fact, traditionally understood as heavenly beings and not created as part of the Earth/universe. He does not directly address the reality of other life forms and their history in the universe.

We return to his words. 'If there were such discoveries, they would, of course, pose the task of defining theologically the relation of such beings to the Logos incarnate in Jesus of Nazareth, and therefore to us.' Since the Word created 'all things' the Trinitarian insight is that the self-distinction of the son from the Father is written into the structure of all things created in the cosmos in and through the Word. It would seem that such life would be open in some way to receive the image of God.

The temptation at this point is to want describe how this relationship can be envisaged in terms of the two natures of the Son of Man, and the Son of God. Does it mean somehow that we need to envisage how the Logos becomes linked to human nature and a series of other natures for other self-conscious creatures? Here on Earth, the Chalcedonian Creed was not able to provide a definition for the relation of the two natures, without even considering the possibility of other 'x' natures. Rather than describe how these natures relate, the Creed affirms who Christ is. What is evident from the apocalypse of Jesus Christ, is that it is not the definitions that make this possible, but the presence of the Word made flesh. The critical question is, who is this Jesus Christ for the Earth, and then who is Jesus Christ for the creation?

The cosmic Christ has incorporated humanity and our creation into the divine realm through his own image, the image of Christ. We know who he is—though he was in the form of God, he "did not regard equality with God as something to be exploited, but emptied himself taking the form of a slave bring born in human likeness." (Phil 2:6) Exulted by God, the cosmic Christ holds the redeemed creation before God. In his disclosure on Earth he has given us the image of Christ, so that in him we are in communion with God. The image of Christ is the gift that he gives to the human life form to discover what it means to be in him, InChrist.

In his ministry on Earth the declaration of the kingdom of God/Heaven discloses the divine love of God for God's creatures in creation. We are convinced that wherever there is life this same love for God's creation and creatures is present. The Logos, discovered as the cosmic Christ, is not alien to any life form since any life form in the created universe has this self-distinction of the Word written into the underlying structure of what it means to be alive. The power of the Spirit is also present there pointing to the promise of the light known there. The corollary then is that any other life form is not alien to humanity, but related to humanity in and through the Word of

God. The cosmic Christ in his radical kenotic ministry to self-conscious intelligent life anywhere, brings the image of Christ to self-conscious intelligent life wherever such life is open to receive from him. First, starting from the uncovering of the self-distinction of the Son from the Father that is written into the very fabric of life, second, through the announcing and living in the kingdom of God/Heaven the restoration of that life, and third the reality of living the gift of being inChrist in the Spirit.

Here is part of the mystery of God's plan from the foundation of the creation. This makes humanity and all other life forms then in some sense of the same family, through the image of God that we all have been given and share, the image that the son fulfills in all of us. As the Word made flesh is truly human, so the Word made flesh is truly the life form wherever there is life in the Spirit. Not only is Adam from the dust, any life form will be from this cosmic stardust. This flesh of the cosmos he takes into himself in whatever form that flesh emerges through evolutionary processes. It is who he is—in the picture language of the Book of Revelation—"the lamb slain from the foundation of the world." (Rev 13:8 KJV) In one sense he holds the whole creation in himself, and in another sense, the whole cosmos already is and will finally be inChrist.

Despite Aquinas's clear delineating between what is humanly possible and what is divinely possible, the question still arises as to how this can be. Vainio [45] presents the wide range of theological options that address how it is possible to conceive of the incarnation, or incarnations, in this cosmic setting. As he shows in the discussion there is no real agreement as to whether there is only one incarnation as it happens on the Earth, or whether this is one of multiple incarnations throughout the galaxy. We cannot know as yet how this 'flesh' or life in the apocalypse of Christ breaks through finitude and death in the image of Christ for these beings.[46] But we know the God who is at work, and the future that is being unfolded in their midst. Not only does the sheer incongruence of the righteousness of God continually surprise and outflank the human view it will enable these life forms to find how God makes it possible for them to live inChrist. What a vision of a diversity of life forms could then be reconciled and enriched in a new heaven and a new cosmos.

The Trinitarian God will in various ways be involved in every life form and the world of which they are a part, taking initiatives of grace, and seeking a response. It would seem that firstly the apocalyptic gospel means that heaven is torn open in some

---

45. Vainio, *Cosmology in Theological Perspective*, 158. The following four options are given for extraterrestrial races.—firstly extraterrestrials are not fallen. Secondly extraterrestrials are fallen and they have their own way to God that is different from ours. Thirdly extraterrestrials are fallen but included in Christ's redemptive work on Earth. Fourthly extraterrestrials are fallen, but their nature is assumed by God in an act of incarnation on their own worlds.

46. Vainio, *Cosmology in Theological Perspective*, 167. Vainio, believes it is possible multiple incarnations could occur. In addition he lists four other possibilities that do not require an incarnation.—that such life forms may be like the heavenly angels and not directly related to the salvation from death and finitude, are able to understand a higher form of natural theology, receive salvation through a divine messenger, or fourthly a messenger from somewhere else. There are proponents for all possible options.

way for every life form. Secondly in some way the Word of God will in each place face death, and defeat death, as the prelude to announcing the end of finitude with the coming of a new heaven and a new cosmos. Thirdly, God's incongruous grace is always at work creating new possibilities for life. The redeeming holiness of the righteousness of God given in faith is always seeking to redeem the darkness. Paul's hymn of praise acknowledges that there is a mystery to the way God works.

> For God has imprisoned all in the disobedience so that he may be merciful to all. O the depths of the riches and wisdom and knowledge of God! How unsearchable are his judgements and how inscrutable are his ways!
>
> For who has known the mind of the Lord? Or who has been his counsellor?
>
> Or who has given a gift to him, to receive a gift in return?
>
> For from him and through him and to him are all things.
>
> To him be the glory forever. (Rom 11:32–36)

The temptation for the observer is to want to have it all worked out. Only the direction can be known because God has disclosed who God is in Christ Jesus. This God who tends all life with light, holding back the darkness, is to be trusted. It is too easy for us to let the tree of the knowledge of good and evil be the source for our evaluation of the 'other' including the way of God, making ourselves the reference point for life, the point that must have answers, rather than glorying in the God who acts to free the creation in grace.

It has been suggested that the new creation was inaugurated on Earth for the whole universe. It gives to the church the task to be stellar evangelists, waiting for the invention of means of travel faster than the speed of light, to spread the message from galaxy to galaxy. That sounds like a grossly inflated form of the nineteenth and twentieth century mission of the church to the world, with the evangelists working unintendedly in tandem with the expansion of western trade to all continents, a mission of light that brought with it the darkness of the west as well. What though of forms of life that have already flowered and died, and of forms of life yet to emerge? Rather than these grand projects that place the pale blue dot in the center of the universe once more, the great discovery of the incarnation, is that it is God who is in the center and has taken the initiative to bring fulfilment to the cosmos in a vast celebration of light.

In the purposes of God it is probable that there are many ways that the tree of life, the apocalypse and the touching of heaven and planets, are involved in the growth and development of self-conscious societies among various forms of life. In terms of the story of the universe it is only a grand outline that we are given; it is wise to be agnostic of much that we do not and cannot know. In life lived within the field of the tree of life, all does not have to be known, because life is lived in relationship with the one who holds everything together. There is the confidence that the love and will of God is there for whatever life forms there are in the cosmos. God has, is, or will offer to embody and liberate that life to live in the light of God's presence free from the darkness that besets the good law of the universe. It is God who is at work in and through the son and the Spirit in all the cosmos, redeeming and restoring the light, given in defeating death and finishing with finitude. As David Wilkinson states, "[t]he Christian conviction is that the God who is encountered in Jesus will do what is necessary."[47]

It is the boldness of this apocalyptic description of the purpose of creation that the present historical view can never give. What the church is learning is that God is far more patient than his people; the end is intimated, but the journey, the Way, maybe longer than we have ever considered. As deep time has pushed back the beginnings of the universe by billions of years, so deep time raises the possibility that the bringing into being of a new heaven and a new earth could also take billions of years. It is more likely that God's house and home is far bigger and more comprehensive than we have ever dreamed, far beyond the limitations we place when we have limited God's house to this Earth, or God's house to the church building.

A NEW HEAVEN AND A NEW EARTH

From Sagan's perspective this good news is surely wish fulfilment on the grandest of grand scales. Yet that is what is implied in what is said and sung Sunday after Sunday in services of worship. Here those implications have been named in terms of a cosmic perspective. At first the early church thought that there would be a short interregnum before this new heaven and a new earth would come. But, as time went on, the church began to realise that there was more to consider. "But do not ignore this one fact, beloved, that with the LORD one day is like a thousand years, and a thousand years are like one day. The LORD is not slow about his promise, as some think of slowness, but is patient with you." (3 Peter 3:8, 9b)

It has taken two days (two thousand years) to discover that a day is but a moment in time given the sheer size of the universe. But the kingdom will come. For much of two thousand years the church succumbed to the view of the wider society that God had inserted a soul in the body. It is only in the last hundred years the church has re-discovered that, "[the] core message of the New Testament is not that our souls fly off to heaven at death, but that our bodies are transformed and resurrected. For example, Jesus, after his resurrection, goes to great lengths to emphasize his bodily presence, albeit a transformed body."[48] Both the results of New Testament research, and the insights of neuroscience support an embodied self, rather than any soul/body dualism.

Most people in church will be surprised to hear of this message of a transformed body for a transformed universe. The apocalyptic disclosures of God's purpose emphasise this involvement with God within the unfolding of time—this embodying of God in the restoration or completion of God's intent for a creation that has never

47. Wilkinson, *Search for Extraterrestrial Intelligence*, 169.
48. Brown et al., *The Physical Nature of Christian Life*, 20

finally succumbed to darkness. It is God who frames the life of the people of God as they live towards the final disclosing of God's neighbourhood.

Over two thousand years the church has born witness to this coming day of the Lord in faltering ways. During the Enlightenment the second coming of Christ has been an embarrassment emphasised by those who keep predicting the cataclysmic end of the planet as almost upon humanity. Now with an extended interregnum moving beyond the denominational paradigm into this age of the pale blue dot, believers are called to live inChrist in this time in which the Kingdom of God/Heaven continues its subversion of the structures of darkness, however long it may take.

13

The Apocalyptic Church

A NEW MODE OF EXISTENCE

Because of the ascension, elemental notions such as "world," "heaven," "time,"
and "place" need to be recast. If Christ has ascended, in his humanity into heav-
en, then humanity and the world in which it is inextricably linked has entered
a new mode of existence. It is not as though Christ has left the world. He now
relates to it in a new way—our humanity has not been discarded in the ascended
Christ. In this sense, heaven, in Christian terms, is not a vague celestial location
but communion with God in Christ in a creation transformed.[1]

THE APOCALYPTIC CHURCH

This description of the apocalyptic church provides a way for the people of God to
envisage the church after the denominational era. It requires a deconstruction of
thought forms that have dominated the life of believers for a long time. Having cleared
some space there will be an opportunity to envision a church for the pale blue dot fit
for the purpose of this apocalyptic paradigm. It is an opportunity to enter into a different ecclesial imagination.

Whatever the century, Theophilus and Cosmophilus share a common reality: in
and through the apocalypse of Jesus Christ they are "inChrist". From the ascension,
to the present time some two millennia later, all things are caught up in the ascended
cosmic Christ, including the body of Christ, the church. In the west the ascension has
not featured largely in Christian thought despite the way the early Church gloried in
this ongoing presence of Christ with the Father as they lived in Christ's new creation.
Jenson and Wihite argue that, "[t]he neglect of Christ's ascension in theology and the
church carries with it an amnesia with regard to Christ's priestly office, which includes

---

1. Kelly, *Upward,* 157.

his self-sacrifice in death (Heb 7:27) but also his role as worship leader (Heb 8:2) and intercessor at the right hand of God.[2]

The ongoing life of the church is lived in this cosmic setting. It lives between the ascension and the time when God brings the new creation to fulfilment in a new heaven and a new cosmos. The coming kingdom gives a cosmic perspective that goes far beyond the future of Israel and this planet. It is time for the people of God to make plans to maintain our house, the Earth, for a more extended time, waiting, ready to be surprised for whenever the master returns. This situation is a radical new setting for the church and has many implications, not the least a re-evaluation of the ascension, and what that means for church in the present.

At the beginning of the twenty-first century, the prevalent focus on a 'Me and God' gospel in the pews constrains a believer's attention to personal experience, the local church and views of God that focus on salvation. Unintentionally, both the majesty of the God who addresses the pale blue dot, and the majesty of the creation of which we are a part, are excluded from the regular ongoing life of the denominational church. In many ways this absence is the end result of decisions made early in the life of the church which have narrowed the understanding of the kingdom of God/ Heaven to the personal, and the restriction of flesh to the body. This narrowing is evident as a result of the kingdom of God being equated with Jesus. The end result is that he was limited 'in Origen's striking phrase', to "the *auto-basileia*, the 'kingdom-in-person.'"[3] This focus on the person of Jesus without his message of the kingdom, greatly influenced the debates that followed about how he could be both human and divine, and the need to describe the trajectory of the individual believer's life within the church from Earth to heaven. This focus on the individual is paralleled by the contemporary affirmation that the kingdom of God is within, with a focus on identity derived from personal inward life.

There are dramatic consequences if the Jesus of the gospels who is a person–in-kingdom is limited to the kingdom-in-person. It changes the answer to Bonhoeffer's question as to who is Jesus. The gospels bear witness that Jesus was first known as the person-in-kingdom, the one who bore witness to the presence of the kingdom of God as well as the kingdom in himself. He refrained from identifying himself with the kingdom. His baptism was an apocalyptic opening of heaven and declaration of his Sonship. He taught about entering this kingdom, spoke of it as the Father's good gift. His ministry displayed this kingdom presence and defined it in healing and teaching and living within the kingdom. He calls his listeners to seek this kingdom and instructs his followers to proclaim this same kingdom and heal also. "He sent them to proclaim the kingdom of God and to heal." (Luke 9:2)

The presence of this kingdom of God/Heaven leads to a reconstruction of human identity through a new seeing, forgiveness, release, freedom, hope, and healing.

2. Jenson et al., *The Church,* 119.

3. Jenson et al., *The Church,* 13.

Instead of being alone in the world, one is known by God in a world with others who are given to each other, as well as God. In the presence of God the divorce between self and world is healed and a person becomes a person-in-world, and person-in-kingdom instead of the world-in-person. The disciples were shocked to find after Jesus crucifixion, resurrection, and ascension, the amazing scope of the expanded reality of this kingdom. They found, as we can, that each of us is a person in the body of the ascended Christ. Even though we are a person in the world of sin and finitude, we are also a person in space and time integrated with each other and God.

If the ascended Jesus is limited to the kingdom-in-person, however, then to be inChrist is focused on him, and it gives rise to a new form of 'Jesus and me' once more focused on the individual relationship. But, if to know him is to know the person-in-kingdom, then the full realization of the cosmic Christ can be discovered for who he is. "For in him all the fullness of God was pleased to dwell, and through him God was pleased to reconcile to himself all things, whether on earth or in heaven, by making peace through the blood of the cross." (Col 1:19, 20)

Jesus is now at the right hand of the Father in heaven, beyond direct human visibility. He now holds the cosmos that came into being through him, in himself as the divine Son. What does this mean for the "body of Christ" with regards to the kingdom, prayer, baptism, and Eucharist, now that the ascension has disclosed this relationship within the Triune God?

There are two important issues to be clarified before attention can be given to what this means for the apocalyptic church. Both flow from how we are to understand the relationship between the church and our ascended Lord, that is, what it means to be inChrist. Firstly, from an Enlightenment immanent perspective of the world the kingdom of God/Heaven has come, but is not yet realized. Christ is absent, and in the power of the Holy Spirit the church must in faith both prepare and wait for God's end time. It is important to hear how the early church describes this 'interval'. Certainly, for Paul, this time of living inChrist is a life lived in the presence of the ascended Christ. In 2 Cor 5: 6–10.

> Paul expects the Corinthians to realize that they are indeed in Christ, but this is only a reality if the Corinthians recognize God's presence. Paul's antithesis again revolves around the way in which one perceives Christ. The Corinthians are only "in the faith" if their lives are defined by the present embodiment of Jesus within and among them.[4] "The stress of Paul's argument rests, therefore, not on the eschatological tension between the now and the not yet but on the present tension that exists in the divide between pleasing God and pleasing humanity."[5]

---

4. Aernie, "A Reassessment," 453.

5. Aernie, "A Reassessment," 449.

The definitive apocalypse of Jesus has led to a radically new relationship between heaven and the cosmos, the formation of a new creation, with the promise of a new heaven and a new earth to flow from what God has done in him.

After Christ's ascension the citizenship of each member of the church is now a heavenly citizenship, hidden inChrist, and through the Holy Spirit the resources of heaven are now available in the continuing finitude and the horizon of death of the cosmos. This heavenly citizenship frees the member to live inChrist in the present ordering our life before God. We are 'being saved' (a present, passive, participle), an ongoing process, rather than being focused on heaven at the end of life, and any other impending endings there may be. Living in the presence of God frees us to allow God's timing for the future to unfold within a cosmos that may include other intelligent self-aware life-forms.

Secondly, living in finitude and sin (but open to the kingdom of God/Heaven) is not the way most churchgoers would describe what is happening in their life. What is the relation between the kingdom of Heaven and everyday life? How is it possible to live before an open heaven? To answer this question it is first vital to explore these words, heaven and cosmos. They each have a history that is important to acknowledge.

In the Hebrew Bible, heaven is the visible heaven above, created by God with the earth. Heaven was created to be the abode of God and angels. Heaven is also a circumlocution for the word God that arose because of the reluctance to speak God's holy name. In the New Testament heaven is Jesus' declaration of the kingdom of heaven at hand, the place of the Father, the throne of God, from whence God makes the sun rise and the rain fall on all, and is the source of manna. Heaven was not only opened at Jesus' baptism, it is the place where he now is as the ascended Lord with the Father.

According to J Gurht, "In Greek philosophy kosmos is the basic term for the world-order, the world system, the sum total of things preserved by this ordering, the world in the spatial sense, the cosmos, the universe, the earth, and also (in Koine Greek) the inhabitants of the earth, humanity."[6] Later, Greek Platonic dualism was accentuated by Neo-Platonism, in which a true intelligible world is opposed by an empirical world of appearances and evil. This dualism was further heightened in Gnosticism. At the same time, Aristotle's view of the world as a central unmoved spherical earth surrounded by layers of heavenly spheres prevailed for almost 2,000 years.

It is quite different in the Hebrew Scriptures. "Nature, cosmic entities are not observed for their own sake but always in their relationship to their Creator and Lord."[7]

In the New Testament, in the gospels, kosmos can denote the universe, the sphere of human life, or humanity.

> The degree to which the word kosmos serves to denote the existent world threatened by futility and need can also be seen in the fact that the future

6. Gurht, "Kosmos," 1: 521.

7. Gurht, "Kosmos," 1: 523.

redeemed world is never called the kosmos, but the 'kingdom of God', and 'a new heaven and a new earth.' There is no phrase corresponding to "this cosmos" such as "the coming", "the future", or "that" cosmos. God and kosmos are strictly disparate. . . . But it is into this world as it is, a world which has fallen into the power of sin and destruction, that God has sent his Son in order to reconcile it to himself.[8]

This is the situation for Paul and in a similar way the writer of John. The gospel dualism between God and the cosmos is not an innate quality of the world. It is a consequence of the sin of humanity. Hence the world does not know God and is blind to God.

Out of love for this world (a completely un-Gk thought!) God sends his Son (John 3:16), not to judge but to save (John 3:17—12:47) . . . Even though believers are no longer conditioned by the cosmos, they are not taken out of the world (John 17:15), but in that they (as the frequently formula says) remain "in him" (i.e. the Son), they are able to demonstrate in the world the belief and practice of the new commandment to love. (John 13:34, 35 ; John 15:9, 10)[9]

These definitions of heaven and the cosmos fill out the background to the experience of the world as one of finitude and sin, humanity's home, but also open to the kingdom of Heaven/God that Jesus the ascended Lord opened to the church. Both the Hebrew Bible and the New Testament have heaven and earth/cosmos linked, existing as parallel realities existing alongside one another.

For most people in the twenty-first century heaven is the end goal rather than the present reality as it was for the early disciples. The last chapter heading of Alister McGrath's *A Brief History of Heaven* states this view. "Journey's End: Heaven as the Goal of the Christian Life." This title summarizes a survey of scripture, literature, expectations of paradise and secular human longings covering more than a thousand years. It is disturbing that, even when Paul says to the Philippians that they are 'citizens of heaven', it is usually reinterpreted that it means the Christian church there is an 'outpost of heaven,' and actually waiting for heaven to arrive. It is not understood that this citizenship is the source of their living in the present. McGrath misunderstands when he writes, "this image thus lends dignity and new depths of meaning to the Christian life, especially the tension between the 'now' and the 'not yet.'"[10] The belief that heaven is the end goal is widely and deeply held and will not easily be changed, even though it is not correct.

What though is the church? How is it described in the New Testament? What is its form and how is it recognized? The word for church *ekklesia* describes a group called to assemble together. In English the word has its origins in *churche* "belonging

---

8. Gurht, "Kosmos," Vol 1, 524.

9. Gurht, "Kosmos," Vol 1, 525.

10. McGrath, *History of Heaven*, 178.

to the Lord". In the New Testament the four primary descriptions of the church are the people of God, the new creation, the fellowship in faith and the body of Christ amongst a slew of ninety-six minor terms.[11] Each of these major terms are a consequence of the ascension of Jesus Christ as the Son of God. They are each related to who Jesus Christ is, as the source of faith, bringing about a new creation, in which the people of God find themselves to be together as his body, the body of Christ. Those who belong to the Lord find themselves in the Lord, or inChrist.

The church in the New Testament gathers together before the ascended Lord. Throughout the centuries the church has been described in many ways depending on particular views derived from scripture and the interaction with the world. Over the centuries the visible church that includes many who are nominal has been contrasted with the invisible church of pure believers, or individual believers. As well, in diverse cultures, various forms of the church have become apparent. Earlier Avery Dulles models of the church helped provide a description for the various views of what constitutes the church. In another way, the marks of the church have sought to define what is essential for a church to be a church. It is not easy, however, to define church. Can an individual be a church, or does it take two or three to be a church, or are greater numbers needed? What does a group of people, or a church need to do or show that they fulfill at least some of the New Testament descriptions?

Dulles six models of the church are helpful.[12]There are also the four marks of a church—one, holy, catholic and apostolic. In the era of the denominational church not only are there a whole range of differing and often competing models of church, each of the marks of the church has to be qualified or defined in ways that mask the divisions in the church about doctrine, leadership, morality, inclusiveness, and message.

Phyllis Tickle has pointed out, about every 500 years the church undergoes a radical transformation—first with Constantine, then the split between east and west, the reformation, and now in the twenty-first century a new ecclesiological ferment. The denominational form of the church faces a bleak future in the west in terms of finding new members in the face of declining numbers, finances, and hope. That is especially so in rural areas. Surveys and denominational church histories predict further stark declines for the church, especially if it maintains business as usual. There are many conferences and books charting the difficulties local congregations are facing and the search for new ways forward. Tickle emphasizes and "underscores an important phenomenon in the present state of ecclesiastical practice and discourse: the emerging church, which represents current concerns in ecclesiastical discourse and is claimed by some to represent the future of ecclesiological practice."[13]

---

11. Minear, *Images of the Church*, 66.

12. As noted earlier, the church as an institution, a mystical communion, a sacrament, a herald, a servant, and community

13. Jenson et al., *The Church*, 96.

Not surprisingly, a key question being asked in this continuing ferment in the life of the church is, 'What is the church?' Cheryl Peterson believes this is the wrong question derived as it is from past views of the church. Instead it should be, 'Who is the church?'

> There is a deeper and more basic issue that must be explored, one that has to do with the church's theological identity, that is, *what it means to be the church.* It is my thesis that the church today is facing an *identity crisis.* It is not simply that the church is culturally irrelevant or inauthentic; these are symptoms of the underlying issue, which is that *we don't know who we are as church.*[14]

She first outlines the two basic forms of the Reformation church. The first is the congregational word event in which the gospel is faithfully preached and God speaks through the scriptures. The other form is a communion ecclesiology where the church's identity and mission are developed in terms of relationship and reconciliation. Both are still caught within Christendom focused on the gathered community. She seeks a post-Reformation church to move beyond Christendom, acknowledging the importance of word and communion but centered on asking who the church is.

> Who is the Church? The church is a Spirit-breathed people who learn to embody the promise of the forgiveness of sins in its own communal life (imperfectly as no doubt will be the case). The church is a Spirit-breathed people who are formed by the word and sacrament around which they gather weekly to become a *koinonia* of sharing and healing. The church is a Spirit-breathed people who are sent out into the world to share God's forgiveness and *koinonia* with a hurting and broken world.[15]

Yet this description still leaves the church at the center whereas in the *missio Dei,* God is at the centre as the one sending the church. Taking Bonhoeffer seriously one must ask a still prior question that arises from Jesus' question to his disciples. "Who do you say that I am?" In Matthew Peter declares Jesus to be the Messiah and the Son of God. Jesus says, "Blessed are you, Simon son of Jonah! For flesh and blood has not revealed (Greek *apocalypse*) this to you, but my Father in heaven. And I tell you, you are Peter, an on this rock I will build my church, and the gates of Hades will not prevail against it." (Matt 16:17,18) The more fundamental question is "Whose is the Church?" It is the church built by Jesus Christ. In Acts, the church of the ascended Lord is empowered by the Holy Spirit at Pentecost. Similarly in John's gospel the Father sent the Son, and the Son sent the apostles and breathed on them the Holy Spirit. (John 20: 21, 22) The church is sent by Jesus Christ.

When Jesus ascended to the Father, it was the church that came into existence. Alfred Loisy made the comment, "Jesus foretold the kingdom, and it was the church

---

14. Peterson, *Who is the Church?,* 4.
15. Peterson, Who is the Church?, 147.

that came. . . ."[16] From this perspective the kingdom is lost when the ascension occurred. Jenson et al., also affirm this point of view.

> Jesus is the one in whom and as whom the kingdom has come. When he announces that 'the kingdom of God has come near', he is not speaking of something other than himself. So when the church focuses its proclamation on Jesus Christ, it does not depart from his message but highlights him as the agent and substance of the kingdom. What, though, is the kingdom? What are Jesus and the church proclaiming?[17]

This explanation assumes Origen's comment that Jesus is the kingdom-in-person. A quite different view emerges if Jesus is also the person-in-kingdom as previously outlined, bearing witness to the reality of the apocalyptic kingdom of God/Heaven, with his ministry pointing to the presence of the Father and the Spirit. This kingdom is the kingdom he also taught his disciples to proclaim and demonstrate. Wherever he went heaven was open and the Holy Spirit was at work. The kingdom was localized in space and time in him and around him. People came to him for ministry. It was while they were in his presence that power went from him. When the Lord ascended to be with the Father he sent his disciples to bear witness to the kingdom of God/Heaven, sent by the Father, and to be empowered by the Holy Spirit. This church, then, is not only a Spirit-breathed church, this church is an apocalyptic church proclaiming the kingdom of God in and through Jesus Christ who is now Lord.

For those inChrist, the ascended Lord, the church empowered by the Holy Spirit, bears witness to this kingdom of an open heaven for any who are in range of hearing, sharing how we have obtained access to this grace in which we now stand through him. His people are the aroma of Christ to God, present before God. The kingdom was disclosed in and about his person.

But they are also ambassadors within finitude and death of this reconciling grace. Where two are three are gathered together Christ is present with them in the kingdom. The sacraments of baptism and communion are apocalyptic sacraments, involving elements of time and space, bread and water and worship as the presence of the kingdom. The experience of koinonia and fellowship become moments, times and places where the Holy Spirit builds the community of joy and peace. The experience of such occasions gives rise to the desire to build places that help such events be a regular part of life. Cathedrals and church buildings emerge from the lived experience of the community that is experiencing the presence of the kingdom. Prayer is both speaking alone with God and addressing our Lord together as part of the community of faith. For the ascended Lord is both in us as a people and we are in him. We are inChrist.

Yet all this is lived in faith. This faith is not subjective belief, but faith that obtains access to the objective grace of God in the midst of one's context. The bold statements

16. Loisy, *The Gospel and the Church*, 166.

17. Jenson et al., *The Church*, 164.

of the New Testament that we are already citizens of heaven, living from the resources of heaven, and are to seek the things that are above (heavenly) are not framed as a 1:1 correspondence, but as realities of which we know in part but do not yet *fully* see or comprehend. The eternal realities go beyond our comprehension, but we do know and experience these realities, though only in part. Paul points to the deepest reality of God's saving presence in our midst. We abide in faith, hope and love, but the greatest of these is agape love. The apocalypse of Jesus Christ given us in the gospels provides us with the events, teaching, and presence that both show and define that self-giving love, for it is the practical data of the kingdom present as it was in and through him. Then after ministry, through cross, resurrection and ascension the abiding reality of his self-giving love keep flowing from the open kingdom of God/Heaven.

The Holy Spirit, named also as the Spirit of Christ, and the Spirit of God, is given with the injunction to actively involve the mind. "To set the mind on the flesh is death, but to set the mind on the Spirit is life and peace."(Rom 8:6) "But if Christ is in you, though the body is dead because of sin, the Spirit is life because of righteousness. If the Spirit of him who raise Jesus from the dead dwells in you, he who raised Christ from the dead will give life to your mortal bodies also through his Spirit that dwells in you." (Rom 8:10, 11) Here the Trinitarian life of God is active in the church witnessing to the people of God that they are children of God.

This transition into living before the ascended Lord is put starkly in Ephesians. "For once you were darkness, but now in the Lord you are light. Live as children of the light—for the fruit of light is found in all that is good and right and true. Try to find out what is pleasing to the Lord." (Eph 5:8–10) How amazing is this injunction for the person inChrist to find out what pleases the Lord! Then, as well, from the Holy Spirit comes the fruit of this reconciliation between God, and others in the growth of love, joy, peace, kindness, generosity, faithfulness, gentleness and self-control, and as well, the gifts of the Holy Spirit. Truth, justice, humility, grace, and holiness constitute and flow in this kingdom.

When the risen Jesus appears to the disciples in John's gospel the practical out-working is put in place for them to be an apocalyptic church living in faith. They are sent as the church, empowered by the Holy Spirit that they then receive, and given the authority to forgive or to retain sins. It seems puzzling to many that this gift from Jesus is given such priority.

The apocalyptic church living from the resources of heaven confronts the practical issues of being a church. This authority to forgive or retain sin is necessary for the church to hold to the marks that define its life. As communities of faith multiplied how were they to recognize each other as one people inChrist. It is the spread of the church that raised the question as to what sort of leadership is needed so that the apocalyptic church can remain one, holy, catholic, and apostolic. Leaders need this authority that is exercised in and through the Holy Spirit.

Over two thousand years much has been learnt and much lost as this one holy catholic and apostolic church has fragmented, adapted, reassessed, wandered, and attempted to return to these marks. These marks ensure the church keeps on witnessing to the kingdom of God/Heaven and lives in the faith that enables God's life and purposes to unfold. This centrality of the apocalypse of Christ requires a new reading of the early church. There are surprising consequences when it comes to the way prayer, baptism, and Eucharist are experienced inChrist for the body of Christ.

What is remarkable in the New Testament is that there is so little about what now is understood as the central act of the church, namely, the service of worship in a church building. There is a huge danger in only experiencing worship this way rather than 'praying in the Spirit at all times in every prayer and supplication' when life is lived in the Lord before an open heaven. Attention can so easily be focused on the ritual, the creativity and energy that leadership brings to this event for passive participants. How extraordinary are the buildings, the music and the liturgies that have come to be in two thousand years. They are a great gift, yet these can so easily be reduced to a performance, a ritual ingrained, or a vehicle for powerful public roles, fame and the exercise of gifts that get in the way of celebrating the kingdom present in the midst of life. Too often in this present time the congregation is an aggregation of individuals each in their own seat, worshiping in their own subjective way. There is little sense of being gathered together as the "church" in the original meaning of the word of "belonging to the Lord". So easily the emphasis is transferred to the place each of us comes to worship God as the house of God. More and more such a place becomes a form of temple that limits God to this place and time, rather than a base for the declaration of the apocalypse of Christ.

This sense of being "inChrist" is so often betrayed by the prayers prayed. Rather than praying to the ascended Lord, open to the kingdom in which we live and move and have our being, the prayers seem prayed to God from outside the kingdom, asking, hoping, wanting God to do things to rectify the ills of the world. How different to the Lord's prayer, Christ's high priestly prayer, the prayers in Acts, or prayers in the letters of Ephesians, Colossians, Philippians, and Corinthians.

These prayers are prayed in the presence of the "Sovereign Lord, who made the heaven and earth, the sea and everything in them." (Acts 4:24) "First, I thank my God through Jesus Christ for all of you . . . that without ceasing I remember you always in my prayers." (Rom 1:8a, 9b). "I pray that the God of our lord Jesus Christ, the Father of glory, may give you a spirit of wisdom and revelation (Greek: *apocalypse*) as you come to know him so that the eyes of your heart will be enlightened, you may know what is the hope to which he has called you, what are the riches of his glorious inheritance among the saints, and what is the immeasurable greatness of his power for us who believe." (Eph 1:17,19) "Blessed be the God and Father of our Lord Jesus Christ! By his great mercy he has given us a new birth into a living hope through the resurrection of Jesus Christ from the dead, and into an inheritance that is imperishable, undefiled, and unfading, kept in heaven for you."(1 Peter 1:3,4)

These are prayers inChrist in the realm of heaven, to the ascended Lord and the Father, rejoicing at what is given, giving thanks for inheritance and new birth and power and wisdom and so much more that flows from the grace in which we stand.

Prayer has become a shopping list of needs and good things for nations and peoples. Sermons are so often trying to convince us that God is our friend, that God is near, that we are loved and cared about. Invitations to chat with God, or play with God have their place, but only when we are clear who this God is with whom we are chatting or playing. The telling moment is after the service as people gather to talk or have tea/coffee fellowship. Rarely is the conversation about the service or how the Lord has blessed us and guided us in the past week, or discussion of the fundamental issues of life. More often it is about the weather, ailments, the last week, TV, or some item of news.

In most congregations there seems little awareness of two thousand years of the rule of this Christ in and through the Holy Spirit, witnessed to in the creation of the church, the canonizing of scripture, the history of mission and evangelical witness, the variety and range of worship and the faithful service of congregations and people throughout the world There is not a lot known about the great story of the spread of the good news to nearly every culture on the face of the planet, or of the times when the gospel has been recovered after periods when the message was compromised or forgotten. It is now rare that groups and members know the history of their own de-nomination beyond a few well-known names and events.

There is little sense of being inChrist, of living in the Lord and of the communion of saints. That sense of God's providence at work in the midst of everyday life has almost disappeared. Genevieve Lloyd speaks of the loss of the sense of God's provi-dence that provides the order sustaining the creation. "The loss of providence from our contemporary social imaging brings with it a new precariousness in the 'buffered' self of modernity."[18]

In the face of startling predictions of decline for the United Church of Canada, Jeff Seaton laments what has been lost in the search for relevance in a secular soci-ety. The Christian story is "reduced to the meanings available within the immanent frame—that Jesus is a teacher of good ethical principles that accord with the modern moral order—it is drained of salvific power."[19] Believers lives are encased within the 'imminent order', locked into historical categories. "We must offer . . . a portal to the riches of our tradition and a window open to transcendence, a view that draws us beyond the constraints of the imminent frame."[20] Yet this yearning for a lost tran-scendence ignores the presence inChrist of the resources of this heaven already given

18. Lloyd, *Providence Lost*, 6.

19. Seaton, *Who's Minding the Story?*, 56.

20. Seaton, *Who's Minding the Story?*, 125.

and available as the good news. The apocalyptic opens up the possibility of speaking about the divine again in an age when Christian belief is so constrained by the human historical perspective.

What is required now is a deconstruction of the life of the denomination and local congregations in order to re-discover and reconstruct what it means once more to be the people on the way inChrist in the kingdom. The denominational church is the body of Christ in so far as its life bears witness to the Kingdom of God as Jesus Christ did. In a society of democratic religious individualism, however, the witness of any congregation is constituted by the decisions of those who belong to the congregation. In most cases the witness affirms their particular understanding of what the church means to them. As a consequence the key elements of the life of the church are focused on maintaining the decisions of the members and reinforcing their views of the church rather than the kingdom of God/Heaven. The result is that the critical elements for decision become those of finance, leadership, recruitment, and the ongoing maintenance of worship in the house of God.

The future of the church depends upon a recovery of the apocalypse, God's disclosure of the kingdom of God, more so than finding and empowering new organizational leadership. The church is called to move from the 'kingdom of God within' to be inChrist in the kingdom of the ascended Christ happening in the midst of time and space—the apocalyptic reality of the presence of God.

The apocalyptic breaches the cocoon of history from within and may yet give birth to more wonderful ways of seeing the creation in which we find ourselves on the pale blue dot. It is time for the church to rediscover its core DNA in a new way that prepares it for a future that is to be part of "'the dawning of a new age'—the new age inaugurated by the death and resurrection of Jesus and proclaimed by Paul."[21]

A NEW GOSPEL URGENCY

Whatever the term that is used in the New Testament—whether it be 'a new creation', 'inChrist', 'in the spirit's power', 'abide in me and God will abide in you', the 'new Adam'—all of these terms are claiming to spell out what is actually made plain in the Lord's Prayer. The work of the church is to witness and live in this new kingdom of the ascended Christ, unfolding toward God's final ending of finitude and sin. Faith is seeing history from God's perspective, living in the new creation that God's divine initiative in Jesus Christ has let loose in our midst. "Significant New Testament scholars, have made it plain that Paul saw the church as a *microcosmos*, a little world, not simply as an alternative to the present one, or an escapist's country cottage for those tired of city life, but as a prototype of what was to come."[22]

---

21. Gorman, *Becoming the Gospel*, 18.
22. Gorman, *Becoming the Gospel*, 37.

There is, of course, a great danger in seeing the church as the prototype of what is to come, for the church has a long history, and has at times sold itself out for less than it is. Since New Testament times, the temptation for the church has been to claim that it is the kingdom rather than living in the kingdom, to limit itself to a subjective spiritual kingdom, to claim that it has a mission from God, to see the kingdom of God as the future beyond death, or to be fractured by competing claims about what is the true church. In these varying ways the church makes itself the reference point for the kingdom or even God, rather than witnessing to God and the kingdom as the fundamental and actual reference point.

THE PEOPLE ON THE WAY INCHRIST

In the task of deconstructing the denomination, the key issue is the recovery of the apocalyptic dimension of the message of Jesus in the time of the Anthropocene. What possibilities may emerge for our communities of faith, inChrist, facing not only wide spread unbelief in God and perspectives locked into an immanent view of the world but climate change, new frontiers from genetics, artificial intelligence, life enhancement, urbanization, the extinction of species, and life beyond the planet.

In the gospels Jesus' life becomes the template for disclosing the kingdom within finitude sin and death. His life, teaching, healing, and ministry show how it is that God rules in the midst of life. What he does is disclose the presence of God, the apocalyptic presence of God, in and beyond a subjugated Israel. This template is not an idea or a thought or a form of motivation as such, but the way to discover what it means to be open to the presence of the kingdom of God. The resurrected Jesus Christ affirms the importance of obeying what he commanded.

> All authority in heaven and on earth has been given to me. Go, therefore, and make disciples of all nations, baptizing them in the name of the Father and of the Son and of the Holy Spirit, and teaching them to obey everything that I have commanded you. And remember, I am with you always to the end of the age. (Matt 28:18b–20)

The rediscovery in the last century of the centrality of his teaching about the kingdom of God provide a clear direction that the kingdom of God/Heaven is at the heart of these commands, especially when it has become so clear that the denominational church was shaped by a fundamental misunderstanding of the kingdom. The way forward is to put his teaching and practice of the kingdom once more at the center of the church's life. Therefore the importance of his direction to "strive first for the kingdom of God and his (its) righteousness, and all these things will be given you," (Matt 6:33) cannot be under-estimated. And similarly the direction on to how to pray to the Father—" Pray then in this way: Our Father in heaven. . . ." (Matt 6:9)

These two commands about the kingdom of God/Heaven lead on to a re-evaluation of the two practices that are at the heart of the life of the church. The two events that Jesus directed his disciples to do together, were to baptize and to celebrate the Eucharist. In Baptism people are to come "alive to God". In the Eucharist the people of God are nurtured and fed along the way by the ascended Jesus Christ. The rediscovery of the gospel that is needed in the life of the church is to be found in and through a life inChrist rather than new methods of organization or grand new plans for growth.

The kingdom of God/Heaven opens us to the "avenues along which the Spirit travels, uniting us with Christ, building us up and sending us (out) into the world to love and serve the Lord."[23]

THE LORD'S PRAYER

The one time and place in which the kingdom is still kept before most congregations is in the saying of the Lord's Prayer, though the prayer is so easily said by rote and fashioned by the culture of the time.

Slowly, but insistently, the importance of the Lord's Prayer has become more evident. Personally it began with the discovery of Anthony Bloom's profound insight that the Lord's Prayer prayed backwards is the history of the Israelite people.[24]. Said backwards it reads like an ascent from Israel's captivity to living before the Father—deliver us from Egypt, remove our sins from us at the Red Sea, give us our daily wilderness manna, your Sinai commandments be done, your kingdom come, your name be kept holy—while prayed forwards it reads as the prayer of the son, the prayer of the church, the prayer of each of us in our togetherness with all. It is a prayer prayed before our Father in the kingdom of heaven, praying for the kingdom to come to the creation. In fact, saying the Lord's Prayer is living in the mission of God. It begins with the mysterious and inclusive "our" God addressed as Father. The "our" has never been satisfactorily defined, or limited, given that it is Jesus who used it. Then our Father in heaven (open to us in our midst), addressed re holiness, kingdom, and will being done, before moving to the requests that acknowledge need under the conditions of finitude—the need for food to be received, sins faced and forgiven, and the acknowledgement that only God can deliver us from evil.

I remember teaching this prayer to our daughter when she was twelve. I was explaining, "At the center is Our Father, then his name is to be hallowed, his kingdom come, etc., to the end." "'Oh dad,' she said, 'You mean it is like a target.'" The center is father God, then God's character is stated, and finally God's provision and expectation to forgive, but there lurking beyond the light of the center at the edge is the darkness that will never overwhelm or overcome the light of this God who has delivered us from evil. Not only is the father at the center, the father is also the source of all life.

23. Jenson et al., *The Church*, 138.
24. Bloom, *Living Prayer*, 20-40, (1990 edition).

The our Father/Mother is like a Babushka doll, containing each petition within, or as in string theory, the nine dimensional vibrations of the string that contain all lesser dimensions within it.

What an amazing prayer Jesus' prayer was, is, and will continue to be. It is a prayer that can be prayed in a capsule dropping from a space station, or wherever a person is on the pale blue dot, or any other dot. We can pray along with Cosmophilus as she says her prayers in a space capsule.

Our Father

I know myself as a son/daughter with others, because you are the source of all family and have given me my identity and a family in this your awe-inspiring creation before me. Here far from any other person you invite me to name you as our Father, and in naming you, know that I am known by you. Beyond all the categories of time and space, I thank you because you found the way for us to know, visualize and name you in and through Jesus Christ.

In heaven

As I am here suspended in inter-planetary space, I live and move in your being, nearer than thinking and closer than breathing, because you opened heaven to us in and through the death and resurrection of your Son. There in your kingdom both the universe and heaven are fully open to you in the fullness of your being beyond our seeing. You are not distant from us, but we are in you, with your providential care sustaining us for life, even as the life support systems on this capsule hum in the background.

May your name be hallowed

You are the Trinitarian God in the majesty of your presence of grace and truth and spirit, living in love and overflowing with a love that has created this world that sustains this world and has redeemed this world. I will sing of who you are, for bringing us the oxygen of life, giving us light for darkness, healing for sickness, forgiveness for trespass, in the great transaction of cross and resurrection. Your promises are sure, your grace is sufficient, your future shown us in picture language worth living for. We will honour your holy name. "Then the angel showed me the river of the water of life, bright as crystal, flowing from the throne of God and of the Lamb through the middle of the street of the city. On either side of the river is the tree of life with its twelve kinds of fruit, producing the its fruit each month; and the leaves are for the healing of the nations."(Rev 22:1, 2)

Your kingdom come.

Here now in this capsule in space, dependent upon machinery, and rockets, and guidance systems, the journey I am on was programmed into the computers an hour or so ago, and even now is being executed. So Lord God, your kingdom made known and realized through Jesus Christ is not only already underway, it has been the imperative from the beginning along the way to the final destination. And even as your rule over all is in some ways disconnected from us, beyond our seeing, you are also connected with us, to me, us, on the way inChrist, as we live the kingdom today in the power of the Holy Spirit to give us the fruits of the Spirit we need for the future journey to your promised end.

Your will be done on earth as in heaven.

Father, your kingdom will has been shown to us in your Son. He gloried in doing your will in our midst as it is done in heaven. His invitation is your invitation. "Come to me all who are tired and doing too much, and I will give you rest. Take my spacesuit upon you, and learn from me, for am gentle and humble in heart me, and you will find rest for your souls. For my suit is easy and my load light." (Adapted Matt 1:28-30) As the spaceship comes into view with its voyaging community enable your will to be a reality in the midst of this varied community from many cultures of the Earth, diverse races, genders, specialists and operators, officers and helpers. In and through us you create a compassionate and supportive community on the way to our destination.

Give us today our daily bread.

To live inChrist, is to live before you Father, the giver of the kingdom requirements for this day—the fruit of the tree of life, the manna in the desert, the bread of the kingdom and the wine of sacrifice in the Eucharist. Resource us for living the kingdom in mess rooms, the walkways and thoroughfares, the engine room, the bridge, the off-duty rooms while, at the same time, fulfilling the tasks wherever we are for which we are responsible.

Forgive us our trespasses, as we forgive those who trespass against us.

Father you are merciful to the systems in which we are all embedded and take for granted which both help some and trespass upon others. The millions sentenced to poverty to pay for this interplanetary mission by those committed to this space program at any cost. In so many ways our society tramples on the rights and lives of its citizens, while we take advantage of any opportunity that comes our way. You call us to mercy that we may be agents of mercy in your kingdom of mercy.

Save us from the time of trial and Deliver us from Evil

In your kingdom, inChrist, in the power of the Holy Spirit rescue us from the unexpected and help us escape from evil—From dangers and disasters that lie on the way, and perverse decisions and vindictive outcomes set in place that threaten our spaceship world. Help us escape pain and destruction. We rejoice that you will act to keep us in the love of your resourceful, merciful and freeing presence.

For Yours is the Kingdom, the Power, and the Glory, forever. Amen

We celebrate your gracious present kingdom, your extraordinary creative power, and the glory of your eternal and loving life here among the planets and stars.

Jesus instructs us to pray this en-globing kingdom prayer that celebrates and worships the nature and character of God. Prayer is a rejoicing in the presence of the Father who knows our every thought and need in our life. Once we have found ourselves in the presence of God, we are ready to receive what God gives, to participate in the apocalyptic mission of God.

In this prayer, the traditional marks of what constitutes the people of God as the church are all here, namely, the one holy catholic and apostolic people. Our Father, the one; the holy name; your kingdom come to all, catholic in extent; and the apostolic reality of your will. The conscious realization of our kingdom identity gives particular roles to the people of God as they meet together to witness to the kingdom of God in witness, service and worship. It will open new possibilities in ministry from the discovery of the apocalyptic Spirit in our midst.

What a delight it is to walk into the community of God's people who show by their actions and language they live in the kingdom, not hoping for it, but giving thanks to God inChrist for how they see the kingdom at work in the midst of society both confronting and bringing blessing as is the case.

This perspective gives rise to the realization that the Lord's prayer is a practical prayer that is about living in the kingdom day by day within the ultimate purpose of God's renewal of the creation in a new heaven and a new earth. "Seek first the kingdom of God and its righteousness and all these things will be given to you as well. So do not worry about tomorrow, for tomorrow will bring worries of its own. Today's trouble is enough for today." (Matt 6:33, 34) Live in the kingdom today.

It is apocalyptic, for this presence is what was uncovered and disclosed before us, as it happened and is available inChrist. We have been brought into the kingdom of light in the midst of life to be lived, not just beliefs or convictions or thoughts or self awareness or words in our heads (which have a part), but a life with others together in community before God in the creation. What is clear to the church in the kingdom is that God loves justice, diversity, and uniqueness and that we are each an "other" to each "other" in gender, age, and culture. As a grander view of creation comes into view it is clear that God loves uniqueness and diversity there as well. How can this people who witness to the kingdom in which they are held not seek peace through reconciliation and not long for the renewal of the whole creation in the shalom of God's presence? We are a pilgrim people on the way to God's promised end.

APOCALYPTIC WORSHIP ON THE WAY

Paul describes the life of the Christian community in more direct apocalyptic ways as communities of the invading Holy Spirit, in which the members live life in the imperative mood, guided by the Holy Spirit, or more precisely 'in step with the Holy Spirit'. These communities live by the commandment "you shall love your neighbor as yourself"(Gal 6:14b) and display the fruit of the Spirit. And the gospel is so specific—Christ crucified: Christ the power of God and wisdom of God. Paul was only too aware his witness would lead to suffering. As Paul wrote from prison in Rome to those on the way in Philippi, "For he has graciously granted you the privilege not only of believing in Christ, but of suffering for him as well—since you are having the same struggle that you say I had and now hear that I still have." (Phil 1:29, 30)

This is the task of the church to witness to what God has done inChrist. As citizens of heaven, as well as citizens of the Earth, kingdom people know the tension, the resistance, and the opportunities to witness to God's disclosure inChrist, as they wait for this disclosure to come to its final culmination in God's time.

This cannot happen unless the church lives this participation in Christ's story. The church needs a rediscovery of the reality of this apocalyptic participation inChrist to be caught up into the activity of the Holy Spirit on the frontier of this present but coming kingdom. The fundamental ways any congregation, or person can make this journey is by discovering the way the resources of prayer, baptism and Eucharist open us to the practicalities of grace in life through the communal sharing (koinonia) of being inChrist, the diaconal transformation inChrist, that in the language of Colossians enables us to be clothed with love.

We are caught up in the invasive presence of the Holy Spirit in a world in which law, lawlessness and forms of love are used to both resist and trespass against the grace of the overflowing love of God. Our mission every moment of every day is to be on the front line, discerning and acting in the Holy Spirit against all that opposes the very being of God. The intensity of this engagement requires that each time the people of God meet, they need to reset what it means to live in the grace in which they stand, that is the kingdom of God/Heaven, and affirm the role of the Holy Spirit as the vital resource for life and discernment. Whether on planet Earth or on the moon, or Mars, or a spaceship, the location is not as important as the gathering together to be clear about the day and the way.

BAPTISM AND EUCHARIST

It is important to ask then how baptism and the Eucharist, the two commands the church has received from Jesus, are integral to the daily living in the kingdom for congregations. At present they come as sacraments—actions that relate to the naming of the individual and a resource for acknowledging the Christ who sustains us. There are many ways that these rituals are practiced in denominations. Too often for Protestants they are additions to worship, tacked on, and even seen as interruptions to "normal" denominational worship. Prayerfully and carefully the discovery of the apocalyptic gospel leads to an awareness of the congregation as the group that is enlivened as the base for the work of the Holy Spirit in our communities. No longer is this the "house of God", the static temple to which people go for times of worship and reflection, instead it is one of many bases for meeting in buildings, homes, halls, any gathering place for a pilgrim people, who, wherever they are, are walking in the kingdom on the way to the promised end.

The gospels and nearly all the epistles in the New Testament are written to communities not individuals. They presume that a community is hearing the letter. The "you" is not an individual you, it is a "communal you". While most of the letters are written to address particular issues that have arisen in the Christian community strangely to modern ears there is not much information about their meeting practices.

Hebrews is a book that does as it speaks to a group of Jewish Christians, who it seems are disillusioned, and want to return to temple worship. The writer reminds them that they are "holy partners in a heavenly calling," (Heb 3:1) and calls them to hold fast to Christ's faithfulness. He reminds them there is no need to offer sacrifice as is done in the temple day after day. "For by a single offering he has perfected for all time those who are sanctified." (Heb 10:1) Instead "Let us hold fast to the confession of our hope without wavering, for he who has promised is faithful. And let us consider how to provoke one another to love and good deeds, not neglecting to meet together, as is the habit of some, but encouraging one another, and all the more as you see the Day approaching." (Heb 10: 23–25)

We meet InChrist to provoke one another to love and good deeds as the living expression of the presence of the Kingdom. As the writer states later, "since we are receiving a kingdom that cannot be shaken, let us give thanks, by which we offer to God an acceptable worship with reverence and awe." (Heb 12:28a)

BAPTISM

Baptism and Eucharist are the sacraments of the kingdom, to be celebrated as the very way our life is constituted in the kingdom, rather than restricted to a rite as the way we join the church, or the way we are fed with heavenly food. After all baptism introduces us to live alive to God in the presence of the kingdom, and the Eucharist is a celebration of the kingdom, remembering the night of institution, the present reception of the bread and the wine, and a foretaste of the celebration of a new heaven and a new earth.

There is a profound need for these events to be at the forefront in our meetings. These are the core marks of our identity that need to come before any agenda and sharing of joys and struggles.

In each of our meetings we need to hear again and participate in how we are caught up in God's mighty purposes. Baptism defines us as those who have died with Christ to live alive to God. Note the use of the word 'we' which is in bold type in the following passage on baptism. This experience is a community experience.

> Do you not know that all of us who have been baptized into Christ Jesus were
> baptized into his death? Therefore **we** have been buried with him by baptism

into death, so that, just as Christ was raised from the dead by the glory of the Father, so **we** too might walk in newness of life.

For if **we** have been united with him in a death like his, **we** will certainly be united with him in a resurrection like his. **We** know that our old self was crucified with him so that the body of sin might be destroyed, and **we** might no longer be enslaved to sin. For whoever has died is freed from sin. But if **we** have died with Christ, **we** believe that **we** will also live with him. **We** know that Christ being raised from the dead, will never die again; death no longer has dominion over him. The death he died, he died to sin, once for all; but the life he lives, he lives to God. So you also must consider yourselves dead to sin and alive to God in Christ Jesus. (Rom 6:3–11)

The remarkable statement that we have been baptized into his death, and united with him, is so often shared as the fact that he 'died in our place'. In fact, that highlights the individual rather than what Christ has done for us. Instead we were co-crucified with him, placed there by God, as he took us where we could never go. There, his death was the death that triumphed over death and sin, and brought resurrection as a new creation. God gathered us up into Christ, and now inChrist we are to consider ourselves dead to sin and alive to God in Christ Jesus.

In baptism we find ourselves inChrist, held in his care even as he is at the right hand of God interceding for life and for the creation. Our life is open to him and we are in time and space open to the resources of this eternal heavenly realm as we respond together, working hard in the Lord. Truly to be inChrist is to be part of the body of Christ. The community is alive to God in Christ Jesus. It is alive to God—open to a continual communion with our Lord in the power of the Holy Spirit, lived in prayer and worship in the midst of joy. Our prayers learnt from the early church, celebrate with thanksgiving what God has done, and has given, to those who are citizens of heaven and part of the creation.

There is so much for the community to celebrate about in what God has done in Christ. The church with hindsight saw that what happened at Jesus baptism in the Jordan was also there in his baptism into death on the cross. The heavens torn open for him at that time, were torn open for us all on the cross. The declaration that Jesus Christ is Lord is not so much a belief which I hold, but a declaration of the reality of what God has done, in opening the presence of God to all believers, releasing the Spirit in and through us as individuals and as communities, members of the family of God caught up in God's purpose.

People are baptized on at least eight occasions in Acts and in each case it is baptism by water and the Holy Spirit. The expectation is that before, with, or after baptism by water, the person being baptized is also baptized by the Holy Spirit. There are no exceptions.

This expectation is far more than is expected or anticipated in the usual baptismal practice in the denominational paradigm. Baptism by the Holy Spirit is subsumed into baptism by water. A prayer asks the Holy Spirit to bless the water used in baptism, so that it will be a baptism of water and the spirit, as the water is used in the triune name to name the child. The result is that the focus in baptism is on the giving of a baptismal name for the individual and the reception of the child or person into the church. What is no longer there is the expectation of the active role of the Holy Spirit. The Holy Spirit drops out of the order, and with it the associated apocalyptic vision of the kingdom, and any possibility that there is an awareness that baptism into Christ is baptism into an open heaven. With the Holy Spirit and the kingdom missing, we are left, meeting together in the "house of God," welcoming a child or new member into the church. Instead we are called to be groups empowered by the Spirit, gathering wherever we are, open to the presence of God, as people on the way, in the joyful event of welcoming a new disciple to participate in Christ's ongoing incarnation in the creation.

It is vital that together we explicitly remember our baptism with water and the Holy Spirit at each meeting in a specific way. Some way is needed in our meetings and services—perhaps a liturgy, or an agreed sharing and response—to help us be more overtly personal and more communal in an open interactive way, instead of belief and conviction subjectively hidden in a withdrawn individual way.

This recovery of kingdom baptism is important in first enabling the expectation of the work of the Holy Spirit in our midst, and secondly in doing this lovingly and respectfully as the Holy Spirit bids us do.

EUCHARIST

Jesus prepares his disciples for what is to come by giving them the bread and the wine in a Passover meal. He declares the bread and the wine are his body and blood, a foretaste of the final heavenly banquet in a new heaven and new earth. Kelly highlights how the ascension provides the context for our celebration of the Eucharist.

> For its part, the Christian community is already embodied in this new creation, assimilated to Christ and indeed assimilating his Body and Blood, to become the Body of Christ.
>
> The ecclesial Body of Christ grows within the boundless field of Christ's universal presence and action. At the right hand of the Father, he inhabits a new space and a new time, within a limitless horizon compared to his previous mode of being. . . . From the here and now of Christ's presence, Eucharistic faith looks forward and outward into the cosmic and universal dimensions of God's saving action.[25]

25. Kelly, *Upward,* 100.

Being inChrist invites human consciousness and action to "expand into new dimensions within the horizon opened up by the ascension."[26] InChrist we are opened to the scope of Christ's incarnation that includes the world, and the cosmos. Planet Earth is not a backdrop; it is part of the divine future and is integral to a faith that will consummate a new Earth/cosmos and heaven. The Anthropocene reminds us of our responsibility as makers of the future. The cosmos in which we now live calls us to move beyond limiting frameworks and consider new horizons for faith, new metanarratives of God's spirit hovering over the galaxies of the cosmos, drawing them into Christ's ultimate incarnation as part of God's new creation.

This expansion in our faith needs new language, new festivals, new ways of earthing the sacraments as the expression of our God given reality and hope. As Catherine Vincie points out.

> Previously, eucharistic theology has stressed we become what we receive, the Body of Christ (Augustine). However we have understood the "Body of Christ" largely in ecclesial terms; we become ever more deeply the Body of Christ, the church. Our increased awareness of Christ as the Cosmic Christ has implications on our understanding of what we think we become in our eucharistic meal. Once again, our horizons are widened to become one with him who is in solidarity with all humanity and with the whole universe. This certainly is a challenge to those who continue to hold a very individualistic theology and spirituality of the eucharist.[27]

The Eucharist, with its focus on the body and blood of Christ, underlines the reality that our union with Christ is not in him as the one on the way to the cross, but our being in him after the ascension within a new creation. Together, in the Eucharist, we remember his death and resurrection. His incarnation grounds the Eucharistic community in the wonder of life, but also the awfulness and tragedy of a world blighted by sin and death. "While "deep incarnation" suggests God's solidarity with all creation, "deep resurrection" also promises transformation beyond death for all creation."[28]

The Lord's Prayer reminds the gathered community that the kingdom is present as part of Christ's purpose and direction for the community. The community eats and drinks as the Holy Spirit holds the group before the ascended Christ, the host for the event. Once more it is the open heaven and the Spirit's presence that enables us to know who we are. "God's action in the Eucharist is not one of descent but one of ascent. It is not so much that Christ descends to us at the Supper, but that the Spirit lifts us up to him."[29] Christ is the heavenly host of the meal, whose glory is the source of our being, feeding us for our ultimate future already held in him. The community

26. Kelly, *Upward,* 99.
27. Vincie, *Worship and Cosmology,* 93.
28. Vincie, *Worship and Cosmology,* 96.
29. Jenson et al., *The Church,* 136.

continues its life already declared in the celebration, singing with the work of the day's mission in the kingdom before them.

This renewed participation in the Eucharist brings all issues before the centrality of who Christ is in the creation of community and the hearing of the good news. Those who lead are called to maintain this apostolic witness to Christ in a church incarnated in the world. Such leadership needs nurturing and preparation and just does not happen. There is a ferment in the way that people are called and prepared for the role of leading the Spirit's base communities. This is not primarily about Church growth but discernment of Christ by the community that is being led.

MEETING ON THE WAY

What could the congregation or group do together as they gather in worship and other meetings?

An Open Heaven Declaration.

The declaration of the Apostles was that Jesus Christ is the Cosmic Lord. The cross has become the place where heaven was torn open and the resources of heaven are now available by the power of the Holy Spirit for the purposes of God in Christ. This reframing of life is there in Paul's statement that his work was not for the Lord, but in the Lord. This is the heavenly framework that redefines life in terms of the intention of the world the Holy Spirit has set out to create, the fulfilling of the dream of God in the midst of the creation.

The Spirit Declaration.

This declaration gives expression to the expectation of being in step with the Spirit in a community that lives from the Tree of Life, embedded in a world that lives from the Tree of the Knowledge of Good and Evil. The very being of the community is to live in sharing of the love of God with neighbor within the community and for others in society. It is this expectation of being guided by the Spirit that distinguishes this group from all others.

> By contrast, the fruit of the Spirit is love, joy, peace, patience, kindness, generosity, faithfulness, gentleness and self-control. There is no law against such things. And those who belong to Christ Jesus have crucified the flesh with its passions and desires. If we live by the Spirit let us also be guided by the Spirit. Let us not become conceited, competing against one another, envying one another.(Gal 5:22–26)

Knowing that we only see the invisible cosmic Christ in part, but that we are fully known to him, provides us with a radical alternative to living from ourselves as the center for human decision and commitment. This profound experience of living in the light is to find ourselves inChrist, working in the Lord. No wonder there is the call for us to be "slaves of righteousness", when this is the slavery of living in the light of what Isaiah calls God's glorious presence. Make us captives Lord and then we will be free.

DISCERNING THE SPIRIT'S DIRECTION

What is unique is the way the Holy Spirit goes about this guiding in and through the ministry of the spirit people. The issues are discerned through local groups and congregations. The people of God have been most effective when they work from the local to the global. It is the way to keep in step with the Spirit in the immediate interaction with those who are either opposed to or suspicious of the fact of creative loving community. The temptation is to do this work far away rather than locally. The early church in the Roman Empire was suppressed, persecuted but kept on with the ministry of love in the Lord with those with who they were in immediate contact. They knew they faced an alien empire that resisted the life of the new future God had in store. This immediacy is still important even though in the present time communication and travel provide new options to be incorporated into this basic approach.

The work on missionary congregations undertaken in the 60s points to the need for revitalized congregations and groups of people who discover in the gospel the holistic world of the kingdom of God/heaven. This regenerated experience of a new identity and view of the cosmos provides a new source for their activity and worship in the Lord. No longer would sociology provide a way of describing the local congregation. Instead the work of the Holy Spirit creates imaginative and creative communities that provide sources of life rather than reflecting the implicit needs of the congregation itself.

The fact is that there is a Spirit war underway, and the front is near and we are involved in the fighting, holding still and resisting with the armor of God to use the language of Ephesians. This conflict is a war of grace against violence, in reality, a subversion of the notion of war-itself, which lives from the world of the tree of the knowledge of good and evil that as we have seen fuels the violence against the creation, society, community, and individuals. It is the Spirit who enables us to rediscover our identity that is given in the kingdom, this reality of the Spirit in both the gifts and fruit given to communities of grace. The early churches realized that it is indeed the life of Christ which is not just the template for life, but also the creator of that template. A people 'inChrist' find that their identity is not just a social creation, it is at the core the discovery of the recreating center of God given identity lived in and through the tree of life, the ascended Christ.

The purpose of God is to create global community in and through particular communities. Historically it is the continuation of the incarnation. Jesus first lived in Nazareth. Through cross, resurrection and ascension the kingdom of God/Heaven is experienced here amongst this group of people. The local global begins with the kingdom of God/Heaven here, and the kingdom of God/Heaven to come. This continuing presence brings a gentle and persuasive revolution that like the tide has ebbed and flowed over the last twenty centuries. It is an account of changing missionary perspectives, unions and divisions, saints and sinners, selfishness and amazing sacrifice, that leaves us even more dependent upon God's grace as we pray.

Perhaps there is more to Isaiah's magnificent vision of the peaceful kingdom than we dare believe; "They will not hurt or destroy on all my holy mountain; for the earth will be full of the knowledge of the Lord as the waters cover the sea."(Isaiah 11:9) This vision issues in the later description of a Glorious New Creation spelled out as the great Shalom of God for all who live in it. "I am about to create new heavens and a new earth" the prophet says in the word of God given sometime in the half a millennium before the birth of Christ. (Isa 65:17). But what is the scope of this new heaven and earth when placed in the context of the universe itself? What is the dream of God for the pale blue dot, the pale red dot, and any other dots in the cosmos? Ernst Conradie sees the Earth as God's house that God intends finally to be God's home. But this view is bound to this planet and now in this century the cosmos can no longer be restricted to planet earth. The question of the Spirit's direction and purpose with regard to the cosmos has also to be taken into account.

But for a people on the way this direction and purpose is the genius of the Lord's Prayer. The prayer is the daily focusing in the presence of God on the way of tackling the world in preparation for God's future. It is the practical way of being caught up in God's plan for the Earth to be at least in someway part of God's home. We keep praying this prayer that lets us witness and declare what God is doing in our midst through justice, forgiveness, discernment and deliverance from the power of the darkness that warped, threatened, and destroyed, until exposed and confronted by the victorious light of the cosmic Christ.

It is remarkable that the kingdom of God/Heaven is here, in the face of the original trespass which issued in finitude and death, and the continuing trespass against God in society and individual life that issues in world views, societies and acts of terrible violence. Yet too the kingdom upholds this universe and suffuses it with the love that led to its creation, and the life that still floods through it. It is an amazing part of the Lord's Prayer. Forgive us our trespasses as we forgive those who trespass against us. Thank God for God's mercy.

Jesus came as a person in the kingdom to prepare the way for us to be persons in the kingdom. His baptism was an apocalyptic event, which framed his ministry as one who lived before God in the power of the Holy Spirit. (His name in Aramaic was Joshua, the one who led Israel into the promised land.) God the Father declared his love for him, who in John's gospel was the Son through whom the creation came into being, a universe conceived in love that did not recognize the source of love.

In the presence of the kingdom of God he forgave sins, healed the sick who came to him, and taught about the kingdom. In doing so he challenged the authority of the temple in Jerusalem, urged all to seek the kingdom of God, and taught about entering it. His teaching showed one who was deeply aware of the world around him, environmentally, socially and politically. He chose a team of twelve men. They were supported by women who accompanied them. His teaching used both male and female perspectives. He sent his disciples to announce this kingdom and to heal as he did. All who came to him for healing were healed. He crossed social barriers, relating to the religious, the sick, out-casts, the military, royalty and foreigners. He lived in the dimension of the Father's presence, and the anointing of the Holy Spirit. He lived in the kingdom he declared, the kingdom of God/ Heaven at hand, with the power of the Holy Spirit flowing in him and through him. At a Passover he challenged the practices in the temple. The temple leadership set out to be rid of him. Dragged into court he was condemned by the High Priest as a blasphemer of God when he admitted to be the Messiah. He was killed, on the altar of hate, violence and sin, crucified for the sake of the kingdom of Israel and the kingdom of God/Heaven.

The early church, knowing him as the crucified risen and ascended Lord realized the cross was God's decisive disclosure, the apocalyptic event, the divine confrontation with sin and finitude. There in and through his Son, God faced the issues of the rejection of the kingdom of God/Heaven by even Israel, the chosen people of God.

> *For the message about the cross is foolishness to those who are perishing (dying), but to us who are being saved, (healed, restored) it is the power of God.(1Cor 1: 18) He (God) is the source of your life in Christ Jesus, who became for us wisdom from God, and righteousness and sanctification and redemption, in order that, as it is written, " Let the one who boasts, boast in the Lord."(1Cor 1:30,31)*

This reality of the kingdom of God/Heaven, the righteousness of God within sin and finitude, is the new creation for those in the ascended Christ. Here is the grace in which we stand, the transforming sanctifying gift of forgiveness, healing, reconciliation, adoption as children of God, the immeasurable greatness of his power with all the spiritual blessings of heaven, given through the Holy Spirit.

The heavenly victory has been won in the cross and resurrection, the apocalypse of Jesus Christ, catching us up into the Trinitarian life of God through being in the ascended Christ. The final outworking of the healing of the creation is in the Father's hands, for Jesus was insistent that only the Father knows when this will be.

14

Epilogue

ON THE WAY

I HAD LITTLE IDEA of the extent to which the lecture on Galatians highlighting "the apocalypse of Jesus Christ" was going to impact on my life. This lecture, heard in the last decade of my working life, provided a different way of hearing the good news of Jesus Christ. As I came to the end of my time as a theologian at the United Theological College the plight of the church in the west was still at the center of my work, and had been all my life. Since then this issue only loomed larger and larger in my observations and experience of the life of the church. I had little awareness of what was to come in the writing of this book. In a very real sense the book shares the journey into the life that has come with this task of following where the apocalypse of Jesus Christ has led.

As described here an apocalyptic event discloses the presence of God through specific events in the midst of the creation. The importance of scripture as the witness to such disclosure is vital. As a follower of Christ I have worked hard in the Lord in the fields of mission, evangelism, social justice and advocacy for more than 60 years. In the last few years the increasing awareness of the apocalyptic gradually led to a questioning of the usual understanding of hermeneutics, the task of bringing a message from the first century to the twenty-first century. The enormous differences in world-view and the understanding of the person, creates 'a ditch' that is not easy to cross—hence the importance and time given to the nature of the text and the interpretation of the text.

It is only the last few years that the realization came that the kingdom of God that Jesus proclaimed was at variance with the world-view of his listeners. They could only vaguely grasp what he was about. For the early church the words of Jesus were to become both the words of the Son of God and the Son of Man. With the rediscovery of the kingdom of God/Heaven in the twentieth century once more the kingdom of

God is at variance with the present world-view, the culture, and also for most in the church. The key then is to discover what Jesus meant by the kingdom of God/Heaven. His words assume a priority over any world-view and culture. There is a gaping hole in the creeds that deal with his person as human and divine and do not mention his ministry, teaching, and embodying of the kingdom of God. The otherness, the impossible possibility of what happened in and through him, opens the possibility that his ministry is about more than logic, existential decision, morality, behavior, values, convictions and words. It meant spending more time focusing on what the early Church wanted us to know about his life, and teaching, and person. Jesus words then have an authority in themselves. That is not to say that it is still essential to bring a questioning mind, and ask the hard questions of reason about him. Nevertheless his words come first.

The scriptures are clear in the four gospels and Acts and stated in the letters in various ways that the ministry of Jesus and the early church saw the miraculous in operation. Paul's question to the Galatians puts it directly. "Well then, does God supply you with the Spirit and work miracles among you by doing the law, or by your believing what you have heard?"(Gal 3:5) for "It was before your eyes that Jesus Christ was publicly exhibited as crucified."(Gal 3:1)

The disclosure of God in our midst, that is the apocalypse of Christ, is about the healing of the creation and that will sometimes be experienced as miraculous. What then of the miraculous now? The world of cause and effect has to explain these events away. When as a scientist I was confronted with miracles I avoided them. That is easy to do, for the miraculous is not highlighted and when it is, it is demythologized as projections and creations of the early church. What a shock it was to read the scriptures and find how integral to the proclamation were the healings that occurred. What would happen if disciples follow their Lord and do what he commanded, proclaim the kingdom and heal the sick, in the twenty-first century? That does not mean believing anything as possible, but it meant for me the need to focus attention on what can happen when one first seeks the Kingdom of God and God's righteousness, and starts from there. There is, when one looks, much evidence of healing through the centuries and from ministries around the world. There are charlatans, and spiritual celebrities, and those too eager to believe anything, credulous people who see miracles around each corner, but that does not vitiate the number of careful and objective reports of healing in the name of Christ. Can what happened in the New Testament ministry of Jesus, and later the disciples, still happen now? Indeed the word salvation in the Greek is *swzw* which can be translated as salvation, healing or restoration. What happens when rather than us projecting our view of God onto God, we allow the light of God to be projected into our midst. And projected into our midst it is through our Lord Jesus Christ. I found that the uncovering of the apocalyptic also uncovered the possibility of the miraculous.

The ministry of Christ as reported in Matthew Mark and Luke, states that all who came to him expecting healing were healed. These events bring wonder and surprise and amazement, and are integral to the New Testament story. Focusing on the words of Jesus made it more difficult to dismiss these events as occasions created by the gospel writers, or the early church, to prove that Jesus really was the Son of God as is often claimed. What happens if one takes at face value one such event reported as the sermon on the plain got underway. "They had come to hear him and to be healed of their diseases; and those who were troubled with unclean spirits were cured. And all in the crowd were trying to touch him, for power came out from him and healed all of them."(Lk 6:18,19)

The claim is made that there is power in the message of the cross, and indeed the New Testament accounts are a litany of such power as well as teaching. If Jesus heals and forgives and commands his disciples to do likewise in the proclamation then the character of God is to heal and heal now.

What a shock it was for me writing about the apocalyptic, declaring the presence of the kingdom and the power of the cross, to be asked about an event that had happened fifteen hundred kilometers away that I knew nothing about. A friend rang to ask how to follow-up a healing weekend with a blind Anglican priest that had had people healed of bodily illness. The priest was the Rev Mike Endicott , the Prior of the Order of Jacob's Well in the United Kingdom, an order instituted by his then bishop Dr Rowan Williams in 1998 to work in the healing ministry.

In one of his books he shares the anguish that followed when the wife of a member of the Order's healing team was diagnosed with lung cancer. In the year it took her to die they tried everything they knew about healing, but to no avail. In the grief and questioning that followed one question firmed. What did Jesus do and what did he instruct his disciples to do in their healing ministry? Several months later he found himself at a conference, bereft of expectation that his past teaching was helpful, in a room filled to overflowing with people wanting to know about healing. With trepidation he asked "Who needs a miracle in their life this afternoon?" Hands went up everywhere. What next? This moment was the moment of truth. He says "I began to preach the good news of Jesus Christ by reminding them that Jesus Christ healed everyone who asked him—everyone with a modicum of expectant faith, and he repeatedly told us he could only do what he saw the Father doing. . . . I drew the simple conclusion from these facts that God's will must be to see healed all who come to Jesus for restoration."[1] After an agonizing silence he said "All heaven let loose." People were healed as they came forward for prayerful proclamation, or as they waited, and amazingly as some walked past the room at this time. That afternoon it was conservatively estimated well over a third who were prayed with had recognized improvement in their condition almost immediately.

---

1. Endicott, *Rediscovering Kingdom Healing*, 16.

He had 'rediscovered' kingdom healing, working alongside the gift of modern medicine, focusing on the proclamation of God's good news in Jesus Christ and his cross, and not the condition of the person. When the kingdom is proclaimed, he was saying we give thanks for who God is and what he has done in Jesus Christ and God's will happens. He whose name can be translated saviour or healer came to save/heal the world, restore it to God's intent. This event was not just words or ideas, but healings happening on a scale he had not seen before. For me, as I read this account, I was being faced with the apocalypse of Jesus Christ. This healing was not thinking about the possibility of healing as revelation, this was faith in the disclosure of Jesus Christ inChrist.

I was intrigued and said yes to working with the group (and eventually became Prior of the Order of Jacob's Well in Australia).

So began a different way of praying in the presence of God and seeing healing in some people coming for healing. What an adventure the last two years has been. Of course there are still issues. Why are some people not healed? I do not know all the answers other than that the apocalypse of Jesus Christ shows us the battle won between light and darkness, grace and sin, healing and sickness. I have seen the joy of seeing many set free of sickness, and encouraging those not yet healed that God's will is still to heal in Jesus Christ. It really has been the rediscovery of ordination vows to preach the good news and expect good news. Healing flows as a by-product of discovering the nature and purpose of God, not focusing on the amount of faith, or trying to manipulate God to act. God loves to act! What is incredible is that this faith is not just words or speeches, but the expectation of seeing God's healing at work in the proclamation of the Kingdom. And indeed this is the task of the church, to be a witness to the Lord of the kingdom through his cross, resurrection and ascension.

What an adventure this kingdom walking has turned out to be, living open to the kingdom of God/Heaven a day at a time. Once more I am acutely aware that I am a disciple, a learner. And not all receive this with approval!

This discovery about healing has happened within the broader issues of ministry on the pale blue dot. Ministry is not only words and the importance of worship witness and service, but the expectation of renewal of the creation happening as well. It means proclaiming the kingdom of God/Heaven for the cosmos, taking seriously the Anthropocene as the context for present ministry inChrist. There are many dangers here for such power draws those who seek power for its own end. It makes it even more necessary for the church to be the body of Christ so that ministry is not the guerilla activity of individual people with gifts, but the ministry of the people of God living in the wisdom and discernment that the ascended Christ gives to his church.

It was with some surprise that in the last five years I realised that the terror of non-being that had dogged my life had gradually ebbed away into the wonder of the cosmic story of a loving Creator and Redeemer God known inChrist. I was given a new lease of life in ministry with the discovery that God acts in the proclamation of the apocalyptic kingdom. New possibilities emerged that called in question my Enlightenment scientific heritage. I discovered the miraculous still happens, and people are saved, healed and restored for God's will is to save, heal and restore the creation. I discovered that this raises new questions and new issues to work through for these events are but a foretaste of God's new heaven and a new Earth (cosmos)—but they are a foretaste.

We are on the way in the kingdom of God/Heaven. Here on the pale blue dot, or any dot, the remarkable fact is that any person can pray the Lord's Prayer. I believe it can be prayed by any life form anywhere in the cosmos. It goes to the heart of the purposes of God. The prayer is a practical living out of the kingdom of God as part of God's creation of a new heaven and a new earth. Prayed in this context it shows the crucial difference between the Denominational Paradigm with the Kingdom of God within, and the rediscovery of the kingdom of God as entering into God's presence, a reality graciously infiltrating and restoring all niches of life towards God's end for the universe.

After two hundred years the denominational paradigm has run its course, embodying the modern era, focussed on the importance of individual decision as the basis of both life and faith. Instead here is the breaking in of the good news of an apocalypse, which has already happened, in which God is the center inviting life in all its diversity into God's gracious purpose.

The Risen ascended Lord is present with his people and creation. He is in the process of fulfilling the prayer he taught us to say, "Your Kingdom come on earth as it is in heaven"

InChrist, we are the children of the Father/Mother of all,

inChrist our lives are hid in heaven,

inChrist all life is hallowed for he shows us the holy, loving, joyful and glorious being of God.

inChrist, the kingdom has come,

inChrist the will of the Father is known and is coming to the Cosmos,

inChrist is our daily life,

inChrist trespasses are forgiven as we live in mercy,

inChrist in a world averse to the kingdom, we are saved in time of trials and delivered from evil,

inChrist is the kingdom, the power and the glory of the eternal Father.

Once this one, the ultimate Other, is known, then all others become part of the story we find ourselves in, whether on this planet, and whatever vast possibilities that a universe like this may contain.

How will this be? The human mind's eye can envisage the way the gracious love of the Spirit will continue to course through generations to come bringing the world closer to the joyous Shalom for which it was created. A Shalom that is a reconciling presence that values all interconnected life and the planets themselves, that helps nurture the life the cosmos was created to bring into being. Now that is a story of love and joy that beats infinite worlds and universes running down, and the loneliness of the Pale Blue Dot.

Bibliography

Aernie, Jeffrey W. "Cruciform Discipleship: The Narrative Function of the Women in Mark 15–16." In the Journal of Biblical Literature No 4 (2016): 779–797.

———. "Faith, Judgement, and the Life of the Believer: A Reassessment of 2 Corinthians 5:6–10". In the The Catholic Biblical Quarterly, Vol 79, No. 3 July 2017: 438–454.

Article, "Big flares doom life on nearby world." *New Scientist*, 21 April, 2018.

Australian Hymn Book 2. Together in Song. Australia: Harper Collins,1999.

Ananthaswamy, Anil. "Perfect Disharmony." *New Scientist*, 14 April, 2018.

Anderson, Alun. "Corridors of the Mind." *New Scientist,* 8 March, 2014.

Aquinas, Thomas. *The Summa Theologica*. 5 vols. English Dominican Province Translation: Christian Classics, 1981

Bachelard, Sarah. *Resurrection and Moral Imagination*. Surrey: Ashgate, 2014.

Barclay, John M G. *Colossians and Philemon*. Sheffield: Sheffield, 1997.

———. *Paul and the Gift*. Grand Rapids: Eerdmann, 2015.

Barth, Karl."Fragebeantwortung bei der Konferenz der World Student Christian Federation in *Gesprache, 1959–1962*," edited by Eberhad Busch, *Gesamtausgabe*. Zurich: Theologischer Verlag, 1995.

Beker, J Christiaan. *Paul's Apocalyptic Gospel: The Coming Triumph of God*. Second ed. Minneapolis: Fortress, 1984.

Bellah, Robert N. *Habits of the Heart*. California: University of California Press, 1985.

Bennett, Denis, J. *Nine O'Clock in the Morning*. New Jersey: Bridge, 1970.

Berkowitz, Jacob. *The Stardust Revolution*. New York: Prometheus Books, 2012.

Bird, Warren and Thuma, Scott. "A New Decade of Megachurches: 2011." Hartford: Hartford Institute for Religion Research on Mega-churches. http://hirr.harsem.edu/megachurch/definition.html

Bloom, Anthony. *Living Prayer*. 1990 Edition. London: Darton, Longman & Todd, 1966.

Blount, Brian. *Invasion of the Dead, Preaching Resurrection*. Louisville:Westminster John Knox, 2014.

Boer, de Martinus. "Paul's Mythologizing Program in Romans 5–8." In Beverly Roberts Gaventa ed. *Apocalyptic Paul*, Waco:Baylor University Press, 2103, 4.

Bonhoeffer, Dietrich. *Christology*. Translated by John Bowden. London: Collins,1966.

———. *Cost of Discipleship*. Translated by R. H. fuller with some revision by Irmgard Booth for SCM, 2001. First published Munich:Ch Kaiser Verlag, 1937.

———. *Ethics*. 6th ed. Translated by Neville Horton Smith for SCM, 1966. First German edition, Munich: Ch Kaiser Verlag, 1963.

Borenstein, Seth. "Cosmic census finds crowds of planets in our galaxy." *Associated Press*, February 19, 2011.

Bosch, David J. *Transforming Mission*. New York: Orbis, 1991.

Botton, Alain de. *Status Anxiety*, Camberwell: Penguin Books, 2004.

Bouma, Gary. *Australian Soul*. Melbourne: Cambridge University Press, 2006.

Breech, James. *The Silence of Jesus*. Minneapolis: Fortress, 1983.

Brown, Warren S. & Strawn, Brad D. *The Physical Nature of Christian Life*. New York: Cambridge University Press, 2012.

Brueggemann, Walter. *Genesis*. Interpretation Bible Commentary, Atlanta: John Knox, 1982.

———. *The Practice of Prophetic Preaching*. Minneapolis: Fortress, 2012.

Buber, Martin. *Meetings: Autobiographical Fragments*. New York: Routledge, 2002.

Bulgakov, Sergius. *The Lamb of God*. Translated by Jakim Boris. Michigan: Eerdmans, 2008.

Calvin, J., *Institutes of Christian Religion, Vol 1*. Philadelphia: Westminster, 1960.

Caputo, John D. *What Would Jesus Deconstruct?* Grand Rapids: Baker, 2007.

Cary, Phillip. *Augustine's Invention of the Inner Self*. Oxford: Oxford University Press, 2000.

———. *Augustine: Philosopher and Saint*. Chantilly: The Great Courses, 2005.

———. *Inner Grace*. Oxford: Oxford University Press, 2008.

Carrington, Damian. "The Anthropocene epoch: scientists declare dawn of human-influenced age." *Guardian* August 30, 2016.

Chardin, Teilhard de. *The Phenomenon of Man*. London: Collins, 1955.

Christie, Ann. *Ordinary Christology*. Surrey: Ashgate, 2012.

Cobb. John B. *The Structure of Christian Existence*. Philadelphia: Westminster, 1957.

Cranfield C. E. B., & Emerton J. A. *The Epistle to the Romans. Vol 1*. The International Critical Commentary. Edinburgh: T & T Clark, 1975.

Davie, G. "Is Europe an Exceptional Case?" 247–258. *International Review of Mission*. Nos. 378/379, July October 2006.

Drayton, R Dean. *A Pilgrim in the Cosmos*. Adelaide: Lutheran, 1995

———. *A Revolution in Understanding Conversion*, Adelaide: Uniting Church, 1982.

Deane-Drummond, Celia, *Biblical eco-theology*. London: Darton. Longman+Todd, 2008.

———. *Christ and Evolution*. Minneapolis: Fortress, 2009.

Dulles, Avery. *Models of the Church*. New York: Bantam Doubleday Bell, 2002.

Dunn, James D G. *The Epistles to the Colossians and to Philemon*. GrandRapids: Eerdmans, 1996.

Editorial. "Hello Neighbour." *New Scientist*, August 24, 2016.

Endicott, Mike. *Rediscovering Kingdom Healing*. Scotts Valley: Create Space Independent, 2015.

Finney, Charles G. *The Autobiography of Charles G. Finney*. Minneapolis: Bethany Fellowship, 1977. Condensed and edited by Helen Wessel.

———. *Revivals of Religion*. Chicago, Fleming H Revell, 1868.

Finney, John. *Finding Faith Today: How does it Happen*. Swindon: British and Foreign Bible Society, 1992.

Flett, John G. *The Witness of GOD*. Grand Rapids: Eerdmans, 2010.

Fox, Matthew. *The Coming of the Cosmic Christ: The Healing of the Earth and the Birth of a Global Renaissance*. New York: Harper Collins, 2010.

Frost, Michael. *Exiles*, Peabody: Hendrickson, 2006.

Fukuyama, Francis. *The End of History and the Last Man*. New York: Avon, 1992.

Fuller, Steve. *Humanity 2.0*. New York: Palgrave MacMillan, 2011.

Gabrielson, Jeremy. *Paul's Non-Violent Gospel*. Eugene: Pickwick, 2013.

Gaustard, Edwin S. *Sworn on the Altar of God*. Grand Rapid: Eerdmans, 2001.

Gorman, Michael J. *Becoming the Gospel*. Cambridge: Eerdmans, 2015.

Gregersen, Niels Henrik, "Christology." In *Systematic Theology and Climate Change*, edited by Michael S. Northcott, 33–50. London: Routledge, 2014.

Gunton, Colin E. *Christ and Creation*. Carlisle: Paternoster, 1992.

———. *Revelation and Reason*. London: T& T Clark, 2008.

Gurht, J. "Kosmos." In *The New International Dictionary of New Testament Theology*, 4 vols. Edited by Colin Brown, 1: 521–526 Exeter: Paternoster, 1975.

Hall, Douglas John. *Waiting for the Gospel: An Appeal to the Dispirited Remnants of Protestant "Establishment"*. Eugene: Cascade Books, 2012.

Havea, Jione. "Engaging Scriptures from Oceania." 11–20. In Jione Havea et al. *Bible Borders, Belonging(s): Engaging Readings from Oceania*. Semeia Studies Book 75. Society of Biblical Literature, 2015.

Hambrick-Stowe, Charles E. *Charles G. Finney and the Spirit of American Evangelicalism*. Grand Rapids: Eerdmans, 1996.

Heath, Elaine. *God Unbound: Wisdom from Galatians for the Anxious Church*. Nashville: Upper Room, 2016.

Hoekendijk, Johannes Christiaan. "Notes on the Meaning of Mission(ary)." *Planning for Mission*, 37–48. Great Britain: Epworth Press, 1966.

Holy Qur'an. English translation of the meanings and Commentary. Revised and edited by The Presidency of Islamic Researches. Medina: King Fahd Holy Qur'a n Printing Complex.

Hooker, Monica. *Gospel According to St Mark*. London: Bloomsbury, 2001.

Horsley, Richard. *Jesus and Empire*. Minneapolis: Fortress, 2003.

Hughes, Philip E. *Commentary on the Second Epistle to the Corinthians*. Michigan: Eerdmans, 1962.

Jacob, Aron. "Christianity's meteoric rise." *New Scientist*, April 25, 2015.

———. "No place like home—or is there?" *New Scientist*, August 29, 2015.

Jayne, Allen. *Jefferson's Declaration of Independence: Origins, Philosophy, and Theology*. Kentucky: University of Kentucky Press, 2015.

Jennings, Theodore, *Reading Derrida/Thinking Paul*. Redwood City: Stanford University Press, 2006.

Jensen, Peter. *The Future of Jesus*. Sydney: ABC, 2005.

Jenson, Matt, and Wilhite, David. *The Church: A Guide for the Perplexed*. London: T&T Clark, 2010.

Johnson, Elizabeth. *She Who Is*. New York: Crossroad,1996.

Johnston, Thomas P. *Examining Billy Graham's Theology of Evangelism*. Eugene: Wipf and Stock, 2003.

Julian of Norwich, edited by Grace Warrack. *Revelations of Divine Love*. London: Methuen 1901.

Jungel, Eberhard. *The Freedom of a Christian*. Minneapolis: Augsburg, 1988.

Käsemann, Ernst. *Commentary on Romans*. Grand Rapids: Eerdmans, 1980.

Kelly, Anthony J. *Upward: Faith, Church and the Ascension of Christ*. Minnesota: Liturgical, 2014.

Kimbrough, S T Jr. and Newport, Kenneth G C. *The Manuscript Journal of the Reverend Charles Wesley, M. A.*, Nashville: Kingswood, 2008.

Kinnamon, Michael. *Can A Renewal Movement Be Renewed?* Grand Rapids: Eerdman, 2014.

Kreider, Alan. *The Change of Conversion and the Origin of Christendom.* Harrisburg: Trinity, 1999.

Kuhn, Thomas. *The Structure of Scientific Revolutions.* Chicago: University of Chicago Press, 1962.

Lambert, Frank. *"Pedlar in Divinity": George Whitfield and the Transatlantic Revivals.* Princeton: Princeton University Press, 1994.

Licona, Michael J. *The Resurrection of Jesus.* Downer's Grove: IVP, 2010.

Lifton, Robert Jay. *The Climate Swerve.* New York: New, 2017.

Lloyd, Genevieve. *Providence Lost.* Cambridge: Harvard University Press, 2008.

Loisy, Alfred. *The Gospel and the Church.* Translated by Christopher Home (New York: Charles Scribner's Sons, 1912.

Malina, Bruce J, and Rohrbaugh Richard L. *Social Science Commentary on the Gospel of John.* Minneapolis: Fortress, 1998.

Martyn, J Louis. *Galatians.* New Haven:Yale University Press, 1997.

———. "From Paul to Flannery O'Connor with the Power of Grace." 279. *Theological Issues in the Letters of Paul.* Edinburgh: T&T Clark, 1997,

Marty, Martin E. *The Public Church.* New York: Crossroad, 1981.

McAfee, David. *No Sacred Cows.* Durham: Pitchstone, 2017.

McFague, Sallie. *Models of God.* London: SCM Press, 1987.

McGrath, Alister. *A Brief History of Heaven.* Oxford: Blackwell, 2003.

McHugh, John F. *John 1–4.*The International Critical Commentary. London: T & T Clark, 2008.

McLaren, Bruce. *Everything Must Change.* Nashville: Thomas Nelson, 2009.

———. *A Generous Orthodoxy.* Grand Rapids: Zondervan, 2004.

———. *A New Kind of Christian.* Chichester: John Wiley and Sons, 2008.

———. *The Secret Message of Jesus.* Nashville: Thomas Nelson, 2007.

Meyer, P W. "The Worm at the Core of the Apple." In *The Conversation Continues in Paul and John in Honor of J Louis Martyn,* edited by R. T.Fortna and B. R. Gaventa, 62–84, Nashville: Abingdon,1990.

Meynell, Alice. *The Poems of Alice Meynell.* London: Burns Oates, 1924.

Middleton, Richard. *A New Heaven and a New Earth: Reclaiming Biblical Eschatology.* Grand Rapids: Baker, 2014.

Migliore, Daniel L. *Faith Seeking Understanding.* 3rd edition. Grand Rapids: Eerdmans, 2014.

Minear, Paul S. *Images of the Church in the New Testament.* Philadelphia: Westminster, 1970.

Moltmann, Jürgen. *The Church in the Power of the Spirit: A Contribution to Messianic Ecclesiology.* Translated by Margaret Kohl. Minneapolis: Fortress Press, 1977.

———. *Jesus Christ to Today's World.* Minneapolis: Fortress, 1994.

———. *The Spirit of Life.* Minneapolis: Fortress, 1992, third impression

———. *The Way of Jesus Christ.* London: SCM Press, 2009, Vol 3.

Mouw, Richard J. *Uncommon Decency: Christian Civility in an Uncivil World.* Second edition, Illinois: IVP, 2010.

Muer, Rachel. *Living for the Future: Theological Ethics for Coming Generations.* London: T & T Clark, 2008.

Myers, Ched. *Binding the Strongman: A Political Reading of Mark's Story of Jesus.* New York: Orbis, 1988.

Norgaard, Karie Marie. *Living in Denial.* Cambridge: MIT, 2011.

Oepke, Albrecht. "Revelation." In *Theological Dictionary of the New Testament*, 10 vols. Edited by Gerhard Kittel and Gerhard Friedrich. Translated by Geoffrey W. Bromiley, 3:563–592. Grand Rapids: Eerdmans 1964–76

O'Meara, Thomas. *Vast Universe: Extraterrestrials and Christian Revelation*. Minnesota: Liturgical, 2012.

Paine, Thomas. *The Age of Reason*, London: Carlisle, 1826.

Pannenberg, Wolfhart, *Systematic Theology*, 3 vols. Edinburgh: T& T Clark, 1998.

Pearson, Clive. "For Christ's Sake: From Expletive to Confession." *Pacifica* 17:2, 2004: 197–215.

Patterson, Stephen J. *The God of Jesus: The Historical Jesus and the Search for Meaning*. London: A&C Black, 1998.

Pearson, Clive. 'For Christ's Sake: From Expletive to Confession', *Pacifica* 17:2 2004: 197–215.

Peperzak Adriaan T., and Critchley, Simon. *Emmanuel Levinas: Basic Philosophical Writings*, Bloomington: Indiana University Press, 2008.

Peters, Ted. "One Incarnation or Many." 271–302 in Ted Peters ed, *Astrotheology*, Eugene: Cascade, 2018.

Peterson, Cheryl. *Who is the Church? An Ecclesiology for the Twenty-first century*. Minneapolis: Fortress, 2013.

Placher, William C. *Mark: A Theological Commentary on the Bible*. Louisville: Westminster John Knox, 2010.

Poewe, Karla A. *Charismatic Christianity as a Global Culture*. Carolina: University of South Carolina, 1995.

Porphyry, "On the Life of Plotinus and the Arrangement of his Works." In Mark Edwards ed., *Neoplatonic Saints: The Lives of Plotinus and Proclus by their Students*, 1.6.6–1.6.9. Liverpool: Liverpool University Press, 2000.

Portier-Young, Anthea E. *Apocalypse Against Empire*. Grand Rapids: Eerdmans, 2011.

Putnam, Robert D. *Bowling Alone*. New York: Touchstone, 2000.

Rasmussen, Larry. "Bonhoeffer and the Anthropocene." NGTT DEEL, Supplementum 1, 2014.

Russell, Robert John. "Many Incarnations or One?" In Ted Peters, ed. *Astrotheology*, 303–316. Eugene: Cascade, 2018.

Rhys, Isaac. *The Transformation of Virginia*. Chapel Hill: University of North Carolina Press, 1982.

Sagan, Carl. *Billions and Billions*, New York: Ballantine, 1997.

———. "In the Valley of the Shadow." Parade Magazine, March 1996

———. *Pale Blue Dot: A Vision of the Human Future in Space*. New York: Random House, 1997.

Schmidt, Hans. "Concerning the Mission of the Church in a Changing World."95–117, *Planning for Mission*, Great Britain: Epworth Press, 1966.

Schweitzer, Albert. *The Mystery of the Kingdom of God*. Charleston: BiblioLife, 2009. Originally published in 1901.

———. *The Quest of the Historical Jesus*. London: SCM, 2000, translated and edited by John Bowden. *Geschichte der Leben Jesus—Forschung*. Tubingen: J. C. B. Mohr, 1913.

Seaton, Jeff. *Who's Minding the Story?* Eugene: Pickwick, 2018.

Sölle, Dorothee. *Thinking about God*. London: SCM Press, 1990.

Spellberg, Denise A. *Thomas Jefferson's Qur'n*. New York: Random House, 2014.

Sprinkle, Preston. "Sex, Science, and Becoming More Like Jesus" September 11, 2015, https:// www.patheos.com/blogs/ sex–science–and–becoming–more–like–Jesus.

Stendahl, Krister. "The Apostle Paul and the Introspective Conscience of the West." in *Paul Among Jews and Gentiles*. Philadelphia: Fortress, 1976.

Storr, Will. *Selfie: How the West became Self-obsessed*. London: Picador, 2017.

Tanner, Katherine. *Christ the Key*. Cambridge: Cambridge University Press, 2010

The Compact Edition of the Oxford English Dictionary. Oxford: Oxford University Press, 1971.

The Uniting Church in Australia, *Constitution and Regulations*. Sydney: Uniting Church Assembly, 2008.

Tillich, Paul. "You are Accepted." *The Shaking of the Foundations*. 155–165. Hammondsworth: Penguin Books, 1949.

Vainio, Olli-Pekka. *Cosmology in Theological Perspective*. Grand Rapids: Baker, 2018.

Valberg, J J. *Dream, Death and the Self*. Princeton: Princeton University Press, 2007.

Vincie, Catherine. *Worship and the New Cosmology*. Minnesota: Liturgical, 2014.

Wallace, Paul. *Stars Beneath Us*. Minneapolis: Fortress, 2015.

Walls, Jerry L. ed, *The Oxford Handbook of Eschatology*. Oxford: Oxford University Press, 2008.

W Reginald Ward and Richard P, Heitzenrater, eds. *The Bicentennial Edition of the Works of John Wesley, Journal & Diaries*, Vol 18. Nashville: Abingdon,1988.

Weiss, Johan. *Jesus' Proclamation of the Kingdom of God.*, Trans by Hiers, R H. & Holland, DL. First published 1892. Philadelphia: Augsburg Fortress, 1971.

Welker, Michael. *God the Spirit*. Minneapolis: Fortress, 1994.

Wenz, John. "20 potential Earth-like worlds." *New Scientist*, November 4, 2017.

Wieser, Thomas ed. *Planning for Mission*, Great Britain: Epworth Press, 1966.

Wijngaards, John N. *How to Make Sense of God*. Maryland: Rowman & Littlefield, 1995.

Wilkinson, David. *Science, Religion, and the Search for Extraterrestrial Intelligence*. Oxford: Oxford University Press, 2013.

Williams, Colin. *Where in the World*. New York: National Council of Churches, 1963.

Wind, James P., and Lewis, James W. eds. *American Congregations*. Chicago: University of Chicago Press, 1991.

Wright, N T. *The Challenge of Jesus: Rediscovering who Jesus Was and Is*. Downers Grove: IVP, 1999.

———. *How God became King: The Forgotten Story of the Gospels,* San Francisco: Harper One, 2012

———. *Jesus and the Victory of God*. Minneapolis: Fortress, 1996.

———. "Jesus is Coming—Plant a Tree." In *Surprised by Scripture*, 83–107. New York: Harper Collins, 2014.

———. *Paul and his Recent Interpreters*. London: SPCK, 2015.

———. *The Resurrection of the Son of God*. Minneapolis: Fortress, 2003.

———. *Surprised by Scripture*. New York: Harper Collins, 2014.

Yong, Amos. *The Future of Evangelical Theology*. Downers Grove: Intervarsity, 2014.

Zizioulas, John D. *The One and the Many*. Alhambra: Sebastian, 2012.

Printed in July 2019
by Rotomail Italia S.p.A., Vignate (MI) - Italy